THE Best-Laid Plans

How Government Planning Harms Your Quality of Life, Your Pocketbook, and Your Future

RANDAL O'TOOLE

CATO INSTITUTE
WASHINGTON, D.C.

Library of Congress Cataloging-in-Publication Data

O'Toole, Randal
    Best-laid plans : how government planning harms your quality
of life, your pocketbook, and your future / Randal O'Toole.
        p. cm.
    Includes bibliographical references and index.
        ISBN 978-1-933995-07-6 (alk. paper)
    1. Central planning—United States.   2. United States—Economic
policy—2001–   3. Capitalism—United States.   I. Cato Institute.
II. Title.

HC106.83086 2007
338.973—dc22

                                                        2007028280

Cover design by Jon Meyers.

Printed in the United States of America.

                        CATO INSTITUTE
            1000 Massachusetts Ave., N.W.
                Washington, D.C. 20001
                        www.cato.org

This book is dedicated to Chip, my fun-loving friend and quiet companion on some 20,000 miles of wilderness walks, urban hikes, and beach tramps over 14 years.

Contents

Acknowledgments

This book should not be necessary. There are already many good books about why government planning does not work. Yet despite books such as Friedrich Hayek's 1944 *The Road to Serfdom* and James Scott's more recent *Seeing Like a State*, federal, state, and local governments continue to plan. So it is time to say, once again, that the emperor of planning has no clothes.

While the story's outline may be familiar to some, I hope the details in this book will be fresh. My education in planning comes from three decades of often-painful experiences with land-use and transportation planners. I hope that some of this book's readers will be able to learn through my experiences rather than having to repeat the process.

Writers such as Hayek, Ludwig von Mises, and Milton Friedman are little more than mythological characters to me. Instead, I am especially grateful to my real mentors: Ed Whitelaw, who taught me the value of economics in studying urban problems; and John Baden and his colleagues in Bozeman, Montana, who provided a framework that helped me interpret the information I gathered when studying the Forest Service and other government agencies.

I am grateful to Stephen Town, who did much of the research contained in the chapter on smart growth and crime, and Kathleen Calongne and Michael Cunneen, who did a considerable amount of the research that went into chapter 31. Kathleen also sacrificed much of her time both in reviewing a draft of this book and in assisting me with some of the other projects described in it. Peter Van Doren of the Cato Institute also made many helpful comments on the draft. Finally, I would like to thank my partner Vickie Crowley for supporting all the efforts that went into this book and for being my most faithful critic. Of course, I take full responsibility for any errors in the book.

Introduction

In proving foresight may be vain;
The best-laid schemes o' mice an' men
Gang aft agley,
An' lea'e us nought but grief an' pain,
For promis'd joy!

—Robert Burns

Somewhere in the United States today, government officials are writing a plan that will profoundly affect other people's lives, incomes, and property. Though it may be written with the best intentions, the plan will go horribly wrong. The costs will be far higher than anticipated, the benefits will prove far smaller, and various unintended consequences will turn out to be worse than even the plan's critics predicted.

People might blame the plan's failure on the officials who wrote it, who may lose their jobs or be voted out of office. More likely, officials and planners will shift the blame to outside circumstances. Who could have known that costs would rise? That new technologies would render the plan useless or pointless? Or that people wouldn't behave in the ways planners expected? Even more likely, few members of the public will even notice that the plan failed because few will remember what the plan said or that it was written at all. Instead, increased traffic congestion, unaffordable housing, declining employment, or other consequences of the plan will be considered "just one of those things."

Few will blame any of these problems on the concept of government planning itself. Government planning has become an accepted part of life in these United States. Almost every city and county in the nation has a planning department and many states have laws requiring cities and counties to plan. Running government without planners seems almost as foreign as running marathons without air to breathe.

1

Yet government planning almost always leads to disaster because government planning is simply not possible. As part two of this book will reveal, the task is too big for anyone to understand and the planning process is too slow to keep up with the realities of modern life. Part four will show that most of the professionals who call themselves *planners* are poorly trained to do the work they set out to do. Even if scientific planning were possible and the right people were doing it, part six will show that politics inevitably distort the results into something totally irrational.

Fifteen years ago, Americans cheered the victory of free markets over the centralized planning that failed so miserably in the Soviet Union and Eastern Europe. Yet we have already forgotten these stark lessons about the impracticality of government planning. Even as government officials in Poland, Hungary, and the Czech Republic were trying to figure out how to restore free markets to their once-planned economies, planners in the United States were seeking greater influence over land use, transportation, health care, energy, and other aspects of our economy. As Boris Yeltsin faced down the tanks of an attempted coup in 1991, the U.S. Congress was passing a law that gave planners more control than ever over our cities and the people who live in them.[1]

Today, the negative consequences of that law and planning in general can be felt in housing bubbles, increased traffic congestion, growing restrictions on what people are allowed to do with their property, and declining employment in some urban areas that should be rapidly growing. Yet planners manage to blame congestion on people who drive alone instead of taking transit; unaffordable housing on speculators and low interest rates; and unemployment on greedy corporations outsourcing to other parts of the world. Few place the real blame where it belongs: in the laps of planners who deliberately created the congestion, cheerfully drove up housing prices, and eagerly wrote regulations hostile to local businesses.

Everybody plans. You plan your day, your vacation, your education, and your career. Companies plan their product releases and long-term strategies. But the planning that is the subject of this book is *government planning*, that is, government officials and planners making decisions about your life, your property, and your future.

I want to further distinguish between broad-based government planning and *mission planning*. Government agencies whose missions are both clear and narrowly defined need to organize their resources to carry out those missions, and such organization might be called planning. Such flexible, short-term mission planning is a necessary part of any organization. Instead, as used here, government planning refers to three kinds of planning:

- *Comprehensive planning* that attempts to deal with both quantifiable (but not always comparable) values, such as dollars, recreation days, or transit trips, and qualitative values, such as "a sense of community." The noncomparable and qualitative nature of comprehensive planning allows or even forces planners and special interest groups to put their own preferences ahead of what the public wants or needs. Part one of this book will show how the U.S. Forest Service spent more than a billion dollars comprehensively planning the national forests and ended up with plans that were obsolete before they were published because political, social, and scientific realities changed faster than the planners could write.

- *Planning of other people's land and resources,* which always fails because planners do not have to pay the costs that they impose on other people and so they have little incentive to find the best answers. Part three will show how state and city land-use planning has made housing unaffordable in many regions and has driven up the cost of most other businesses as well.

- *Long-range planning* that attempts to dictate activities 10, 20, or more years in the future. Long-range planning always fails because no one can predict the future and so, as with comprehensive planning, it leads planners to write their preferences into the plan and gives opportunities for special interest groups to manipulate the plan for their own benefit. Part five will show how many long-range transportation plans written for the nation's metropolitan areas ended up favoring a tiny minority of the residents of those areas at everyone else's expense.

There are several important differences between private planning and government planning. When you plan, you are primarily deciding how to use your time, your money, and your property. The costs of any mistakes you make will fall mainly on you, so you have an incentive to get it right. When government agencies plan, they are making decisions about other people's time, money, and property.

3

When the planners make mistakes, someone else bears the costs, so planners have little incentive to get it right. As a result, they often repeat their mistakes.

Second, because your time, money, and property are your own, few people other than members of your family have a significant interest in the decisions you make. Government planning agencies, however, have the power to make people very wealthy or send them into bankruptcy. This kind of power attracts people, corporations, and interest groups who will put enormous pressure on the agencies and the elected officials who oversee them to see that the plans work in their favor. This pressure inevitably distorts the planning process into something other than the rational system planners claim it to be.

A third difference between private and government planning is flexibility. If your boss offers to take you to lunch at Benihana, you won't hesitate to abandon the peanut butter and jelly sandwich you planned to eat. If your rich uncle offers to take you to Hawaii next summer, you don't say, "No, I was planning to do my laundry that week." If Toyota or Ford makes a car that no one buys, it can switch production to a more popular model.

Government planning agencies lack this flexibility. Once a plan has been written, it is almost impossible to change because the interest groups that benefit from that plan have an incentive to ensure it is followed to the letter. In fact, the preparation of a plan often leads to the formation of new special interest groups aimed solely at enforcing the plan. Many planners welcome these interest groups, because what is the point of spending years writing a perfect plan if politicians can ignore it or change it the next day?

This doesn't mean that the plan will be followed. It usually doesn't take long after a plan has been written for reality to intrude and either the agencies charged with its implementation or the people affected by the plan to realize it isn't going to work. The best-case scenario is that the agencies abandon the plan. The more likely case, however, is that they try to implement the plan anyway and those people affected by it respond in unexpected ways so that the outcome differs completely from what was planned.

When I first began studying issues related to federal lands, urban growth, and transportation, I thought I was dealing with questions of policy. But I soon realized that what tied these and many other issues together is that elected officials have turned these issues over to the planners. To the extent that elected officials create policy, it is haphazard and usually a side effect of some budgetary compromise. The planners respond to these indiscriminate budgetary incentives and overlay them with their own preferences. The results are far from the rational planning promised by the textbooks.

Whether it is urban growth, air pollution, traffic congestion, or national forest management, planners advertise their method as the solution to any problem or controversy. This is attractive to elected officials who gladly turn thorny issues over to the bureaucracy rather than make the decisions—and take the heat—themselves. Planning bureaucracies, in turn, are run by the tens of thousands of well-intentioned but often clueless people called planners who, having graduated from architecture schools and other universities, are eager to bring their visions of utopia to the American people.

The bitter irony, freely admitted by numerous planners, is that many if not most of the problems that the planners propose to solve were caused not by the free marketplace, but by past generations of planners and other government bureaucrats. Instead of trying to figure out how to make the market work, planners today seek even more power to act as a substitute for the market and attempt to solve the problems created when their predecessors interfered with that market.

This leads to round after endless round of failed plans, each imposing more restrictive rules on and more costly fixes to the previous plans. The plans waste the time of people who try to participate in the planning process and impose huge costs on the people who are ultimately burdened with more taxes to pay for the plans and then suffer a lower quality of life that results from the plans.

Even if planning worked, almost every problem that plans are supposed to address can be more easily solved through other means. Part seven will present guidelines and examples of how to do that. The main barrier is often just the inertia that accompanies the status quo.

Americans routinely translate the Robert Burns poem that introduces this book as "the best-laid plans of mice and men." Yet the word that Burns uses is "scheme." My dictionary reveals that in the United Kingdom, including Canada, Australia, and Burns's Scotland, "scheme" means "a plan, policy, or program carried out by a government or business." But in the United States, the dictionary adds, "scheme" has a dark undertone; it is "a secret and cunning plan, especially one designed to cause damage or harm."[2] British politicians may scheme to their hearts' content, but American politicians caught scheming are soon voted out of office if they don't resign first.

The ultimate goal of this book is to inspire federal, state, and local governments to repeal planning laws and shut down their planning departments as not only a burden on taxpayers but also a source of costly mistakes. In the short run, I will consider this book a success if it leads more people to view long-range, comprehensive government planning with the same suspicion they give to cunning and sinister schemes.

Part One
Forest Planning

*Once we have seen how simplification, legibility, and manipulation
operate in forest management, we can then explore how the modern
state applies a similar lens to urban planning, rural settlement,
land administration, and agriculture.*

—James C. Scott[1]

Between 1952 and 1976, the Forest Service went from being one
of the most popular agencies in government to one of the most
controversial, with debates raging over clearcutting, road construction, herbicide spraying, grazing, mining, and other activities on
the nation's 193 million acres of national forests. Senator Hubert
Humphrey thought that the controversies could be resolved by having each national forest write a comprehensive, long-range plan.
Each plan would rationally consider all the various competing
resources and alternative ways of managing the forests and would
find the alternative that maximized net public benefits. Humphrey
also expected that the national forests would revise their plans every
10 to 15 years.

When Humphrey's legislation passed in 1976, the Forest Service
estimated that it could write the plans in four years at a cost of
about $120 million. Fifteen years later, the agency had spent at least
10 times that much on planning and some of the plans were still
unfinished.

- Far from resolving controversies, the plans created opportunities for interest group leaders to further polarize the public.
- Far from rational planning, the plans often relied on fabricated
  data and computer models that used highly questionable
  assumptions designed to confirm the preconceived notions of
  top forest officials.
- Far from maximizing net public benefits, the plans proposed
  to spend billions of dollars on highly controversial and environmentally destructive activities that would produce negligible
  returns to the Treasury.

- To add insult to injury, the plans that cost taxpayers at least a billion dollars and required a decade or more to write ended up being virtually ignored by on-the-ground forest managers, who quickly realized that they were worthless.

What went wrong? After spending years reviewing scores of forest plans, including all the background documents and computer runs associated with those plans, I realized that the Forest Service was heavily influenced by its budgetary incentives. Those incentives rewarded national forest managers for losing money on environmentally destructive activities and penalized those managers for making money or supporting environmentally beneficial activities. If misincentives caused the original controversies, planning was simply the wrong solution, since the planners themselves, and the officials who supervised them, were subject to the same incentives that led to the controversies in the first place.

I also realized that long-range, comprehensive planning would not have been feasible even if the incentives had been correct initially. A one- to two-million-acre national forest capable of producing dozens of different resources that sometimes complement but often conflict with one another is simply too complex to plan, especially when planners were also expected to predict such things as timber prices and demand for various forms of recreation. Planners who tried to gather all the necessary data and understand the various relationships among resources soon discovered that their plans were obsolete before they were completed because new information, political trends, or physical events such as forest fires had a way of intruding into their virtual realities.

Finally, the notions that planning can be "rational" in a highly politicized environment or that competing interest groups would gladly sit down to negotiate the goals of their members proved to be as unrealistic as many of the numbers the Forest Service put into its computer models. For all these reasons, planning proved to be such a failure that a recent chief of the Forest Service referred to it as "analysis paralysis."[2] Sadly, the Humphrey law is still on the books, and many national forests are busily but uselessly revising their plans for the next 10 to 15 years.

1. The Case of the Fake Forests

"Fake Forests!" blared the headline on the front page of the April 13, 1985, *San Francisco Chronicle*. The accompanying article by *Chronicle* writer Dale Champion revealed that Forest Service employees in California had pretended to reforest thousands of acres of land, and then spent the reforestation money on something else. The article noted that they sometimes also spent reforestation money to reforest land that didn't need it.[1]

The revelation was so stunning that in July 1985, the House Forest Management Subcommittee held hearings in San Francisco about the phantom forests. The star witness was a Forest Service employee named Cherry DuLaney, a reforestation specialist on the Tahoe National Forest. In late 1984, as part of a Forest Service–sponsored leadership-training program, DuLaney had surveyed Forest Service silviculturists (reforestation experts) in California. Nearly two-thirds of them returned the 32-page questionnaire within three weeks.[2]

"Twenty-three percent of the respondents acknowledged reporting ghost acres," she told the subcommittee.[3] In other words, nearly a quarter of the reforestation experts admitted to having reported reforestation or other work that hadn't actually been done.

After DuLaney completed her testimony, Subcommittee Chair Jim Weaver (D-OR) turned to Zane Smith, the forester in charge of the Forest Service's California operations, and asked what the agency had done to publicize DuLaney's report. "Randy O'Toole noted it in his land-management planning newsletter," answered Smith.[4]

That newsletter, which we called *Forest Planning*, followed the Forest Service's efforts to write comprehensive land-use and resource management plans for each of the 120 or so national forests in its care. When I wasn't writing articles for the newsletter, I spent much of the 1980s sitting in Forest Service offices reading computer printouts and other planning documents. In doing so, I often ran across interesting memos such as DuLaney's study and reported them to the newsletter's readers.

When I found DuLaney's report, I knew it was interesting, but I never suspected it would lead to front-page headlines or congressional hearings. Representative Weaver's office asked me to testify, saying, "The subcommittee will want to know why you think Forest Service employees would fabricate the numbers." To answer that question, I had to put together everything I had learned in the previous 10 years about the Forest Service and its budgetary process.

In 1952, *Newsweek* magazine reported that the Forest Service was one of the most popular agencies in government. In addition to the Forest Service being the only federal agency that actually earned a profit, *Newsweek* noted that the Forest Service's management of the national forests produced huge nonmonetary benefits for recreation, wildlife, watersheds, and other uses. Members of Congress "would as soon abuse their own mothers as be unkind to the Forest Service," added the magazine.[5] *Newsweek* traced the agency's success and popularity to its decentralization, a view later endorsed by social scientists studying government bureaucracies.[6]

During the four decades before this *Newsweek* article, the Forest Service budget was dominated not by timber, recreation, wildlife, or water, but by fire. In 1908, Congress had taken the unusual step of giving the Forest Service a blank check for extinguishing wildfires that started anywhere on the 193 million acres of national forests. This made the agency into, above all, a fire suppression agency.

This was changing, however, even as *Newsweek* published its article. In 1952, the Forest Service sold about three billion board feet of timber, a board foot being the amount of wood needed to cut a board of lumber 1 inch by 12 inches by 12 inches. Most of the timber sold by national forests was cut using *selection cutting*, meaning that Forest Service experts selected individual trees, based on their maturity, and marked them for cutting, leaving behind most other trees in the vicinity. If carefully done, selection cutting could leave a forest looking like a well-manicured park or even (to the untrained eye) untrammeled wilderness.

Over the next 15 years, postwar demand for housing led the Forest Service to ramp up annual timber sales to more than 10 billion board feet. Along with the increase in sales, the Forest Service switched from selection cutting to *clearcutting*, that is, the removal of all trees, regardless of size or maturity, within a perimeter marked by Forest Service employees. The change was not the result of a national directive but was made by individual forest managers over three decades in the 1950s through the 1970s.

Clearcutting, the managers argued, was less expensive (partly true) and was needed by many species for reforestation (rarely true[7]). But clearcutting led to waves of protests from hunters, anglers, hikers, and other recreationists who considered clearcuts ugly and responsible for soil erosion, stream pollution, destruction of wildlife habitat, and numerous other problems. Controversies over clearcutting led to numerous congressional hearings, blue-ribbon reports, and lawsuits. In 1974, one of those lawsuits convinced a federal judge that clearcutting violated an 1897 law that required the Forest Service to cut only mature trees and mark every tree to be cut. Under pressure from the timber industry, which claimed this law was archaic, Congress was forced to take action.

Led by Senator Hubert Humphrey, Congress decided to turn the national forests over to the planners. Humphrey's National Forest Management Act of 1976 directed the Forest Service to write comprehensive land-use and resource-management plans for each national forest. The plans would determine where clearcutting was "optimal," which lands were suitable for other sorts of timber cutting, how much timber could be cut each year, and which lands should be set aside for recreation or other purposes. The law also required the Forest Service to revise the plans every 10 to 15 years. One of the last of the New Deal Democrats, Humphrey saw the planning process as a "vehicle that will get the facts needed to make wise decisions ... to set national goals, [and] to get public input into policy making."[8]

The Forest Service was no stranger to planning, but before the 1970s its plans were short and simple. Most of them focused on calculating how much timber could be cut from a national forest each year. Each national forest wrote such *timber management plans* (sometimes called *multiple-use plans*) about once every 10 years.

Private timber companies tended to cut all the trees in a given forest in a few years, leaving nothing more to cut until the forests grew back. In contrast, the Forest Service had long promised that no national forest would sell so much timber in one year that it would ever have to sell less in some future year, a policy that came to be known as *nondeclining flow*.[9] To ensure that future cutting levels did not decline, plans written before about 1960 tended to be very cautious. Managers were conservative in their projections of how fast timber would grow, and they excluded large amounts of land from timber cutting because either it wasn't economically suitable for timber or it helped to protect recreation, wildlife, or watershed values.

As the market for national forest timber grew in the 1950s and 1960s, Forest Service managers began using a variety of tricks to increase timber sale levels. They added land to the timber base that had previously been set aside for other uses. They included low-valued timber in the base in anticipation that its price would eventually rise enough to make it economic to cut. They inflated the yield tables that predicted timber growth rates. They changed their method of measuring trees to increase the amount they could sell.

In 1969, a Forest Service research report called the *Douglas-Fir Supply Study* revealed that many national forests had overshot their mark.[10] The cutting rates they had set in the 1960s were higher than they could sustain in the future. To keep the Forest Service from immediately reducing timber sales, the timber industry urged that the agency simply abandon its nondeclining flow policy. But in 1973, the chief of the Forest Service sent a directive to the forests requiring them to continue following the policy, even if it meant reducing timber sales now.[11]

Meanwhile, in 1970, Earth Day energized all sorts of people who were critical of national forest management. Recreationists hated the growing clearcuts that spread across the forests like leprosy. Wilderness lovers detested new roads that penetrated remote areas. Organic farmers and gardeners living near the national forests felt threatened by the herbicides and other chemicals that forest managers routinely dumped on clearcuts.

The Forest Service responded to the many local controversies by becoming more centralized. The Forest Service hierarchy has four levels: In the 1970s, about 600 district rangers did the actual on-the-ground management and reported to about 120 national forest supervisors, who were overseen by 9 regional foresters, who answered to the Washington, D.C., chief of the Forest Service. (Due to budget cuts and mergers, the numbers of district rangers and supervisors have declined by about 20 percent since 1990.) As late as the mid-1960s, the chief trusted the district rangers to make most of the decisions about on-the-ground management. When those decisions led to public debates in the late 1960s, the chief progressively moved decisionmaking authority up to the forest supervisors and regional foresters.

In 1970, President Nixon signed the National Environmental Policy Act directing federal agencies to write environmental impact statements for all major federal actions significantly affecting the human environment. Many agencies resisted this mandate, but the Forest Service welcomed it, hoping that an open planning process with public involvement would reduce the criticism it had been getting from all sides. In the early 1970s, the Forest Service directed regional and forest offices to write environmental impact statements for at least three kinds of plans:

- Timber management plans that calculated how much timber could be cut from each national forest;
- Land-use plans that allocated land to recreation, wildlife, timber, and other uses, usually for planning units that ranged in size from a tenth to a quarter of a national forest; and
- Herbicide spray plans that analyzed the effects of chemical herbicides, usually written for groups of several national forests.

To handle the wilderness question, the Washington office itself wrote a national Roadless Area Review and Evaluation (RARE), which analyzed all roadless areas for their wilderness suitability. The Sierra Club took this plan to court, arguing that a national plan could not adequately deal with the nuances of local conditions. When the courts ruled RARE inadequate, the Forest Service followed with RARE II, which the courts again ruled inadequate.

In contrast to RARE's failure, splitting up the rest of planning into discrete decisions made each plan appear more manageable. But the interdependency of the plans created problems for both planners and the public. The amount of herbicide spraying depended on how much timber was cut. The level of timber sales depended on the allocations in the land-use plans. The land-use plans depended on the results of the RARE analyses. The amount of land the Forest Service was willing to set aside for wilderness in the RARE analyses depended on how fast it thought timber would grow on the remaining lands, which was calculated in the timber management plans.

The separation of the herbicide spray plans from timber planning created a particularly gaping hole in the analyses. Herbicides were needed after clearcuts and not generally needed after selection or other cutting methods. The timber management plans, which decided whether to clearcut, ignored the effects of herbicides because they were analyzed in the herbicide plans. But the herbicide plans were only written after the clearcuts had been accomplished. So the planning process never factored the effects of herbicides into the decision to clearcut.

After Congress passed the National Forest Management Act, the Forest Service decided to collapse all these plans, and their interdependencies, into one comprehensive land-use and resource management plan for each national forest. The then chief John McGuire called the anticipated planning process the "largest planning effort in the western world"—a backdoor allusion to soviet "eastern world" planning that should have made people wary.

Developed with the help of a committee of nationally known forest scientists, the Forest Service's new planning process would include national, regional, and forest plans. The national plan would set timber, grazing, and other targets for each region. The regional plans would distribute those targets to the forests. The forest plans would attempt to meet those targets at the lowest possible cost. If individual forests could not possibly meet their targets, they could negotiate a reduction. But they were expected to try to meet them, even if the cost to taxpayers was far greater than the resources were worth.

The process was almost a perfect parody of Soviet-style government: 5- and 10-year plans, targets, and a complete disregard for profits or value. Anyone who really believed that this process could result in "wise decisions" that would pacify Forest Service critics was in for a rude awakening. Instead, timber, environmental, and other interest groups used the plans as organizing tools to polarize the public and demonize the Forest Service. Members of the public challenged every plan using an internal agency appeals process and, when they lost some of those appeals, often took the plans to court. My job during the 1980s was to provide conservation groups with the technical tools and support they needed to make those challenges.

2. Garbage In, Gospel Out

Writing a 150-year plan (or even a 10-year plan) for a 1.5- to 2.0-million-acre forest that produces a wide variety of goods (and bads) that often compete and conflict with one another requires more than the back of an envelope. In the 1970s and 1980s, managers of both public and private forests increasingly turned to computers to help plan their lands, schedule timber harvests, and coordinate resource management.

A number of competing computer models were available for forest planning, and some might have been more appropriate for certain forests while others would work best on other forests. But as part of its growing centralization, the Forest Service directed all forests to use the same computer program, which was called FORPLAN, short for forest planning. FORPLAN allowed planners to enter information about the forest into the computer and then ask questions, such as "What is the maximum amount of timber that can be cut?" or "How much timber would be cut each decade if the forest were managed to earn maximum profits?" Forest officials gushed that FORPLAN would simultaneously allocate land and schedule timber cutting for the next 150 years.[1]

To build their FORPLAN models, planners would break their forests up into hundreds of different zones based on such factors as vegetation, the age of the timber, wildlife habitat, steepness of slope, whether the zone had roads, or any other criteria that seemed important. For each zone, planners had to identify management costs, timber values, timber yields, and the values and yields of other resources such as recreation, water, forage, and specific species of wildlife. Planners would set a goal such as maximizing timber or net economic value and could also set constraints, such as floors or limits on the amount of timber that could be cut. They could then give FORPLAN a goal, such as maximizing timber or profits, and it would allocate zones to timber, recreation, and other prescriptions and tell how much timber could be harvested from the forest for each of the next 15 decades.

As parodies of soviet planning, the forest plans were quite humorous. The data used in the models were often erroneous or fabricated. Many plans assumed, for example, that timber was worth 50 to 100 percent more than timber companies were actually paying for it. Others assumed that trees could grow far faster than is realistic. One actually projected that trees could grow 650 feet tall, nearly twice the height of the tallest trees in the world.

Many people described FORPLAN as a *black box*, that is, a machine whose inner workings were too complicated for most people to understand.[2] Technically, FORPLAN used linear programming methods to find the optimal solution to any problem the planners gave it. But FORPLAN's inner workings were much less important than the quality of the data planners entered into the computer. As an outsider, I suspected that the Forest Service would bias FORPLAN models toward timber, and I set a goal of reviewing at least a third of the plans to find out if this was true. Ultimately, I collected and read every draft and final plan and reviewed the actual FORPLAN computer runs and background data for well over half the 120 forest plans.

To write the forest plans required by the National Forest Management Act, the Forest Service hired hundreds of recent graduates in economics, planning, operations research, and other technical fields. These people enthusiastically and often idealistically embraced the opportunity to prepare objective plans that would determine the future of nearly 10 percent of the nation's land. Almost immediately, however, they ran into serious obstacles.

Data collection is one of the most important early steps in any planning process. Forest Service rules required planners to use the "best available data"—but the emphasis was on *available*. Historically, the Forest Service usually did a complete forest inventory before each 10-year timber management plan. An inventory would not measure every tree in a forest but would measure randomly or systematically selected plots scattered across the forest. In one common inventory procedure, one plot was measured for every 1,850 acres, so each plot was assumed to represent that many acres. If 10 plots were found to have 100-year-old Douglas fir trees, planners assumed the forest had 18,500 acres of 100-year-old Douglas firs.

Inventory specialists planned to measure the same plots every 10 years, providing information on how fast trees were growing and other changes in the forest. Reinventories also made it possible to identify and correct any errors in the previous inventory. In the 1970s, managers of one Oregon forest realized that one of its inventory crews had made a serious mistake in the 1960s: Contrary to directions, if a plot fell in a meadow or a lake, they moved the plot to the nearest forest. This led managers to underestimate the number of acres of meadows and lakes and overestimate the number of acres of productive forest.

Given planning deadlines and the fact that they were spending so much money on computer runs and newly hired experts, forest planners in the 1980s were rarely able to do new inventories. So they relied on data that were anywhere from 10 to 30 years old. These data were updated by subtracting the volume of timber cut in that time and adding the amount that planners thought trees would grow in that time. Obviously this meant they had no opportunity to correct errors in earlier inventories or their growth projections.

The few forests that did new inventories often took shortcuts to save time and money. Previous inventories collected a huge amount of data, including the height, age, diameter, and species of every tree in each plot, plus more general information such as the steepness of the slope, the direction the slope faced, and the species of shrubs growing under the trees. The computer age is supposed to enable people to consider and analyze ever-greater quantities of data. But FORPLAN could deal with only a limited number of variables, so planners decided not to collect any data FORPLAN couldn't handle. This saved money in the short run, but reduced the reliability of the inventory and made it impossible to compare the inventory results with any future inventories that did collect more data.

Other forests completed their reinventories only after forest planning was well under way. A reinventory of Oregon's Malheur National Forest found that trees measured in the previous inventory subsequently "shrank" in both diameter and height. This prompted speculation that the person in charge of the previous inventory had inflated the numbers to get answers more in keeping with the Forest Service's timber goals.[3] Since the reinventory was completed in the midst of forest planning, planners continued to use the older discredited data in FORPLAN.

Given information, however unreliable, about how much timber was standing in the forest, the next question planners had to answer

17

was how fast trees could grow. Under the nondeclining flow policy, forests that had lots of old-growth timber couldn't cut that timber any faster than the next generation of trees could grow. So second-growth *yield tables* that projected rapid growth allowed for more cutting of old-growth trees today.

The first plan I reviewed was for the Okanogan National Forest. Though located in arid eastern Washington, it based most of its growth projections on yield tables written for moist western Washington, which receives as much as four times the rainfall. Timber inventory data collected by the forest revealed that Okanogan growth rates were only about 60 percent of the rates projected by the western Washington yield tables.[4]

The Santa Fe National Forest itself discovered that actual timber volumes were only 80 percent of the numbers it had entered into FORPLAN. Rather than reenter all the yield tables, it decided to simply reduce the timber harvests proposed by FORPLAN by 20 percent. This seemed simple enough—except that planners asked FORPLAN to maximize the forest's net economic value. Given the overestimated volumes, FORPLAN calculated that timber cutting was more lucrative than it really was. The higher volumes made it appear that only 11 percent of the forest would lose money on timber sales. I found that correcting the volumes increased this to 48 percent.[5]

Some forests had already cut much of their old growth, so—if you believed their second-growth yield tables—the main limiting factor to timber-cutting levels was the growth rate of the old growth. California national forests used yield tables that stunningly predicted old-growth forests would double in volume in as little as 20 years.[6] Since old growth is normally considered to grow very slowly, these predictions were not credible and greatly distorted the plans.

Other national forest yield tables were even more absurd. University of Montana forestry professor Alan McQuillan found computer-generated yield tables used by Idaho's Clearwater National Forest that predicted trees could grow 650 feet tall in 150 years.[7] That's nearly twice as tall as the tallest tree in the world and close to three times as tall as the tallest trees in Idaho.[8] No one on the forest noticed the error, and planners didn't correct it after McQuillan pointed it out.

When they weren't overestimating timber growth rates, many planners overestimated timber prices. Timber prices had risen rapidly during the 1970s, partly due to speculation fueled by contracts that allowed purchasers to pay for timber up to five inflation-filled years after they bid.[9] Many forests presumed that prices would continue to rise at similar rates for the next 50 years. Since FORPLAN did its calculations in decades, planners applied the prices predicted for the midpoint of each decade to that entire decade. Yet planning was taking place during the deepest recession in the second half of the 20th century, and actual prices had crashed well below the levels of the late 1970s. So planners found themselves in the odd position of using prices for the first decade that were higher than the forests had ever received at a time when actual prices were their lowest in years. Average FORPLAN prices were often two or three times actual prices, and in some forests they were more than five times as high as the highest amounts ever paid for timber on those forests.[10]

Even in the long run, planners' predictions of future timber prices were unlikely. The price surge of the 1970s was due to timber purchasers' discovery that, in an inflationary era, they could take advantage of Forest Service timber contracts that gave them years to cut and pay for the trees without indexing the price they paid to lumber or other wood values. At 5 percent inflation on a five-year contract, purchasers could bid 25 percent more than the trees were worth at the time of sale and still make a profit. This led to furious speculation as some companies that didn't even have processing facilities started bidding in anticipation of reselling the logs to some other buyer several years down the road.[11]

All of this came to a screeching halt when the Federal Reserve Board raised interest rates enough to curb inflation, effectively shutting down the homebuilding industry in the process. Purchasers found themselves holding contracts for trees they couldn't afford to cut at the time they bid on them, much less after interest rates rose. But in the world of FORPLAN, many forest planners pretended that the party would continue another 50 years.

While timber price *trends*—an assumption of increasing timber prices over time—were built into many FORPLAN models, costs and competing resource values were usually assumed to remain constant. In reality, costs were rising and recreation values had historically risen even faster than timber values. Forest planners in

Oregon and Washington were so disturbed by this "strong and unjustifiable bias" toward timber that they wrote a memo to the Washington office arguing that the trends were "unstable" and of questionable accuracy.[12] The Washington office replied that "it would be an error to ignore the substantial documentation of long-term real prices" for timber and ordered them to use the trends.[13] Of course, the reason the Forest Service had documentation of future timber prices and none for the future prices of other resources was that the agency had directed its researchers to study the one and not the others.

Even if the researchers' work was valid, many forests misapplied it. For example, the research predicted that lodgepole pine prices in western Montana would reach $116 per thousand board feet by the year 2030. The Bitterroot National Forest told FORPLAN that this value would exceed $350 by the same year.

Rather than justify timber sales using overestimated timber yields or prices, some forests relied on the relationships between timber and other resources. Typically, they would tell FORPLAN that recreation was very valuable, but that no recreation could be produced without roads. The only way FORPLAN could get roads was by cutting trees. As one forest planner derisively wrote, "The mechanic has just modeled a nation of people who like to camp in clearcuts!"[14] Timber values on some of these forests were so negative that, without the recreation values, FORPLAN would cut no timber. But with recreation, FORPLAN would cut over the entire forest.

Research showed that, on virtually all forests, the use of roaded recreation at the current price—which was zero—was far less than the supply offered by the 300,000 miles of roads that laced through the forests. The recreation that was in short supply was wilderness and roadless recreation. Yet some planning teams designed FORPLAN to calculate that even wilderness recreation would increase after more roads were built.

One of the first forests to include these recreation-timber relationships in FORPLAN was Indiana's Hoosier Forest. The formal documentation included a table claiming that the demand for roaded recreation greatly exceeded both the supply and current usage. Since demand (technically, the *quantity demanded*) cannot exceed use when the price is zero, I asked to see all the background documents relating to recreation demand. The planners brought me a stack of papers about three feet high.

Reading through the papers, I found several earlier demand projections that were much lower. Near the bottom of the stack, I found a memo from the regional office in Milwaukee questioning the later, higher demand numbers. A note was written on the memo in handwriting that I recognized as belonging to the forest's recreation specialist. "I would agree that my 7/7/82 calculations are high!" said the note. "I was told by the forest planning team to make sure that demand was higher than our capability. I did as I was told."[15] By that time, he had transferred to another forest and nervously refused to talk with me on the telephone about the demand figures.

Two years later, when I was reviewing the Mark Twain Forest plan in Missouri, I found a memo from the Eastern Regional Office of the Forest Service to all forests in the Midwest and Northeast. The memo said that the Hoosier Forest had found a way to make FORPLAN cut trees even where timber sales lost money: simply tell FORPLAN that there was a huge, unmet demand for roaded recreation. Samuel Clemens no doubt would find it amusing that the Mark Twain Forest joined most of the other forests in the region in following the Hoosier's example.

Planners' assumptions about the relationships between timber and wildlife were also often questionable. The grizzly bear, a threatened species in Montana, is vulnerable mainly to humans. To minimize conflicts, biologists recommended isolating the bear by building few new roads and closing existing ones. So the Gallatin National Forest, which borders Yellowstone Park, put over 120,000 acres in "grizzly-timber emphasis." This prescription called for building new roads, selling timber, then using revenues from the timber sales to close both the new and the existing roads.

In practice, however, Gallatin timber values were so low that few, if any, timber sales sold by the forest generated enough revenues to close any roads.[16] The result was that each new timber sale built more roads that increased the vulnerability of the grizzly to humans. Planners didn't consider the possibility of simply closing existing roads, which would have cost less than the subsidized timber sales, because Congress freely appropriated funds for timber sales but disliked funding road closures.

The Flathead National Forest, which borders Glacier National Park, went a step further and presumed that a mere decision not to build roads in a roadless area would lead to a 20 percent increase in

21

grizzlies, thus allowing more timber cutting somewhere else without threatening overall grizzly populations.[17] Seemingly, forest planners believed that grizzlies would read the plan and increase their numbers as soon as the decision was made to not build roads.

Another important question was how much land was suited for timber management. Congress had directed the Forest Service to exclude from timber management land that was not physically or economically suited for timber production. The Forest Service neatly sidestepped the question of economic suitability through its definition of the term. Each forest was given a timber target based on what the forest had previously produced or what forest managers thought—before doing any economic analyses—it could produce. Economically suitable land, said forest planning rules, included all the land needed to meet that target. That this might require taxpayers to lose money on most or all of a forest's sales was irrelevant to the Forest Service.

Questions of physical suitability were often sidestepped as well. Planners on the Mt. Hood National Forest carefully studied 141 randomly selected plots and calculated that 16.4 percent of the land that had previously been included in the forest's timber base was basically just rockslides and talus slopes, incapable of producing any wood at all. Since these areas were too small to map in FOR-PLAN, they asked for permission to reduce yield tables by 16.4 percent. However, regional timber staff approved only a 10 percent reduction, suggesting that wishful thinking prevailed over the analysts.[18]

The problems with the data used in FORPLAN were pervasive, yet Forest Service officials based important decisions on how to manage land and how much timber to cut on this computer program. One Forest Service economist told me that his FORPLAN motto was "Garbage in, gospel out."

Most of these errors could be explained away by bias on the part of Forest Service officials. They do not necessarily prove that there is anything wrong with the concept of planning itself. Nor do they explain the fake forests uncovered by Cherry DuLaney. But it turned out that both the fake forests and the garbage-like data in the computer models were closely related.

3. A Process of Natural Selection

Since many FORPLAN runs supposedly aimed to maximize net economic values, some of the most important data in FORPLAN related to timber prices. To verify these data, I reviewed reports for all timber sales sold by individual forests in the years before my visits. The Forest Service sold timber in auctions, and the bidding was often vigorous. Timber sale reports included the Forest Service's appraisal, which was used to set a minimum bid, as well as the actual bids made by the various purchasers.

The timber sale reports also revealed something I had not known, which was that the Forest Service was allowed to keep some of the receipts from the timber it sold. Each timber sale report had an entry with the cryptic title of *Plan'd SAB Col*, which stood for *planned sale area betterment collection*. This represented the portion of the timber sale's receipts that the Forest Service expected to keep.

A 1930 law known as the Knutson-Vandenberg Act allowed the Forest Service to keep an unspecified (and therefore unlimited) share of timber receipts for reforestation. The 1976 National Forest Management Act expanded the purposes for which these funds could be used to include wildlife habitat improvements, recreation facilities, or any other "sale area improvements." This law greatly shaped the Forest Service's view of the world and how it designed timber sales, because certain designs allowed it to keep more money while others allowed more money to go back to the U.S. Treasury.

In essence, the Knutson-Vandenberg Act encouraged the Forest Service to use timber sales as a fundraising tool for all sorts of forest activities. Would you like to improve wildlife habitat? Plan a timber sale. Want to build a hiking trail? Design another timber sale. Need to repair some of the watershed damage done by past timber sales? Sell more timber.

Detailed K-V documents written for each sale revealed something else: Although the law allowed the Forest Service to spend K-V funds only in the timber sale areas (defined by the Forest Service to include any area within a quarter mile of a cutting unit), the Forest Service actually kept a significant share of K-V funds as "administrative overhead." After each K-V dollar was spent on the ground, the Washington office of the Forest Service received 4 cents; the regional offices kept about a dime; and the national forest offices kept anywhere from 20 to 50 cents. The result was that about a third of K-V money was actually spent on overhead.

The bureaucracy's dependence on K-V overhead funds explained Cherry DuLaney's fake forests. DuLaney did her survey in 1984. In the early 1980s, the timber industry was suffering from a severe recession and was cutting very little national forest timber. This meant there were few opportunities for reforestation, herbicide spraying, or other activities funded by K-V monies. But the Washington and regional offices wrote their budgets three years in advance. Because they did not anticipate the decline in K-V spending, their budgets counted on a continued flow of K-V overhead funds. When the funds didn't come in, rather than reduce spending, the regional office pressured local reforestation specialists to plant more trees, spray more herbicides, and do other K-V activities.

"Many times, unnecessary projects are proposed and accomplished to finance the personnel to accomplish very necessary jobs such as planning and prework on future projects," one silviculturist commented.[1] This created a chain of incentives: to fund the planners, they had to plant trees, and to plant the trees, they had to sell trees to timber companies.

"The natural tendency of the bureaucracy to maintain and increase its budget provides a strong motivation for the Forest Service to make targets, not on-the-ground needs, the driving force in project work," I told Representative Jim Weaver's subcommittee. "Targets are easily budgeted; on-the-ground needs are not, since they are less predictable from year to year. As Mr. Zane Smith testified, the targets are set three years in advance. So targets set in 1979 through 1981, which anticipated high levels of timber cutting and high levels of need for reforestation, were overestimated because in 1982 through 1984 much less timber was cut and fewer acres needed reforestation." Saying this was not "impugning the integrity of anyone in the Forest Service, which has some of the most honest and well-intentioned employees in the government," I added. "But honesty and good intentions are not enough; bureaucratic and institutional forces overrule."[2]

After the hearing, I realized that the Knutson-Vandenberg Act helped explain many of the other controversies that swirled around the national forests. They included clearcutting, herbicides, roadless areas, below-cost timber sales, and the nondeclining flow policy.

Clearcutting

Congress appropriates funds for the Forest Service to arrange and administer timber sales, while timber receipts provide the funds for postsale activities, such as reforestation. From the forest manager's viewpoint, the funds available for arranging sales are fixed, whereas funds for postsale activities are limited only by timber values and the number of acres included in sale areas. The ideal cutting method, then, is one that cuts the greatest number of acres at the lowest presale cost per acre.

That means clearcutting. As the Forest Service often pointed out, clearcutting had the lowest presale costs since managers only needed to mark the perimeter of areas to be cut. This allowed them to stretch appropriated funds to the greatest possible number of acres. A typical timber sale might include a dozen clearcuts, each located some distance apart. Since the Forest Service defined "sale area" as the land within a quarter mile of trees that are cut, managers could locate clearcuts up to one-half mile apart and apply K-V funds to all the land between them.

At the same time (and contrary to repeated Forest Service claims), clearcutting often imposed the highest postsale costs because it created the harshest environment for reforestation: hot, dry sites, with soil temperatures sometimes reaching levels lethal to seedlings because of the lack of shade. Of course, this simply allowed managers to keep more K-V funds for reforestation, including, in many cases, funds to shade each individual seedling.

During the 1950s and 1960s, individual national forests discovered, either on their own or by the transfer of personnel from one forest to another, that clearcutting was much more lucrative than other cutting methods. Managers may not even have been aware that the budgetary process was shaping their decisions. They just knew that they got a more positive response from some activities than from others. No doubt some people within the Forest Service genuinely believed that clearcutting was economically and ecologically a superior practice. These people might be promoted over those who believed in selection cutting, not because of their position on clearcutting but because their decisions led to larger budgets for the agency, and thus they were viewed as more successful than supporters of other cutting methods.

Herbicides

The Forest Service often claimed that the softwood timber species they wanted to grow, such as Douglas fir and ponderosa pine, "needed" clearcutting for optimal growth. In fact, in many areas the harsh conditions created by clearcutting were more ideal for less valuable hardwood trees and shrubs, such as alders, maples, and oaks. Forest managers applied herbicides, often from helicopters, to kill the hardwoods and allow the softwoods to grow. Because of differences in the way that hardwoods and softwoods grow, managers had a small window of opportunity every spring during which herbicide spraying would kill hardwoods without hurting the softwoods.

Herbicide opponents charged that the Forest Service sprayed chemicals whether or not they were needed. DuLaney's report proved this to be true. As part of reforestation, many national forests routinely built one or two herbicide applications into the K-V plans for every sale. In turn, regional offices would give the forests an annual target to spray so many acres with herbicides so the regional offices could forecast their share of K-V overhead. Forest managers who were rated on their ability to meet targets had no incentive to find out whether herbicide spraying was actually needed on a particular clearcut because the money was available and if they didn't spend it, they might fail to meet their target. Many managers admitted to DuLaney that, during the years when cutting rates were low, they sprayed herbicides during the wrong time of the year, when they knew spraying wouldn't do any good, just to meet their targets.

Below-Cost Timber Sales

In the 1950s, the Forest Service claimed, with some justification, that it was the only federal agency that earned a profit. It continued to make this claim through the 1970s, but by this time it was spending hundreds of millions of dollars more to manage the national forests than it returned to the Treasury.

Moreover, as Natural Resources Defense Council analyst Tom Barlow found when he compared timber receipts with timber-related costs, most national forests lost money on their timber sales alone, not counting the costs of recreation, wildlife, and other resource management.[3] Barlow coined the term *below-cost timber sales* and inspired Congress to include a requirement in the National Forest Management Act that forest plans identify lands "not suited for timber production, considering physical, economic, and other pertinent factors" and exclude those lands from timber management.

Whatever Congress's intent, the effect of the Knutson-Vandenberg Act was to reward forest managers for losing money on timber sales. I once asked a timber staff officer how long the Forest Service had to revise K-V plans after a sale was completed. "The plan can be revised until the sale is closed," he said, meaning when the last trees were cut and the last dollars paid for the sale. "And if you want to do it, you had better do it by then or the money is lost—*it goes to the U.S. Treasury*." Two decades of timber sales transmogrified an agency that had been proud to return more money to the Treasury than it spent into an agency that viewed returns to the Treasury as "losses."

The Knutson-Vandenberg Act authorized the Forest Service to collect money for reforestation and other activities "in addition to the payments for the timber." Up until 1956, that's what the Forest Service did: purchasers paid for K-V activities separately from their payment for timber. Starting in 1957, however, K-V funds were simply incorporated into the total payment for timber. At this time, the Forest Service required managers to return only 50 cents per thousand board feet to the Treasury.

This number was selected because, at some point in the remote past—presumably soon after Congress passed the Knutson-Vandenberg Act in 1930—50 cents per thousand represented the cost to the Treasury of arranging and administering timber sales. But by the 1970s, this cost was approaching $15 per thousand. Although timber purchasers usually built the roads, the cost of designing the roads was paid with tax dollars, and it could more than double sale costs. But the Forest Service never changed the 50-cent rule, and it remains in effect to this day.[4]

Timber values in many national forests were so low that forest managers would keep nearly all timber receipts in the K-V fund to pay for reforestation and other activities. The sale would be below cost because the 50 cents returned to the Treasury failed to cover the $15 to $30 cost of arranging the sales and engineering the roads.

Other forests had at least some timber that could earn a profit. But these forests became adept at *cross-subsidizing* timber, that is, designing timber sales to include both valuable timber and worthless timber elsewhere on the same forest. The purchaser would pay less for the valuable timber than it was really worth in exchange for also removing worthless timber.[5]

For example, suppose a forest had a stand with a million board feet of valuable ponderosa pine trees worth $60 per thousand board feet. The reforestation specialist says that reforesting the site would cost $9,500, including administrative overhead. Selling the trees for $60,000 would allow the forest to keep $9.50 per thousand board feet for reforestation and the remaining $50.50 would go to the Treasury. Elsewhere, the same national forest has a stand of a million board feet of low-value lodgepole pine trees worth negative $40 per thousand board feet—that is, the cost of cutting and transporting the trees to a sawmill would be $40 less than the mill would pay for the logs. If it can sell the trees, the Forest Service could spend more money on reforestation and, of course, have more money for administrative overhead. To sell the lodgepole pine, the forest combines both stands in the same sale. It sells the trees for $10 a thousand board feet, or $20,000. Costs to the Treasury double but receipts to the Treasury fall from $50,500 to just $1,000. Meanwhile, the Forest Service doubles its K-V collection to $19,000.

Such cross-subsidization was extremely common in the national forests. In 1984, I analyzed every timber sale sold by the Forest Service in 1983—roughly 10,000 of them. I was surprised to discover that the forests with the most valuable timber did the most cross-subsidization. The reason was simple: timber values in some areas were so great that managers could not possibly spend all of the receipts within a quarter mile of the timber cutting. Rather than return the maximum amount to the Treasury, forest managers "spent" some of that timber value subsidizing the cutting of other worthless trees on the same forests.[6] Timber purchasers went along with the game, but were known to call the worthless areas "punishment units" because the losses they took on those units were their punishment for getting other valuable timber at such low prices.

Roadless Areas

National forests tended to sell the most valuable timber first, meaning species of trees that had the highest value or that could be reached at the lowest cost. By 1970, national forest areas that were still roadless tended to include mainly less valuable species or be the most expensive to access due to steep slopes, poor soils, or other problems.

Thanks to the cross-subsidies encouraged by the K-V fund, negative timber values presented no problem for the Forest Service. One leading forest planner in California joked about "helicopter lodgepole" sales, because helicopter logging was the most expensive way of removing trees from remote or sensitive areas and lodgepole pine was the least valuable softwood tree in the West. Yet it was no joke: many national forests did have sales with helicopter lodgepole areas, most of which were cross-subsidized by valuable timber in some other part of the same sale.

Wilderness was probably the most valuable use of many roadless areas, if only because timber and other resources in those areas cost more to remove than the resources were worth. Moreover, Forest Service studies of recreation values consistently found that recreationists placed the highest value on wilderness recreation because of the solitude that it provided. But Congress did not allow the Forest Service to charge for most recreation, so wilderness added little to Forest Service budgets. The budgetary process encouraged forest managers to dedicate these areas for timber, even though those areas would cost taxpayers, because they could use them to boost their own budgets.

Nondeclining Flow

Some argue that the Forest Service has merely been "captured" by the industry it was supposed to regulate, namely, the companies that purchased timber from the national forests.[7] But the timber industry could not have its way with the Forest Service either, particularly on the question of the nondeclining flow policy. The industry managed to convince Congress to allow departures from nondeclining flow in the National Forest Management Act, but the industry could not budge the Forest Service from its policy.

The explanation for this can also be traced to the Forest Service's budget and, eventually, to the Knutson-Vandenberg fund. Given

29

the nondeclining flow rule, timber sales on many national forests with large old-growth inventories were limited by how fast the second-growth forest could grow. This meant that investments in thinnings, fertilization, and other activities that stimulated the growth of second growth could lead to immediate increases in old-growth cuttings. In essence, the Forest Service was using nondeclining flow to hold timber harvest rates hostage to get Congress to appropriate more money for timber management. Congress responded in 1976 by allowing the Forest Service to use K-V funds for those management activities.

It is possible that no one in the Forest Service was consciously aware of the influence the K-V fund had on these controversies or on agency decisionmaking in general. But most were aware that K-V formed a huge part of the agency's budget, particularly after 1976, when Congress expanded the use of K-V funds to include nonreforestation activities. In 1977, K-V collections exceeded $100 million, more than the appropriation for timber sales, and collections more than doubled over the next 11 years. Including three other funds that worked similarly to K-V—timber revenues used for specific purposes such as road maintenance, brush disposal, and timber salvage sales—timber sales contributed hundreds of millions of dollars to national forest budgets. The K-V funds were the most valuable because they were highly discretionary: they could be spent on any sale area improvements. This encouraged wildlife, recreation, watershed, and other experts inside the Forest Service to support timber sales.

Congress did not intentionally write the Knutson-Vandenberg Act to give forest managers incentives to lose money on timber sales. When the law passed in 1930, there was little support for national forest timber sales in Washington, D.C. The Depression had wiped out the value of private timber inventories, and major timber companies actually lobbied to prevent the Forest Service from driving down prices still further by flooding the market with cheap wood. Senator Vandenberg and Representative Knutson's original goal was to ensure that there would always be funds for reforestation despite the Depression that was deepening at the time the law was passed.

After World War II, however, rising demand for wood and diminishing private timber supplies made the industry more supportive of national forest timber sales. In addition, timber made excellent pork barrel because sawmills were highly visible parts of a region's economy. So Congress enthusiastically funded timber even when it was reluctant to fund other parts of the Forest Service program. In 1972, Weber State University economist Richard Alston reviewed 19 years of budget requests and found that Congress had given the Forest Service more than 95 percent of its requests for timber funds, but less than 80 percent of its requests for wildlife funds and only 70 percent of its requests for recreation, watershed, and reforestation funds.[8]

While the Forest Service was aware that Congress liked to fund timber sales, it was even more aware that the K-V fund allowed the Forest Service to turn every dollar Congress appropriated for timber sales into at least one more dollar for reforestation and other activities. No other resource provided that opportunity. By 1980, when forest planning began under the National Forest Management Act, all the biases resulting from the Knutson-Vandenberg Act were deeply ingrained in the Forest Service.

Natural selection explains how the idealistic young people who began working on forest plans straight out of school ended up biasing all their FORPLAN models so strongly toward more timber cutting. In any institution, a process of natural selection favors those who work best in that institution. In the Forest Service, the people who truly believed that all timber grows fast, that timber prices will rise rapidly, and that wilderness recreation benefits from new road construction were more likely to be promoted than the doubters.

This process of natural selection did not immediately affect the young FORPLAN planners, but it had worked on many of the people who submitted the data to use in FORPLAN. Most timber yield tables, for example, were designed by timber staff who had worked in the agency for years. Few of the economists, planners, and computer jockeys who ran FORPLAN had the expertise to question the yield tables, so they merely entered the numbers into the computer.

Economics was different. Few if any forests had staff economists before 1979, so the economists hired to work on the plans had to develop their own resource value and cost data. Even so, they usually followed guidelines set by the regional offices, leading to a situation in which all forests in a given region tended to make the same mistakes. National forest planners attended frequent meetings of planners in their regions during which the regional leaders presented the rationale for the numbers they used, with no dissenting views presented. Skeptics were sometimes allowed to go their own way. But often, as in the case of the Oregon and Washington economists who questioned the assumption of rising timber prices, they were told to follow the rules.

Forest planners were given more discretion to prepare some sorts of data, such as the relationships between timber and other resources. But any data or assumptions that threatened to reduce timber sales would be met with sharp criticism and require extensive documentation. Data or assumptions that supported high levels of timber sales would produce a pat on the back. With the presence of promised promotions and, in some cases, cash bonuses for getting the plans done on time, planners soon realized that those payoffs were more likely to come about if they supported timber. No doubt many reasoned—with some justification, as it turned out—that they needed to make some compromises so they could advance far enough in the agency to really make a difference.

The natural selection process eventually worked on the planners. One frustrated FORPLAN modeler in Montana quit the Forest Service and moved to Hawaii to surf. Some got jobs in other agencies. But those who could bend their ideals stayed in the Forest Service and a few went on to become district rangers and forest supervisors. The results would be surprising to everyone.

4. Analysis Paralysis

Far from helping the Forest Service resolve controversies over clearcutting, herbicides, wilderness, and other issues, forest planning ended up devastating the agency. In the 1970s, the Forest Service was still known as a can-do agency, famous for its esprit de corps and popular among members of Congress despite growing criticism that came mainly from environmental groups.

When Congress passed the National Forest Management Act, the chief of the Forest Service confidently predicted that the plans would be written in four years at a cost of about a million dollars a forest. The reality turned out to be far different: in the end, it took some 15 years and more than a billion dollars to write all the plans.

The first delay was in the preparation of rules to govern forest planning. The law specified that the rules should be written within two years of the law's passage, but the Forest Service took three. Just two years later, the White House changed hands, and the new administration appointed former timber industry executive John Crowell as assistant secretary of agriculture in charge of the Forest Service. Crowell decided to rewrite the rules, and the changes he made forced some forests to start over.

Just months after the new rules were approved, Crowell fired another salvo at the Forest Service. The draft plans that had been passing through his office were unsatisfactory, he warned. "Appropriate changes would be made unless review drafts begin to improve significantly soon."[1] Many within the Forest Service took this as a threat that the administration would replace the chief and regional foresters, who historically had all been promoted from within the agency, with political appointees. In response, the regional forester for Oregon and Washington ordered all his forests—including one that was about to send its final plan to the printer—to start over from scratch.[2]

Planners were frustrated by a variety of other delays. If the Fish and Wildlife Service listed a species as threatened or endangered, planners would have to revise their FORPLAN model so they could track the effects of the plan on that species. New timber inventories revealed that the data used in some FORPLAN models were hopelessly optimistic. Major forest fires in 1987 burned enough timber in California to force several forests to start over. It became clear that planners couldn't plan fast enough to keep up with the pace of everyday change. As one planner explained, "There is never enough time to do it right, but always enough time to do it twice."

Even when the plans were done, they weren't done. Environmental groups appealed almost every plan to the chief of the Forest Service, and some of those appeals were successful. The Santa Fe National Forest was ordered to redo its plan with corrected yield tables. Embarrassed by the "did-as-I-was-told" memo of its recreation specialist, the Hoosier National Forest withdrew its plan and didn't sell any timber sales for years after. The chief or the secretary of agriculture sent plans for the Black Hills, San Juan, George Washington, Ouachita, Texas, and many other national forests back to the planners. Plans for the Rio Grande and other national forests survived their appeals only to be overturned in court.

Eventually, the Forest Service came up with the curious legal argument that plans made no decisions and so there was nothing anyone could challenge in court. The Supreme Court bought this argument in 1998, but by that time the damage was long done. No one could explain why the agency had devoted more than a billion dollars to a planning process that the agency itself said reached no decisions.

Far from taking just four years, some forest plans remained unfinished a dozen years after planning began. Far from costing a mere million dollars a plan, many plans cost tens of millions of dollars. Far from resolving controversies, the plans just increased polarization as environmental and industry leaders used the plans as rallying points for their troops. Delayed by, among other things, the Reagan administration's new planning rules, forest fires, and the spotted owl, the Klamath National Forest started over from scratch five different times and did not publish its final plan until 1994—18 years after Congress passed the law requiring forest plans.

Things didn't get any better when the completed plans were turned over to managers to implement. Many managers soon found that the data in the plans didn't jibe with the conditions they found on the ground.

- After doing "site-specific analyses" on 20 percent of the forest, the supervisor of Idaho's Clearwater National Forest (home of the 650-foot computer-projected trees) informed the regional forester in 1990 that the forest could sell only about two-thirds as much timber as FORPLAN had calculated.[3]
- Timber managers on Utah's Wasatch-Cache National Forest reported in 1991 that many acres that planners had considered suitable for timber management weren't really suitable. They also found that planners had overestimated timber growth rates and that planned timber sales weren't as compatible with wildlife as planners presumed. Managers estimated they could sell less than half as much timber as FORPLAN had calculated.[4]
- The General Accounting Office, working closely with officials of the Flathead National Forest, concluded that the Montana forest could only sustain about three quarters of the timber cuttings scheduled by FORPLAN.[5]

The years of indecision and the transfer of scarce funds and resources from management to planning frustrated on-the-ground Forest Service workers. By 1990, Forest Service employee surveys found that morale had sunk to its lowest levels ever. Internal memos revealed that employees felt that the agency suffered from a lack of leadership and had lost its identity as one of the nation's leading conservation agencies. "The Washington office leadership is in a situation where the oars are out of the water and the Diesel engines are shut off," one regional memo bitterly reported in early 1989.[6]

Regional officials told the chief that they couldn't achieve the timber targets Congress was expecting, and became upset when the chief turned around and promised Congress that they *could* meet those targets. Dissension over timber targets reached a peak in November 1989, when the forest supervisors from the 19 national forests in Oregon and Washington prepared a videotape for the chief.

"I understand why targets are emphasized and how those targets generate dollars," said Umpqua Forest Supervisor Robert Devlin on the video. But he warned that he could not meet his targets without unduly harming other resources. "The people who I am familiar with on the ground are not comfortable with this, and neither am I." Unless this problem is solved, he told the chief, "I can't be the steward of the public lands that you depend on me to be."[7]

Thirteen forest supervisors in Montana and northern Idaho wrote a memo supporting the video. Because of timber targets, they said, "We are not meeting the quality land management expectations of our public and our employees." They added, "A 'can-do' attitude cannot save us this time."[8] A second memo signed by 63 forest supervisors from throughout the interior West noted that "our timber program has been 35 percent of the National Forest System budget for the last 20 years while recreation, fish and wildlife, and soil and water have been 2 to 3 percent each." Because of this imbalance, "the allowable sale quantity [ASQ] issue will continue to be a problem for us and some supervisors feel our ASQs are unrealistic even with full funding."[9] As a narrator on the videotape told the chief, "It's time to reconsider program emphasis and round out multiple use."

The chief apparently listened. The national forests offered 11 billion board feet of timber for sale in 1990, but sales fell to just 6 billion in 1991, 5 billion in 1992, and under 4 billion in 1994.[10] By 2000, the agency was selling around 1.5 billion board feet a year, though sales recovered slightly to about 2.8 billion board feet in 2006.[11]

Many people blame this reduction in sales on the northern spotted owl, which was listed as a threatened species in 1990. The spotted owl lives in only about a dozen national forests in the Pacific Northwest. Yet national forests throughout the West, and to a lesser degree in the East, significantly reduced timber sales. It is clear that national forest sales declined largely because forest managers did not believe the forest plans and concluded instead that historic sale levels were too high.

The only forest plans that foreshadowed this decline came out of Oregon and Washington, known in the Forest Service as Region 6. Region 6 had historically been the Forest Service's leading timber region. Though Oregon and Washington forests comprised less than 13 percent of the land area of the national forests, they typically produced 40 percent of the volume and more than half the revenue. Insiders sometimes said, "The real chief of the Forest Service is the Region 6 director of timber management."

Yet when Jeff Sirmon, the regional forester, responded to John Crowell's pressure to boost timber sales by ordering planners to start over, he apparently let it be known that he would support reductions in sales proposed by the forests provided they could present an airtight case for such reductions. While previous Region 6 regional foresters were known as "timber beasts" who might have welcomed Crowell's timber imperative, Sirmon did not have a long history of working in forests dominated by timber sales: his previous job had been in Utah, a state not known for having particularly productive forests.

Yet it wasn't just Sirmon vs. Crowell. People throughout the region were disturbed by the recession's effects on the industry. They felt they had an unwritten agreement with the timber companies: the Forest Service would sell lots of timber each year, and the industry would cut it, thus keeping the revenues flowing into the Knutson-Vandenberg and similar funds. But the recession of the early 1980s was so bad that timber companies almost completely stopped cutting public timber. Lacking the anticipated revenues, Region 6 had to lay off thousands of employees. Even many of the most hard-core timber supporters felt that the agency should diversify its sources of revenue and political support.

Around this time, the 1970 Environmental Teach-In (Earth Day) began to influence the Forest Service. Before 1974, most forestry school graduates came from rural areas and were sympathetic to a commodity-production view of forestry. But Earth Day inspired many urban high school students (including this writer) to go to forestry school. As a result, by 1974, most forestry school graduates came from urban areas and were more sympathetic to wildlife, wilderness, and other amenities. By the late 1980s, many of these people were rising to positions of power within the agency.

Partly because of this change, the new plans from nearly all the national forests in Region 6 significantly reduced timber sales. Over-all, the plans would have reduced Region 6 timber sales by 45 percent, from 5.5 billion board feet to 3.0 billion. The timber industry did its best to delay implementation, including pressuring Congress to try to stop the plans. But what really killed the plans was the spotted owl.

Abandoning the goal of "comprehensive planning," the Forest Service responded to the spotted owl controversy by dealing with the owl in a separate plan—ultimately, a series of plans—that would cover all spotted owl national forests as well as other federal lands managed by the Department of the Interior (the Forest Service is in the Department of Agriculture). The 3 billion board feet that came out of the forest plans did not take the owl plans into account. When the president's Northwest Forest Plan was finally approved in 1994, it rendered obsolete the plans for all the owl forests and many of the other forests in the region.

Despite the plan's effects on the timber program, many Forest Service employees welcomed the final spotted owl plan. Having convinced themselves that they were cutting too much timber, national forest managers were happy to let the owl take the blame for reductions. By 1996, timber purchasers cut only three-quarters of a billion board feet of wood from all 19 Region 6 forests—less than they had cut from just one Oregon forest, the Willamette, in 1989.

Practically overnight, the Forest Service was transformed from an agency dominated by timber to one that attempted to focus on ecosystem management. Yet a billion dollars and more than a decade invested in planning had almost nothing to do with this transformation, except to the extent that the plans had failed so badly that they exposed many of the other problems with the agency.

Comprehensive forest planning turned out to be a demoralizing nightmare for the Forest Service. There are many reasons for planning's failure, but three stand out:

- The Forest Service's incentives conflicted sharply with what most people regarded as the best way to manage the national forests.
- Comprehensive planning for 1- to 2-million-acre national forests is simply too complicated, especially when the plan depends on information about the future that no one can accurately predict.
- Finally, planning cannot be rational in a political environment, even if the politics are only the internal politics found in any bureaucracy.

Congress had carelessly designed a budgetary process that rewarded forest managers for losing money on environmentally destructive activities, and penalized the agency for earning a profit. As a result, managers came to believe that it was in the public interest for them to lose money, impose ugly clearcuts on the landscape, spray thousands of gallons of chemical herbicides on the clearcuts, and build tens of thousands of miles of expensive roads. Planners built these beliefs into their FORPLAN models: beliefs that timber was so scarce that people would pay a fortune for helicopter-logged lodgepole pine; that managers could make trees grow far faster than nature; and that cutting trees produced such positive effects on other resources that those effects alone justified below-cost timber sales.

The Forest Service is far from the only government agency whose incentives conflict with its mission. Congress lets the Park Service keep 25 percent of construction and reconstruction costs as overhead, so the agency lets national park ecosystems decline while it spends millions of dollars rebuilding housing for employees who could easily live in private housing outside the parks.[12] Some state land agencies that are required by law to earn revenues for local schools fail to do so because they are funded out of tax dollars and have no incentive to produce revenues.[13] Everywhere, agencies learn that failing to solve a problem can be more lucrative than solving it because, when the problem becomes a crisis, Congress or state legislatures will deal with it by dumping money on the agencies.

Perverse incentives pervade government agencies and create real conflicts about how the agencies fulfill their missions. These conflicts will not be resolved by legislatures passing the buck to planners. They will only be remedied when Congress or state legislatures change the incentives within agency budgets.

Even if there had been no conflict between the Forest Service's incentives and the public good, forest planning would still have failed. To paraphrase forest ecologist Jerry Franklin paraphrasing J. B. S. Haldane, a 1- to 2-million-acre national forest is not only more complicated than we understand, it is more complicated than we *can* understand.[14] Forest planning might have been useful when each plan focused on a single resource, such as timber, wildlife, or recreation, but comprehensive planning of all resources required more variables than any human or any computer could deal with. Adding to this complexity is the fact that new issues arise and public tastes change faster than planners can plan.

How is it that private timber companies can plan a forest but the government cannot? Private forest plans rarely attempt to be comprehensive. Instead, they focus on the resources that are valuable to the company doing the planning. They also tend to be relatively short-term, committing the company to actions for only a few years instead of a decade or more. Since they are short-term in nature, they are also very flexible, and since they are narrowly focused, they do not lead to the formation of special interest groups dedicated to carrying out an absurd program.

The real reason national forest planning failed is that it was a solution for the wrong problem. Senator Humphrey proposed planning because he erroneously assumed that national forest controversies resulted from inadequate data collection, poor analyses, and insufficient public involvement. But the Forest Service had always been good at these things; indeed, its ability to collect data and work with the public declined when it began writing comprehensive forest plans. So it was no surprise when, in 2001, the chief of the Forest Service described the planning process as "analysis paralysis."[15]

Ultimately, the real problem with national forest management was that Congress failed to align the Forest Service's incentives with the public interest in the national forests. *Newsweek* magazine praised the Forest Service of 1952 for earning a profit, avoiding conflicts between resources, and being responsive to the public. Although the Forest Service at that time sold timber, its use of selection cutting minimized public objections to those sales. If the incentives inadvertently built into the Knutson-Vandenberg Act had not encouraged the Forest Service to switch to clearcutting, sell money-losing timber, and increase timber cutting to the point where it conflicted with almost every other resource, then most of the controversies over wilderness, herbicides, the spotted owl, and other issues might never have happened and no one would have proposed to solve those problems with an unwieldy and unworkable forest planning process.

5. The Return of Fire Dominance

As the decline of national forest timber sales reduced the controversy over clearcutting, a controversy over fire management has taken its place. Like timber, the fire issue also has its roots in budgetary incentives. In 1908, Congress passed a law that effectively gave the Forest Service a blank check for "emergency fire suppression." In 1924, Congress passed the Weeks Act, which provided the Forest Service with funds to distribute to the states to encourage the formation of state and local fire protection districts. Together these laws "helped to bring political power to the Forest Service," says fire historian Stephen Pyne.[1] Yet "as that power grew, the Service found itself subtly corrupted in spirit and imagination."[2]

Initially, that corruption was expressed in the Forest Service's attitude toward prescribed burning. Private landowners and university researchers found that, in many parts of the West and South, frequent light fires favored commercially valuable trees and prevented the buildup of fuels that could lead to catastrophic fires. But for several decades, the Forest Service ignored this research and sometimes suppressed publications by its own researchers who came up with similar results.[3]

For many years after passage of the Weeks Act, the Forest Service also refused to distribute federal fire protection funds to states that allowed prescribed burning. Many private landowners, particularly in the South, refused to join forest protection districts until the Forest Service completely reversed this policy in the 1950s. Until landowners joined those districts, Forest Service officials spitefully recorded all prescribed fires on their lands as "wildfires."

The 1970s were the wettest decade of the 20th century, and as a result, the United States experienced the fewest number of acres of wildland fires. Despite this, the costs of the blank-check emergency fire suppression program rose rapidly, raising alarm bells in the Office of Management and Budget. In 1978, Congress repealed the blank-check law and instead gave the Forest Service a fixed amount of money for fire suppression each year. When fire costs exceeded this amount, the Forest Service was expected to borrow the money from its Knutson-Vandenberg (K-V) fund and then repay it in future years when costs were less than the annual appropriation.

The Forest Service responded with many cost-cutting measures, including allowing forests to let natural fires burn instead of suppressing every fire and changing strategies from suppressing fires on every acre to containing fires within natural boundaries. Average annual fire costs fell dramatically for several years. However, droughts in 1987 and 1988 forced the Forest Service to severely deplete the K-V fund. So in 1990, Congress gave the Forest Service a supplementary appropriation of nearly $280 million to replenish the fund.[4]

Congress's action effectively restored the blank-check mentality and reduced the incentive for forest managers to control costs. An internal Forest Service review in 2003 found that fire managers continued to act as though "suppression funds [were] unlimited." They spent millions of dollars on little-used rental cars, unnecessarily purchased upscale camping gear for crews, and paid exorbitant rates for firefighting equipment.[5]

Such free spending offers many opportunities for corruption. In 2006, a Forest Service purchasing agent in Oregon was discovered to have paid her boyfriend more than $640,000 in firefighting funds. No one in the agency missed the funds; she was caught only after someone tipped off the local district attorney that the couple was gambling away unusually large amounts of money.[6]

In 2000, a prescribed fire lit on the Bandolier National Monument escaped control and swept across the Santa Fe National Forest into Los Alamos, where it burned hundreds of homes. Congress responded by increasing the Forest Service's budget by a whopping 38 percent and asking the Forest Service and other federal land agencies to write a national fire plan.

The Forest Service long ago agreed with private landowners that some forests benefit from frequent light fires. But not all do: while 85 percent of the mostly private forests in the South need frequent fires, only about a third of forests in the West, where most federal lands are located, fall into this category. Without making any effort to determine where the money would be most effectively spent, the National Fire Plan simply asked for huge appropriations for treating forests to reduce fire hazards.

Congress accommodated the agency by passing the Healthy Forests Restoration Act of 2003, which allowed the Forest Service to spend timber sale revenues on activities aimed at reducing fire hazards. This effectively laid the perverse incentives created by the Knutson-Vandenberg Act on top of the perverse incentives created by the blank check. Predictably, in 2006 the U.S. Department of Agriculture inspector general's office charged that the Forest Service had failed to "ensure that the highest priority fuels reduction projects [were] being implemented."[7]

In the meantime, the Forest Service is rewriting the plans for each national forest. Because no one in the Forest Service dared tell Congress that its billion-dollar planning process was a failure, Congress did not change the law requiring forests to revise their plans every 10 to 15 years. So the agency continues to spend money on a process in which no one, from the chief of the Forest Service on down, seriously believes.[8] The status quo suits Congress, which finds it easier to let government agencies waste taxpayers' money than to agree on a sensible public lands policy. It suits the Forest Service, which gets bigger budgets and a larger bureaucracy. And it suits some forest users, who vaguely hope they can use the planning process to get what they want out of the national forests. Taxpayers who must pay the cost and members of the public who are frustrated by bad forest management have no influence.

Part Two
Why Planning Fails

It is a popular delusion that the government wastes vast amounts of money through inefficiency and sloth. Enormous effort and planning are required to waste this much money.

—P. J. O'Rourke[1]

Because they can grow a tree, planners think they can plan a million-acre forest. Because they can build a house, planners think they can design an entire urban area. But there is a qualitative difference between these activities that is more than just a matter of scale. Ecosystems and cities are complex systems that are inherently unpredictable, even chaotic. This term is used in the sense of *chaos theory*, best known for the aphorism, "A butterfly stirring the air today in Beijing can transform storm systems in New York next month."[2] Since even the near-term future of chaotic systems cannot be accurately foreseen, any attempt to plan the distant future will fail.

Any who say they can write a comprehensive, long-range plan for a city or region necessarily presumes that

- they can collect all the data they need about the values and costs of the land, improvements, and proposed and alternative projects in the planning area;
- they can accurately predict how those values and costs will change in the future;
- they can properly understand all the relationships between various parts of their region and activities in those areas;
- they can do all this quickly enough that the plan is still meaningful when they are done; and
- they will be immune to political pressures and can objectively overcome their own personal preferences.

Consider an urban area with a million people and a million parcels of property, each of which could be used for dozens of different purposes. Each of those people places a different value on each potential use of each parcel of land, resulting in trillions of different pieces of data to collect. Add transportation and other infrastructure (each item of which will be separately valued by each of the million people), changes in tastes and trends over time, and the way different uses on different properties influence the values of other nearby properties, and the data requirements reach into the quadrillions. No one can ever collect or understand this much data.

What do scientific, rational planners do when confronted with problems of this magnitude? They simplify.

- Instead of comprehensively planning for all resources, they focus on one or two resources.
- Instead of measuring the actual relationships between resources, they rely on preconceived notions and the latest planning fads.
- Instead of predicting the future, they envision what they want and try to impose that vision on the future.
- Instead of finding out what the people in the region really want, they succumb to pressures from powerful interest groups.

In *The Death and Life of Great American Cities*, Jane Jacobs called planning a "pseudoscience."[3] That remains true today not because of any flaws in the planners but because the promises planners make are simply impossible to keep. As a result, plans end up doing far more harm than good to the cities and regions for which they are written.

6. Radical Doctrine or Rational Decisionmaking?

Imagine a world free of politics. Imagine everyone has the best of intentions. Imagine the sharpest experts are at your disposal. Is it possible to plan? That is, is it possible for a government agency employing those experts to write a long-term, comprehensive land-use plan for your city, region, watershed, or other large area of land?

Many believe the answer is yes. "Planning is not radical doctrine," say planners. "It is rational decision making. It is time the country gives up its fear of planning and embraces its benefits."[1] Yet there is little evidence in history that government-controlled, centralized planning can work. The Soviet Union failed spectacularly not because it was communist, in the sense of common ownership of the means of production, but because the government had turned over all production questions to planners. Yet the above defense of planning was written less than five years after the collapse of the Soviet Union.

There are several technical barriers to the success of planning. These barriers prevented planning from working in the Soviet Union, and they are just as much of a problem for American planners.

- The Data Problem: Planning requires more data than can be collected in time for it to be useful to planners;
- The Forecasting Problem: Planners cannot predict the future;
- The Modeling Problem: Models complicated enough to be useful for planning are too complicated for anyone to understand; and
- The Pace of Change Problem: Reality changes faster than planners can plan.

The Data Problem

In 1952, the California legislature invented *tax-increment financing*, or TIF, to help cities finance urban-renewal projects. It allows a city to declare a particular neighborhood or district blighted and to promote redevelopment of the area. From that point on, all property taxes on any new development would go not to the schools, fire, police, and other services for which they were intended but to the city to subsidize the redevelopment.

In effect, developers would get to use the taxes they pay to subsidize their own developments. Meanwhile, the cost of police, fire, educational, and other urban services consumed by the redevelopment district would have to be covered by other taxpayers. Typically, cities would project future tax revenues and sell bonds to be repaid with those revenues. The bond proceeds would then be used to subsidize the redevelopment, sometimes by buying land with the help of eminent domain and turning it over to developers; sometimes by building infrastructure that developers would normally have to build themselves; and sometimes by giving the developers outright grants.

Today, 10 percent of all property taxes paid in California go to TIF, and every state but Arizona allows cities to use TIF for urban renewal.[2] From one point of view, TIF is just a scheme by city officials to divert taxes to favored developers. But TIF-supported urban-renewal projects are always backed up with lofty documents written by urban planners. What makes planners think they can know that a particular neighborhood or district would be better off with condos instead of offices, mixed-use developments instead of single-family homes, or skyscrapers instead of low-rise buildings?

As law professor Bernard Siegan points out, land-use planners must consider "questions of compatibility, economic feasibility, property values, existing uses, adjoining and nearby uses, traffic, topography, utilities, schools, future growth, conservation, and environment" for each parcel of land. Just to determine the feasibility of one use for one site at one time "would require a market survey costing possibly thousands of dollars."[3] Planning requires data, and the amount of data needed to ensure that a plan is both efficient and equitable is simply overwhelming.

A small suburb may have thousands of parcels of land; a major city may have hundreds of thousands; a large urban area may have millions. Any given parcel might be put to dozens of different uses: single-family residential at various lot sizes; multifamily residential at various densities; small-, medium-, and big-box retail; low-, medium-, or high-rise office space; light, medium, or heavy industrial use; developed and undeveloped open space; and so forth.

No planning agency has the budget needed to do a market analysis of all the possible uses for all the parcels in their jurisdiction. Yet planners claim they can determine the optimal uses for most or all sites in an entire region—not just for today but for many years into the future, and not just considering market factors but considering social, environmental, and other nonmarket factors as well.

If the data needs for land-use planning are daunting, transportation data requirements are impossible. Transportation planners must deal not with chunks of inanimate land but with people whose preferences and tastes can vary widely. As an expression of that variation, most people make several trips each day to different work, school, shopping, home, recreation, and other locations. Imagine a million people leaving roughly 400,000 different homes and going to a similar number of different destinations several times each day. No one could possibly collect the data needed to understand all those trips.

Many planners rely largely on information provided by their hierarchical bureaucracy. As information filters up the bureaucracy, much of it is necessarily left out. The models that the planners build contain only a tiny fraction of the information available at the lowest levels of the bureaucracy. Nor is the information provided by the bureaucracy unbiased. At each level, officials with their own goals tend to pass on information that they think will promote those goals. As Anthony Downs notes, "Each official tends to distort the information he passes upward into the hierarchy, exaggerating those data favorable to himself and minimizing those unfavorable to himself."[4]

Planners simplify their data collection problems by lumping things into a few classes and averaging the data for each category. Land-use planners writing the 50-year plan for the Portland urban area lumped land uses into just 10 classes. Only two of these classes, "inner neighborhoods" and "outer neighborhoods," represented all the variation of residential land in the urban area.[5] The detail that is lost from such lumping is staggering. Yet Portland's plan has had an enormous effect on the lives of Portland-area residents since planners began implementing it in 1995.

The Forecasting Problem

During World War II, Kenneth Arrow—who would later win a Nobel Prize in economics—was ordered to help with long-range weather forecasts for the Army Air Corps. His group soon realized that their forecasts were no better than numbers pulled out of a hat, and they asked to be assigned to more useful work. "The Commanding General is well aware that the forecasts are no good," they were told in reply. "However, he needs them for planning purposes."[6]

In addition to needing data about the present, planners need data about the future. According to one planning advocate, planners "can take account of processes which are occurring so slowly, or will begin to occur so far in the future, that no single producer could be aware of their existence."[7] Economist Gerald Sirkin scoffs, "What is this mysterious prophetic vision that comes to a man when he sits at a desk in the central authority but not when he sits at a desk in a business or university?"[8]

Planners typically write plans for the next 10 years or more. Some plans are even ostentatiously called "20-year plans" or "50-year plans." For such plans to be worthwhile, planners must be able to accurately answer such questions as

- What technologies will be available in the future?
- How much will land, energy, and other resources cost?
- How will individual tastes and preferences change?
- How will people earn their incomes?

None of these questions can be answered with any degree of confidence. Yet any plan that is based on inaccurate answers to even one of these questions is likely to be drastically wrong, locking people into expensive but unnecessary policies and programs. Despite the absolute need for accurate predictions, planners must contend with the rather unstartling *Law of the Future*:

Planners have no better insight into the future than anyone else.

So government plans written today are unlikely to make any sense to the people in the future that the plans are supposed to benefit.

Imagine, for example, writing a 50-year plan for your city in 1950. In 1950,

- few people had ever flown, and no one had ever flown in a commercial jet;

- few people had ever worked with computers, and not even the most far-seeing science-fiction writers had predicted microcomputers or the Internet;
- few people could afford to regularly make long-distance phone calls, and no one had ever made a direct-dial long-distance call;
- few married women worked, and the highest-paid jobs were all held by men; and
- few other countries could match the United States as a manufacturing powerhouse, and no one had ever imported a transistor radio from Japan, Korea, or China.

With the information available in 1950, your plan for the year 2000 would make the airport too small and the train station too big. You would assume that high telecommunication costs would force jobs to cluster tightly together. Because you would assume that few married women would work, the homes you would plan would have one-car garages. You would plan for the wrong ratio of blue-collar to white-collar jobs, and you would never imagine that large numbers of people would want a home office.

Although planners cannot truly know the future, they rely on *forecasting* to provide projections about future populations and demand for various goods and services. Forecasting is generally based on projecting current trends into the future while taking into account demographics—for example, aging baby boomers—and other changes that planners think they can foresee.

Planning forecasts can be very intimidating. But "the technical complexity of forecasts is in fact quite misleading," says University of California planning professor Martin Wachs. "While equations, computers, and enormous data bases give the forecasts an aura of 'science,' which invests them with certain authority in the political arena, the most critical data needed to make a forecast often consists of assumptions about the future." These assumptions, Wachs admits, "can never be known with certainty."[9]

Wachs adds, "Forecasters are usually drawn from the ranks of social scientists, engineers, and planners whose education and professional identities are based primarily on technical methodological skills." While we can train these people to run complicated computer models, "we don't—and probably can't—educate them to make better assumptions."[10]

Since the forecasts are very sensitive to these assumptions, it is easy for elected or politically appointed officials to "cook the books" by directing planners to use particular assumptions. The apparent complexity of forecasting, says Wachs, is often used to "hide from the public the fact that the assumptions included in the forecast can be selected to help advocate certain courses of action for political purposes."[11] "A wise colleague has pointed out to me," continues Wachs, "that politicians who agree with her recommendations have never challenged her assumptions, while those who oppose her recommendations almost always challenge her assumptions."[12]

Planners' inability to see the future might not be fatal if plans can be easily revised to account for unforeseen changes. But changing plans that take years to write is slow and tedious. Moreover, any plan will favor certain groups over others, and the favored groups will work especially hard to prevent any changes, no matter how sensible they may be.

Contrary to the quaint belief of Kenneth Arrow's commanding general, planning is the wrong response to uncertainty about the future. If "the only certainty about the future is that the future is uncertain," says Harvard economics professor Stephen Marglin, "if the only sure thing is that we are in for surprises, then no amount of planning, no amount of prescription, can deal with the contingencies that the future will reveal."[13]

The Modeling Problem

All plans are based on models. The most sophisticated plans use computers for modeling. Other models are simply in the heads of the people doing the planning. Models are simplifications of reality, but such simplifications are necessary simply because reality is too complicated.

For some purposes, simplifications are useful. For example, a company or government agency might use a model to forecast the need for its products or services. But when writing plans that make complex decisions about such things as how people should be allowed to use their property, planning runs up against a barrier that can be expressed as the *Law of Modeling Limits*:

Before a model becomes complicated enough to be useful for planning, it becomes too complicated for anyone to understand.

Forest Service planners ran into this barrier when writing plans for the nation's forests during the 1980s. Each national forest covers one to two million acres, ranging in many cases from lush wetlands to alpine or desert tundra. Various competing uses for these lands include timber cutting, livestock grazing, mining, oil and gas exploration, wildlife habitat, watershed, fisheries, and numerous (and often incompatible) forms of recreation. Each of these uses had positive or negative effects on many of the other uses.

The computer models planners developed to plan these forests vastly oversimplified the forests. The computer program that the Forest Service used allowed planners to divide their forests into just a few hundred different kinds of land. This limit meant that such variables as steepness of slope, soil erodability, and even land productivity were often left out of the models. The program also allowed planners to model relatively few resources: timber along with a few species of wildlife or two or three kinds of recreation.

Despite these and other oversimplifications, the models were so complicated that few understood how they really worked or how to interpret the results. While most of the computer programmers who designed the models probably understood them, many other members of the planning team did not, nor did the agency officials who were basing their decisions on those models.

As just one example, most of the computer "runs" aimed at maximizing the net economic return from the timber and other resources in the forest, with future values and costs discounted by 4 percent per year. At a 4 percent discount rate, $1 in a hundred years is worth only 2 cents today. While it is perfectly appropriate to use a discount rate, when combined with the Forest Service's nondeclining flow rule the results could be bizarre. Given the requirement that no less timber be cut in the future than is cut in the first year, the computer would decide to cut all the valuable timber first, when it greatly contributed to the net returns, while leaving the money-losing timber for the distant future, when the 4 percent discount rate would render the losses negligible.

This is not the way the Forest Service actually manages national forests, and any national forest manager who practiced such "high grading" would be severely criticized by his or her colleagues. Yet high grading was built into most forests' computer models. This effectively allowed the models to cut more timber today than if the models had been constrained to ensure that both timber volumes and net returns did not decline in the future. It is possible that forest officials understood this deception and accepted it to get more timber cutting. But it is also likely that many did not even realize that the computer runs were proposing cutting rates that were economically unsustainable.

Models simple enough for the decisionmakers to understand would be dangerously oversimplified. In fact, the models were already dangerously oversimplified, but making them complicated enough to account for more variables would make them so complicated that even the programmers would be unable to understand them. If they can't understand the models, then they won't know when the model results make sense or when they are just gobbledygook.

The point of a model, of course, is to simplify reality so that it becomes easy to understand. But the simplifications necessary to make a forest, much less an urban area, understandable are so great that the model is no longer reliable. Such a simplified model might be useful for a city to project future tax revenues or to estimate the costs of providing schools, sewer, water, and other urban services. But urban planners want to go much further: they want to practically dictate how every single parcel should be used.

"Regional planning efforts should not stop short of creating detailed physical plans for the development and redevelopment of neighborhoods, especially for areas near transit stations," urges architect Andrés Duany. "Merely zoning for higher density in these locations is not enough. . . . The most effective plans are drawn with such precision that only the architectural detail is left to future designers."[14] Developers may get to decide what color to paint their buildings, but planners will decide exactly how each parcel will be used and the size and shape of each building on the parcel.

Despite this overwhelming task, with the appropriate simplifications, the plan practically writes itself. Since planners imagine there are only a dozen or so different land uses, they can write off entire lifestyles, such as urban farmers or exurbanites, as being too messy or somehow immoral. Since planners imagine there are only a few dozen origins and destinations, they don't have to plan for automobiles because a light-rail transit system should adequately serve everyone in the region.

"In urban planning," warns Yale political scientist James Scott, "it is a short step from parsimonious assumptions to the practice of shaping the environment so that it satisfies the simplifications required by the formula."[15] In other words, planners who rely on oversimplified models are more likely to try to impose the model's results on reality than to build more accurate models. As absurd as this sounds, some planning advocates actually endorse such a policy. "If economic reality is so complex that it can only be described by complicated mathematical models," says planning guru Herman Daly, "then the reality should be simplified."[16] Under this ideal, planners should regulate choice and complexity out of existence and require everyone to adopt the lifestyle choices that planners think best.

The Pace-of-Change Problem

Imagine you can collect all the data you need. Imagine that you have made the best possible predictions about the future and that you have developed the best possible models for your plan. Then you start to plan, and what happens? Something changes. Congress passes a new law. Someone finds an endangered species. A natural disaster completely alters the area you are planning. Scientists discover a new pollution problem. Such events reveal the *Law of Change*:

Reality changes faster than planners can plan.

As part one showed, the Forest Service encountered the law of change when planning the national forests in the 1980s. Planning began in 1979. But then, the Reagan administration revised planning rules in 1982; fires burned large areas of California forests in 1987; the spotted owl was listed as a threatened species in 1989; and President Clinton ordered the creation of a Northwest Forest Plan to address old-growth forest protection in 1993. Each of these events led many forests to scrap the plans they had written and start over. One result was that more forests took more than 10 years to write plans that were supposed to last for 10 years.

One way planners respond to change is to pretend it isn't happening. Oregon's Deschutes National Forest was nearly done with its plan when a new inventory revealed that the data planners had relied on were faulty. Planners decided it would be too much trouble to revise the plan so they simply used the faulty data. When planners do respond to change, it can significantly delay the plans.

Urban planners have had the same experiences. Portland's plan called for higher-density housing on all available vacant land within the region's urban-growth boundary. Then the northwest salmon was declared a threatened species and the National Marine Fisheries Service issued guidelines for protecting salmon habitat that specified that no more than 10 percent of any undeveloped area should be rendered impermeable by paving it or covering it with new buildings. Only low-density developments—one home per acre or less—could comply with these guidelines. Since they were only guidelines, planners ignored them because they did not fit preconceived preferences for high density.

7. Human Barriers

Any one of the technical barriers described in chapter 6 would be sufficient to render planning impossible. Yet planners simply ignore them and go on planning. If they cannot really do the jobs they say they are doing, how do they do them? First, since their work has no scientific basis, planners rely on fads—ideas that become popular, for a time, in the planning community even if they have no scientific bases. Zoning, urban renewal, public housing projects, and smart growth are all examples of such fads.

Second, to support these fads, many planners turn to pseudoscience, that is, the use of assumptions or claims that either are wrong or cannot be verified. Third, planners support many of their proposals with a public involvement process that is inherently undemocratic. Finally, no matter how good the process, the people who make the final decision for any plan have preconceived biases and inadequate information.

The Fad Problem

Any one of the technical problems—collecting data, predicting the future, building models, and dealing with the pace of change—would render planning infeasible. Rather than admit that planning is technically impossible, planners simply ignore these problems. But if they are not collecting data, accurately calculating the future, and building useful models, what are they doing?

Since planners can't really do the rational planning that they advertise, they instead follow fads. In the 1920s, the fad was zoning. In the 1950s, it was urban renewal and public housing. Today, it is smart growth (which before 1996 was called New Urbanism), meaning policies that encourage high-density development and discourage driving. Given the technical barriers that prevent planning from working, it is not surprising that these fads end up doing more harm than good.

Planning is susceptible to fads for at least two reasons. First, because planning is so complex, planners must simplify, and fads are the ultimate simplification. Fads provide a substitute for real thinking. Rather than try to figure out the best transportation system or the best land-use plan, planners can simply apply the latest fad.

A second reason for planning fads relates to the nebulous nature of planning. While a private development is easily judged by whether it earned a profit, planning is supposed to produce all sorts of difficult-to-measure social benefits. The difficulty is greatly increased when a plan is written for a long period, such as 20 or more years; until the last year is reached, no one can know whether even a plan's measurable goals will be attained, much less the nonmeasurable ones. By that time, most planners will have taken other jobs or retired.

Planners are therefore judged on other criteria, and most of the judges are other planners. The American Planning Association and other planning groups issue an endless series of awards to planners whose plans meet the approval of their peers. Because the awards are presented before the plans can be evaluated on the ground, these awards have nothing to do with whether the plans improve the livability of the cities for which they are written or otherwise accomplish their goals, and everything to do with whether the plans follow the latest fads.

Planners who win such awards may be more likely to get pay raises, promotions, or better-paying jobs in other cities. At the very least, they win the praise and admiration of their peers at conferences and other planning forums. Other planners respond by imitating the award-winning plans and few bother to ask whether the plans will really work. Except in the political sphere, where planners must do their wily best to sell their ideas, this means that actual innovation is extremely limited.

The Pseudoscience Problem

To provide a patina of support for the fads they follow, many planners turn to pseudoscience. As used here, *pseudoscience* means the use of data to give a patina of scientific validity to various claims that, when closely examined, are not really supported by the data. Urban planners and planning advocates using pseudoscience claim to have proven that

- it costs more to provide urban services to low-density developments than to high-density developments;
- expensive rail transit projects cost-effectively reduce traffic congestion;
- suburbs reduce people's sense of community; and
- low-density suburbs cause obesity and other health problems.

Pseudoscientists start by finding a database. It doesn't matter if the data were scientifically collected or even if they measure anything that is very closely related to what the pseudoscientists are trying to prove. For example, if they are trying to prove that cities are better than suburbs, they do not seem to need a database that actually compares cities and suburbs. If they cannot find a database, they will sometimes just fabricate data to make a database.

Once they have a database, they search the data to see if they can find some correlations between two sets of numbers. If they find any correlations, they presume that correlation proves causation. For example, if they find a correlation between suburbs and obesity, they assume that suburbs are causing the obesity and not that, perhaps, obese people prefer to live in the suburbs. They then declare that they have proven that suburbs are evil and high-density urban areas are good.

Planners use the term "the costs of sprawl" to describe the belief that providing urban services to low-density developments costs more than to higher densities. The original costs-of-sprawl study was based almost entirely on hypothetical—otherwise known as fabricated—numbers. Rather than actually measuring the costs of providing services to various low- and high-density communities, the authors of the study simply made up numbers. Not surprisingly, the numbers they made up "proved" their case.[1] However, when a researcher at Duke University actually looked at the cost of urban services in hundreds of communities of various densities, she found that, at anything above very rural densities, higher densities were associated with higher urban-service costs.[2]

The most widely cited recent update to the original costs-of-sprawl study, *The Costs of Sprawl 2000*, is still partly based on hypothetical data. Yet its claims are extremely modest: the study estimates that low-density suburban development imposes about $11,000 more in urban-service costs on communities than more compact development.[3]

As modest as it is, this calculation is still questionable. When researchers at the Heritage Foundation looked at actual government expenditures in more than 700 cities, they found that local governments spend $1,180 per person per year in the highest-density cities and only $106 to $135 less in medium- to low-density cities. While they found costs of $1,265 in the very lowest–density cities, this is only $85 more than in the highest-density cities. They also found that other factors such as the age and growth rate of the city had as much to do with urban-service costs as density.[4]

Even if urban services to homes in a low-density area cost $11,000 more than to houses in higher densities, homebuyers can more than make up the difference by getting access to the lower-priced land that is typically found in suburban areas. Most homebuyers would gladly add $11,000 to the cost of a $150,000 home to have a good-sized yard and not share an interior wall with next-door neighbors. On the other hand, chapter 14 will show that smart-growth policies designed to increase urban densities create artificial housing shortages that drive up housing prices by far more than $11,000 per home.

Another pioneer in the use of pseudoscientific databases in the cause of urban planning is Robert Putnam, the author of the 1995 bestseller *Bowling Alone*. Putnam heard that American participation in bowling leagues had declined even though bowling itself remained popular. It never occurred to him that people might be bowling with families and friends; he presumed that this meant people were bowling by themselves. He declared this was proof that Americans' sense of community had declined. When people questioned the validity of this proof, Putnam gathered scores of data sets, none of which directly measured community, but which together proved, he claimed, that America's sense of community was declining. For example, the data he found measured such things as "dwindling trust between adults and teenagers" and "the changing observance of stop signs."[5]

Only two of Putnam's data sets compared suburbs with cities. One measured the percentage of people who served as officers or committee members of a local group. The other measured the percentage of people who had attended a public meeting on town or school affairs. Both data sets showed higher participation in the suburbs than in the central cities.[6] If these things measure a sense of community, Putnam's conclusion should have been that people have a higher sense of community in low-density suburbs than in high-density cities. Instead, Putnam made the amazing claim that mobility and sprawl somehow "undermines civic engagement and community-based social capital."[7]

Furthermore, Putnam somehow calculated that "suburbanization, commuting, and sprawl . . . account for perhaps 10 percent" of the decline in community participation.[8] To "fix" this, he recommended New Urbanist planning: "It is surely plausible that design innovations like mixed-use zoning, pedestrian-friendly street grids, and more space for public use should enhance social capital."[9] In other words, Putnam proposed to apply to the suburbs the same features that are found in the cities that (according to his measures) have a lower sense of community than the suburbs.

Contrary to Putnam's presumption, sociologists have worried more that dense cities, not low-density development, reduced people's sense of community.[10] A new study from University of California economist Jan Brueckner confirms Putnam's data (but not his conclusions) by finding that suburban residents have more friends, more contact with neighbors, and greater involvement in community groups than residence of dense urban neighborhoods.[11]

New Urbanists, however, are fond of claiming that their higher-density housing projects will provide a stronger sense of community than low-density suburbs. But they have a very restricted sense of community. To them, *community* is solely geographically based. Yet as University of California–Berkeley planning professor Melvin Webber pointed out more than 40 years ago, thanks to automobiles, telephones, and (more recently) the Internet, Americans no longer rely on their immediate neighbors for a sense of community.[12] Instead, they form communities with people all over the country and indeed all over the world.

I myself belong to communities of road cyclists; people who love trains and restore historic rail equipment; and owners of Belgian Tervuren dogs, among others. Very few members of any of these communities live in my town, yet I feel a strong sense of community with them all. If people were restricted to forming communities only with their geographic neighbors, their lives would be far shallower and narrower. Since they are no longer so restricted, they do not feel a need to form a strong sense of community with neighbors with whom they share few interests. Planners who mourn the loss of geographic community ignore the much larger gains in other forms of community.

More recent studies have claimed to prove that low-density suburbs cause obesity and other health problems. The databases used to support these allegations often do not actually compare suburbs with cities. One obesity study compares low-density counties with higher-density counties. A health study compares low-density urban areas with higher-density urban areas. Neither finds much statistical significance in the data, but that does not stop the pseudoscientists from making their claims.

The obesity study is based on the ominously named *Behavioral Risk Factor Surveillance System*, a telephone survey of 200,000 Americans conducted each year by state health departments. Among other things, surveyors ask people how much they exercise each day as well as their height and weight, which can be used to estimate the amount they are overweight or obese. It is likely that people responding to a telephone survey overestimate their height and underestimate their weight, but surveyors merely assumed that everyone lies equally. Because the database was so large, the Centers for Disease Control, which coordinated the survey, did not feel the need to do any statistical analyses testing the validity of the data.

The database indicates a very strong correlation between income and obesity. According to the data, among people with household incomes of less than $10,000, 27.5 percent are obese. As household incomes rise, this percentage steadily falls to as low as 15.1 percent in the $75,000 plus category. There is also a strong correlation between education and obesity: 28.3 percent of people with a grade-school education are obese, steadily decreasing with more education to 15.4 percent among college graduates.[13]

The surveillance system does not ask people whether they live in a city or suburb. So pseudoscientists at Smart Growth America and the Surface Transportation Policy Project compared obesity rates in counties with various amounts of "sprawl."[14] They adjusted for age, race, and education, but not for income, even though incomes vary widely by county and the data indicate that income has a huge effect on obesity. Their results show that sprawl is far less important to physical fitness than income or education.

For example, their results indicate that about 2 percent more people in Atlanta are obese than in San Francisco, which is about the same as the difference between people who ended their education in high school and people who went to, but did not finish, college. Or to use an example raised by planning critic Wendell Cox, Cook County, Illinois, is 70 times denser than Grundy County, Illinois, and the obesity formula indicates that people in Cook County exercise an average of 40 seconds per day longer and weigh 1 pound less than people in Grundy County.[15] Despite these tiny differences, which could easily be accounted for by socioeconomic variations, flaws in the survey data, or other factors, the Smart Growth America study blames obesity on the suburbs.

To gain scientific credibility, the smart-growth pseudoscientists even submitted their report to a peer-reviewed journal. To get their report into the journal, however, they had to seriously weaken the claims. "Sprawling development has had a hand in the country's obesity crisis" says the press release issued by Smart Growth America. This demonstrates "the urgent need to invest in making America's neighborhoods appealing and safe places to walk and bicycle," which to Smart Growth America means rebuilding the suburbs at higher densities.[16]

In contrast, the journal article says sprawl "had small but significant associations with minutes walked [and] obesity."[17] In popular use, *significant* means "having a major effect," but in statistics, significant can refer to very tiny effects as long as they are "not mere chance." So the article finds only small, nonrandom "associations" between sprawl and obesity. Unlike the press release, the article carefully does not assert that sprawl "had a hand" in causing obesity, merely that they are "associated," which could mean that some other factor caused the obesity that was also associated with sprawl.

One such factor was revealed by a Canadian study that found "no evidence that urban sprawl causes obesity." Instead, the study revealed, "Individuals who are more likely to be obese choose to live in more sprawling neighborhoods." It appears that obesity contributes to sprawl, not the other way around. As a result, the researchers concluded, any effort to change "the built environment to counter the rise in obesity is misguided."[18] A study from Oregon State University confirms that "the association between sprawl and obesity reported in earlier studies is largely due to self-selection rather than to the impacts of the urban environment on physical activity and weight."[19]

If sprawl does not cause obesity, there is no justification for Smart Growth America's call to rebuild the suburbs. People who actually want to reduce obesity should work on increasing incomes, education, or other factors that have much larger effects on obesity and health and that would cost less and produce far more benefits than rebuilding neighborhoods to fit some planning utopia.

A similarly flawed study recently blamed chronic health problems on low-density suburbs. It was based on a telephone survey that asked people how many chronic diseases they had in their households. Like the obesity study, the survey did not distinguish between suburbs and cities, so the pseudoscientists who did this study compared answers for low-density urban areas versus high-density urban areas. The urban areas with the most diseases were in Florida, which was not surprising because the average age in those areas was much higher than most other areas. After adjusting for age, incomes, and education, they still found sprawl to be a factor, but the statistical reliability was low. For example, the sprawling Atlanta and Minneapolis–St. Paul regions both had lower incidences of chronic diseases than the much more compact San Francisco and New York regions.[20]

Instead of relying on a crude telephone survey, researchers could have compared actual health and mortality records in cities and suburbs. One study that did found that mortality rates are significantly higher in cities than in rural areas, while suburban rates are only slightly higher.[21]

The application of databases to problems for which they were not designed, the assumption that correlation equals causation, and claims of strong results from weak correlations are all indicators of pseudoscience. Planners are especially ready to use and rely on pseudoscience because the scientific basis for their own work is so weak.

Many of the pseudoscientific studies were conducted by planning advocates and they are widely cited by planners who firmly believe that suburbs reduce people's sense of community and increase obesity and other health problems. These planners also take for granted that improved urban designs will go far toward solving these problems.[22]

The Democracy Problem

When confronted with criticisms about their plans, planners often point to their public involvement processes. "Hundreds of people came to our meetings and commented on our plans," they say. "So we must be doing something right."

Wrong. Planning is inherently undemocratic. Efforts to involve the public mainly attract people who have a special interest in the outcome of the plans. As one Oregon pollster dryly reported, the people who actually commented on Portland's regional plan "hold views that are not necessarily reflective of the community as a whole."[23]

There is a good reason for this. People have a limited amount of time in their lives. They are inclined to spend that time on things that they can influence and that affect them the most. They will spend time studying cars because when they buy a car, they get the benefits and, if they make a mistake in their purchase, they pay most if not all the costs. But few people will spend much time on elections because their vote is unlikely to influence the outcome and, even if it does, the cost of any mistake they make is shared with everyone else.

Planning processes are even less likely to attract the public than elections. Getting involved in planning requires a much greater commitment of time than simply voting, and the process is so nebulous that there is no assurance that planners will even listen to the public. The planners in charge will rarely commit to any kind of voter democracy, that is, to agreeing to abide by the preferences expressed by the public during the process.

At the same time, some groups have a strong interest in getting involved in planning either for ideological reasons or because planning can enrich their businesses. The usual result when a few special interests get involved in a process ignored by everyone else is to develop a plan that accommodates the special interests at everyone else's expense. This is why rail transit, for example, has become so popular: although it does nothing that buses can't do as well or better, it costs far more than buses, and the companies that stand to profit from it promote it among politicians and are even hired by planners as "independent experts" to develop regional transit plans.

Even if public involvement processes could be truly democratic, planners are not sure they want them to be. This is confirmed by a national survey of planners. While more than three out of four believed that public involvement was important for identifying problems, less than half the planners surveyed believed that members of the public "[had] the requisite reflective ability to contribute" to later stages in planning. Instead of truly believing in public involvement, most "planners think of the planning process as an intellectual activity in which substantive expertise, the planners' forte, is the primary requirement," so the average member of the public is not qualified to participate.[24]

In fact, many planners viewed public involvement as merely an opportunity for politicians to stifle the good recommendations made by planners. As a result, "some planners advocate increasing the statutory authority of planning departments, so that planners' recommendations can have the force of law." "There is little recognition," comments the planner who did the survey, "that political constraints on planners' influence may reflect public concerns about limiting the role of experts in democratic decision making."[25]

In public, most planners give lip service to democracy, but among themselves they take a very different attitude. A guest speaker at a recent conference of a state chapter of the American Planning Association was an elected city councilor who, before her election, worked as an urban planner. She told her audience of planners, "Planners are the brains of our city. They tell the neighborhood groups what must be done, and the neighborhood groups then make the city councils do it."[26]

"From conventional planners' point of view, participation of laypeople in the planning process is not desirable, or even nonsensical," writes one disapproving planner. "Planning is a technical matter which has to be carried out on the basis of rationality; ordinary people who are not technically trained have to submit to the intellectual authority of planners."[27]

The Decisionmaker Problem

No matter how smart the planners or how good their intentions, no plan will ever reduce every variable to a number that can be put into a computer program. Even things that can be quantified are not always comparable; for example, how should we rationally weigh the tradeoff between saving endangered species and saving jobs? Due to the subjective nature of planning, different people will interpret many elements of the plan differently. Into this pool of vagueness steps the decisionmaker—an elected official, legislative body, or director of a bureaucracy—who is conditioned by incentives to make a particular decision regardless of the plan.

The decisionmaker may be corrupt, motivated by under-the-table bribes, or promises of cushy jobs once retired from his or her current position. More likely, the decisionmaker has a set of goals that are heavily conditioned by the years spent climbing the bureaucratic or political ladder. Decisionmakers know that certain decisions will likely be rewarded by voters or the legislators who fund the agency, while others might be punished. No matter what the plan says, the decisionmaker will listen to those who cast their ballots or write the checks or face replacement with someone who will.

Elected officials' incentives differ from agency officials', but neither guarantee that the public interest is foremost in their minds. Government agencies are best thought of as ecosystems in which various ideas compete and evolve in response to outside forces— the most important of which is the agency's budget. Most environmental and social problems have vague or uncertain causes, and there is often wide disagreement within agencies like the Forest Service, Environmental Protection Agency, and Department of Transportation about what the actual goals of the agencies should be and how they should achieve those goals. The ideas that win out are the ones that add the most to the agency's budget.

For example, timber cutting was a dominant part of the Forest Service's management of the national forests from about 1960 through 1990. When environmental challenges and internal dissension led to an 85 percent reduction of timber sales, something of a vacuum formed within the agency. If not growing and cutting trees, what should now be the primary mission of the Forest Service: Ecosystem management? Recreation? Watershed restoration? Advocates for each of these views competed for attention within the agency.

The answer came in 2000, when the Los Alamos fire burned several hundred homes and Congress responded by giving the Forest Service a 38 percent increase in its budget, nearly all for fire. Today, fire prevention and suppression dominate the Forest Service's budget, staffing, and operations. No one in the agency deliberately said, "I am going to maximize the Forest Service budget by manufacturing a fire crisis." But thanks to a fire crisis that some say is not real, the agency now enjoys the largest annual budgets in its history.[28]

If the goal of government agencies is to maximize their budgets, the goal of elected officials is to get reelected. While they might need to please voters, it is more important to please campaign contributors. One reason why rail transit has become so popular in U.S. cities is that its high cost to taxpayers translates to significant profits for engineering and design firms, construction companies, railcar manufacturers, and others in the rail industry—profits none of them would get if cities relied exclusively on buses. In 2000, Portland city commissioner Charles Hales encountered a strong challenge for his seat on the city council from someone who opposed rail transit. Hales easily raised nearly three times as much money as the challenger, much of it coming from firms that built either rail transit or subsidized real-estate developments near rail stations.[29]

Given the imperative to maximize budgets or get reelected, decisionmakers will not spend much time wading through planning data, forecasts, and models. Instead, they are likely to base their decisions on preconceived notions shaped by their budgetary and electoral experiences. The decisions they make, then, will be subjective and unscientific no matter what the quality of the actual planning process.

8. Planning Is Not Necessary

The ultimate argument for government planning is that, even if it does not work very well, it is the only way to deal with certain social and environmental problems. In fact, almost everything that planners do could be done better, at lower cost, and with less intrusion into people's lives, with properly designed user fees, markets, and incentives. While part seven will provide detailed examples of such proposals, it is appropriate here to examine the justification for planning.

The original justification for zoning was the need to protect residential neighborhoods from unwanted intrusions. Someone building a rental apartment in a neighborhood of high-quality single-family homes could charge higher rents because of the surrounding neighborhood, but the apartment might reduce the value of the nearby homes. As the U.S. Supreme Court wrote in its 1926 decision affirming the power of cities to zone, such an apartment building would be "a mere parasite, constructed in order to take advantage of the open spaces and attractive surroundings created by the residential character of the district."[1]

But the market-based alternative to zoning—private neighborhoods protected by covenants, conditions, and restrictions—was created even before zoning. The first such private neighborhood, Gramercy Park in New York City, actually preceded zoning by nearly 90 years.[2] By the time New York City passed the nation's first zoning code in 1916, private communities had been created in New York, Boston, St. Louis, and other cities.

Such private neighborhoods had all been created from scratch. A developer subdivides land, writes the protective covenants, sells the lots or homes, and creates a homeowners' association to enforce and, when needed, modify the covenants. This process did not work for neighborhoods that already existed without such covenants. Zoning was created for such neighborhoods. In retrospect, however, it was a mistake to give planners the authority over zoning, as today they use that authority to force some neighborhoods to accept high-density housing in the name of smart growth.

The better solution would have been to do as Houston has done. In place of zoning, many Houston neighborhoods have protective covenants. For those that do not, the city created a process allowing residents to petition their neighbors to create a homeowners' association. If a majority of the neighborhood's residents agree, the homeowners' association is allowed to write new covenants. In essence, the Houston system allows every neighborhood to be its own zoning board.

Early 20th-century planners said planning was needed because of "market failure." Since then, several generations of planners have left their marks on cities in the form of increasingly restrictive zoning codes. As a result, planners today no longer blame urban problems on market failure. Instead, they candidly admit that those problems are due to their predecessors' mistakes. Past planners dedicated too much land to low-density housing, thus preventing people from learning the benefits of high-density, mixed-use developments. Past planners spent billions on highways, thus denying people the benefits of public transit.

There is some truth to this argument, though less than planners claim. To the extent that it is true, the appropriate solution is to relax existing rules, end subsidies, and let the market work. Instead, convinced they know best and are somehow immune to making the mistakes their predecessors made, many planners want to pass even more restrictive zoning codes mandating high-density housing and to devote huge subsidies to transit and other nonautomotive forms of travel.

Another argument for planning is that certain problems are regional and only regional government staffed by regional planners can solve those problems. This argument has been strongly promoted by former Albuquerque mayor David Rusk.[3] In fact, most of the supposedly regional problems—including housing, open space, solid waste, infrastructure, and transportation—can easily be handled at the local level. The few problems that are difficult to solve locally are not made any easier by magnifying those problems to a regional scale. As Jane Jacobs wryly observes, a region is "an area safely larger than the last one to whose problems we found no solution."[4]

Proponents of regional government often point to the hundreds of local governments, including fire, water, sewer, school, and other special districts, as well as counties and cities, that characterize most urban areas, as if this is a problem. But why should this be more of a problem than having hundreds of different homebuilders, retailers, doctors, lawyers, accountants, and other providers of goods and services competing for people's business? Each special service district can concentrate on its particular problem and not get distracted by the complexity of regional issues. Moreover, local governments have long demonstrated that they can cooperate with one another on such issues as roads, water, and other infrastructure just as private parties cooperate on issues that they care about.

There are a few problems that markets cannot fully solve, but they are far less common than planning advocates will admit. Moreover, even for these problems, part seven will show that there are nongovernmental alternatives that work far better than comprehensive government planning.

In sum, the technical barriers—data, forecasting, modeling, and pace of change—to comprehensive, rational planning of land or other resources by government agencies are insurmountable. Because they cannot overcome these technical barriers, planners rely on junk science and resort to fads—and those fads cause far more problems than they solve. Instead of planning, governments should find alternative means of solving their problems, with an emphasis on user fees, markets, and incentives.

Part Three
Land-Use Planning

A man is not a whole and complete man unless he owns a house and the ground it stands on.

—Walt Whitman[1]

The latest fad among land-use planners is to write 50-year plans for entire urban regions housing millions of people. As noted in chapter 6, some believe that such regional plans should be "drawn with such precision that only the architectural detail is left to future designers."[2] How much effort would be needed to accomplish this?

An urban area of a million people may have a million parcels of land, each suitable for dozens of different uses. Each person in the region may have a different idea about the best use of each parcel, and picking any particular use for a given parcel will influence the best possible uses of other nearby parcels. This means that the number of data needed to find the optimum use of each parcel in the region is literally in the quadrillions. This is far beyond the ability of anyone to collect, much less comprehend.

In response, planners simplify. Too often, that simplification is not limited to the models planners use to understand what they are planning. Instead, it extends to actually simplifying reality. Oregon planners, for example, believe that the only legitimate lifestyles are urban and rural. State planning rules prohibit anyone from building a house on their own land in the 95 percent of the state that is zoned rural unless they own at least 160 acres, actually farm the land, and earned $40,000 to $80,000 (depending on land productivity) farming it in two of the past three years. This rule was needed, said the state, to prevent "lawyers, doctors, and others not really farming [from] building houses in farm zones."[3]

Planning a complex regional economy becomes more feasible once planners simplify the economy to just a few possible lifestyles. But that does not mean that the economy planners get will be as productive or desirable as one that is allowed to evolve with minimal planning and regulation.

New Urban design, the idea of high-density, mixed-use developments, often located on transit lines, is another simplification. Though planners deny it, such so-called transit-oriented developments have become a one-size-fits-all solution to any urban problem.

- Do you have a decaying warehouse district near your downtown? Build a transit-oriented development such as Portland's Pearl District.
- Do you have a thriving suburb where most people drive to most places they go? Build a transit-oriented development such as the Round in the Portland suburb of Beaverton.
- Do you have an undeveloped greenfield inside the urban-growth boundary whose owner is eager to subdivide? Build a transit-oriented development such as Orenco near the Portland suburb of Hillsboro.
- How about a town so small it does not even have any regular transit service? Build a high-density, mixed-use development such as one recently proposed in my current hometown of Bandon, a town of 3,000 people.[4]

The simplifications planners make may change over time. In the 1950s and 1960s, planning was all about urban renewal: slum clearance and construction of high-rise luxury housing or high-rise low-income housing projects. In the 1990s and early 2000s, planning focuses on suburban renewal: redevelopment of suburbs to higher densities. Perhaps in another couple of decades planning will turn to exurban renewal, with planners attempting to impose their visions on the increasing number of telecommuters who choose to live in rural areas. But in all these cases, the plans are based on planners' simplified notions of how people should live rather than on how people actually live.

9. Urban Renewal

In June 2005, five members of the U.S. Supreme Court agreed that New London, Connecticut, could take people's homes by eminent domain and give or sell the land to private developers, even if the area was not blighted. While this decision provoked widespread outrage, few noted that Justice Stevens's majority opinion specifically approved of the taking because New London had "carefully formulated an economic development plan that it believes will provide appreciable benefits to the community."[1] Justice Kennedy concurred, saying, "The taking occurred in the context of a comprehensive development plan."[2] As the American Planning Association gleefully observed, "The decision validates the essential role of planning"—at least, essential to the process of taking people's homes by eminent domain.[3]

In other words, the majority of the Court was seduced by the claims of urban planners. These five justices never asked whether the outcomes of plans ever turned out as well as the planners promised. They merely presumed that, if a plan had been "carefully formulated," the benefits would be greater than the costs.

Tell that to the former owners of homes and businesses in the Bronx, Ft. Lee, New Jersey, or many other places whose properties were taken by eminent domain decades ago and reduced to rubble for "urban renewal." On many of these sites, that rubble can still be seen today as no urban renewal ever took place.

Or tell it to the nearly one million low-income families—80 percent of which were black—displaced by urban renewal—sometimes called "Negro removal"—between 1950 and 1980. Since urban renewal often replaced slums with luxury housing, one study found that urban renewal "succeeded in materially reducing the supply of low-cost housing in America."[4] Another study concluded that urban renewal cost the average displaced family "20 to 30 percent of one year's income."[5]

Or tell it to residents of Greenwich Village, New York, whose neighborhood was saved from urban renewal bulldozers by the efforts of people like the late Jane Jacobs. Today, property in that neighborhood is extremely valuable, no thanks to the urban planners of the 1950s and 1960s who considered it a blighted slum and slated it for demolition.

In 1954, the U.S. Supreme Court ruled that a government agency could use eminent domain to take property from private owners for redevelopment if land around the property was "blighted"—even if the property itself was not blighted. Just as in 2005, the fact that the agency in question had written a comprehensive plan swayed the Court's decision.[6] The ruling led many cities to prepare grandiose urban-renewal plans, some of which proposed to sweep away entire neighborhoods of thousands of families. One of those plans called for leveling 14 blocks in Manhattan and displacing nearly 10,000 residents and workers to build an eight-lane elevated freeway connecting the Holland Tunnel with the Williamsburg and Manhattan bridges.

Jacobs, then a critic for *Architectural Forum* magazine, responded by writing *The Death and Life of Great American Cities*, which she described as "an attack on current city planning and rebuilding." Urban planning, she said, was no better than "the pseudoscience of bloodletting" because it has "not yet broken with the specious comfort of wishes, familiar superstitions, oversimplifications, and symbols, and [has] not yet embarked upon the adventure of probing the real world." "Having swallowed the initial fallacies and having been provisioned with tools," planners "go on logically to the greatest destructive excesses."[7]

Since urban renewal was legitimized by the existence of blight, Jacobs focused much of the book on proving that many high-density, mixed-use urban neighborhoods were not blighted at all but were living, vibrant communities. A journalist at heart, she took a journalist's approach to the problem: "The way to get at what goes on in the seemingly mysterious and perverse behavior of cities," she wrote, "is to look closely, and with as little previous expectation as is possible, at the most ordinary scenes and events, and attempt to see what they mean and whether any threads of principle emerge among them."[8]

By looking closely at her neighborhood, Jacobs concluded that cities need "a most intricate and close-grained diversity of uses that give each other constant mutual support, both economically and socially." To attain the diversity necessary to allow a city to thrive, she continued, "four conditions are indispensable": mixed uses, short blocks, a mixture of old and new buildings, and a dense concentration of residents as well as workers. "The necessity for these four conditions is the most important point this book has to make."[9]

There is a contradiction here. First, Jacobs tears down the science of urban planning. But then, by reducing to a simple formula all the conditions needed for a lively, thriving city, she creates the foundation for a new science of urban planning. "By deliberately inducing these four conditions, planning can induce city vitality," she claims.[10]

Jacobs cautions readers not to "try to transfer my observations [about great cities] into guides as to what goes on in towns, or little cities, or in suburbs." But it is a half-hearted warning: she admits she likes "dense cities best" and considers suburbs, with their separated uses, to be "city destroying." Eventually, as suburbs are "engulfed in cities," she expects that her observations will "have somewhat wider usefulness."[11]

Jacobs was unaware that, as she was criticizing urban planning as a pseudoscience, she herself was creating another pseudoscience. One person who was aware of this irony was Herbert Gans, a sociologist whose research far exceeded Jacobs's amateurish efforts. Gans spent a year living in an inner-city neighborhood like Greenwich Village, and then spent a year living in a low-density suburb. His books *The Urban Villagers* and *The Levittowners* dispel many of the myths propounded by urban planners to this day, including some that were accepted or promoted by Jacobs.

Like Jacobs, Gans was often critical of urban planners, whose "values are those of the professional upper-middle class." Among other things, Gans found, planners acted as though lower-class people were simply people with middle-class values who lacked "access to opportunities and services available to the middle class." So planners assumed "that cultural change can be induced by providing the improved residential conditions and . . . educational, health, and other facilities."[12] This is the *design fallacy*—the idea that urban design shapes human behavior—that pervades much of urban planning.

In his 1961 review of *The Death and Life*, Gans admits that Jacobs's observations of inner-city neighborhoods "are far more closely attuned to how people actually live than are those of orthodox city planning." But he points out that Jacobs's emphasis on such things as short blocks is simply another example of the design fallacy, and her claim that cities need diversity is "not entirely supported by the facts."[13]

Instead of focusing on design, Gans presents a cultural interpretation of inner-city neighborhoods. In the 1950s, ethnic, working-class families dominated these neighborhoods. "In this culture, the home is reserved for the family, so that much social life takes place outdoors." Thus, the active street life in these neighborhoods "stems not so much from their physical characteristics as from the working-class structure of their inhabitants." This active street life also attracts "intellectuals, artists, and bohemian types [such as Jacobs], contributing further to the street life." The resulting "exotic flavor then draws visitors and tourists, whose presence helps to make the district even livelier."

Middle-class people enjoy the "charm and excitement" of such lively neighborhoods as tourists, but few—Jane Jacobs and Herbert Gans being exceptions—actually tried to live in them. Gans pointed out that those charmed by Jacobs's description of Greenwich Village or their own visits to such neighborhoods often failed to see that, from the point of view of residents, "the houses in these traditional districts are often hard to maintain, that parking is often impossible, that noise and dirt are ever present, that some of the neighbors watch too much, and that not all of the shopkeepers are kind."[14]

"Middle-class people," Gans wrote, "especially those raising children, do not want working-class—or even bohemian—neighborhoods." Their social lives take place indoors, which leads people on the outside to erroneously conclude that their neighborhoods are dull. "But visibility is not the only measure of vitality, and areas that are uninteresting to the visitor may be quite vital to the people who live in them." Middle-class people do not necessarily socialize with their neighbors; "their friends may be scattered all over the metropolitan area, as are the commercial and recreational facilities which they frequent." This means they need a car, not pedestrian-oriented, mixed-use housing.

Gans recognized, as Jacobs did not, that the inner-city neighborhoods "were built for a style of life which is going out of fashion with the large majority of Americans who are free to choose their place of residence." Young people raised in these neighborhoods moved out as soon as they were old enough to have their own children. As working-class families moved to the suburbs, some were replaced by bohemians—mainly young people with no children who appreciated the lively streets. But it is likely that many of the lively neighborhoods would have disappeared with or without urban renewal.

While Gans himself enjoyed living in one of these neighborhoods, he "made no recommendations for or against urban villages or ethnic enclaves, because they are desirable only if people want to live in them, and that is up to them." His objection to urban renewal was "first and foremost economic and political" because it often imposed high costs on low-income people in order to subsidize high-income housing and because it deprived people of the right to choose how they wanted to live.[15] He feared that Jacobs's colorful descriptions of these neighborhoods would "win her the support of those who profit from the status quo" and those "who want to bring back the city and the society of the 18th and 19th centuries."[16]

This is exactly what happened when a new generation of urban planners read Jacobs's book. Instead of finding in *The Death and Life* a warning that urban planning does more harm than good, planners used the book as a model for how they should do urban renewal. If Jacobs's high-density, mixed-use communities were so good in the inner city, the planners reasoned, then they should be built everywhere else too, and particularly in the suburbs. Calling themselves New Urbanists, they proposed that all new developments be like Greenwich Village: high densities, mixed uses, with limited room for the automobile. They also urged that existing suburbs be redeveloped along these lines. "There's no question that [Jane Jacobs's] work is the leaping-off point for our whole movement," says the executive director of the Congress for the New Urbanism, which was formed about 30 years after *The Death and Life* was published.[17]

Few would question *The Economist*'s judgment that *The Death and Life* "was among the most influential and controversial books of the twentieth century." However, the magazine erroneously added that the book "stopped America's urban renewal movement in its tracks."[18] While it did help stop the Lower Manhattan Expressway, if it had stopped urban renewal, Susette Kelo would never have become famous as a U.S. Supreme Court case. Though Jacobs demolished the theory behind inner-city urban renewal, the tools that made urban renewal possible, including eminent domain and tax-increment financing, remained in place. As a result, cities continue to "renew" urban areas to this day, with results that are often as controversial and devastating to neighborhoods as they were in the 1950s and 1960s. Since New Urbanism is the current planning fad, much of that urban renewal aims to recreate Jane Jacobs's vibrant streets in quiet suburban settings.

While the *Kelo* decision set a precedent by allowing cities to use eminent domain even in areas that are not blighted, many state laws still limit the use of eminent domain and other urban-renewal tools to blighted areas. But to the New Urbanists, any low-density suburb is blighted simply because it does not have mixed uses or small blocks, or meet Jacobs's other standards. For example, in 2002, the city of San Jose declared a full third of the city to be blighted. One neighborhood of Victorian and Craftsman-style single-family homes was considered blighted because planners found wet leaves on the tennis court behind one of the houses—which happened to be the home of San Jose's representative in Congress.[19]

If there is a difference between urban renewal in 1960 and urban renewal today, it is that highways are no longer a major tool to clear slums. This is partly because inflation in construction costs led cities and states to reduce their plans for new highways and partly because planners today are more interested in discouraging driving than in building new roads.

Planners could use eminent domain to force sales of land in neighborhoods they considered blighted, but they still needed to pay for the land. With freeway funds out of the picture, they turned to another tool: tax-increment financing. Tax-increment financing allows urban-renewal agencies to divert all property taxes on new developments in an urban-renewal area to subsidies for that development. Typically, the agency designates an area an urban-renewal or redevelopment zone and makes specific plans for how that redevelopment should take place. Planners project the tax revenues from the new development and sell bonds that will be repaid out of those revenues. The money from the bonds is used to buy the land, build streets and other infrastructure, and provide other subsidies to the developers. First authorized in California in 1952, tax-increment financing is now legal in every state but Arizona.

Armed with these tools—eminent domain; tax-increment financing; and various other federal, state, and local grants and subsidies—

planners remain very much in the business of urban renewal. Only now they call it something else: smart growth. And the most famous smart-growth plan in America was written for what was then my hometown, Portland, Oregon.

10. Turning Portland into L.A.

In the late 1980s and early 1990s, Portland was one of the fastest-growing urban areas in America. Environmentally conscious Oregonians worried that this growth would "Californicate" Oregon and "turn Portland into Los Angeles." Indeed, Los Angeles is the bogeyman for people all over the West who worry about the effects of growth on their community.

"Los Angeles is the granddaddy of sprawl," says the Sierra Club.[1] Data show that Los Angeles is the most congested[2] and most polluted[3] urban area in the United States. The Sierra Club and other planning advocates blamed these problems on Los Angeles's low-density sprawl and its extensive freeway network.

In 1992, planners told Portlanders they could save their region from becoming like Los Angeles if only the area's residents voted to create Metro, a regional government that would write land-use and transportation plans for 24 cities and 3 counties in the Portland area. Voters agreed and Metro immediately began writing its plans.

By 1994, Metro's plan was mostly written if not yet set into concrete. Although Metro anticipated an 80 percent population increase in the Portland area in the next 50 years, it decided to expand the region's urban-growth boundary by only 6 percent. To accommodate everyone else, Metro ordered the 24 cities and 3 counties to rezone existing neighborhoods to higher densities. Metro claimed such compact development, the opposite of sprawl, would reduce congestion because people wouldn't have to drive as far to get to their destinations.

Other aspects of Metro's plan included the construction of more than 100 miles of light-rail and commuter-rail lines so that people would have alternatives to the automobile. Metro wanted developers to build scores of high-density, mixed-use developments so that people could walk to cafés, shopping, and perhaps even to work. Such transit-oriented developments would be located on major transit corridors so people could ride the bus or light-rail to get to places that were too far to walk. With all the emphasis on transit, Metro proposed to build very little new road capacity, and that would mainly serve industrial areas, not commuters or shoppers.

After reaching these decisions, Metro planners looked at the nation's major urban areas to see which one was closest to the future Metro planned for Portland. The nation's most compact urban area— that is, the one with the highest number of people per square mile— also turned out to have the fewest number of miles of freeway per capita, which Metro liked because it proposed to build few new freeways. Moreover, this urban area was also spending billions of dollars building new rail transit lines. It also had an excellent balance between jobs and housing in its various communities, which planners believed would allow residents to minimize driving by living close to work. Clearly, this urban area came closest to representing the future Metro planned for Portland.

What urban area was it? The surprising answer: Los Angeles. While New York City is denser than the city of Los Angeles, New York is surrounded by low-density suburbs in Connecticut and New Jersey. Los Angeles, which itself contains the nation's largest expanse of land with more than 10,000 people per square mile, is surrounded by fairly dense suburbs. Far from being low-density sprawl, the Los Angeles urban area is, according to the 2000 census, 33 percent denser than the New York urban area. Moreover, unlike most urban areas, Los Angeles's density has steadily increased over the past 60 years.

In addition, far from it being "a great big freeway," Los Angeles turns out to have the fewest miles of freeway per capita of any major U.S. urban area. While the average U.S. urban area has about 110 miles of freeway per million people, and some have more than 140, Los Angeles has only 53.[4] Los Angeles also operates commuter, light-rail, and subway trains on nearly 400 miles of track, and in 1994, it had plans for many more.

It barely occurred to Metro that this might mean there was something wrong with its plan for Portland. Instead, it merely attributed the results to a disparity "between perception and measurement." "In public discussions we gather the general impression that Los Angeles represents a future to be avoided," noted Metro. Yet "with respect to density and road per-capita mileage it displays an investment pattern we desire to replicate" in Portland.[5]

84

Instead of a disparity between perception and measurement, the real disparity is between how planners think people should live and how people really do live. The characteristics that planners valued, high densities and low per capita road mileage, were the ones that made Los Angeles so unlivable. Los Angeles is the most congested urban area in America because it has so many people crammed into a compact region and they have so few freeways to drive on. It is the most polluted urban area in America because cars pollute more in congested traffic. Construction of rail transit proved so expensive that the regional transit agency was forced to cut bus service, leading to a 17 percent drop in bus riders in the decade after 1985. Urban residents who hate traffic congestion and polluted skies have good reasons to fear that their region might be following Los Angeles's development patterns.

Yet when asked at a public hearing why Metro was trying to replicate Los Angeles in Portland, Metro's executive director, Michael Burton, responded lamely, "There's lots of people who like to live in L.A."[6]

The same report that promised to "replicate" Los Angeles by increasing Portland's population densities casually noted that there were "welfare tradeoffs" for higher densities that "appear to take the form of higher housing prices."[7] While high densities themselves don't cause higher housing prices, the factors that lead densities to increase, such as high land prices, usually force increases in housing prices.

Some might ask how a plan that was supposed to save Portland from becoming as congested as Los Angeles got turned into a plan that specifically aimed to "replicate" Los Angeles–like congestion in Portland. But the real question should be: why did anyone think that planning was the solution to Portland's growth problems in the first place? Unfortunately, few people were willing to ask, much less answer, this question.

I first became aware of Metro's plan when planners came to my suburban neighborhood of single-family homes promising to make it easier to walk and bicycle. Since I encountered no problems walking my dog five miles a day and few problems cycling six miles each way to work, I wondered how they were going to do that. Eventually, the planners revealed that their plan called for

- promoting mixed uses, including residential, retail shops, and offices in the same developments;

85

- building new streets to reduce the size of the large blocks that characterized our suburb;
- building new four- and five-story complexes among (or replacing) the historic homes, including some of the oldest homes in the Portland area; and
- quintupling the population density of the neighborhood.

These happen to be the four steps that Jane Jacobs said were necessary to "induce city vitality."[8] However, no one in my neighborhood was particularly interested in living in a Greenwich Village, and they loudly said so at several public hearings on the plan. Planners said they were willing to drop the plan, but warned, "If you don't let us approve this plan now, Metro will impose even more density on you next year." It turned out that Metro had targeted some three dozen neighborhoods for densification and planners were using mine as a sort of proving ground. What Metro learned from this test was not to hold public hearings that would give people a forum to speak out and organize against the plans. Instead, Portland and other cities created "public involvement committees," most members of which did not actually live in the neighborhoods being densified. As a result, Metro's plans succeeded in the other 35 or so neighborhoods where they failed in mine.[9]

The plan to replicate Los Angeles in Portland dates back to at least 1990, when 1000 Friends of Oregon commissioned a study aimed at discouraging construction of a new freeway in the region. One Thousand Friends of Oregon is a classic example of a special interest group formed to support a plan, or, in this case, a planning law. In 1973, the Oregon legislature passed Senate Bill 100, which required all cities and counties to write comprehensive plans that followed rules set by a seven-member Land Conservation and Development Commission (LCDC) appointed by the governor.

Soon after the law was passed, it occurred to Henry Richmond, the staff attorney for the Ralph Nader–inspired Oregon Student Public Interest Research Group, that he could probably convince 1,000 people to each donate $100 a year to a group formed to monitor and enforce LCDC's rules. While some say he never reached that target, he raised enough money to hire two recent law school graduates, Robert Stacey and Richard Benner.

For its first 15 years, 1000 Friends of Oregon appealed plans and took cities or counties to court if its attorneys believed their plans did not do enough to safeguard Oregon's quality of life. Their goal was to protect farms, forests, and open space, and they lobbied LCDC to strengthen its standards, first requiring 40-acre minimum lot sizes in rural areas, then increasing them to 160 acres, then requiring that landowners actually farm the land before allowing even a single home to be built on 160 acres.

When LCDC approved the last local plan in 1986, all the land in the state could be grouped into one of four zoning categories:

- Less than 1.25 percent of the state was included in an urban-growth boundary, which supposedly included enough vacant land to accommodate 20 years of growth.
- More than 94 percent of the state was zoned for a minimum of 40—later 160—acre lot sizes.
- Less than 1.75 percent of the state, mostly land near an urban-growth boundary, allowed for 5- to 10-acre lot sizes.
- The remaining 3 percent was mostly parks, public facilities, water, or Indian reservations.[10]

At this point, nearly all the effects of state land-use planning rules fell on rural landowners who were denied the right to use their land for things other than traditionally rural purposes. Since they made up only a small minority of the state's voters—in 1980, more than two out of three Oregonians lived in urban areas—their efforts to overturn or modify the law were unsuccessful. Few urbanites cared that the LCDC, prodded by 1000 Friends, wrote increasingly stringent rules for rural residents, saying, for example, that 75 percent of the goods sold by farmers' roadside stands must be locally grown or that farmers must actually earn $80,000 a year from farming before being allowed to build a house on their own land.

The first hints that the state would become more prescriptive inside the urban-growth boundaries came in 1989, when the Oregon Department of Transportation proposed a new freeway in the Portland area. After recovering from a deep recession in the early 1980s, the Portland area was growing rapidly, with much of that growth taking place in Washington County, which includes the suburbs west of Portland. The new highway would serve those suburbs and the high-tech factories that were providing much of the region's job growth. However, 1000 Friends of Oregon decided to oppose the highway, partly because a portion of it would be outside the growth boundary.

To prove that there were alternatives to more highways, 1000 Friends commissioned the Land Use, Transportation and Air Quality (LUTRAQ) study.[11] The group claimed that the study proved that alternative land-use patterns, such as higher densities, pedestrian-friendly design, and transit-oriented development would do more to reduce congestion than building new roads.

As University of Southern California planning professor Genevieve Giuliano observed, however, most of the reductions in driving projected by LUTRAQ were not due to increased densities or urban design. Instead, LUTRAQ presumed that all workers would be given free transit passes and that they would be required to pay for parking if they chose to drive to work. LUTRAQ projected that these two changes would have more effect on driving than all the land-use changes combined.[12]

In addition, the higher densities required by smart growth more than make up for any per capita reductions in driving.[13] Doubling density will reduce congestion only if per capita driving is cut by more than 50 percent. The actual reduction in per capita driving that would be associated with a doubling in density is more like 5 or 10 percent, which would mean an 80 to 90 percent increase in driving per square mile. Unless more roads are built, which 1000 Friends would oppose, that means more congestion. Moreover, since cars pollute the most in stop-and-go traffic, the increased congestion in compact cities greatly increases air pollution. Reducing per capita driving by 5 percent but getting 25 percent more pollution from the remaining cars is not a very good tradeoff.

By glossing over LUTRAQ's weak findings, 1000 Friends of Oregon persuaded Oregon's LCDC to issue a 1991 transportation planning rule directing planners in all of Oregon's major urban areas to change "land-use patterns and transportation systems" so as to reduce per capita driving by 10 percent in 20 years and 20 percent in 30 years.[14] To reach these goals, the rule specified that planners must increase residential densities, promote mixed-use developments, mandate pedestrian-friendly design, and apply other policies that would come to be known as smart growth.[15]

Directing cities to reduce per capita driving is like directing water to run up hill. Since the rule was passed, per capita driving in

Portland has increased by 19 percent and would have increased more were it not for the 2001 recession.

By 1993, land available for development was increasingly scarce and land prices were rising fast. Yet 1000 Friends of Oregon lobbied against any additions to Portland's urban-growth boundary. Portland-area homebuilders went to the Oregon legislature seeking a law that would force planners to expand the urban-growth boundary to accommodate growth, as they had promised in 1979. But Metro, Portland's regional planning agency, opposed the measure until it was amended to allow Metro to accommodate growth by rezoning existing neighborhoods to higher densities. After the law was passed, Metro gave the Portland region's 24 cities and 3 counties population targets and required them to rezone land to meet those targets.

To meet their targets, cities rezoned many neighborhoods of single-family homes to multifamily densities. While past zoning had specified maximum densities—so that homes could be built on acre or half-acre lots in an area zoned for quarter-acre minimum lot sizes—the new zoning was minimum-density zoning, requiring that all development be at least 80 percent of the maximum density allowed by the zone. In some areas, zoning was so strict that, if people's homes burned down, they would be required to replace them with apartments.[16]

Yet Metro's plan for the Portland area gave no comfort to those who argued that higher densities and better design would reduce auto driving. The plan called for increasing population densities within the urban-growth boundary by 70 percent, building 125 miles of rail transit, and redeveloping dozens of neighborhoods into high-density, mixed-use regional and town centers. Planners projected that this would more than double transit's share of trips from 2.8 percent to 6.4 percent and increase walking and cycling's share of trips from 5.2 percent to 5.8 percent. Yet this meant that the automobile's share of trips would fall by less than 5 percent, from 92.1 percent to 87.8 percent.[17] Since auto trips tend to be longer than transit, cycling, or walking trips, the auto would still be used for well over 90 percent of travel when measured in passenger miles.

Of course, a slight reduction in the automobile's share of trips would not reduce congestion because Metro also projected a 70 percent increase in the region's population. Given that increase, Metro projected that overall driving would increase by 67 percent.

Since Metro was planning only a few small additions to the region's road system, it projected a quintupling of congestion and a 10 percent increase in smog by the year 2020.[18]

When asked about these projections in a public hearing, Metro's executive, Michael Burton, replied that "no one at Metro or Tri-Met" (Portland's transit agency) believed the numbers.[19] So Metro had spent hundreds of thousands of dollars developing transportation models whose results were ignored because they did not support the planners' preconceived notions.

At the same hearing, Richard Benner, executive director of the state Department of Land Conservation and Development (and former attorney for 1000 Friends of Oregon), denied that his agency was responsible for controversial neighborhood densifications. His department's planning goals and guidelines, which all cities are required to follow, never even mentioned the word "density," he said.[20] This is disingenuous, as the goals and guidelines are only the top level of the department's planning requirements. The department's transportation planning rule uses the words "density" or "densities" a dozen times and requires planners in Oregon's major metropolitan areas to consider "increasing residential densities" and in particular to increase densities near "major transit stops" to reduce per capita driving.[21]

Metro's projections included an assumption that all employers and retailers would charge their employees and customers for parking.[22] Confirming LUTRAQ's finding, Metro planners concluded that this assumption produced half the projected reduction in driving. Yet Metro's plan has focused on density and urban design, and so far Metro has made no attempts to force shopping malls and office parks to charge customers and employees for parking.

Nor have the numerous "transit-oriented developments" that have been built along Portland's light-rail lines had a significant effect on the region's driving. Indeed, developers quickly learned that these developments only work if they are automobile oriented. Despite being next to a transit line, they need plenty of parking or people won't live in them and the retail shops will remain vacant.

One development, Center Commons, has fewer than two parking spaces for every three housing units. To compensate, residents illegally park in fire lanes or on sidewalks.[23] The development's managers know that if they enforced the parking rules, they would lose many of their tenants. Due to the lack of parking, the only occupied retail shop currently in the development is an H&R Block office that is closed most of the time.

Another mixed-use development, Beaver Creek, is located next to a huge parking lot, but it is reserved as a park-and-ride station. As a result, almost every retail shop in the development remains vacant.

A third development, Beaverton Round, was supposed to include retail shops, offices, and condominiums or apartments encircling a light-rail station. After receiving $9 million in subsidies, the developer went bankrupt because no private party would finance a development that didn't have enough parking. After sitting uncompleted for three years, another developer finished it on the condition that it could put in 300 parking spaces. Even today, the development remains only partially occupied.

When Portland built a light-rail line to its airport, it paid for the construction in part by giving a 99-year lease to 120 acres of vacant land to Bechtel. Planners zoned the land for pedestrian-oriented retail shops and offices. Although served by two light-rail stations, after four years not a single shop or office had opened in the area. The rules restricted shops to no more than 60,000 square feet, and there was little demand for a new area of small shops.[24]

Under pressure from Bechtel, the city finally relented and rezoned the land to allow at least three big-box stores, the first of which will be a 280,000-square-foot IKEA. The city insists that the development will still be "pedestrian friendly"; apparently, planners think Portland yuppies will load their purchases of bookshelves and bedroom furniture on the light-rail trains or on the bicycles they park at one of the 75 bike racks they are requiring IKEA to provide. IKEA knows better, and has insisted on providing 1,200 parking spaces in its part of the development.[25]

Portland's great success story, a development Metro proudly shows to people touring the region, is Orenco Station. Orenco (which stands for Oregon Nursery Company) was built on prime farmland after a light-rail line was deliberately routed across the land so the region could build a transit-oriented community from scratch. The area was zoned for a combination of apartments, mixed uses, and single-family homes on small lots. As Cascade Policy Institute researcher John Charles observes, the areas with no parking limits were quickly developed, while areas that were zoned for limited parking remain vacant. Since the limited parking areas were closest to the light-rail station, this means that, until recently, most of the development is not within walking distance of the rail line.[26]

A survey of Orenco residents by Lewis and Clark College researcher Bruce Podobnik found that most of them liked the development but that few had changed their travel habits. "Though some have increased their reliance on mass transit for occasional trips since moving into Orenco Station, most residents of the neighborhood report using alternative modes of transportation far less than do their counterparts in Northeast Portland," says Podobnik. "A key objective, that of significantly altering resident transportation habits, therefore remains to be achieved in Orenco Station."[27]

The other problem with Orenco—one that wouldn't particularly interest planners—is that it was not very marketable. The developer who built much of it called it "our non-profit wing," implying that his company built it only to get permits to build more lucrative developments of single-family homes on larger lots.[28] Many other transit-oriented developments have high vacancy rates. Smart growth thus follows in the planners' tradition of creating surpluses of things people don't want and shortages of things they do want.

Metro can be proud of one achievement. A recent Environmental Protection Agency analysis finds that Oregon has the third-most toxic air in the nation after California and New York. Oregon's air was even dirtier than New Jersey's.[29] The drive to turn Portland into Los Angeles is succeeding.

11. How Smart Is "Smart Growth"?

Urban planners in Portland and many other cities today base their plans on a belief that Americans are too *auto dependent*, and that we have become that way as a result of land-use patterns that force people to drive and discourage transit, walking, and cycling. *Smart growth* is a land-use and transportation planning concept that calls for higher-density, compact urban areas, mixing commercial with residential uses, and emphasizing pedestrian-friendly design and transit-oriented development over automobile-oriented development, all aimed at reducing the amount of driving people need to do.[1]

The term "smart growth" was first used in this way by Maryland Governor Parris Glendening in 1996. As one of Glendening's staff members later admitted, "The name 'Smart Growth' represented one of the Glendening Administration's smartest strategies," because it was "hard to oppose": anyone who questioned smart growth could be (and usually was) immediately accused of favoring "dumb growth."[2] The clear implication is that anyone who wants to allow people to live the way that a majority of Americans actually do live must be dumb.

Before 1996, the concepts known as smart growth were often referred to as New Urbanism. Since then, at least some of the New Urbanists have distinguished themselves from smart growth by saying that smart growth is coercive, whereas New Urbanists simply want to relax existing zoning codes so they can build for those people who would prefer to live in New Urban communities.[3] Although few object to building New Urban projects where there is market demand, many smart-growth advocates want to use coercive policies to shape people's transportation choices.

A major problem with smart growth is that its advocates have badly mistaken the causal relationships that lead people to drive rather than walk or ride transit. Smart growth is based on the design fallacy, the idea that urban design shapes human behavior. In fact, the design features that smart growth would impose on urban areas have little effect on people's travel habits. They do, however, have significant negative effects on such things as congestion and housing prices.

Herbert Gans pointed out that few middle-class families with children want to live in dense, lively neighborhoods such as Jane Jacobs's Greenwich Village. But in a typical planner fashion, smart-growth advocates reason that since most residents of dense, mixed-use neighborhoods are childless, therefore most child-free households will be glad to live in such neighborhoods. ("All dogs have four legs, so anything with four legs is a dog.") They imagine, for example, that as baby boomers become empty nesters, large numbers of them will want to move back to the high-density neighborhoods they enjoyed before they had children.[4]

There is no doubt that some people prefer living in high-density, mixed-use neighborhoods. As Gans hints, they are mainly young singles or childless couples.[5] But between 1990 and 2000, the vast majority of growth of these groups—in fact, in virtually every population group—was in the suburbs, not in cities.

Claims for a recent "downtown rebound" based on changing preferences toward high-density, mixed-use housing, for example, are greatly exaggerated. "'Downtown is Back' seemed to be a common observation in the 1990s," says a Fannie Mae study. "This was more than wishful thinking," the study says optimistically, but then adds, "The actual numbers of downtown growth are relatively small."[6]

That's putting it mildly. The study looked at 24 urban areas and found that, during the 1990s, downtown populations had grown in 18 of them. But total population growth in those 18 downtowns was just over 54,000 people, an average of about 3,000 per downtown. During the same period, the cities surrounding those downtowns grew by more than 77,000 people and the suburbs of those cities grew by 5.54 million people, or more than 100 times as much as the downtowns.[7] Considering that at least some of the cities in the study, including Denver and Portland, subsidized their downtown population growth, it is hard to see in these numbers much of a signal that Americans desire to live in smart-growth neighborhoods.

If anyone is interested in finding out what people really want, it is homebuilders and realtors, whose livelihoods depend on providing products that people will buy. A 2002 opinion poll commissioned by the National Association of Home Builders and National Association of Realtors revealed that the vast majority of Americans still aspire to live in a single-family home with a yard, and less than 20 percent are eager to live in New Urban neighborhoods. The poll found that

- 64 percent of Americans want to live in a larger home than their current one;
- only 17 to 23 percent want to live closer than they do to work, shopping, entertainment, and restaurants;
- only 7 to 9 percent want to live closer to "the city" or public transportation;[8]
- 82 percent prefer a single-family home in the suburbs; and
- only 18 percent want a "home in the city, close to work, public transportation, and shopping."[9]

Yet most smart-growth advocates are not content to build to the market. As Urban Land Institute researcher Douglas Porter notes, there is a "gap between the daily mode of living desired by most Americans and the mode that most city planners . . . believe is most appropriate." While most Americans "want a house on a large lot and three cars in every garage," planners believe this leads to an urban development pattern "that is expensive in terms of public and private infrastructure costs, quality of life, and environmental damage."[10]

To ensure that planners would have their way, in 1991 the founders of New Urbanism called for having "government take charge of the planning process" rather than allow "developer-initiated, piecemeal development."[11] They went on to form the Congress for the New Urbanism, whose goals included that "all development should be in the form of compact, walkable neighborhoods" with "a diverse mix of activities (residences, shops, schools, workplaces and parks, etc.) . . . in proximity."[12] Not only did the group think that all new development should follow its model, it supported "the reconfiguration of sprawling suburbs into communities of real neighborhoods and diverse districts."[13]

In other words, if they had their way, no one except a few rural residents would be allowed to live anywhere but in New Urban neighborhoods. Pressure from some of its members led the group to delete these phrases from its charter, but many smart-growth advocates remain committed to coercive policies. To be fair, some New Urbanists today say that these goals were merely "aspirational," and the Congress for the New Urbanism has removed some of the more extreme statements from its website. But many planners still seek to impose New Urbanism on the residents of their communities.

For example, Porter says that the problem with government is that democratically elected local officials are unwilling to try to impose huge lifestyle changes on their constituents. So Porter, the Brookings Institution's Anthony Downs, and others have recommended that planners use regional governments to impose smart growth on urban areas. As Downs says, regional governments "can take controversial stands without making its individual members commit themselves to those stands. Each member can claim that 'the organization' did it or blame all the other members."[14]

Officially known as *metropolitan planning organizations*, regional governments were imposed on urban areas by the federal government in 1965. Sometimes called *councils* or *associations of governments*, the original purpose of these regional governments was not to govern but to submit housing and transportation grant proposals on behalf of urban areas to the federal government and in turn to distribute those federal funds to local governments in each urban area. Each council of governments is supposed to be overseen by mayors or city councilors representing a majority of the people in the urban area. Over time, some regional governments have gained actual planning and governing powers over their regions, most often through their power to deny federal funds to local governments that refuse to cooperate with the rest of the region.

Mostly through the power of their regional governments, a number of urban areas in the United States have applied New Urbanism or smart-growth principles to their entire regions. Denver, Minneapolis–St. Paul, Portland, San Diego, and San Jose are the most comprehensive examples, but some smart-growth principles have been tested in such varying regions as Austin; Baltimore; and Missoula, Montana.

The fundamental premise of smart growth—that urban design can and should be used to change people's transportation choices—is based on a misunderstanding about cause and effect. Smart-growth planners correctly recognize that there is a connection between transportation and land use; but they fail to accept that it is a one-way street: transportation technology influences land use, but land use does not significantly affect people's transportation choices. Part five of this book will take a closer look at transportation planning, but this chapter will examine the influence that land-use planning supposedly has on transportation choices.

Steam trains in the 1830s, horsecars in the 1850s, cable cars in the 1870s, electric streetcars and subways in the 1890s, and automobiles in the 1910s each reduced transportation costs and allowed more people to live in their preferred styles of housing.[15] For many, that meant a single-family home with a yard. While early technologies such as steam trains and horsecars were accessible only to the wealthy, electric streetcars helped create a growing middle class while Henry Ford's automobiles were affordable to the working class.

By the 1920s, the suburbs were fast becoming the dominant lifestyle, not only in America but in many other countries as well. "In the days of electrical transmission, the automobile and the telephone," said Frank Lloyd Wright in 1922, urban concentration "becomes needless congestion—it is a curse."[16] "Cities are doomed," agreed Henry Ford in the same year. "There is no city now existing that would be rebuilt as it is, if it were destroyed."[17] Ford was right: where early-19th-century cities had high population densities with concentrated job centers—think Brooklyn—late-20th-century cities have low population densities with widely dispersed jobs—think Phoenix.

While the Depression and World War II put a damper on suburbanization, it greatly accelerated after 1945. Between the 1950 and 1990 censuses, many major cities lost population while the overall urban areas in which they were located grew. The 2000 census revealed that some—though far from all—cities made a slight recovery, but in most cases their suburbs continued to grow far faster than the cities.

Despite all the suburbanization of the 20th century, America's suburbs haven't come close to destroying the nation's stock of rural open space. The 2000 census found that all urbanized areas (including unincorporated lands) of 2,500 people or more occupy just 2.6 percent of the United States.[18] The U.S. Department of Agriculture estimates that all urban developments, large and small, occupied just 3.5 percent of the nation's land area in 1997, and all rural developments, such as highways, added just 1 percent more.[19] Either way, some 95 percent of the United States is rural open space, which hardly makes rural open space the scarce commodity that planners claim it to be.

Whatever the value of rural open space, suburbanization does not "consume" such space as much as it transforms that space into another kind of open space. People's homes are going to occupy land one way or another, and from an open-space view, the main difference between smart growth and low-density suburbs is the size of people's yards. But suburban residents regard their yards as a form of open space, one that receives far more recreational use than, say, cropland or rangeland.

Sprawl opponents also claim "sprawl kills," as the title of one recent book screams.[20] Planning advocates link air pollution, obesity, and a variety of other health problems to low-density suburbs. Yet as chapter 7 showed, these claims are little more than pseudoscience.

While it doesn't threaten rural open space, health, or community, suburbanization did cause a number of feuds that set the stage for the modern anti-sprawl movement. Central city officials resented the suburbanites who seemed to take advantage of the city without paying their fair share of taxes toward it. Downtown property owners resented suburban shopping malls that quickly captured most of their retail business and suburban office and industrial parks that left some downtowns nearly vacant. Neighborhood residents resented the highways that took many homes and imposed noise and traffic on the homes that were left behind. Although most of the leaders of these groups lived in their own single-family homes with large yards, their solution was to demonize the suburbs and anyone who wanted to live in them.

For most people, automobiles provided access to low-cost land where they could afford to own their own homes. Far from causing congestion, the resulting low-density development was actually the solution to congestion. "Suburbanization has been the dominant and successful mechanism for coping with congestion," say University of Southern California planning professors Peter Gordon and Harry Richardson.[21] People in suburbs don't necessarily want to drive more than people in cities. But because the suburbs are less congested, driving costs less, and so they may in fact drive a little more. At the same time, the growth of driving in dense cities has matched and in some cases exceeded driving growth in the suburbs.

If traffic is the problem, then smart growth is entirely the wrong solution. The notion that higher densities lead people to drive less appeals to planners who suffer from the design fallacy, yet there is no merit to this belief. In 1999, a U.S. Department of Transportation researcher reviewed numerous studies on the relationship between density and driving. He found that those who claimed that density reduced driving were "spurious" because they failed to account for differences in such factors as income and household size. When such factors are considered, changes in driving are significant only at very high densities.[22] For example, one study found that increasing suburban densities (1,000 to 2,000 people per square mile) to 25,000 or more people per square mile would reduce driving by only 11 to 25 percent.[23] Another found that increasing densities from 3,600 people per square mile (the average for U.S. urban areas in 1990) to 5,400 people per square mile would reduce driving by less than 3 percent.[24]

The weak link between density and driving can be seen in figure 11.1, which compares data from the 2000 census on how people usually traveled to work with population densities in the nation's 452 urban areas. In the vast majority of regions, more than 90 percent of commuters take autos to work. This group ranges from Kingsport, Tennessee, with a density of less than 1,000 people per square mile and where 98.5 percent of people drive to work, to Los Angeles, the nation's densest urban area at more than 7,000 people per square mile and where 91.5 percent of people drive to work. If density is a factor at all in these urban areas, it appears that multiplying density by seven times will get little more than 7 percent of commuters out of their cars.

Fewer than 90 percent of commuters choose to drive to work in just 49 of the 452 urban areas measured in the 2000 census. The 49 exceptions are almost all university towns or cities with major job centers in pedestrian-oriented downtowns. The university towns, including Davis, California; Ithaca, New York; and State College, Pennsylvania, have large percentages of young people who walk or bicycle to work. The major cities with large concentrations of downtown jobs, such as Boston, New York, and San Francisco, have many commuters who take transit to those jobs.[25]

Figure 11.1
DENSITY VS. COMMUTE BY AUTO

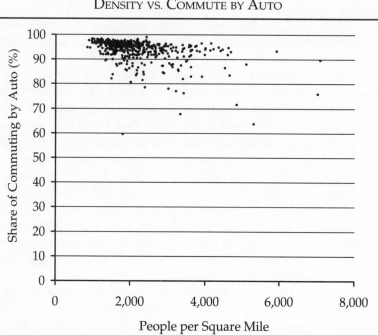

The nation's densest urban area is seven times denser than the least-dense areas, yet the auto's share of commuting in the denser area is only about 7 percent lower. The automobile's share of commuting is under 90 percent in fewer than 50 urbanized areas, most of which either have highly concentrated job centers or are university towns. SOURCE: 2000 census.

Unless planners outlaw middle age, they are unlikely to have much of an influence on the age distribution of individual urban areas. So the best opportunity they have to reduce auto commuting is by influencing the job distribution. Yet job distributions are influenced more by history than by government planning or regulation. American cities were built in three periods:

- Before 1890, cities were designed for pedestrians because few people could afford to travel except on foot. They had highly concentrated populations close to or intermingled with highly concentrated jobs.
- Between 1890 and 1930, streetcars were a dominant form of travel, especially for the middle class. Cities built during this

period tended to have dense residential areas of single-family homes on small lots, but they were not necessarily close to the jobs. Jobs also spread out a little more and could be located in multiple centers instead of just downtown.

- After World War II, the automobile was the dominant form of travel. Cities built during this period tended to have low-density residential areas of single-family homes on large lots, and jobs were widely distributed throughout the area. These cities often lacked traditional downtowns unless the city had gone out of its way to subsidize high-rise construction.

Today, the only American cities with significant remnants of the pedestrian era are Boston, Chicago, New York, Philadelphia, San Francisco, and Washington. These urban areas still have concentrated job cores and a dense central-city population, surrounded by younger, lower-density suburbs. Most other cities that had been densely built before 1890 lost so much of their populations to the suburbs after 1945 that they no longer qualify as pedestrian cities. St. Louis, a once-dense city that lost 60 percent of its population to its suburbs after 1950, is a classic example.

The remnants of a classic streetcar city—a dense city of single-family homes—can be found today in much of Los Angeles. Many other northern cities such as Cincinnati, Minneapolis, and Seattle retain significant characteristics of the streetcar era. These urban areas have multiple job centers, but their population densities are much higher than the densities of their suburbs.

Many cities that have grown since World War II have virtually no characteristics of pedestrian or streetcar cities. They include Atlanta, Houston, and other Sun Belt cities that did not really start growing until air conditioning became affordable. These regions tend to have low densities and numerous job centers, and the central cities are often no denser than the suburbs.

Table 11.1 compares the percentage of people who take transit to work with population densities in all American urban areas of one million people or more. All six pedestrian regions have transit shares of 10 percent or more. All 10 regions with transit shares of 5 to 10 percent are streetcar regions. The regions with transit shares under 5 percent are mostly automobile regions, though some, such as St. Louis, have seen such drastic declines in inner-city populations that

101

Table 11.1
TRANSIT'S SHARE OF COMMUTERS AND TOTAL TRAVEL BY
URBAN AREA

Urban Area	Transit's Share of		2000 Population	Density/ Sq. Mile	Type
	Commuters (%)	Total travel (%)			
New York	29.8	9.7	17,799,861	5,309	Pedestrian
San Francisco–Oakland	16.8	4.2	3,228,605	6,130	Pedestrian
Washington	13.9	4.1	3,933,920	3,401	Pedestrian
Chicago	12.9	3.7	8,307,904	3,914	Pedestrian
Boston	12.7	3.1	4,032,484	2,323	Pedestrian
Philadelphia	10.2	2.6	5,149,079	2,861	Pedestrian
Pittsburgh	8.2	1.4	1,753,136	2,057	Streetcar
Seattle	7.9	2.5	2,712,205	2,844	Streetcar
Baltimore	7.8	1.4	2,076,354	3,041	Streetcar
Portland	7.8	2.2	1,583,138	3,340	Streetcar
New Orleans	7.5	1.5	1,009,283	5,102	Streetcar
Los Angeles	6.1	1.8	11,789,487	7,068	Streetcar
Minneapolis–St. Paul	5.6	1.1	2,388,593	2,671	Streetcar
Milwaukee	5.1	0.8	1,308,913	2,688	Streetcar
Cleveland	5.1	1.3	1,786,647	2,761	Streetcar
Denver	5.0	1.4	1,984,889	3,979	Streetcar
Las Vegas	4.6	1.1	1,314,357	4,597	Automobile
Atlanta	4.3	1.1	3,499,840	1,783	Automobile
Houston	3.9	1.0	3,822,509	2,951	Automobile
Cincinnati	3.7	0.7	1,503,262	2,238	Streetcar
San Diego	3.7	1.3	2,674,436	3,419	Automobile
San Jose	3.6	0.9	1,538,312	5,914	Automobile
San Antonio	3.5	0.9	1,327,554	3,257	Automobile
Miami	3.4	1.0	4,919,036	4,407	Automobile
Columbus	3.0	0.3	1,133,193	2,849	Streetcar
St. Louis	3.0	0.8	2,077,662	2,506	Streetcar
Sacramento	3.0	0.7	1,393,498	3,776	Streetcar
Providence	2.7	0.7	1,174,548	2,332	Streetcar
Phoenix	2.3	0.6	2,907,049	3,638	Automobile
Dallas–Ft. Worth	2.3	0.7	4,145,659	2,946	Automobile
Detroit	2.1	0.4	3,903,377	3,094	Streetcar
Orlando	2.1	0.7	1,157,431	2,554	Automobile
Norfolk–Virginia Beach	2.0	0.5	1,394,439	2,647	Automobile
Riverside–San Bernardino	2.0	0.5	1,506,816	3,434	Automobile
Indianapolis	1.7	0.2	1,218,919	2,205	Streetcar
Kansas City, Kansas	1.6	0.2	1,361,744	2,330	Streetcar
Tampa–St. Petersburg	1.6	0.3	2,062,339	2,571	Automobile

SOURCE: 2000 census; transit's share of total travel from 2005 *National Transit Database* and 2005 *Highway Statistics*, except for New Orleans, which is based on 2004 data.

they might best be called former streetcar regions converted to automobile regions.

Notice that population density is almost totally irrelevant. Las Vegas, Miami, and San Jose have greatly increased their densities in the past two or three decades, yet with both populations and jobs evenly spread out, transit plays a minimal role in commuting and travel. The overall densities of Boston, Philadelphia, and Washington are low, but with dense concentrations of jobs and people at their cores, transit plays a much larger role in commuting than in regions with denser populations but no significant job concentrations.

These numbers tell us that job concentration, not overall population density, is the key to making transit work. Even if the overall population density is low, it helps if a dense central city is located next to the concentrated jobs. This is confirmed by research in Montreal, one of the densest cities in Canada. "Denser areas have lower [per capita] auto ownership," the research found. "But it takes a large increase in density to reduce the number of vehicles a household owns."[26] Moreover, because "people who don't want to drive are likely to choose locations where they don't have to," merely increasing population density won't reduce driving.[27] The most important influence on reducing car ownership was "having a central-business district worker in the household." Overall, "centrality [of jobs] has more effect [on auto ownership] than population density."[28]

Despite this, smart-growth planners do not call for concentrating jobs downtown. Instead, they seek a "jobs-housing balance" so that every part of an urban area has enough jobs to meet the needs of the residents of that portion of the area. This way, planners hope, people will live close enough to their jobs that they can walk or cycle to them. The problem is that, in a mobile society, people no longer consider proximity to work a high priority when locating their homes. In fact, one University of California study found that people actually prefer to live some distance from work.[29] So it is not surprising that University of California planning professor Robert Cervero found that jobs and housing in many San Francisco Bay Area communities "are nearly perfectly balanced, yet fewer than a third of their workers reside locally, and even smaller shares of residents work locally."[30]

Smart growth is based on fundamental misunderstandings of how people, cities, and urban areas work. Yet it has become a dominant paradigm in many cities and regions that rely on urban planners to help them prepare for their futures. The results are proving to be even more disastrous than the effects of the urban renewal programs of the 1950s and 1960s.

12. Smart Growth as Oppression

Joe Neal is a representative in the South Carolina legislature who owns 110 acres of land in Richland County, the state's capital county. Most of this land can be traced to Neal's great grandfather, a slave before the Civil War. After the war, he and his fellow freedmen worked hard for many years to purchase the plantations on which they had formerly worked as slaves. Today, southeastern Richland County has the greatest extent of African American–owned land in the eastern United States.

Much of the land has multiple owners as 40- or 60-acre parcels of land are handed down to children and cousins. Family members often live and work elsewhere and regard the land as a safety net, a place they can retreat to if they lose their jobs. Most of the homes on the land are either mobile homes or very old and in poor condition.

Recently, wealthy whites in the Sierra Club and other environmental groups began pushing for Richland County to adopt a "town and country plan." This was named after the 1947 Town and Country Act, a British law that forced many working-class English families to live in ugly high-rises and made English housing some of the least affordable in the world. Richland County's town and country plan declared that most of the land owned by blacks would be placed in a "preserve," greatly restricting what they could do with their land.

For example, anyone who left a home for one year would not be able to reoccupy the house. Anyone who wanted to make minor improvements to a mobile home would be required to put it on a permanent foundation, which could easily cost more than the mobile home was worth. Planning rules even micromanaged such things as how many yard sales a family could hold each year and whether they could use signs to advertise such sales.

The plan's supporters said they were only trying to stop sprawl and leapfrog development. Yet the plan included a number of leapfrog villages called "nonemployment centers," where housing would be provided for people displaced from their land. As the name implies, there would be no jobs in these villages, so workers would have to commute to Columbia, the capital of South Carolina and Richland County seat. No matter how much traffic this generated, the plan required that the roads between these villages and Columbia remain only two lanes wide. Instead, the villages were to be connected to Columbia with commuter trains, thus allowing the black residents of the villages to come and go from Columbia only on the schedules dictated by the state's wealthy elite.

"The Sierra Club is now a chapter of the KKK," says Richard Jackson, one of Neal's constituents.[1] Despite protests from Neal, Jackson, and numerous other rural residents, Richland County approved the town and country plan in 2004.

Not all government plans are so blatantly racist. But plans nearly always fall short of the promises made for them by the planners. By focusing on using urban design to reduce per capita driving, smart-growth planners end up with increased congestion, dirtier air, unaffordable housing, childless cities, and crime-friendly neighborhoods. In too many cases, the plans become a source of oppression instead of a way for people to improve their lives and their regions.

Consider the San Jose urban area, which in 1970 had a density of about 3,700 people per square mile. In 1974, San Jose and Santa Clara County drew an urban-growth boundary that has never been expanded. This boundary led the region's population density to increase by 60 percent to more than 5,900 people per square mile by 2000, making it the third densest urbanized area in America after Los Angeles and San Francisco–Oakland.

In addition to increasing density, San Jose and the state of California built and operated several light-rail and commuter-rail lines, and developers built dozens of high-density, mixed-use, transit-oriented developments along those lines, many subsidized with tax-increment financing. Although planners predicted that these actions would attract fewer than 2 percent of auto users out of their cars, they did not hesitate to impose them on the region anyway.[2]

So far, the 2 percent projection appears to be optimistic. Census data say that about 2.4 percent of San Jose commuters rode transit to work in 1970. Significant improvements to the region's bus system increased this to 3.2 percent in 1980. By 2000, the region's population density was 56 percent denser than it had been in 1970 and it had built several rail transit lines. Yet the share of commuters taking transit to work increased by just another 0.4 percent to 3.6 percent. Getting 0.4 percent of commuters out of their cars does not take much of a bite out of congestion. Meanwhile, per capita driving increased by nearly 40 percent and the Texas Transportation Institute estimates that the amount of time San Jose auto users waste sitting in traffic has more than doubled.[3]

San Diego's regional government wrote a plan in 1980 that restricted development outside the existing urban fringe, imposed stiff system development charges for new homes in suburban areas, but waived any system development charges for infill in the urban core. According to San Diego State University planning professor Nico Calavita, this plan led to "frantic overbuilding . . . in the urbanized tier. One after another, single-family neighborhoods were invaded by multifamily dwellings, many of them insensitively designed." Though the purpose of the plan was to "manage growth," in fact community facilities were "overwhelmed," Calavita says. "Freeway congestion and sewer breakdowns became commonplace," and by 1990 the city estimated that "it would cost over $1 billion to make up the infrastructure shortfall."[4] Meanwhile, per capita driving grew by 30 percent between 1982 and 1990. Despite the failure of this plan, in 1999 the regional government approved an even more prescriptive smart-growth plan.[5]

Other regions that have written smart-growth plans include Charleston, South Carolina; Denver; Minneapolis–St. Paul; and Missoula, Montana. The plan for Minneapolis–St. Paul uses urban-service boundaries instead of urban-growth boundaries. This theoretically allows development outside the boundary, but prevents the extension of sewer, water, or other infrastructure to such developments. This approach effectively keeps developers from doing subdivisions outside those areas. Inside the boundary, the regional government uses its power to distribute federal funds to local cities to force those cities to promote the high-density developments that smart growth demands.[6]

Planners refuse to learn from their failures. To ensure successful transit-oriented developments, "reverse the normal parking rules," one planner recently wrote. "Instead of worrying whether there will be enough parking, make sure there is not too much. You may need

107

parking maximums instead of parking minimums."[7] As Portland's experience reveals, that is a prescription for failure.

Despite the lip service given to congestion by smart-growth advocates, reducing congestion really isn't their goal. Increased congestion will "signal positive urban development," says Portland's Metro,[8] adding, "transportation solutions aimed solely at relieving congestion are inappropriate."[9] In fact, Metro has declared that "level of service F"—the transportation engineer's term for near gridlock—is "acceptable" during rush hour throughout most of the Portland area. Why? Because, says Metro's leading transportation planner, relieving congestion "would eliminate transit ridership."[10] Similarly, the Twin Cities Metropolitan Council decided in 1996 that "expansion of roadways will be very limited in the next 25 years." "As traffic congestion builds," planners hoped, "alternative travel modes will become more attractive."[11]

Because congestion is such a hot-button issue, planners rarely reveal to the public that their real goal is to increase it. But smart-growth planner Dom Nozzi specifically urges "sprawl busters" to seek more congestion because "congestion is a powerful disincentive for urban sprawl. With congestion, the market for development in outlying areas withers."[12] This isn't true—the reality is that growth avoids congested areas. But since planners think it is true, they deliberately promote policies that will increase congestion.

Edge City author Joel Garreau notes that many planners "rather hope" that the future "might look like Paris in the 1920s."[13] Yet even Paris doesn't look like Paris in the 1920s anymore. Indeed, since the automobile was invented, inner Paris (*arrondissements* I and II) has lost 72 percent of its population.[14] Many other European inner cities have seen similar population declines.

In 1999, two Australian planners published a detailed database for dozens of major cities comparing densities, driving, and transit use.[15] Their goal was to prove that people drive less in higher-density regions. Unwittingly, they actually showed that people are driving more and more in all urban areas, no matter what the density.

Between 1960 and 1990, their data revealed, per capita driving in European urban areas such as Brussels, Copenhagen, Hamburg, London, and Paris increased by two to five times. Meanwhile, 1990 per capita transit ridership in those same areas was about the same or less than in 1960, so transit's share of travel typically declined by

50 percent or more. As Europeans acquired cars, they left the high-density inner cities and moved to the suburbs, with the result that the average population densities of most European urban areas declined by 30 to 50 percent. So even as American planners are trying to model U.S. cities after European ones, European cities are looking more American every year.

These examples provide further evidence that the fundamental premise of smart growth—that urban design, and in particular higher densities, mixed-use developments, and a jobs-housing balance, can reduce driving—is fatally flawed. Not only does urban design have little influence on driving, the one factor in urban design that might reduce driving—concentrating jobs in a central transit hub—is not even a part of smart growth.

13. Homeownership

The congestion created by smart growth is bad enough, but its effects on housing affordability are far worse. Regions that have adopted smart growth or similarly restrictive planning programs tend to have the least affordable housing, whereas affordable regions remain relatively free of strict planning rules.

Coldwell Banker says that, in 2006, $155,000 would buy a home in Houston suitable for a "corporate middle manager"—a four-bedroom, two-and-one-half bath, 2,200-square-foot home with a large family room and two-car garage in a nice neighborhood. The same house would cost more than twice that much in Portland, close to four times that much in Boulder, and more than eight times as much in San Jose.[1] Such huge variations in the cost of housing from city to city did not exist 50 years ago, and today they are mainly due to artificial housing shortages created by land-use planning.

Homeownership is the ultimate American dream and the aspiration of families all over the world. In the wake of the postwar boom, U.S. homeownership rates soared from less than 44 percent in 1940 to 62 percent by 1960.[2] Since then, however, the rate of increase has slowed so that only 7 percent more families own their homes today.[3]

Although Americans like to believe they are number one, many other countries have higher homeownership rates. Homeownership rates exceed 80 percent in Italy, Spain, and even Mexico; 75 percent in Ireland and Portugal; and 70 percent in Belgium and Britain.[4] Due to postcommunist privatizations, several Eastern European nations also have high homeownership rates, though admittedly many of the homes in these countries are tiny condominiums in Soviet-built apartment buildings.

When more than 80 percent of families in other countries own their own homes, why has the growth of American homeownership virtually halted in the high 60s? One important reason is the increasing number of states, regions, and communities that have adopted some form of smart growth or another version of *growth-management planning,* a term embracing planning practices that seek to control either the rate of growth or where that growth will take place.[5]

Economist Paul Krugman divides the country into what he calls the "Zoned Zone," where "land-use restrictions" make "it hard to build new houses," and what he calls "Flatland," where housing prices have not increased much faster than inflation. Writing in 2005, Krugman observed that prices were rapidly increasing in the Zoned Zone but remained very affordable in Flatland.[6]

Krugman's colorful terms are a bit misleading because most of the cities in Flatland have zoning. Before 1970, zoning rarely made housing unaffordable because it tended to be very flexible. Areas zoned for single-family residential were restricted to this use. But multifamily residential zones allowed single-family homes; retail zones allowed residential; commercial zones allowed retail and residential; and industrial zones were effectively open to any uses. Land on the urban fringe, if it was zoned at all, might be zoned for low-density residential but only as a sort of holding pattern until cities could see what developers wanted to do with the land. Even as zoning got a little more rigid, with only industrial uses allowed in industrial zones, cities commonly adjusted to changing needs or demand with frequent variances and zoning.

All that began to change in the 1970s as communities in California, Colorado, New York, Oregon, and elsewhere began to try to manage growth. Some tried to slow growth by limiting the number of building permits issued each year. Others only tried to control where growth would take place. In addition, once an area was put in a particular zone, nearby residents began to feel zoning had conferred a right on them to think that the use of that area would never change. In the end, the following planning policies restricted the supply of new homes and drove up housing prices:

- Urban-growth boundaries, urban-service boundaries, large-lot rural zoning, or other restrictions on the amount of land available for development;
- Purchases of greenbelts and other open spaces that reduce the amount of land available for development;
- Design codes requiring developers to use higher-cost construction methods or designs;
- Historic preservation ordinances, tree ordinances, and other rules restricting or increasing the cost of development;

- Impact fees aimed at discouraging development;
- Growth ceilings limiting the number of building permits that can be issued each year;
- Concurrency rules requiring adequate financing for all urban services before building permits can be issued;
- Lengthy permitting processes that force developers to hold land for several years before they are allowed to develop it;
- Planning processes that allow people to easily appeal and delay projects, creating uncertainty about when a project can begin; and
- Inclusionary zoning programs that require developers to subsidize some housing for low-income people, effectively increasing the price of the remaining housing. (Like so many planning programs, inclusionary zoning actually has the opposite of its intended effect.)

By 2006, what Krugman calls the Zoned Zone included the Pacific Coast states; New England to Washington, D.C.; Florida; and a few interior metropolitan areas such as Denver and Minneapolis–St. Paul. What Krugman calls Flatland includes much of the South other than Florida; much of the Midwest other than Chicago, the Twin Cities, and a few smaller cities; and most of the Rocky Mountain region other than Arizona, the Denver–Ft. Collins area, and a few smaller cities.

If asked, Krugman could point to numerous research studies showing that land-use regulation has increased housing prices in many parts of the United States. "Government regulation is responsible for high housing costs where they exist," say Harvard economist Edward Glaeser and Wharton economist Joseph Gyourko. In particular, they add, "difficult zoning seems to be ubiquitous in high-cost areas."[7] Other researchers have found that rapid growth in housing prices is strongly "correlated with restrictive growth management policies and limitations on land availability."[8]

Homeownership has been identified with the American dream for more than a century, but it is more than just a dream. In a housing market unfettered by planning restrictions, it typically costs less to buy a house than rent one. Buying a home also allows people to build equity, while renters merely help someone else pay off his or her mortgage. The equity homeowners have in their homes can be used to put their children through college, start small businesses, carry them through emergencies, or help them retire.

Peruvian economist Hernando de Soto attributes the wealth of the developed world in large part to the ease with which people can buy their homes. In most undeveloped and developing nations, it can take years for people to acquire title to land. In contrast, obtaining a title in the United States and most other developed countries takes just a few days. In Peru, de Soto observed that when people had title to their land, they lived in nicer homes and had faster-growing incomes than those of similar incomes who did not. The reason was simple: with a title, they could use their home as collateral for loans to improve their homes or start small businesses.

"The single most important source of funds for new businesses in the United States is a mortgage on the entrepreneur's house," de Soto observes.[9] But this was not always the case. In the early 19th century, the United States was a developing nation, and west of the Appalachian Mountains most people found it hard to obtain title to land. "It took more than one hundred years, well into the late nineteenth century, for the U.S. government to pass special statutes that integrated and formalized U.S. assets," de Soto says. "The result was an integrated property market that fueled the United States' explosive economic growth thereafter."[10]

Ownership gives people incentives to take better care of their dwellings, so people who own their own homes tend to live better than people who rent; similarly, neighborhoods dominated by owner-occupied homes tend to be nicer than neighborhoods dominated by renter-occupied homes. This has many ramifications for society. For example, after adjusting for income and other factors, children who live in owner-occupied homes score an average of 7 to 9 percent higher on math and reading tests than children who live in renter-occupied homes.[11] As a result, some economists suggest that promoting homeownership could do more to improve educational outcomes, at a lower cost, than spending more money on the schools themselves.[12]

Children raised in owner-occupied homes are less likely to drop out of school and more likely to end up owning a home themselves. The effect of homeownership on educational attainment, earnings, and welfare independence is greatest for low-income children, so policies that restrict homeownership help maintain a permanent underclass of low-income families.[13]

114

Homeownership provides other social benefits as well. The opportunity to own a home and the need for a down payment encourages people to save money—which is good for the economy—and the tendency to save more money seems to continue after the home is purchased. Homeownership also leads to measurable increases in self-esteem, which probably helps contribute to the better educational outcomes, and neighborhood stability.[14]

Some people think homeownership has a downside. A researcher in England has found higher levels of unemployment among people who own their homes. But this is because Britain's growth-management planning has made housing there the least affordable in the world.[15] Such high-priced housing greatly increases the cost of moving and discourages people who own homes from relocating to a city with more jobs. To date, this effect is much weaker in the United States, but continued housing shortages could potentially reduce American mobility.[16]

Many planning advocates blame suburban sprawl on federal mortgage programs that offered loans to people buying single-family homes in suburbs but often denied loans to people buying multifamily, mixed-use, or even single-family homes in cities. But this merely reflected the market reality: Americans were leaving the dense, mixed-use housing in cities in droves. Since the market value of such housing was declining, it did not make good collateral for loans.

Although there is no doubt that federal programs such as the mortgage interest tax exemption represent subsidies to homeownership, those subsidies have produced an important social good by extending the value of homeownership to lower-income people. Whether those benefits justify the subsidies is debatable. But, while many might argue that government should not subsidize homeownership, it is much more difficult to argue that government should actively try to reduce homeownership.

14. Housing Affordability

Planners and elected officials often use the term *affordable housing* to describe specific units of subsidized housing provided for low-income families. In contrast, *housing affordability* refers to the general level of affordability of all housing in a particular city or housing market.

One common measure of housing affordability is the *value-to-income ratio*, that is, the value of a median home divided by the annual income of a median family. Until 1970, median homes in nearly all U.S. metropolitan areas typically cost about twice as much as median family incomes in those areas. Depending on the prevailing interest rate, this meant that a family dedicating a quarter of its income to a mortgage could pay off a loan for a home in a little more than 10 years.

In an unfettered market, a house costs little more than the cost of building it plus the cost of the land, which at the urban fringe tends to be low. But planning restrictions can greatly increase new home costs by creating artificial shortages of land or impeding the ability of homebuilders to meet the demand for new homes. Economists say that housing demand is *inelastic*, meaning, in essence, that most people need a place to live and will pay whatever it takes to have one. So a small restriction on the supply of new homes can lead to large increases in price. For example, one study estimates that a 1 percent decline in the supply of new homes can lead to a 2.5 to 3 percent increase in prices.[1]

Moreover, the price of new homes is a tide that lifts all boats: when sellers of existing homes see the price of new homes rise, they raise the prices they ask for their homes. Seemingly trivial rules can therefore make housing significantly less affordable for everyone.

Today, San Francisco is notorious as the least affordable major housing market in the United States. But as late as 1969, housing in San Francisco and almost every other U.S. metropolitan area outside of Hawaii was affordable to most of the people who lived in those

117

areas. Census data show that in 1969 median home values in the San Francisco metropolitan area were less than 2.3 times median family incomes.[2] This meant that a family could pay off a home in less than 13 years at the interest rates prevailing in 1969.

Since 1969, housing has remained affordable in many parts of the country, particularly (with important exceptions) the Midwest, South, and interior West. But it has grown unaffordable—in some cases grotesquely unaffordable—in other areas, particularly (also with important exceptions) in coastal states. In almost every case, rapid declines in affordability followed soon after the imposition of growth-management plans or other land-use restrictions.

Ramapo, New York, a suburb of New York City, pioneered growth-management planning in the United States. In 1970, Ramapo passed the first *adequate public facilities ordinance*, also known as a *concurrency* ordinance. Instead of allowing developers to build homes and commercial areas and then providing the sewer, water, and other urban services needed by those areas, Ramapo decided that it would only approve new developments once the capital improvements needed for the development were fully financed.[3]

In 1972, the city of Petaluma, California, took a different approach. Instead of conditioning growth on urban finances, the city simply decided to issue no more than 500 residential building permits a year.[4] Soon after, Boulder, Colorado, decided to limit the number of building permits so that it would grow no faster than 2 percent per year. Boulder was also the first city in the United States to pass a tax dedicated to open space preservation, and the city and county of Boulder have since purchased a greenbelt around the city that is several times the land area of the city itself.[5]

Petaluma and Boulder set out to slow growth, but other growth-management advocates said they only wanted to control where growth would take place. In 1974, the city of San Jose and Santa Clara County agreed to draw an urban-growth boundary outside of which development could not take place. Inside the boundary, growth could continue unabated, but outside it would be strictly limited. The growth boundary effectively placed tens of thousands of acres of marginal pasturelands east of San Jose off limits to development.

Taking after Ramapo, San Jose said it would add land to the growth boundary when financing could be assured for the urban services needed for new developments. But in 1978, California voters passed Proposition 13, which strictly limited the property taxes cities could collect for urban services. This made California cities dependent on sales taxes and therefore reluctant to devote more land to residential areas. As a result, San Jose has never expanded its urban-growth boundary.

Even before Proposition 13, cities throughout the San Francisco Bay Area had approved a variety of growth-management policies, including growth boundaries, density limits, and purchases of land for open space. While growth-management planning supposedly aims at protecting environmental quality, it is vulnerable to manipulation by not-in-my-backyard (NIMBY) advocates whose real goal is to boost their property values by limiting the supply of housing for others. As Bernard Frieden notes in his 1979 book *The Environmental Protection Hustle*, one important limit to growth was a public involvement process that made it so easy for people to challenge proposed developments that "even a lone boy scout doing an ecology project was able to bring construction to a halt on a 200-unit condominium project."[6]

David Dowall's 1984 book *The Suburban Squeeze* points out that people living in a neighborhood of $200,000 homes will fear that an adjacent development of $100,000 homes will bring down their property values, while they would welcome a development of $300,000 homes. When NIMBYs object to plans, developers respond by eliminating affordable housing and proposing only expensive homes. For example, one proposal to build 2,200 homes selling for $125,000 to $135,000 on 685 acres in Oakland was, due to public opposition, scaled back to a mere 150 homes that would sell for $175,000 to $200,000.[7]

Federal, state, county, city, and regional governments were able to tie up a huge amount of potential residential land in the Bay Area as open space. By 1984, says Dowall, "Over 15 percent of the region's total land supply is in permanent open space controlled by" various government agencies.[8]

Today, parks and preserves in the nine-county San Francisco Bay Area total more than one million acres, or almost 23 percent of the land area of those counties, not counting areas outside of urban-growth boundaries that are subject to restrictive zoning. By comparison, only 761,000 acres have been urbanized.[9] Ostensibly, these

119

reserves were for environmental protection, but the hilltops that were reserved tended to have the lowest values for fisheries, wildlife, and streams. The main effect of such reservations was to significantly boost land prices throughout the region.

Proposition 13 spurred city governments to go further than ever before in beggar-thy-neighbor efforts to force residential developments into adjacent cities while capturing retail developments, and the sales taxes they generated, for themselves. As one city put up barriers to growth, that growth would spill over into nearby cities, leading them to erect their own barriers. "Santa Clara County cities have become extremely combative," observed Dowall, "fighting back with a variety of growth-restricting mechanisms that have made each community a 'tight little island.'"[10]

Given this history, it is not surprising that Boulder and the San Francisco Bay Area suffered a tremendous decline in affordability during the 1970s. By 1979, median home values in these areas were more than four times median family incomes.[11] At the then prevailing interest rates, a family devoting 40 percent of its income to a mortgage could not pay off a home in 30 years.

During the 1970s, housing also became unaffordable in Oregon. State planners required every city in the state to draw urban-growth boundaries outside of which development was limited to 40-acre minimum lot sizes—later increased to 160 acres. The boundaries did not go into effect until the late 1970s, so Oregon housing was more affordable in 1979 than housing in California. Still, the value-to-income ratio in the typical Oregon metro area increased from about 1.75 in 1969 to 2.75 in 1979.

Over the next few decades, other cities and states followed Boulder, the San Francisco Bay Area, and Oregon's pioneer efforts at managing growth, and most suffered from declining affordability. Boston and other New England cities had been affordable in 1979, but became unaffordable in the 1980s due to land-use restrictions passed by individual cities and suburbs and the purchase of conservation easements to turn farms into agricultural reserves. Harvard economist Edward Glaeser observes that cities in the Greater Boston Metropolitan Area issued more than 170,000 permits for new homes in the 1970s, but only 141,000 in the 1980s and fewer than 85,000 in the 1990s. By 2005, Glaeser estimates, the planning rules that led to this slowdown added $156,000 to the cost of a median home in the Boston area.[12]

Housing was affordable in most Florida cities in 1989.[13] But the Florida legislature required all cities in the state to put growth-management plans in place by the mid-1990s. The result was that housing prices turned sharply upward. By 2005, affordability had dramatically declined in every Florida metro area.

As growth-management planning spread across the country, differences in affordability between regions greatly widened.

- In 1969, only Honolulu and Stamford, Connecticut, had value-to-income ratios greater than 3.
- By 1979, 33 metro areas had exceeded this threshold, most of them in California.
- In 1989, the number increased to 45, now including many in New England.
- By 2005, more than 85 metro areas had value-to-income ratios greater than 3, including many in Florida, Washington state (which passed a growth-management law in 1991), and Arizona (which passed a "smarter growth" law in 1999).[14]

We can estimate how much planning costs homebuyers by comparing value-to-income ratios in metro areas with growth-management planning with the ratios in more normal areas. From 1959 through 1999, the median value-to-income ratio in the nation's metropolitan areas remained very close to 2.0.[15] However, from 1999 to 2005, it rapidly increased to 2.4. Part of this increase is due to the high cost of housing in California and other states with growth management, but part is due to a shift in money from the stock market to the real-estate market.[16]

In urban areas with growth-management planning, home prices increased by 4 to 13 percent per year between 1999 and 2005. But in areas with little or no such planning, prices increased by only 1 to 3 percent per year. If median home values nationwide had increased by 2.5 percent per year, the price-to-income ratio would have been 2.24 in 2005.

Even metro areas with no growth-management planning exhibit some variation in value-to-income ratios over time. Based on census data from 1959 to 1999, value-to-income ratios might vary as much as 20 percent due to economic cycles. So the value-to-income ratio in a metro area could be as high as 2.69 without indicating a serious housing shortage.

In 2005, about a third of the metropolitan areas in America had value-to-income ratios greater than 2.69. In all but a handful of cases, these high housing prices could be traced to smart growth or some other form of growth-management planning. This cost can be considered the penalty homebuyers must pay to own a home in a region that uses growth-management planning. The penalty in Boston, for example, is $171,000, which is very close to the penalty calculated by Harvard economist Edward Glaeser using a completely different methodology.

- In nearly 50 metropolitan areas, the cost of a median home in 2005 was at least $100,000 more than it would have been if the value-to-income ratio in those areas had been only 2.69.
- In another 50 areas, the cost was $25,000 to $100,000 more.
- The record, of course, was the San Francisco metro area (which includes Marin and San Mateo counties), where the penalty for planning was $850,000.

Recall that *The Costs of Sprawl 2000* estimated that low-density housing cost cities about $11,000 more in urban services than more compact development. To the extent that planning is supposed to remedy such a cost, this remedy costs far more than the ill it supposedly cures.

In 2005, for example, planning-induced housing shortages added at least $275 billion to the cost of homes purchased in the United States. Nearly 95 percent of this cost was in just 12 states with the most restrictive land-use laws. By comparison, *The Costs of Sprawl* estimated that, over a 25-year period, low-density housing had added $225 billion to urban-service costs—less than the cost planning imposed on homebuyers in 2005 alone.[17]

This is only the cost of planning to homebuyers. Home renters and purchasers of commercial, retail, and industrial properties also paid additional costs due to land shortages, permitting delays, and other aspects of growth-management planning. Land-use regulation that doubles the price of housing is likely to roughly double the cost of developing industrial, commercial, and retail property as well.

Growth-management planning that limited the land available for development in California also imposed huge costs on renters. But more recent smart-growth planning in Oregon offered renters an escape from high housing costs. Since one goal of smart growth is to increase the percentage of people who live in multifamily housing, such planning often ends up creating a surplus of rental housing. Owners of rental properties in Pacific Coast cities that have used smart growth have not seen their rents grow as fast as home prices.[18] Some landlords have responded by converting rentals to condominiums, but there is a limit to the number of people willing to accept condominium living as opposed to single-family homes.

Some argue that the cost of planning to homebuyers is balanced by the benefit to home sellers. There are two problems with this argument. First, the people who lose outnumber the people who benefit from higher home prices. Losers include most homebuyers as well as owners of property downzoned by planners in an effort to control sprawl. However, home sellers win only if they plan to trade down to a smaller home or move to a less restrictive part of the country. People who want to trade up to a larger home or move to a more restrictive city encounter barriers as formidable as first-time homebuyers. As described in more detail later, home sellers also lose if they find themselves on the wrong side of a deflating housing bubble, having to sell because, perhaps, their job is moving at a time that their mortgage is more than they can get by selling their home.

Second, growth-management planning is regressive because families who already own their homes when growth-management plans are adopted tend to be wealthier than renters and other first-time homebuyers. Growth-management planning is effectively a tax on low-income people that is immediately transferred to wealthier people.

Tufts University economist Matthew Kahn has found that "sprawling" urban areas tend to have more affordable housing and higher rates of minority homeownership.[19] This is true at least in part because the low-density areas have fewer land-use restrictions that drive up housing costs.

Nearly three out of four white families in America own their own homes, whereas fewer than half of black or Hispanic families own their own homes. This leads Portland economist Randall Pozdena to call smart growth "the new segregation." "Insidiously, the burden of site-supply restrictions will fall disproportionately on poor and minority families," says Pozdena. "Families who already owned homes at the time that smart-growth policies were embraced, of course, enjoy some immunity from the effects of smart growth on housing costs. However, for new or young families, and families that rent their homes, the impact of higher home values and rents is a significant burden." Pozdena estimates that, if Portland's planning measures had been applied nationwide during the 1990s, more than a million young and low-income families would have been prevented from buying homes.[20]

Peter Hall sums it up by calling growth management "environmentally-conscious NIMBYism." He adds, "It is very difficult to combine it with any concept of social equity, whether for the less fortunate in the local community, or still more for the less fortunate in other places, or for younger generations, or for generations still unborn."[21]

Unaffordable housing can dramatically slow the growth of a community or region by leading employers to locate offices or factories elsewhere. Although slow growth was the goal of early growth-management plans such as those adopted by Boulder and Petaluma, smart-growth supporters claim they only want to manage growth, not slow it. But the numbers show that smart growth actually does slow growth.

Census data show that the San Jose urbanized area grew by more than 42,000 people per year throughout the 1950s and 1960s. In the 1970s, when the region adopted its urban-growth boundary, growth was slowed to less than 22,000 people per year, declining still further to 19,000 people per year in the 1980s and only 10,000 people per year in the 1990s. From 2000 to 2005, it grew by only about 3,000 people per year. High housing and land prices have clearly slowed the region's growth.

The Portland area grew in the 1990s partly because it was so much more affordable than San Jose in 1990 that many Silicon Valley employers opened new factories in Oregon. But the fastest-growing part of Portland since 1990 has been Clark County, Washington, which welcomed families who wanted a home with a yard.

Growth-management planning is not the only thing that can make housing unaffordable. In 1959, when Hawaii entered the union, it was the nation's least affordable state. Government agencies and just 72 private entities own 95 percent of the land in the state.[22] The private owners have historically chosen not to develop most of their land, which explains why it was unaffordable in 1959. Since then,

124

Hawaii has imposed urban-growth boundaries and created a formidable planning process, but it is hard to estimate how much of the state's current unaffordability is due to planning and how much is due to the landownership problems that preceded planning.

Nevada is the nation's seventh-largest state, but the federal government owns nearly 90 percent of the land. Until recently, Las Vegas and Reno were able to rapidly grow without becoming unaffordable because the Bureau of Land Management regularly sold land to developers to accommodate new homes. However, increasing resistance from environmental groups has slowed such sales in recent years. Such resistance might be considered a form of growth-management planning, and it explains why these two Nevada cities have become unaffordable since 2001 despite the lack of any state or local growth-management planning.

Despite these examples, true shortages of land are rare because urban areas, even low-density areas, simply do not require much land. Nearly 95 percent of the 34 million people in California, America's most populous state, live on just 5 percent of the land in that state. As previously noted, urban areas cover only about 3 percent of the nation as a whole and only five states—Connecticut, Maryland, Massachusetts, New Jersey, and Rhode Island—are more than 15 percent urbanized.

If every family in the United States built a home on a quarter-acre lot, they could all comfortably fit in Ohio or Tennessee—which each occupies about 1.1 percent of the nation's land area—with plenty of room left over for connecting streets, parks, and other amenities. All the nation's retail, commercial, and industrial areas could easily fit in Kentucky—another 1.1 percent—leaving the remaining 97.8 percent of the nation for farms, forests, or untrammeled wilderness. While parts of the country have shortages of affordable housing, there is no shortage of rural open space anywhere in the United States. Government programs to buy or otherwise protect rural open space from development represent a tragic misplacement of priorities.

15. Housing Bubbles

Growth-management planning not only makes housing less affordable, it makes housing prices more volatile. If small restrictions in supply can push prices sky-high, small reductions in demand, such as during a recession, can cause prices to plummet. Over the past 30 years, median U.S. housing prices have grown at a fairly steady 1 percent per year faster than inflation. But places that rely on growth-management planning, such as California, New England, and Oregon, have prices that zoom up and down.

Inflation-adjusted prices in coastal California housing markets, for example, grew by 60 to 70 percent in the late 1970s, dropped by 5 to 10 percent in the early 1980s, grew another 50 to 60 percent in the late 1980s, dropped 20 to 30 percent in the early 1990s, then grew by 80 to 100 percent through the early 2000s.[1] If experience is any guide, prices will fall at least 30 percent in the next five years or so.

Unfortunately, each successive boom just makes housing even more unaffordable than it was in the previous boom. In 1969, no California housing market had a value-to-income ratio greater than 2.3. By 1979, most were more than 3 and a few were more than 4. In 1989, several were greater than 5, and in 2005, almost all were greater than 5 and a few were more than 10.

Recent studies have firmly tied such volatility to land-use regulation. A 2005 economic analysis of the housing market in Great Britain, which has practiced growth management since World War II, found that planning may drive housing prices up, but it also makes housing markets more volatile, that is, more susceptible to booms and busts. "By ignoring the role of supply in determining house prices," the report says, "planners have created a system that has led not only to higher house prices but also to a highly volatile housing market."[2]

Harvard economist Edward Glaeser agrees that land-use rules that restrict "housing supply lead to greater volatility in housing prices." Glaeser found that "if an area has a $10,000 increase in housing prices during one period, relative to national and regional trends, that area will lose $3,300 in housing value over the next five-year period."[3]

One reason why land-use rules make housing prices more volatile is that the same rules drive employers away, either because the employers try to avoid high-cost areas or because they seek to locate in places where their employees can afford to buy homes. Glaeser also found that "places with rapid price increases over one five-year period are more likely to have income and employment declines over the next five-year period."[4]

Investment analysts agree that the market price for the stock in a company should have some relationship to the profits that company can be expected to earn in the future. One way to estimate this is to compare current earnings with the stock price. If the ratio of price to earnings is too high, then the stock price is probably too high. The dot-com boom grew because investors expected that companies whose profits were zero or negative today would soon grow to have huge profits, so they ignored the price-to-earnings ratio as a criterion for buying. This led to wild speculation and a huge crash in 2001.

Between 2001 and 2005, much of the money that was once put into the stock market was put into the real-estate market, and people made the same mistakes. The real-estate equivalent of the price-to-earnings ratio is a price-to-rental income ratio. In a normal housing market, owners of rental properties set rents to cover the cost of their mortgage plus a little more for profit and risk. This means buying a house can be less expensive than renting, that is, the monthly mortgage payment is less than the monthly rent. In a market driven by speculation, however, buyers lose perspective and pay far more for homes than can be supported by rental prices. This is made even worse when smart-growth planners stimulate the construction of multifamily housing with tax breaks and other subsidies, thus creating a surplus of rental housing even as they create a shortage of single-family homes.

In the past few years, housing prices in some markets have shot upward even as rents have stayed flat.[5] In 2000, the rent on a two-bedroom apartment in San Antonio would have covered the cost of a median-priced home in less than 14 years. In San Francisco, however, it would take 26 years.[6] Yet from 2000 to 2005, San Francisco home prices grew much faster than those in San Antonio. This suggests that investors are ignoring the real value of the properties they are buying just as they once ignored the real value of the dot-com stocks they once bought. Lenient loan policies, including zero-down-payment loans, interest-only loans, and 40- to 50-year mortgages, are promoting more speculation, with the result that an increasing percentage of homes purchased in the early 2000s were not owner occupied.[7]

Unlike stock-market bubbles, housing bubbles do not burst; they slowly deflate. The risk is that when the bubbles deflate, they will leave many homeowners with mortgages far greater than the actual value of their homes. Imagine you make a 10 percent down payment on a $400,000 house and borrow the remaining $360,000. But then home prices start falling. You try to wait it out, but after five years your house value falls to $300,000 while you still owe more than $330,000. If someone offers you a higher-paying job in another part of the country, you can't accept because you can't afford the $30,000 or more that it would cost to sell your house. You can let the bank foreclose, but that just passes the problem onto someone else. When this happens to enough people, the result is a drastic slowdown of the economy.

While housing prices are not likely to crash the way dot-com stock prices fell, home prices in many regions are likely to decline significantly over several years. In California and Massachusetts, housing prices fell by 15 to 25 percent between 1989 and 1994. As measured by price-to-rental-income ratios, prices in many housing markets are even more unrealistic today than California prices were in 1989, suggesting that the next bubble deflation will reduce prices by an even greater percentage.

PMI Mortgage Insurance Company publishes a quarterly estimate of the nation's riskiest housing markets.[8] Most of the markets at the top of this list are in California, Massachusetts, and other states or urban areas that practice heavy doses of growth management. Collectively, regions with high-risk housing markets include close to half the housing stock in the nation.

San Jose, for example, is in a classic bubble. Between 2001 and 2004, the region lost 17 percent of its jobs and office vacancy rates increased from 3 percent to 30 percent.[9] Yet housing prices over the same time period grew by more than 20 percent, an increase that cannot be supported by any fundamental economic measure. As a result, PMI has consistently rated San Jose as one of the two riskiest housing markets for the past several years.

In contrast, regions such as Houston are considered to have little risk of a bursting bubble. While not entirely immune from the recent increase in housing prices caused by low interest rates, Houston's prices remain much more reasonable than in places such as San Jose. While San Jose home prices increased by 15 percent in 2004, prices in Houston increased by less than 4 percent.[10]

In general, the places with the least affordable housing and the greatest risk for deflating housing prices are places where growth-management planning has been applied. Other causes of land shortages can also play a role, as Las Vegas illustrates, but they are the exceptions that prove the rule: anything that restricts housing supply can make housing less affordable and more volatile. While it is unfortunate if such restrictions have natural causes, it is absurd to adopt government policies that will make housing unaffordable and create housing bubbles.

Planning-induced housing bubbles not only threaten individual families and local economies, they threaten the world economy. Housing has played a major role in keeping the U.S. and world economies going for the past few years. Europe's and Japan's economies are still sluggish, with high unemployment and slow growth. Only the fast-growing U.S. economy has kept the world from suffering a major recession. Yet that fast growth is driven by borrowings against the equity in people's homes—equity that in too many cases has been created by planner-induced speculation. This is not a sound basis for a healthy economy.

The total value of America's owner-occupied housing stock in 2005 was about $18 trillion. More than $5 trillion of this value was due to inflated prices caused by planning-induced housing shortages. Prices in many Western European countries are similarly inflated by growth-management planning. If all this value disappears in a general price deflation, it could cause the world to go into a severe recession.

In 2004, *The Economist* estimated that "two-thirds (by economic weight) of the world ... has a potential housing bubble."[11] "The whole world economy is at risk," the magazine added in 2005. "It is not going to be pretty."[12]

The effect of a deflating housing bubble on an economy can be seen in Japan, which at least since World War II has strictly regulated land use to prevent urban encroachments on agricultural lands. The result was such a huge property bubble that downtown Tokyo was at one time supposedly worth more than all of the private real estate in the United States. The bubble burst in 1991, and home values have since fallen to less than half their 1990 peak.[13] The result has been 15 years of stagnation.

Housing prices began to level off in many U.S. markets in 2006. The question is how many metropolitan areas will suffer the 15 to 25 percent declines that California saw in the early 1990s—and how much greater a decline will California have to endure this time.

16. It's Supply, Not Demand

Planning advocates often blame housing affordability problems on demand. They reason that the rules they write are aimed at making cities more livable, and the rise in housing prices that follow the rules is proof that the rules are working: people are willing to pay more to live in their livable cities.

Paul Danish is a former Boulder city councilor who so strongly advocated limits on building permits and open space purchases that these policies are known in Boulder as "the Danish plan." According to him, Boulder prices are high solely because his policies have made it "a really desirable place to live." Any place that is more affordable—which includes 90 percent of the urban areas in the United States—must be, according to Danish, "a really awful place to live."[1]

Danish's simplistic analysis ignores basic economics. No matter what the demand, the cost of existing homes is limited by the cost of building new ones, and the cost of new homes depends on four factors: construction materials, labor, land, and government regulation. At least in the contiguous 48 states, construction materials are sold on a national market, and except for very short-term situations, such as right after a major disaster, local material prices are not going to vary much from the national average no matter what the local demand.

Labor is almost as mobile as materials. Labor costs may vary from region to region if the cost of living is higher in one region than another. But in the contiguous 48 states, differences in the cost of living are due mainly to differences in housing costs. In other words, high labor costs may be an effect of high housing costs, but they are not the cause.

Unlike labor and construction materials, land is not mobile. But, as previously noted, land is not only plentiful, it is actually more abundant than labor or many raw materials. Except in rare circumstances such as those found in Las Vegas, suburban land will be a major component of the cost of housing only if there are artificial restrictions on land use such as urban-growth boundaries.

In the absence of restrictions on land supply, homebuilders have proven themselves able to meet the demand for housing in the fastest-growing areas. San Jose grew by nearly 14 percent per year in the 1950s, yet housing remained affordable in 1959. During the 1990s, the Atlanta, Dallas–Ft. Worth, Houston, and Phoenix urban areas all grew by 900,000 people or more, while the Denver, Los Angeles, and Portland urban areas grew by only about 400,000, and San Jose grew by only about 100,000 people. The relatively unregulated regions also grew faster in percentage terms than the regulated ones. Yet the fast-growing regions all maintained or even increased their housing affordability, while the slower-growing regions either remained unaffordable or significantly lost affordability during the 1990s.

Nor are the regulated regions attracting people with higher incomes who buy more expensive housing. As the value-to-income data show, housing prices in Denver and Portland both significantly increased relative to family incomes, whereas they did not in Atlanta, Dallas–Ft. Worth, Houston, or Phoenix.

It is undeniable that housing quickly becomes unaffordable in regions that adopt smart-growth policies. Planning advocates then turn their attention to the "greedy developers" who are demanding higher prices for their homes and attempt to rectify the situation with more subsidies or regulation.

During the 1990s, San Jose provided some $180 million in subsidies to 6,000 units of low-income housing. Yet San Jose's land-use policies have added at least $200 billion to the cost of all homes in the San Jose metropolitan area, or more than a thousand times as much as the housing subsidies.[2] As Glaeser and Gyourko say, "Building small numbers of subsidized housing units is likely to have a trivial impact on average housing prices."[3]

Subsidies can also be inequitable: San Jose uses federal funds to subsidize housing for "below median-income families." But San Jose's median family income is $105,000 per year, while the national median income is only $58,000. This means taxes paid by U.S. families earning $50,000 or $60,000 per year are used to subsidize some San Jose families who earn $100,000 a year.

Worse, many planning responses to unaffordable housing often make housing even less affordable. San Diego charges homebuilders a "housing impact fee" that is then used to subsidize low-income housing. The builders pass this fee onto their customers. This leads owners of existing homes, who see that new housing now costs more, to charge more when they sell their houses. So everyone, including the vast majority of low-income homebuyers, pays more so that a few people can get affordable housing. Though San Diego has charged this fee since 1990, it has been able to build only 6,500 low-income dwellings—a drop in the bucket in a city that had some 470,000 new homes in 2000.[4]

An even more popular policy is *inclusionary zoning*, which requires homebuilders to sell a certain percentage of all their new homes to low-income people at below-market prices. Several studies have shown that inclusionary zoning, like a housing impact fee, merely drives up the cost of housing for all those not fortunate enough to get the subsidized homes.[5]

For example, San Jose State University economists Benjamin Powell and Edward Stringham found that, in the 30 years since San Francisco Bay Area cities began passing inclusionary zoning ordinances, only 7,000 affordable units have been built as a result of those ordinances. That is just 4 percent of what the Bay Area Association of Governments says is needed.[6] One reason why so few units were produced is that the ordinances lead to a slowing of overall home construction: Powell and Stringham found large declines in construction rates after ordinances were passed by California cities.[7]

Despite these problems, inclusionary zoning remains popular in communities that consider themselves "progressive," perhaps because some people want to assuage their consciences for promoting policies that drive up housing costs. "If policy advocates are interested in reducing housing costs," Glaeser and Gyourko observe, "they would do well to start with zoning reform," not affordable housing mandates.[8]

While growth-management, inclusionary zoning, and other planning policies impose high costs on homebuyers, they also confer a windfall on existing homeowners, leading Glaeser and Gyourko to conclude that zoning has changed "cities from urban-growth machines to homeowners' cooperatives."[9] In effect, just as the Organization of Petroleum Exporting Countries provides a vehicle for oil-producing countries to drive up oil prices, urban planning provides a vehicle for homeowners to drive up housing prices.

In fact, few homeowners are aware of the relationship between planning and home prices. People living in a fast-growing city often worry about the effects of growth on their taxes and the livability of the city. Planners offer policies they say will protect urban livability, and so the public approves them. Almost immediately, home prices rise. The first response is, "We passed these policies just in time. Look at how the demand for housing is increasing." Later the response is, "Our policies must have truly increased the livability of our city. Look at how much people are willing to pay to live here!"

If the plan is a smart-growth plan, it probably calls for more compact development and multifamily housing. Most of the plan's supporters already own their own homes on large lots. *The Onion* once humorously reported, "98 percent of U.S. commuters favor public transportation for others."[10] Similarly, many supporters of compact cities want density for someone else rather than for themselves. Though 70 percent of their community may currently live in single-family homes, they see nothing wrong with dictating that, say, half of all future inhabitants will have to live in multifamily housing. "You are going to love living on our lively streets," they say before they get into their SUVs and drive to their suburban estates.

Of course, those who do understand the relationship between planning and housing prices will fight doubly hard against any relaxation of the planning rules for fear it would reduce their home values. Many Boulderites support the purchase of more open space because they think the open spaces make their homes more valuable by adding to the city's livability. The real reason open space makes their homes more valuable is that it creates an artificial scarcity of land available for housing. Either way, however, the result is the same: most people are priced out of the market.

17. Portland Housing

Portland-area housing was very affordable in 1969, with value-to-income ratios of less than 1.6. Although the city of Portland had passed a zoning ordinance in 1924, it was highly flexible, allowing a wide range of densities over much of the city.[1] As a result, the city had, if anything, a surplus of multifamily housing. Many Portland suburbs had no zoning at all.

In 1969, the Oregon legislature passed a law requiring all cities and counties to write comprehensive plans. In 1973, the legislature created a Land Conservation and Development Commission with the authority to write rules that those plans must follow.

By 1979, increasingly strict planning requirements had doubled Portland-area housing prices after adjusting for inflation. This drove the region's value-to-income ratio up to 2.9. The bubble burst in the 1980 recession when high interest rates devastated the home construction market, which, in turn, decimated the timber industry that was Oregon's largest employer. The recession hit Oregon so hard that the state's population actually declined in the early 1980s. By 1988, housing prices had fallen by nearly 30 percent and Portland's value-to-income ratio was less than 2.0.

In 1991, 1000 Friends of Oregon reported that Oregon's land-use planning system had made Portland housing more affordable "than in comparable West Coast markets where land use is not regulated," such as San Diego, San Francisco, and San Jose.[2] The report ignored the fact that California's economy was booming due to defense contracts while Oregon was still recovering from the second-worst recession in its history. More importantly, the notion that California had no land-use regulation was ludicrous—the difference between the two states was that a state land-use planning law drove Oregon's regulation while local governments influenced by Proposition 13 drove California's. In any event, the rise of Portland-area housing prices in the next six years would prove the report to be embarrassingly wrong.

Portland's housing was more affordable in 1991 than Silicon Valley's. So high-tech companies such as Intel located numerous factories in the Portland area, figuring that their employees could afford housing at the wages the companies were willing to pay. Thus, as California housing markets deflated in the first half of the 1990s, Portland's market boomed. But as housing developers bumped up against the urban-growth boundary, Portland's affordability rapidly declined.

In 1991, when 1000 Friends put out its housing report, developers could buy land suitable for residential development for less than $25,000 an acre. By 1995, such land would cost more than $80,000 an acre.[3] Within two more years, the price of such land, if you could find it, had doubled again and the National Association of Home Builders ranked Portland the nation's second least-affordable housing market after San Francisco.[4] While the Portland area still had plenty of undeveloped land, it was all outside the urban-growth boundary. A stroke of the pen had enriched landowners inside the boundary while it impoverished those outside.

During the 1990s, Portland experienced the greatest decline in affordability—that is, the greatest percentage increase in value-to-income ratios—of any urban area in the nation. Including Portland, four of the top five greatest declines in affordability were in Oregon or Oregon-Washington urban areas. The fastest growing part of the Portland area was Vancouver, Washington, which, being outside Oregon's jurisdiction, was able to offer families affordable homes with yards. While Portland grew by 22 percent and its Oregon suburbs grew by 40 to 50 percent, Vancouver grew by 210 percent during the decade.

The 1000 Friends report of 1991 found that one thing that would keep Portland more affordable was a state rule requiring cities to zone more land for apartments and small-lot subdivisions. Even if land prices increased, the report claimed, housing would remain affordable because people could live in multifamily housing or in homes on tiny lots. The only problem, it turned out, was that people did not want to live in multifamily housing and were unenthusiastic about living in homes with virtually no yards. Thanks to Portland's 1924 zoning ordinance, which had zoned 41 percent of the city for multifamily housing, the region's market for such housing was saturated.[5]

138

For example, when Portland opened its first light-rail line in 1986, the city zoned all the land near light-rail stations for high-density transit-oriented developments. Ten years later, Portland city planner Mike Saba reported to the city council that "we have not seen any of the kind of development—of a mid-rise, higher-density, mixed-use, mixed-income type—that we would've liked to have seen" along the light-rail line. Even though Portland was "the hottest real estate market in the country," observed city Commissioner Charles Hales, "most of those sites" near light-rail stations "are still vacant."[6] The reason for this was simple, developers told the council: there was no market for high-density housing; people wanted single-family homes with yards.

The region responded by offering hundreds of millions of dollars in subsidies to high-density housing:

- Portland waived property taxes for 10 years on all high-density residences built near light-rail lines;
- Cities waived impact fees that would have been charged to low-density developments;
- Metro, Portland's regional planning agency, purchased land and resold it to developers for half price on the condition that they build high-density developments;
- The state of Oregon and local governments sold land to developers at below-market prices;
- Portland even sold some of its city parklands to developers at below-market prices;
- Portland and other cities used tax-increment financing, which uses the property taxes on the new developments to subsidize those developments, both to build light-rail lines and to subsidize high-density housing; and
- Some favored developers even received direct grants, such as funds from the federal Congestion Mitigation/Air Quality fund.

Those subsidies, not good planning or the stimulating effects of light-rail, were for many years the only reasons developers built denser housing in Portland.

Developers initially responded by building row houses in areas previously occupied by single-family homes, effectively doubling densities. But in 1999, Portland planners decided row houses were not dense enough: they wanted four- to five-story apartment buildings, preferably with retail shops on the ground floor.[7] With plenty of subsidies, many such projects were built, but their vacancy rates were high.[8] Moreover, they devastated the market for existing rental housing, leading many landlords to convert their apartment buildings to condominiums.

To meet the demand for single-family homes, developers would find narrow lots, or tear down older homes on regular lots, and build 15-foot-wide "skinny houses" on 25-foot lots. While there were superficial differences between them, all the skinny houses followed the same basic plan dictated by the automobile: the front of the two-story homes had just enough room for a front door and single-car garage, a kitchen-living area was in back, and bedrooms were upstairs. So much for reducing Portland's auto dependency by increasing housing densities.

The artificial shortage of single-family homes was not the only shortage created by Portland-area planners. Under the comprehensive plans written in the 1970s, Clackamas County, which includes all the suburbs south of Portland, had plenty of residential land but little industrial land. Washington County, which includes all the suburbs west of Portland, zoned plenty of industrial land but not enough retail and residential land. This made Washington County the region's new employment area, but its residential land was quickly built out. Planners expected increasing numbers of Washington County workers to commute from Clackamas County, where they could find new homes. But the highway connections between the two counties were, to put it mildly, inadequate. During rush hour, someone could drive 70 miles from Seaside, on the Oregon coast, to Washington County jobs in less time than they could drive 25 miles to those same jobs from Clackamas County.

People responded to high housing prices in different ways. Some gentrified low-income neighborhoods, forcing former renters to disperse to other parts of the city where they lacked the community ties that once helped maintain their families.[9] Families with children fled to suburban areas where they could afford homes with a yard. Portland's school district was forced to close several schools a year as Portland's under-18 population fell to 21 percent of the city's total (compared with a nationwide average of 26 percent).[10] While many families moved to Vancouver, Washington, others moved to Salem,

45 miles south of Portland, which overtook Eugene as Portland's second-largest city in 2001.

In 2005, planners were elated to announce that Portland's suburbs had reached a "tipping point" so that developers were willing to demolish existing single-family homes and replace them with apartments or other high-density housing. All that was necessary for this to happen, says a suburban planner, was for "land value [to] become so much greater than its improvement value." Thanks to the urban-growth boundary, land prices have reached that level, so planners hope developers will eventually turn many of Portland's suburbs into New Urban communities.[11]

Effectively, planners were admitting that they had deliberately driven up housing prices to force residents of the region to accept higher densities. Driven by the state's mandate to reduce per capita driving, planners were imposing congestion and unaffordable housing on residents throughout the region. Yet these are not the only negative effects of smart growth: planners' prescriptions also turn out to make homes and businesses more vulnerable to crime.

18. Smart Growth and Crime

Burras Road was a pleasant cul-de-sac of 21 new homes in Bradford, England. Residents were blissfully unaware that, just east of the site, approval for a proposed new shopping center required the breaching of their cul-de-sac by a bicycle-pedestrian path. Planners favored this because, they say, cul-de-sacs are "auto dependent" and "anti-urban." Opening up the site would connect residents to local services, and the cycle route would promote walking and cycling.

The path connecting the shopping center to the cul-de-sac opened in 2000. Although there is no evidence that the path has led residents to drive less, it did have a profound effect on their lives. Suddenly, a neighborhood that had been virtually crime free saw the burglary rate rise to 14 times the national average, with matching increases of overall crime, including arson, assault, and anti-social behavior.[1]

Cul-de-sacs are a particular target of New Urbanists and smart-growth planners because, they claim—without any evidence, of course—cul-de-sacs increase congestion and reduce people's sense of community. But Burras Road reveals just one more flaw with smart growth: in addition to increasing congestion and making housing unaffordable, smart growth makes neighborhoods more vulnerable to crime.

In 2001, the American Planning Association published a book titled *SafeScape*, which purported to show how neighborhoods could be designed to reduce crime. The book's recommendations included all the standard New Urbanist policies: higher densities, mixed-use developments, gridded streets instead of cul-de-sacs, alleys, pedestrian paths, and large common areas. However, the book offered no data to show that its recommendations actually made neighborhoods safer.[2] There was a good reason for this: all available research shows that these New Urbanist policies actually make homes and businesses more vulnerable to crime.

Instead of presenting data or research to show that New Urbanism made places safer from crime, the book relied heavily on designs that supposedly create "a sense of community."[3] They also endorsed the concept of "eyes on the street," a term used by Jane Jacobs. Jacobs wanted to show that high-density, mixed-use inner-city neighborhoods were not overwhelmed with crime, so she suggested that the shopkeepers and residents kept watchful eyes out at all times, discouraging any would-be burglars or other criminals. The fact that she provided no evidence that eyes on the street were effective did not prevent the authors of *SafeScape* from adopting the phrase as their mantra.

An architect named Oscar Newman was the first to take a hard look at the relationship between urban design and crime. Newman observed that the high-rise housing projects that were popular in the 1950s and 1960s suffered such high crime rates that many were almost unlivable. Yet nearby neighborhoods of single-family homes occupied by people in the same socioeconomic class enjoyed minimal crime. With support from the National Science Foundation, Newman carefully compared crime rates with the design features of thousands of blocks in hundreds of neighborhoods that collectively housed nearly half a million people.

Newman found that the safest neighborhoods maximized private ownership and minimized common areas. Private yards were more defensible, he concluded, because the owners could immediately know whether or not someone belonged in their yard. Public areas were less defensible, particularly in mixed-use developments, because no one could tell whether a stranger in these areas had good or bad intentions. Newman also found that safer neighborhoods minimized "permeability," that is, the ease of entry to and exit from the neighborhood or housing area. For example, apartment buildings with several entrances providing access to dozens of apartments were less safe than buildings with each entrance providing access to a minimal number of units. Similarly, alleys and pedestrian paths that increase the number of public entrances to private properties tend to make them more vulnerable than properties with only one entrance on the street.

Newman called his concepts *defensible space*, and he published a book by that name in 1973.[4] Newman's work proved highly influential in England, and today all British police departments have *architectural liaison officers* who review proposed developments and help developers find ways to minimize crime. English police have significantly reduced crime in many neighborhoods by breaking up common areas and assigning them to individual apartments or homes.

The authors of *SafeScape* specifically misrepresent Newman's findings, claiming "he argued that the reason 'eyes on the street' provide safety in urban, mixed commercial and residential areas is because there is a visible link between residents and the street."[5] In fact, Newman rejected Jane Jacobs's assertions about the safety of high-density, mixed-use neighborhoods. In contradiction to what he called "the unsupported hypotheses of Jane Jacobs," Newman's data revealed that these neighborhoods suffered from higher crime than single-use neighborhoods.[6]

Since New Urbanism has recently become popular in Britain, the architectural liaison officer for one of England's police departments compared a neighborhood built to New Urbanist standards with one built at the same density but to defensible space standards. He found that the New Urban neighborhood had five times the crime and cost police departments three times as much to keep secure as the secured-by-design neighborhood.[7]

A close comparison of New Urbanism and defensible-space standards indicates that they make exactly the opposite recommendations for many design features:

- Where New Urbanism calls for small private lots and large common areas to create a sense of community, defensible space calls for maximizing private yards to create defended space;
- Where New Urbanism calls for mixing uses to put eyes on the street, defensible space separates uses to keep strangers out of residential areas;
- Where New Urbanism calls for a gridded street pattern and strongly objects to cul-de-sacs because they supposedly force people to drive too much, defensible space finds that cul-de-sacs are one of the best crime-prevention tools because they minimize the number of escape routes open to criminals;
- Where New Urbanism promotes alleys (and *SafeScape* suggests that buildings face the alleys to provide "eyes on the alley"[8]), defensible space suggests that existing alleys be closed to minimize public entrances to private properties;

- Where New Urbanism proposes to increase pedestrianism by building numerous bike and pedestrian paths across private properties, defensible space would restrict such paths to along public streets; and
- Where New Urbanism wants to hide automobiles in rear parking areas, defensible space suggests that ungaraged autos should be parked in highly visible areas to discourage thefts and break-ins.

While no one has yet conducted a study comparing crime in New Urban and traditional suburban neighborhoods in the United States, studies of all the above individual New Urbanist features—mixed uses, alleys, gridded streets, and so forth—have clearly shown that each makes neighborhoods more vulnerable to crime. While some people have associated increased population densities with more crime, at least part of this effect is due to the difficulty in designing safe neighborhoods when densities are higher; for example, higher densities offer less room for private defensible yards.

The New Urbanist infatuation with gridded streets and opposition to cul-de-sacs seem particularly unfathomable, as there is no evidence that cul-de-sacs increase congestion as New Urbanists sometimes claim. Yet several cities and suburbs have rewritten their zoning codes to prohibit the construction of cul-de-sacs in new developments and have tried to breach existing cul-de-sacs with streets or pedestrian paths.

SafeScape claims that converting cul-de-sacs to gridded streets somehow increases eyes on the street.[9] Yet research in the United States and England shows that the opposite is true. Newman himself helped Dayton, Ohio, reduce crime in the city's Five Oaks neighborhood by 25 to 50 percent (without increasing crime elsewhere in the city) by blocking many streets, effectively turning gridded streets into cul-de-sacs.[10] Many other cities, such as Berkeley and St. Louis, have followed this example. *SafeScape* included 17 case studies, but only 1 actually reported a reduction in crime, and that was in a community that turned gridded streets into cul-de-sacs.[11]

"The design of streets and buildings should reinforce safe environments," says the Congress for the New Urbanism, "but not at the expense of accessibility and openness."[12] With *accessibility* a euphemism for mixed use and *openness* a euphemism for permeability, it is clear that New Urbanists make safety from crime a low priority. That is fine if residents know and accept that open and accessible will mean more crime. However, *SafeScape* claims the opposite, possibly because the authors sense people will not accept needless vulnerability just to fit into the latest planning fad.

"I am not very impressed with the work of the New Urbanists," Oscar Newman wrote to an English architectural liaison officer shortly before Newman passed away in April 2004. "The residential environments they are creating are very vulnerable to criminal behavior."[13] As Jane Jacobs wrote more than four decades ago, "To build city districts that are custom made for easy crime is idiotic. Yet that is what we do." And that is what New Urbanists are still having us do today.

19. Portland Planning Implodes

Planners' intrusiveness into the lives of Portland-area residents may have peaked in 2000, when a planner told the Sunnyside Centenary Methodist Church in southeast Portland that it could allow no more than 70 people to worship at one time in the church's 400-seat sanctuary.[1] After a firestorm of protest from the region's religious leaders, this decision was overturned by the Portland city council.

In fact, voter dissatisfaction with Portland's planning had been growing for several years. But it took a major sex scandal to shake the faith of the region's leaders in their highly regulatory plans.

As previously noted, the effects of Oregon's land-use planning system originally fell mainly on rural landowners. But after 1990, planners' efforts to replicate Los Angeles in Portland upset many urban residents. It was one thing to talk about "growing up, not out." It was another thing to find 55-foot-tall apartment buildings popping up in your neighborhood of single-family homes. The result was that Portland-area residents—especially those in the suburbs— were increasingly disenchanted with the plans.

Planners hoped that Metro, a bureaucracy with plausible deniability, would deflect this unhappiness. As Brookings Institution urban analyst Anthony Downs observed, a regional government "can take controversial stands" because "each member can claim that 'the organization' did it or blame all the other members."[2] At first, this seemed to work: cities that rezoned neighborhoods to higher densities responded to fierce opposition by saying, "Metro is making us do it." Meanwhile, Metro responded to complaints by saying that the cities had all voluntarily accepted their population targets.[3]

Almost every neighborhood targeted by Metro for densification fought bitterly against rezoning to higher densities. Thanks to the system of plausible deniability, almost every neighborhood that fought densification lost the battle. But this built up a reservoir of resentment that voters expressed in other ways. For example, Oregon is one of the states that gives voters the power to recall elected officials from office. In 1996, the voters in the Portland suburb of Milwaukee decided to recall their mayor and a majority of their city council when the council passed a high-density plan for part of the city. Officials in other cities held their collective breaths and were relieved when the recall movement did not spread.

In 1998, 53 percent of Portland-area voters rejected a proposed new light-rail line. This was a major shift from the 75 percent of voters who had approved the previous light-rail line in 1990. In subsequent elections, support for light-rail had steadily declined, from 65 percent in 1994 to 55 percent in 1996, as increasing numbers of voters realized that light-rail was really a land-use tool used to justify increased densities in neighborhoods along the route. It is significant that there were no plans to build light-rail to Lake Oswego, the one suburb whose voters supported light-rail in the 1998 election, so residents in that suburb did not fear densification.

In 2000, 54 percent of Oregon voters approved a property-rights measure that allowed anyone whose property values had been reduced by zoning or land-use regulations to ask local governments to either compensate them or waive the rules. Such a measure could never have passed before 1990. In 2002, Portland-area voters over-whelmingly supported another ballot measure that prohibited Metro from densifying any more neighborhoods, at least until 2015.

When the courts overturned the 2000 property-rights measure on a technicality, the measure's supporters fixed the technicality and put it back on the ballot in 2004. Planning supporters outspent the measure's advocates by four to one trying to convince voters that this measure would devastate Oregon's land-use planning system. If anything, this argument simply gave residents of densified urban neighborhoods just one more reason to vote for it. As a result, 61 percent of Oregon voters, including a majority of voters in every county in the Portland area, voted for the measure. When opponents took this measure to court, Oregon's Supreme Court unanimously rejected every one of their arguments.

While Portland voters were becoming more and more disgruntled with land-use planning, a consensus in favor of planning persisted among most of the region's political leaders, including elected offi-cials, members of appointed boards and commissions, editorial writ-ers, and many business leaders. That consensus began to fall apart when a scandal broke regarding Portland's former mayor, Neil Goldschmidt.

Goldschmidt was just 32 years old when he was elected mayor in 1972. The highly charismatic former legal-aid attorney was considered a reformer, and is best remembered for canceling construction of a planned freeway and funneling the funds into Portland's first light-rail line. This attracted the attention of President Jimmy Carter, who made Goldschmidt his secretary of transportation. When Carter left office, Goldschmidt returned to Oregon where he was elected governor in 1986. Even though most observers regarded him as a shoo-in for reelection, he mysteriously left office after one term and started a political consulting firm.

Out of office, Goldschmidt was revered as a senior statesman. "Portland never had a better mayor," the city's *Willamette Week* newspaper gushed in 2001.[4] But over the years, some began to see him as "nothing but an influence-peddling money grubber," the "big dog" of Oregon politics, working behind the scenes for large corporations such as Weyerhaeuser and the State Accident Insurance Fund.[5]

Still, people were stunned when the same *Willamette Week* newspaper revealed in 2004 that Goldschmidt had a lengthy sexual relationship with his children's babysitter when he was mayor of the city and she was 14 to 17 years old.[6] He had not run for reelection as governor because the woman had asked him for (and he provided) a $200,000 trust fund to make up for problems the relationship had created in her life, and he reportedly feared it would become public. Though the statute of limitations had long since passed, this was statutory rape, and Goldschmidt immediately resigned all of his memberships on various boards and commissions in disgrace.

The significant result of the sex scandal was that it suddenly allowed the region's media leaders to openly criticize things that had previously been off-limits, such as the fact that Goldschmidt had earned huge fees for brokering a backroom deal giving construction giant Bechtel a no-bid contract to build one of Portland's light-rail lines.[7] "The term 'light-rail mafia' is tossed around by journalists, planners and elected officials to describe the Goldschmidt-connected people working on regional transit projects," reported the *Portland Tribune*. The paper listed many members of this "mafia," including contractors who build the rail, developers who build transit-oriented housing, and politicians who get contributions from the contractors and developers.[8]

For example, Goldschmidt helped his friend, homebuilder Tom Walsh, get the job of running Portland's transit agency. While there, Walsh promoted federal, state, and local subsidies for transit-oriented developments. Walsh Construction Company just happened to build many of these developments.

Homer Williams, the builder of many other transit-oriented developments, was a Goldschmidt client. Goldschmidt helped Williams steer millions of dollars of federal money to the Pearl District, a former warehouse district near downtown that Williams converted to hundreds of expensive condominiums, many of which pay practically no property taxes thanks to other tax breaks.[9] The city also spent up to $234 million in tax-increment-financed bonds to subsidize redevelopment of the River District, of which the Pearl District is a part.[10] Williams bristles at the idea that Portland is "unfriendly" to business; after all, with Goldschmidt's help, his heavily subsidized business has thrived.[11]

Between tax waivers and tax-increment financing, subsidies to the Pearl District and similar developments divert tens of millions of dollars each year away from schools, libraries, fire, police, and other public services. Eventually, this raised the ire of public employees unions, which could see the budget squeezes in the agencies their members worked for while money appeared to be freely flowing to New Urban developers.

On September 17, 2006, for example, Williams was eating dinner on the patio at the Bluehour, the ritziest restaurant in the Pearl District, when he saw police subdue a man on the sidewalk outside. Williams was struck by the "casualness" of the situation.[12] But it was anything but casual for James Chasse, the man in custody. A talented musician who had mysteriously come down with schizophrenia, Chasse was known to Portland mental health workers to be fine as long as he took his medications. But they had received a report on September 15 that he was not eating and probably stopped taking his medicine. When someone working for a Portland non-profit mental health clinic tried to find him, Chasse fled in panic.

Two days later, police officer Christopher Humphries saw Chasse and assumed he was drunk or on drugs. When Humphries tried to approach, Chasse ran away. Humphries tackled him and, according to witnesses, punched and kicked him several times.[13] Chasse later died in custody of chest injuries.

Portland mental health advocates were outraged that many of the programs that could have saved Chasse's life had suffered recent budget cuts: community policing,[14] a crisis triage center,[15] and the city's mental health program.[16] Yet the city continued to spend tens of millions of dollars a year subsidizing high-density developments. "So while some poor mentally ill guy lay there with his life ebbing away," says popular blogger (and law professor) Jack Bogdanski, "the big-shot real-estate sharpie sat with his cloth napkin on, eating his braised veal ravioli with truffles."[17]

The latest controversy deals with a $2 billion high-density development—and the $290 million or more subsidies that it will receive—on Portland's waterfront south of downtown. With Homer Williams's heavy involvement, the South Waterfront project will include an extension of the Oregon Health and Science University, whose main campus is located with several other hospitals on "Pill Hill," two-thirds of a mile away and 500 feet above the waterfront.

As early as 1998, Goldschmidt, who sat on the university's board and whose clients owned the waterfront properties, began promoting the idea of an aerial tramway connecting Pill Hill with the waterfront. Goldschmidt lobbied the then mayor of Portland, Vera Katz, to have the city help fund the tramway.[18] City and Oregon Health and Science University planners estimated the tram would cost $15.5 million. Since the city was spending $50 million per mile on light-rail lines, this seemed such a good deal that one urban planner suggested that the city build an entire network of aerial trams.[19]

Typically, the planner never asked whether people would really want to ride on 12-mile-per-hour tramways. But that was a moot point because the $15.5 million cost was a complete fantasy. Though they did not bother to tell the city council, planners knew the cost would be much greater months before the council approved what it thought was a $15.5 million tram.[20] Soon after approval, cost estimates increased and the final construction cost was $57 million. The annual cost of operating the tram also grew from a projected $480,000 to $1.7 million.[21]

The aerial tram is not the only tax subsidy to the South Waterfront district that went over budget. As a part of the project, the city agreed in 2003 to spend $50 million building streets, parks, and affordable housing. But when detailed cost estimates were made in

2006, the costs of streets and parks alone were estimated to exceed $100 million. A representative of one of the landowners in the district called the new estimates "bizarre" because they still understated many of the costs.[22]

Meanwhile, the city seemed to give up on the idea of affordable housing. In 2004, the city modified its policy of granting developers 10 years of property tax waivers along transit corridors to require that the developers dedicate at least 15 percent of the units to "moderate income" renters or buyers. At least $92 million worth of developments were taken off the tax rolls by this policy. But when the developer of a planned South Waterfront high-rise apartment building applied for such a waiver, the city commission turned it down and put a moratorium on any further waivers.[23] Some members of the commission may have been swayed by the fact that the property taxes they would have given up were the same taxes needed to pay for all the cost overruns.

To top it off, in May 2006, Portland Commissioner Sam Adams—no doubt heavily coached by Portland's transit agency—announced that the "success" of the South Waterfront district "depends" on spending $550 million on a new light-rail line from downtown, crossing the Willamette River and running to the southern suburb of Milwaukee. This surprised other members of the city commission, who "never heard that before" in all the discussions about the South Waterfront district.[24] Meanwhile, the nearby Sellwood Bridge is crumbling and has been put off-limits to heavy trucks and buses. The bridge carries far more people than any light-rail bridge would carry, and its replacement would cost far less to build than a light-rail line. But no money is available for its replacement even as Portland leaders freely talk about spending six times as much money on a new light-rail line.[25]

For many, the South Waterfront district's tax subsidies, cost overruns, and huge payoffs for a select few friends of Neil were symbolic of everything else that is wrong with Portland planning.

- Multnomah County, which includes Portland and its eastern suburbs, spent $59 million building a new jail (including $600,000 spent on "one percent for art") that sits empty because the county has no funds to run it. This has forced the county sheriff to give early release to 5,000 criminals a year, at least one of whom committed a murder a few days after being released.[26]

154

- Columbia Sportswear, one of Oregon's largest companies, wanted to relocate its headquarters to central Portland but was told it could not have any surface parking at the site because "it's a light-rail station." There was no light-rail line anywhere nearby, and voters had turned down funds to build such a line, but the transit agency hoped to build the line anyway, so the parking rule was "nonnegotiable."[27] The company moved to suburban Washington County instead, and its chief executive officer (CEO) blasted the city for its anti-business climate.[28]

- The Portland Development Commission, which oversees the city's urban-renewal projects, bought a building for $1.3 million and spent $700,000 remodeling it, then sold it for $400,000 to a company whose CEO just happened to chair one of the commission's advisory committees.[29]

- The Portland Development Commission purchased another property for $1.2 million and proposed to sell it to a developer for condos. The commission allowed the developer to design the appraisal process for the sale, and when the resulting appraisal claimed the property was worth minus $1.9 million, the commission proposed to give the land away.[30]

- Despite closing five to six schools a year for lack of students, Portland's school district was projecting a $57 million budget shortfall in 2007, which is remarkably close to the property taxes it lost from taxes waived or diverted to tax-increment financing for various high-density projects.[31] When Portland's mayor suggested a city income tax to help schools, the idea sank like a lead aerial tram.[32]

All these controversies are leading left-leaning Portlanders to question the region's land-use planning consensus. Liberal bloggers such as Bogdanski and writer Bill McDonald are scathing in their critiques of urban renewal projects such as the aerial tram and South Waterfront district.[33] Newspaper columnist Phil Stanford freely compares the aerial tram with Portland's light-rail lines, as both were promoted by Goldschmidt, cost taxpayers a bundle, and carry only a tiny portion of the region's residents.[34]

These controversies are leading even the region's leaders to lose faith in planning. The Portland Business Alliance was joined by the Oregon Department of Transportation and even congestion-loving

Metro in paying for a study that estimated congestion would cost Portland businesses nearly $1 billion a year in 2025 unless steps were taken to relieve it.[35] Metro's plans called for relieving congestion only in industrial areas, but planners were surprised to learn that freight is delivered to all parts of the region.

"It used to be our trucks could make six to 10 deliveries a day in the Portland area," reports the representative of a building supply company. "But over the past three years, that dropped to only five to eight deliveries a day because of increased congestion. The only way to keep our customers stocked was to buy two more trucks and hire two more drivers."[36] Businesses such as this one are "prisoners of congestion," said the study.[37]

For years, Portland has cultivated a reputation as a mecca for sound urban planning. The Goldschmidt scandal revealed that much of this planning was little more than a cover for a cabal of developers and contractors centered on Goldschmidt who enriched themselves at taxpayers' expense. This light-rail mafia was supported by anti-auto groups who turned Metro's "comprehensive planning" into a single-minded effort to reduce per capita driving, while ignoring the effects on housing costs, businesses, crime, tax rates, schools, and watersheds. The only questions left are whether Portlanders can repair the damage planners have done to their region and how many other regions will follow Portland's descent into folly.

Part Four
Why Planners Fail

Experience should teach us to be most on our guard to protect liberty when government's purposes are beneficial. Men born to freedom are naturally alert to repel invasion of their liberty by evil-minded rulers. The greater dangers to liberty lurk in insidious encroachment by men of zeal, well-meaning but without understanding.

—Justice Louis Brandeis[1]

More than half of all planners graduated from planning schools that are affiliated with colleges of architecture, and architects have heavily influenced most of those who did not. Whether the architect is Frederick Law Olmsted, Le Corbusier, or Peter Calthorpe, their significance for urban planning is the belief that particular architectural designs will improve human behavior, increase our sense of community, reduce our environmental impacts, or otherwise make us better citizens.

"We shape our cities," planners love to say, "and then our cities shape us." If the pronouns are a bit vague, planners hope that the "we" who shape the cities consist of architects and planners while the "us" who are shaped include everyone else. It is not enough for these planners to merely ensure that development pays for itself out of taxes and user fees (indeed, urban finance is not even part of the curricula of many planning schools) and does not create nuisances that harm other property owners (nor do many schools include courses on common law). Planners want to use urban design to shape human behavior.

These planners are guilty of believing the *design fallacy*, the notion that architectural design is a major determinant in shaping human behavior. While design does play a role at the margins of certain things—for example, certain patterns can make housing more vulnerable to crime—the effects that planners project are often highly exaggerated.

157

To make matters worse, planners rarely test whether the influences they claim are accurate. After adjusting for incomes, education, and family size, do people living in high-density neighborhoods really drive less and participate in the community more than people in low-density neighborhoods? And if there are differences, are they large enough to justify the huge costs that planners' visions would impose on cities? Planners do not know and many seemingly do not care as they continue to support ideas long after they have proven not to work in other cities and countries.

The worst thing about having a vision is that it confers upon the visionary a moral absolutism: only highly prescriptive regulation can ensure that the vision overcomes an uncaring populace responding to a free market that planners do not really trust. But the more prescriptive the plan, the more likely it is that the plan will be wrong, and such errors will prove extremely costly for the city or region that tries to implement the plan.

Early zoning plans, for example, allowed only single-family housing in single-family zones, but allowed any kind of housing in multi-family zones, allowed residential uses in commercial zonings, and allowed any use at all in industrial zones. The only costly error such a plan might make would be to underestimate the amount of land needed for industry, since an underestimate of any other use would simply result in that use overlapping another zone. Modern plans are much more prescriptive, with only industrial uses allowed in industrial zones, only commercial in commercial zones, and so forth (not to mention various prescriptive subzones for each use). This not only creates many more opportunities for costly errors, it generates a sense of entitlement among residents that a particular parcel of land will always and forever be dedicated to a particular use even if there really is little or no market for that use.

Problems such as these stem from the design fallacy that is shared by so many planners and the architects who inspire them. Correcting these problems will require more than improved research or better education. It will require a fundamental revolution in how we manage our cities and the regions that surround them: a change from a focus on design to a focus on public finance.

20. The Planning Profession

Part two showed that comprehensive government planning is impossible no matter who is doing it. But ignore that for the moment and imagine government planning *is* possible. Are planners the people to do it?

A few years ago, some planners and economists built a computer model of an urban area. They assumed that jobs were located downtown and that people wanted to minimize the sum of their costs of housing plus commuting. Those who lived close to downtown had lower commuting costs but higher housing costs. Living farther from downtown meant higher commuting costs but lower housing costs.

After entering the appropriate data into the model, the planners and economists asked, "How far will people live, on average, from their jobs?" The computer said one mile. Yet the modelers knew that, in reality, people lived an average of seven miles from their jobs. When they improved the model by assuming there were many job centers instead of just one downtown center, the modelers found that the model still came up with average commute distances of a little over two miles—less than a third of reality.

The economists and planners had very different responses to these results. "Naturally we don't expect the real world to fit the . . . model perfectly," said the economists, "but being off by a factor of seven or even three is hard to swallow."[1] The economists decided there must be something wrong with the model.[2] Perhaps people use factors other than proximity to work when deciding where to live. Improving the results meant identifying those factors and adding them to the model.

In contrast, the planners concluded instead that something must be wrong with reality. The cities are inefficiently designed, they decided, leading people to waste their time commuting. Numerous articles in planning journals address "excess" or "wasteful" commuting and how cities should be redesigned to eliminate it.[3] By failing to ask the right questions, planners ended up with a totally wrong-headed view of urban problems.

Who are the planners who make these kinds of errors? As of 2005, the Bureau of Labor Statistics estimated that there were 31,650 practicing planners in the United States. Their average annual salary was $57,620, which means America spends more than $1.8 billion a year on planning salaries alone.[4]

Based on its 30,000 members, the American Planning Association says about two-thirds of planners work for state and local governments.[5] Many of the rest work for consulting firms that are either hired by state and local governments or hired by developers to help them interpret and comply with government plans.

"Regulatory problems tying you up?" one consulting firm asks developers. "Let our experienced planners help you deal with local government and regulatory agencies."[6] This suggests a revolving door of planners writing complex rules for government agencies, then working for consulting firms extorting money from developers to interpret the rules they wrote.

The contrast between planners and developers is stark. Developers can easily judge the success or failure of their projects by the bottom line: did they make or lose money? Developers generally must put up their own money to finance at least part of each development, so if it fails, they pay much of the cost. This gives them a powerful incentive to get it right, as determined by what potential buyers and renters want. As Joel Garreau observes, developers' "unshakable observation was this: if they gave the people what they wanted, the people would give them money."[7]

Developers can rapidly learn from their mistakes because they carefully watch how projects by other developers fare in the marketplace. The development world quickly evolves in response to changing tastes, changing costs, and changing regulations. While developers may grumble about government regulation, in the end those rules are just a part of the development environment. Most regulations passed by a city council apply to all developers in that city, so they simply pass the costs onto the buyers or renters.

In contrast, planners working for government agencies don't have to back up their plans with their own money. This means that success or failure is not determined by whether the plans can make or lose money. If the regulations written by planners force developers to do projects that would lose money, the developers, of course, won't do the projects. Planners tell themselves this is a market failure and respond by looking for tax breaks or other subsidies that they can offer the developers to entice them to do the projects. The projects may get built, though at a net loss when the subsidies are subtracted from any benefits they produce.

The Design Fallacy

Most planners graduated from 1 of 69 planning schools accredited by the American Planning Association. Of these schools, 39 are affiliated with architecture schools, 13 with social science or science schools, 5 with public affairs or public administration schools, 5 with environmental science schools, and 7 are independent. Only one is in the same school as an engineering department.

The strong emphasis on architecture reveals a major weakness of urban planning: most planners share with architects an undue faith in the power of design to improve or control human behavior. "Winston Churchill's dictum, 'We shape our cities, and our cities then shape us,' was an axiomatic precept in city planning circles," says University of California planning professor Melvin Webber.[8] (Actually, what Churchill said was "We shape our buildings, thereafter they shape us.")

Notice that there are two forms of hubris here. First is the arrogance of architects who believe that, because they can design a house for one family, they can design an entire urban area for a million families. That is something like gardeners believing that, because they can grow a rose bush, they can design an entire ecosystem for a million-acre forest. Second is a faith in the design fallacy: that by influencing urban design, architects and planners can create a new, utopian society in which people are happier, have a stronger sense of community, and spend less time isolated in their automobiles.

"The planners seemed to think that human behavior was malleable, and that nobody was better equipped by dint of intelligence and education than they to do the malleting," says *Edge City* author Joel Garreau. "They believed that the physical environment they wanted to shape could and would shape society. The places they would like to plan would lead, they believed, to fundamental, welcome, and long-overdue changes in human mores and human attitudes."[9]

Planning's focus on design grew out of the profession's long history as an offshoot of architecture. Many of the first planners in the

United States were architects such as Daniel Burnham or landscape architects such as Frederick Law Olmsted. Throughout the history of the urban planning profession, planners have looked to architects such as Le Corbusier and Frank Lloyd Wright for inspiration. The leading heroes of the planning profession today are architects Andrés Duany and Peter Calthorpe.

How valid is the notion that urban design can shape human behavior? As noted in chapter 18, architect Oscar Newman observed that differences in design could make a neighborhood more or less vulnerable to crime. Newman's recommended designs, including cul-de-sacs and private yards, are remarkably similar to modern suburban layouts, perhaps because homebuyers intuitively understand that these features make neighborhoods safer.[10]

By comparison, smart-growth planning is based on the unproven notion that certain urban designs will lead people to drive less. Planners reason that, before the automobile was invented, people lived in dense housing often mixed with retail shops, offices, and other uses. If cities mandate the construction of dense, mixed-use developments, planners hope it will reduce congestion, air pollution, and other detrimental effects of driving.

There are three main differences between defensible space and smart growth. First, defensible space works. Newman observed a correlation between certain designs and crime, and he showed that this correlation represented a cause-and-effect relationship: certain designs resulted in more crime while others resulted in less. Smart-growth planners also observed a correlation between certain designs and driving, but they failed to find out whether there was a cause-and-effect relationship. It turned out that the designs they noted do not reduce driving but instead are an effect of people's limited mobility before they had automobiles.

Second, almost everyone agrees that crime is bad. In attempting to apply the same philosophy to driving, planners are implicitly equating auto driving with the evils of crime. Considering that 88 percent of all passenger travel in the United States is by car, it is clear that not everyone agrees that driving is as evil as burglaries, rapes, and vandalism.

The third difference is an ethical one. It is one thing to offer people designs that can make their lives safer from outside invaders. It is quite another to impose designs on people that are aimed at shaping their own behavior in ways that they might not want to be shaped. Such imposition is often called *social engineering*, an ugly term that planners may resent. Yet the ugliness fits because so many planning efforts that have attempted to shape human behavior have ended in disaster.

The first problem with social engineering is, who gets to set the goals? Most people would agree that reducing crime is a good idea, but some people might be willing to accept a slightly higher vulnerability to crime to get other benefits. For example, mixed-use developments tend to suffer higher crime than pure residential areas, but some people might accept that to get easy access to shops and services. A regionwide ban on anything that might reduce defensible space would ignore such preferences.

Other goals, such as reducing driving, are even more debatable. *The Onion* points out that most Americans would be happy for other people to drive less, but don't want to drive less themselves.[11] As described in chapter 27, automobility provides enormous benefits, and efforts to reduce driving risk reducing those benefits by more than any savings in air pollution, congestion, or other costs.

The second problem with social engineering is that planners so often get it wrong. With their attraction to fads over analyses, they frequently write plans that do the opposite of what they want. Smart growth, with its goal of reducing driving, is a classic example. The cities with the least amount of driving are those with large concentrations of jobs at their centers. Yet smart growth calls for a "jobs-housing balance," meaning the distribution of jobs throughout the urban area. Urban transit cannot serve such a job pattern and, since people base their home locations on many factors other than their work location, smart growth's prescription does little or nothing to reduce driving.

Slow to Learn

Developers learn rapidly from their mistakes because they pay the cost of those mistakes in lost investments or credit. Planners rarely face such a reckoning. Many years, typically a generation or more, are required to determine whether or not planners' experiments are successful. This makes it possible if not probable that planners will significantly harm entire regions before anyone can correct their errors.

For example, in 1959, Kalamazoo, Michigan, tried to "revitalize" its downtown by closing a street to auto traffic and turning it into a pedestrian mall in a conscious attempt to compete with suburban shopping malls. Over the next 30 years, U.S. and Canadian cities created roughly 200 such pedestrian malls. Many won awards from planning groups.

Yet far from revitalizing retail districts, most of the pedestrian malls killed them. Vacancy rates soared, and any pedestrians using the malls found themselves walking among boarded up shops or former department stores that had been downgraded to thrift stores or other low-rent operations.

"The street was more vibrant before the pedestrian mall," says a Tampa resident familiar with that city's Franklin Street mall. "The businesses started moving out about the same time the mall came in and the situation has only worsened," she says. First, the five-and-dime stores left. Then in the late 1980s, the Maas Brothers Department Store went under. The last major store in the area, a Woolworth's, closed in the early 1990s.[12]

Despite these failures, cities continued to create pedestrian malls 25 years after Kalamazoo's initial experiment. In 1984, Buffalo closed 10 blocks of its Main Street to autos. In the following years, Main Street vacancy rates increased by 27 percent and property values declined by 48 percent.[13]

By 1990, many cities began restoring auto traffic to their pedestrian malls. Eugene, Oregon, spent $2.4 million reopening its downtown to autos. Greeley, Colorado, spent $2.6 million scrapping a pedestrian mall that had cost $4 million to create two decades before.[14] Kalamazoo reopened its pioneering mall to auto traffic in 1998.[15] Baltimore, Pittsburgh, Seattle, and many other cities followed suit.[16]

As of 2002, only about 30 pedestrian malls remained, and cities were considering reopening many of these to auto traffic.[17] A study by the city of Buffalo, which is considering reopening its mall, found only nine malls that were successful. Seven of them were in university or resort towns, which have higher-than-usual concentrations of pedestrians, while the other two were open to transit buses.[18] In other words, malls could not create pedestrians out of auto drivers. They only worked when the pedestrians were already there.

Despite this record, some planners still promote the idea of pedestrian malls.[19] Businesses in Ketchum, Idaho, stopped planners from turning a street into a pedestrian mall in 1998.[20] Quincy, Massachusetts, proposed a pedestrian mall in 2004.[21]

Why did it take 25 years or more for planners to give up on the idea of pedestrian malls, and 20 to 40 years for cities to reopen their failed malls to autos? One reason is that, unlike the developers' bottom line, planning goals were nebulous and difficult to measure. Businesses might close on pedestrian malls, but planners could tell themselves that new businesses would take their place or that there were other compensating benefits. Or they might argue that the businesses would have closed anyway due to competition from the suburbs, and that the pedestrian mall may have even delayed this closure.

No one likes to admit failure, and because of the difficulty in measuring benefits, planning champions could, for a time, claim success no matter what actually happened. Thus, it could take a literal generation for the original planners to retire, move, or otherwise be replaced by new planners who were more willing to see the failure of their predecessors' plans.

In 1961, Jane Jacobs observed that "theoretical city planning has embraced no major new ideas for considerably more than a generation."[22] The urban-renewal concepts that were popular when Jacobs wrote have morphed into smart growth, but those smart-growth ideas have not significantly changed in at least 15 years. In the 125 years since modern city planning began, there have been about five generations of planners. In that time, planners have been able to learn about as much from their mistakes and rare successes as developers can learn in about five years.

In short, while urban design can influence behavior, the influences claimed by planners are often exaggerated or flat-out wrong. In the case of driving, factors such as income and family size are far more influential on the amount that people drive than urban design. In the case of obviously bad things such as air pollution, urban design is far less effective than simple technical improvements to autos and other pollution sources. Even where urban design does influence behavior, it is ethically questionable whether planners—or anyone else—should have the power to impose such designs on unsuspecting residents.

The ethical question is one planners rarely ask. As Peter Hall points out, "All the different urban forms in the world might not

165

make that much difference" in the amount people drive. Yet, he adds, "planners should do what they could to make people virtuous."[23] Hall may say this with tongue in cheek, but many planners clearly believe their mission is to make people virtuous whether they like it or not and no matter what the cost.

21. The History of Planning

The planning profession grew out of a perception that something was wrong and a conviction that scientific managers and government regulation could fix it. The perception was not always right, and the conviction was almost always wrong.

"Twentieth-century city planning, as an intellectual and professional movement, essentially represents a reaction to the evils of the nineteenth-century city," says Peter Hall in his history of urban planning, *Cities of Tomorrow*.[1] Those evils included slums so crowded that often two or more families shared a single room; poor sanitation; rampant disease; high rates of crime; and (perhaps "most shocking" of all to Victorian sensibilities) prostitution and other forms of immoral behavior.[2]

Hall identifies six different responses to the 19th-century city that came together to form today's planning profession:

1. Ebenezer Howard's *Garden City*, the idea of moving people to new, self-contained cities, featuring both jobs and housing, outside the periphery of existing cities;
2. *Regional planning*, the idea that experts should plan not just individual cities but entire regions;
3. Frederick Law Olmsted's *City Beautiful* movement, which focused on building large monuments and parks to give people a sense of pride and community;
4. Swiss architect Le Corbusier's *Radiant City*, which consisted of modern, concrete high-rises separated by green spaces and connected by broad avenues and highways;
5. *Democratic planning*, in which people essentially build their own homes and cities, deciding for themselves how they want to live; and
6. The *City on the Highway*, that is, city planning centered on the auto and the truck, most famously practiced by New York's Robert Moses.[3]

Hall, who is fond of irony, notes that most of these strains can trace their origins to the 19th-century anarchist movement.[4] "The anarchist fathers had a magnificent vision of the possibilities of urban civilization, which deserves to be remembered and celebrated," opines Hall.[5] The major exception is Le Corbusier (1887–1965), who Hall calls "the Rasputin of this tale," both because his Radiant Cities turned out to be so wrong and because of his authoritarian approach to planning, "the evil consequences of which are ever with us."[6]

Hall points out that the Swiss "are an obsessively well-ordered people," and Le Corbusier sought to impose this sort of order on the buildings and the cities that he designed.[7] To ensure that the designs were properly carried out, Le Corbusier favored the appointment of a "master architect" whose will would be followed without question. "The design of cities was too important to be left to citizens,"[8] said Le Corbusier. Of course, he was doomed to be frustrated by most governments, and he envied authoritarian leaders of the past, such as Louis XIV and Napoleon, who could order urban redevelopment simply by saying "'we wish it,' or 'such is our pleasure.'"[9]

The irony is that, despite planning's anarchistic roots, it was Le Corbusier's authoritarian strain that has become dominant in urban planning for the past 60 or more years. An even more "central irony" of urban planning, Hall adds, is that it was "the market," not planners, that managed to "dissolve the worst evils of the slum city through the process of mass suburbanization."[10] This started taking place as soon as streetcars allowed white-collar families to escape the crowded cities and accelerated as automobiles became affordable to blue-collar families.

While suburbanization would have taken place without urban planners, planners initially welcomed it. The Garden City and City Beautiful movements in particular supported the idea of mass suburbanization because they regarded dense inner cities as unhealthy. As the director of the Denver Planning Commission wrote in 1930, "To avoid the evils of congestion and overcrowding attendant upon excessive use of land, Denver has aspired to spread widely rather than reach high."[11] Such spreading allowed for increased ownership of single-family housing rather than housing in tenements.

One 1928 suburb, Radburn, New Jersey, has in many ways become a model for suburban development since that time. Radburn has a street layout with numerous cul-de-sacs. The streets were treated as little more than utility corridors, and the houses faced their backs to those streets. The fronts of the houses faced large green spaces that separated the homes. Within these green spaces, walking paths formed the borders between individual properties.

Planners today think highly of Radburn, but the part they applaud, the walking paths, is the only part that did not survive in postwar suburbs. Homeowners soon realized that such walking paths offered vandals and thieves easy access to their properties and private developers omitted them from later suburbs. Through the 1970s, however, government planners in England built numerous housing projects known as "Radburns" that emphasized such walking paths. These projects suffered much higher crime than English neighborhoods without the walking paths.[12] Modern planners revile many of the ideas that American suburbs have taken from Radburn, including cul-de-sacs and house orientation.

Further irony is found in the fact that, as soon as working-class people started moving to the suburbs, which was the goal of some of the early, non-Corbusian strains of planning, planners began complaining about the evils of the suburbs. By the 1930s, British suburbs were "universally derided and condemned," says Hall. "The fact was that the prosecutors were all upper-middle class and the offenders were mostly lower-middle class in a typical such suburb."[13] The residents of these new suburbs "were enjoying a quantum leap in their quality of life." But that was not good enough for the architects and planners, who "repeatedly in their journals, at their congresses, during the 1930s . . . railed about the suburbs."[14] "The suburbs' chief fault," comments Hall, "seems to have been that they conspicuously diverged from either of the then main standards of good taste: the neo-Georgian . . . or the uncompromisingly modern."[15]

Harvard historian John Stilgoe makes similar observations about American suburbs. Until the 1920s, he says, "most intellectuals favored their creation." But when working-class people moving to the suburbs were "slow to accept the European avant garde," then "urban writers, especially in New York, turn[ed] on the suburbs as the home of narrow-mindedness." In particular, "architects entranced with the flat-roofed, cement apartment houses of 1930s Berlin reeled from steadfast urban love of single-family, pitched-roof houses," and "city planners championing great boulevards and public parks learned of gardeners anxious to shape their own private spaces."[16]

Hidden beneath this aesthetic view was class prejudice. The critics, says Hall, had "a terror of what Anthony King has called the democratization of the countryside: the lower-middle-class and working-class invasion of an area that had hitherto been the preserve of an aristocratic and upper-middle-class elite."[17]

"Tradition has broken down," one English critic, Thomas Sharp, stridently declared. "Taste is utterly debased. There is no enlightened guidance or correction from authority."[18] Another critic, C. E. M. Joad, complained of "hordes of hikers cackling insanely in the woods" and "people, wherever there is water, upon sea shores or upon river banks, lying in every attitude of undress and inelegant squalor."[19] The countryside, obviously, should be preserved for those who know how to properly appreciate it.

To achieve such preservation, urged Joad, "the extension of the towns must be stopped, building must be restricted to sharply defined areas, and such re-housing of the population as may be necessary must be carried out within these areas."[20] That housing, added Sharp, should be in "great new blocks of flats which will house a considerable portion of the population of the future town."[21]

This, of course, is Le Corbusier's vision: not only his Radiant City but his authoritarianism. Le Corbusier promoted a "famous paradox": cities are congested because they were too dense, and the solution is to increase their density by building Radiant Cities. This fit right into the elitist view that most people should be confined to high-density areas because, after all, they would at least get to enjoy the green spaces between the high-rises.

Le Corbusier's Radiant City and his authoritarianism inspired planners throughout the world. Not surprisingly, some of his most devoted followers could be found in the Soviet Union and its satellites behind the iron curtain.

22. The Ideal Communist City

The Ideal Communist City, a book written by planners at the University of Moscow in about 1965, provides insight into the attitudes of postwar planners not just in Russia but throughout Europe. The principles in this book formed a blueprint for residential construction all across Russia and Eastern Europe. Construction in much of Western Europe was not significantly different. Smart-growth advocates bristle at the suggestion, but—with a couple of minor changes—these principles could also be the blueprint for much of today's urban planning.

Echoing the English critics of the 1930s (and echoed by American critics today), *The Ideal Communist City* described suburbs as "a chaotic and depressing agglomeration of buildings covering enormous stretches of land." Because the cost of providing services to such "monotonous stretches of individual low-rise houses" is too high, the book said, "the search for a future kind of residential building leads logically to high-rise structures."[1]

Mixed-use developments, the Moscow planners added, allow people easy access to "public functions and services" such as day care, restaurants, parks, and laundry facilities. This, in turn, would minimize the need for private spaces, and the authors suggest that apartments for a family of four need be no larger than about 600 square feet.[2] Before the late 1960s, the Soviets built 5- to 6-story brick apartment buildings, but the authors accurately projected that new, reinforced-concrete building techniques would allow 15- to 17-story apartment buildings.

The soviet planners saw several advantages to high-rise housing. First, it would be more equitable, since everyone from factory managers to lowly janitors would live in the same buildings. Second, the Soviets believed apartments would promote a sense of community and collective values. Single-family homes were too "autonomous," they said, while the apartment "becomes the primary element in a collective system of housing."[3]

Third, high-density housing was supposed to allow easy access to public transportation. "Private individual transportation has produced such an overwhelming set of unresolved problems in cities that even planners in bourgeois societies are inclined to limit it," the Russians prophetically observed. With their high-density apartment buildings, as many as 12,000 people could live within 400-yard walking distances of public transit stations. That's about 70,000 people per square mile, slightly greater than the density of Manhattan. "The economic advantages of [public transit] for getting commuters to and from production areas are obvious," says the book, "and it is also an answer to congestion in the central city."[4]

Soviet-bloc countries were building such new cities even as the University of Moscow planners were writing their book. In 1970, East Germany developed a standard building plan known as the WBS 70 (WBS stands for *Wohnungsbausystem*, literally, "house-building system") that was applied to nearly 650,000 apartments in East Berlin and other East German cities. "The WBS 70 was the uniform basis of the accelerated housing construction until the end of the GDR [German Democratic Republic]," says Christine Hanneman, a researcher at Humboldt University in Berlin.[5] The WBS 70 offered a generous 700 square feet in its three-room apartments, not counting 75 square feet of private balcony.[6]

The WBS 70 was one of the major designs used in Halle-Neustadt, a bedroom community built between 1964 and 1990 for about 100,000 people on the outskirts of the East German manufacturing city of Halle. As planned in the 1960s and 1970s, Halle-Neustadt consisted of rows of apartment buildings surrounded by pleasant-looking green spaces, with a central commercial area and road corridor featuring large, articulated buses. The new city was also connected to Halle by an extensive streetcar system and an S-Bahn (commuter-rail line), and the city met the Ideal Communist City density of about 70,000 people per square mile.

At a 1998 conference on sustainable transportation, two planners from the University of Stockholm praised Halle-Neustadt as one of "the most sustainable" (i.e., least "auto-dependent") cities in the developed world. The Stockholm planners' paper noted that almost all the apartments had two bedrooms because government planners decreed "that the ideal family consisted of four family members and that the number of flat rooms should be one less than the number of family members." They also noted that the government discouraged car ownership by placing most of the parking on the outskirts of the city "at a relatively large distance from the residential houses."[7]

What the Swedish researchers failed to note in their 1998 presentation, but faithfully recorded in their full paper, was that Halle-Neustadt was only "sustainable" during the socialist period.[8] When Germany reunified, many residents moved out, and those who stayed bought cars so that auto ownership rates "reached nearly the level of western Germany." Naturally, this created major congestion and parking problems: "Every day there are about 7,400 wrongly parked cars in the city," noted the researchers. "The cars are parked everywhere—on pavements, bike-ways, yards and lawn."[9] The Swedes feared that proposed construction of new parking garages would "undermine" the "planning concept of concentrating the parking places on the city's outskirts."[10]

The residents and former residents of Halle-Neustadt do not share the same ideals as the Swedish planners. Since reunification, the city's population has fallen from 94,000 to 60,000 people.[11] Many moved to find work in western Germany, but others moved to single-family or duplex homes in low-density suburbs that are not much different from older, inner-ring suburbs in the United States. Today no one in Germany refers to such suburbs as "monotonous." This term is instead reserved for the gray slabs of concrete that people are abandoning as fast as they can. They commonly refer to the apartments as *die Platte*, meaning "the slab," referring to the method of construction.[12] Because Germans pronounce the letter *h* as "ha" while "neu" is pronounced "noi," Halle-Neustadt residents often refer to their town as "Hanoi," an ironic reference to the bombed-out nature of much of the city.[13]

Halle-Neustadt includes both 6-story mid-rise buildings built in the 1960s and 11-story or taller high-rise buildings built in the 1970s and 1980s. The mid-rise buildings have no elevators, so it is not surprising that many of the upper apartments are vacant. Some of the high-rise buildings are in good condition, but others are entirely vacant.[14] After reunification, these buildings were sold to private companies that rent them out at market rates. To deal with the glut of apartment housing, these companies lobbied the government to pay for demolition of at least 28 of Halle-Neustadt's buildings, and even when that is done the remainder will still have a high vacancy rate.

The people who stayed in Halle-Neustadt have turned most of the green spaces between the buildings into parking lots. The city center enjoys a modern new shopping mall supported by a multi-story parking garage as well as at least one auto dealership. A number of new big-box stores can be found not far outside the city, including a home improvement center, a furniture store, and a hypermart (the European version of a Wal-Mart supercenter). Following reunification, many of Halle's inefficient factories went out of business. The city has partly compensated by doubling the size of its university. Halle-Neustadt's central corridor still has frequent streetcar service to the university, but the commuter line connecting Halle-Neustadt with Halle's factories receives little use.

It would be nice to think that Le Corbusier's authoritarian planning was found only east of the iron curtain, but it was not. As sociologist David Popenoe has documented, an almost identical set of principles moved Swedish planners after World War II. They, too, elected to build mainly high-density, mid-rise and high-rise housing. "A public opinion poll at the time in Stockholm showed that a majority of people wanted single-family homes," says Popenoe. "Needless to say, the people did not get them."[15] In fact, at the time Popenoe did his research, 76 percent of Stockholm residents lived in apartments.[16] "The housing desires of individual residents was not a serious input" into this decision, says Popenoe. "Swedish housing densities are a planners' alternative, and for better or worse, Swedish cities are planners' cities. In this sense Swedish urban development is much more akin to that of the Eastern European socialist countries than it is to the United States."[17]

The Swedes did more than plan for and build at high densities in the 1950s and 1960s. Like the Soviets, they tried to discourage auto use, partly by heavily taxing both autos and fuel. In addition, to encourage people to ride transit instead of driving, "they have even gone so far, in some areas, as deliberately to locate car owners' private parking places further from their residences than the nearest public transportation stop."[18] As a result of such policies, "only 7 percent of households have two cars, while 45 percent own no automobile at all."[19]

Popenoe thinks that these policies should be applied in the United States. He notes that the metropolitan boundary of an American city "is by no means clear-cut." Instead, the city "signals its presence well in advance: scattered houses, shops, and gas stations begin to thicken." As a result, "one is never quite sure at what point the rural countryside ends and the physical metropolis . . . actually begins," frets Popenoe.[20] By comparison, "Stockholm has very little rural-urban fringe: the use of land is either rural or urban, not a mixture of the two." When approaching it, "suddenly pristine countryside gives way to a high-density build environment." Popenoe finds this appealing: "Visually, this yields a strong sense of order, and signals a clear ideological separation of town and country as two very distinct worlds."[21]

Unless, like Le Corbusier, you are "obsessionally well-ordered," why is this clear ideological separation so appealing? It assumes that only two lifestyles are legitimate: the urban and the rural. If you don't have a rural occupation—farmer, fisher, logger, miner—then you must live in an urban area. Anything in-between—suburb, exurb, hobby farm—is for some mysterious reason unacceptable.

Even if you believe this, planning didn't work in Stockholm any better than it did in Halle-Neustadt. Peter Hall's study of Stockholm reveals that, though Popenoe's book was published in 1985, his data were from 1970.[22] That year, Hall discovered, was a turning point for Swedish planners. Much of the high-density housing had been "completed at top speed, with little attention to the quality of the surrounding environment; much of it was industrialized, highly monotonous, and built at too high a density." As a result, "around 1970 came a quite sudden reaction against" both high-density housing and "the planning system itself."[23] Vacancy rates soared, which critics blamed on a housing-industrial complex consisting of the construction industry and the planning bureaucracy."[24]

"The new mood blew up in 1971," says Hall, with protesters taking to the streets to object to various urban plans. "Protesters no longer accepted politicians' arguments of economy and functionality, and exposed 'official' plans as inconsistent, misconceived, and inaccurately based."[25] After 1972, housing "tipped sharply towards owner-occupiership" and new construction tipped "towards single-family homes." Before 1970, "nearly three-quarters of all new units were multi-unit apartments," but "by 1980 the proportions were reversed."[26] As a result, the apartments were increasingly left to low-income people and foreign guest workers. In short, says Hall, "attempts to persuade everyone to live in apartments failed." Today,

Stockholm is largely suburbanized and much of it "is almost indistinguishable from its counterparts in California and Texas."[27]

Contrary to Popenoe's outdated data, Stockholm planners are also losing their war on the automobile. Auto ownership in the greater Stockholm area increased from about one car per four people in 1970 to one car per two people in 1990, while per capita driving increased by 30 percent.[28] Nor is Sweden unusual. If anything, population densities are declining and per capita driving is increasing even faster in most other European cities.

Hall points out that, in 1977, Popenoe asked, "Why, in a country so affluent, with high car ownership, so recently rural, and with so much land [and, incidentally, virtually undamaged by World War II], was it necessary to put so many people into small high-density apartments?"[29] One answer is "that the influential architects favored high-density development, and they dominated the planning profession in Sweden," says Hall. "They were able to get their way, it seems, because of rent controls and rent subsidies, which created a built-in demand for housing. Public preferences, it seems, carried little weight." An "even deeper" explanation is that "from 1932 to 1976," the Swedish democracy "voluntarily maintained a one-party system of government," giving Social Democrats, who favored planning, virtually all the power to run the country.[30]

Hall doesn't say so, but Europe's parliamentary systems can also be credited with giving planners more power than they normally enjoy in the United States. Parliamentary systems are essentially serial dictatorships, allowing leaders to enact radical legislation with little public input. People may vote for their party based on a few highly visible issues such as foreign policy or education, but they end up with the whole package, high-density housing, anti-automobile programs, and all. While this can also be true in the United States, the U.S. separation of the executive and legislative branches creates a check on the ability of either branch alone to run roughshod over voter preferences.

As in Sweden, the revolt against high-density housing also took place in Britain and most other Western European nations after World War II. In Britain, the postwar Labour government passed the Town and Country Planning Act of 1947, which greatly restricted the development of rural lands. In implementing this law, the government disregarded the preferences of most of its subjects for living

176

in single-family homes.[31] Instead, housing was provided by building hundreds of new mid-rise and high-rise apartment buildings.

In many of these apartments, "the architect was uninspired or non-existent, and where tenants found themselves uprooted into hurriedly constructed system-built flats lacking amenities, environment, community: lacking, in fact, almost everything except a roof and four walls," says Hall.[32] "The remarkable fact was how long it took for anyone to see that it was wrong."[33] Unlike Sweden, Britain at least had the excuse that such apartments were an improvement over the housing that remained after the war in many of England's bombed-out cities, where families often had to share both kitchens and baths with other families. Yet, as planning critic Wendell Cox has found, the average size and quality of housing for British residents were dramatically lower in the 1950s, and remained lower in the 1990s, than they had been in the 1920s.[34]

In 1965, a housing official visiting a new development in Greater Manchester found it to be of "an appalling dimness and dullness." Soon, such apartments became "hard-to-let, i.e., lettable only to the poorest and most disorderly families." As a result, by about 1970, in Britain as in Sweden, "the great Corbusian rebuild was over."[35]

The main problem with these dense developments, says Hall, "of which Corbusier is as fully culpable as any of his followers, was that the middle-class designers had no real feeling for the way a working-class family lived." The rich could live in high-rises but for ordinary people, "the suburbs have great advantages: privacy, freedom from noise, greater freedom to make a noise yourself. To get this at a high density requires expensive treatment, generally not available in public housing." It especially didn't work for children. "Corbusier, of course, was blissfully unconscious of this, because he was both middle-class and childless."[36] Plus he never lived in a Radiant City; "as the media delighted to discover," Hall says, the architects who designed such developments "invariably lived in charming Victorian villas."[37]

23. Urban Renewal in the United States

The New Deal, which created a National Resources Planning Board and dozens of other planning agencies, had given planning a major boost in the United States.[1] Yet as European voters turned left after the war, preferring Labor and Social Democratic parties over more conservative ones, U.S. voters turned right, selecting Republicans over Democrats.

Thus, the United States was not as quick as Europe to follow either Le Corbusier's authoritarianism or to build his Radiant Cities after the war. Aside from providing low-interest home loans to returning GIs and mortgage-interest income-tax deductions to all homeowners, the United States preferred to let the market work and allow people to choose their own preferred form of housing. The result may have been the largest land rush in history as the postwar boom allowed millions of families to escape the crowded cities and move to suburbs built by William Levitt, Henry J. Kaiser, and other homebuilders.

Between 1950 and 1970, 24 of the nation's 50 largest cities collectively lost more than two million people. By 1990, 30 of the cities that had been among the nation's 50 largest in 1950 had lost more than 6.2 million people.[2] Places that lost population tended to be high-density cities with large urban cores built in the pre-1890 pedestrian era, such as Boston, Chicago, and Philadelphia. Cities that gained population tended to be those that were already low in density because they were largely built in the post-1890 streetcar era, such as Los Angeles, or the post-1920 automobile era, such as Phoenix and San Jose. Meanwhile, the suburbs of every one of these cities grew rapidly.

Suburbanization was not new; villages had been growing around the fringes of American cities for more than a hundred years before World War II. But never before had suburbanization been tied to a depopulation of the great cities: from 1950 to 1990, St. Louis lost 54 percent of its residents; Buffalo, Cleveland, and Pittsburgh lost 40 to 50 percent of their populations; while Baltimore, Boston, Chicago, Cincinnati, Minneapolis, and Washington lost 20 to 30 percent of theirs.

In the previous century, cities would have merely annexed their suburbs, which most suburbs willingly accepted to obtain city services. But in 1873, Brookline, Massachusetts, became the first suburb to reject a major city's offer to be annexed.[3] By the mid-20th century, many suburbanites viewed the cities, with some accuracy, as cesspools of corruption, and they didn't want to see their taxes going into the pockets of aldermen or their contractor friends. Most states did not allow cities to annex without the permission of the people being annexed, and that permission was often difficult to obtain.

City officials, however, complained that the average incomes of the people left behind were lower than those of the people who moved out, which in turn tended to mean lower tax revenues for the cities. The cities came to view suburbanites as parasites, enjoying the benefits of the cities without paying their full share of the costs.

The depopulation of these older cities had two major effects. First, the intellectuals who hated the suburbs found new allies in the mayors and other officials of the big cities that were most threatened by the suburbs. Like most people, these officials were glad to blame the problems of their cities on anyone but themselves, and if they could blame them on the suburbs that were increasingly their rivals for federal housing and transportation dollars, so much the better. Some of these officials would get elected to Congress or other high office, taking with them pro-urban, anti-suburbanism clichés and platitudes. This would be especially important as complaints about urban sprawl grew in the 1990s.

The second major effect was to give New Deal planners who survived into the 1950s an opportunity to carry out some of their idealistic prescriptions: not the Garden City prescription, as urban mayors did not want to lose more people—or the taxes they paid— to the suburbs. Instead, the mayors favored planners who promised the City Beautiful or the Radiant City. They called this *urban renewal*: the wholesale removal of "blighted" areas and their replacement with various urban monuments: theaters, museums, and high-rise housing. Public-housing advocates supported urban renewal in the hope that it would improve housing for the urban poor. Instead, too often it destroyed affordable housing and replaced it with either high-priced housing or no housing at all. From 1950 to 1961, urban renewal destroyed four times as many housing units as it built. By 1965, urban renewal programs had evicted more than a million people, 90 percent of them ending up in substandard housing at higher rents.[4]

The public housing that was built too often followed the Radiant City model: high-rise apartment slabs not much different from those found in Halle-Neustadt. The most infamous example was St. Louis's Pruitt-Igoe apartments. Designed by Minoru Yamasaki, the same architect who would later design the World Trade Center, Pruitt-Igoe included more than 2,800 apartments in 33 identical 11-story buildings. The project won several architectural awards, but initial construction bids were so much higher than anticipated that the public housing authority made major cuts.[5] When the project opened in 1955, new residents found that locks broke, doorknobs fell off, windowpanes blew out, and elevators did not elevate.[6]

The real problem, as Oscar Newman later demonstrated, was that a design that might have worked for upper-middle-income families was totally unsuited for low-income families. Residents could not defend the complexes' common areas, including entrances, corridors, laundry rooms, and surrounding green spaces, which became havens for muggers, rapists, and, later, drug dealers. Despite a city-wide shortage of affordable housing, Pruitt-Igoe was never more than 75 percent occupied. In 1965, the city spent $5 million trying to cure the problems, but by 1970 occupancy fell to 35 percent. In 1972, Pruitt-Igoe reached its peak of fame when the city imploded the entire complex.[7]

While Pruitt-Igoe inspired Newman's research on defensible space, Chicago, Newark, New York, Philadelphia, and many other cities built similar complexes—many of which have also been imploded. The problems with such complexes were so widespread that in 1995 the federal government began funding the demolition of projects once built with federal funds. By 2002, Philadelphia had blown up 20 high-rise public housing projects.[8] Chicago blew up most of the Robert Taylor homes—28 16-story buildings with nearly 4,300 apartments—and expects to demolish the rest of its high-rise public housing by 2009.[9] Housing authorities replaced many of these projects with low-rise, low-income housing that is designed to blend in with adjacent neighborhoods.

Urban mayors seeking federal pork, downtown property owners seeking the removal of low-income and particularly black residents from their neighborhoods, and construction companies and unions seeking juicy government contracts all enthusiastically supported urban renewal and public housing. But urban renewal was also endorsed, promoted, and given respectability by architects and urban planners whose goals were to revitalize downtowns and remove urban blight.

Many planners were also enthused by that other great postwar federal program, the Interstate Highway System, which they saw as a way both to shape cities and to remove blight. As transportation historian Mark Rose observes, the different varieties of planners in the 1930s all had at least one thing in common: they viewed highways as an important part of the solution to urban problems, and not just as transportation.

A ring road around the cities, they believed, "would discourage outward movement and promote 'uniform development of whole areas,'" that is, development at more uniform densities.[10] Radial roads connecting downtowns with the ring roads like spokes would divide neighborhoods, which planners considered a good thing because the roads would "act as barriers to residents traveling cross-town but allow easy access to the central business district, thus promoting neighborhood social cohesion and downtown sales."[11]

The radial and ring highways that most cities built are now objects of derision by today's planners who bitterly complain that they promoted urban sprawl while they destroyed existing neighborhoods by dividing them. As far as the sprawl argument goes, the earlier planners may have been more accurate. Harvard transportation professor Alan Altshuler notes that downtowns declined more rapidly in the late 1940s and 1950s than in the 1960s, after many interstate highways were completed. "If the circumferentials had been built, but no radials, the decentralizing consequences might have been even greater than they were," says Altshuler.[12]

The planners had even greater ambitions for the interstate highway program. They urged that cities be allowed to do "excess condemnation" when purchasing rights of way for urban interstates. In other words, instead of just condemning the land needed for the highway, the city or state should also condemn a broad swath of land around the highway. The blighted areas of this land could be removed and the areas revitalized and sold, allowing the state to benefit from the increase in economic value created by proximity to the highway.[13] Planners who today complain that urban interstates destroyed existing neighborhoods can be grateful that their predecessors' even more grandiose ideas were not approved.

The shallowness behind the supposed expertise that architects and planners brought to urban renewal was brought sharply to light when Jane Jacobs, an architectural writer then living in Greenwich Village, wrote *The Death and Life of Great American Cities*, first published in 1961. "This book is an attack on current city planning and rebuilding," Jacobs began. Urban renewal, she went on, has produced

> low-income projects that become worse centers of delinquency, vandalism and general social hopelessness than the slums they were supposed to replace. Middle-income housing projects which are truly marvels of dullness and regimentation. . . . Luxury housing projects that mitigate their inanity, or try to, with a vapid vulgarity. Cultural centers that are unable to support a good bookstore. Civic centers that are avoided by everyone but bums, who have fewer choices of loitering place than others. Commercial centers that are lackluster imitations of standardized suburban chain-store shopping. Promenades that go from no place to nowhere and have no promenaders. Expressways that eviscerate great cities. This is not the rebuilding of cities. This is the sacking of cities.[14]

So far, this is a critique of Le Corbusier's Radiant City. But Jacobs's real argument was that the supposedly blighted areas that the planners wanted to "renew" were not slums at all but living, vital neighborhoods. Jacobs described in detail how these high-density, mixed-use neighborhoods operated and thrived.

Somewhat defensively, Peter Hall argues that it is unfair to blame the failures of urban renewal and Radiant City–like housing projects on "planning." If planning is "an orderly scheme of action to achieve stated objectives in the light of known constraints," then urban renewal was not planning, Hall asserts. But, he admits, if planning is "a rationalist paradigm, built on abstract ideas" rather than "the experience of precedents that have worked well," then perhaps urban renewal *is* planning.[15]

24. From Radiant City to Smart Growth

The failures of City Beautiful–inspired urban renewal projects and Radiant City–inspired public-housing projects caused the planning profession to fall out of favor in the 1970s and 1980s. The number of graduates from planning schools declined, and Peter Hall observes that the fastest-growing county in England actually abolished its planning department.[1]

In an irony that Hall would appreciate, the planning profession was reinvigorated when it replaced the Radiant City fad with a fad based on anti-planner Jane Jacobs's urban villages. This transition began in a book titled *Compact City: A Plan for a Livable Urban Environment*. By a curious coincidence, this book appeared just two years after the 1971 publication of the English translation of *The Ideal Communist City*. Like the latter book, *Compact City* promoted high-density development as an alternative to suburban sprawl and based its ideal "on Radiant City lines—it would have a central work core ringed by residences and there would be a general separation of functions." But, as an alternative, the authors suggested that Jacobs's "lively neighborhoods" could work just as well.[2]

The advantage of a compact city, the authors claimed in parallel to *The Ideal Communist City*, is that congestion would be reduced because neighborhoods would be so dense that people could get around on foot or by transit rather than by driving. By 1972, research by Northwestern University economist Edwin Mills had disproven this claim.[3] That didn't stop the U.S. House of Representatives from holding hearings in 1980 titled *Compact Cities: A Neglected Way of Conserving Energy.*[4]

In the 1980s, a number of architects, notably Andrés Duany in Florida and Peter Calthorpe in California, began consciously emulating Jacobs's urban villages in what would otherwise be considered suburban developments. Duany said that his developments were modeled on what he called "traditional neighborhoods" built during the streetcar era in the 1920s, and that his goal was to increase residents' "sense of community."[5] Calthorpe said that his goal was to create "pedestrian villages" that would reduce the amount of driving people needed to do.[6]

In 1991, Duany, Calthorpe, and other architects and planners met at the Ahwahnee Hotel in Yosemite Park and wrote the "Ahwahnee Principles." The principles emphasized designing neighborhoods so that "housing, jobs, daily needs and other activities are within easy walking distance of each other," and planning regions "around transit rather than freeways."[7] These architects called their ideas *New Urbanism* and soon formed the Congress for the New Urbanism to promote them.

Despite the apparent departure from Radiant City, New Urbanism in fact shared many things in common with the principles of Radiant City as defined in *The Ideal Communist City*. New Urbanism retained planners' historic animosity toward low-density suburbs, coupled with a new animosity toward the automobile that they shared with the soviet planners but not Le Corbusier. New Urbanism retained the goal of high-density housing, merely substituting Brooklynesque mid-rise developments for Radiant City high-rises. Both models shared the ideas of mixed-use developments, mixed-income housing, and transit-oriented and pedestrian-friendly design. While New Urbanism accepted that people would want dwellings much larger than 600 or 700 square feet, both models minimized the size of private yards and substituted common areas.

Moreover, New Urbanism, or at least its smart-growth incarnation, is just as authoritarian as Le Corbusier or *The Ideal Communist City*. The Ahwahnee Principles required that "government take charge of the planning process" rather than allow "developer-initiated, piecemeal development."[8] As noted in chapter 11, the Congress for the New Urbanism at least at one time urged that all new developments be required to follow New Urban designs and that all existing suburbs be reconfigured to such designs.[9]

Andrés Duany and a few other New Urbanists have distanced themselves from such authoritarianism, saying they merely want to build New Urban developments for those people who would prefer to live in them. Duany distinguishes between New Urbanism and smart growth by saying the former is voluntary and the latter is coercive. In a bow to critics, the Congress for the New Urbanism deleted some of the more authoritarian statements from its website, though they still can be found on other New Urbanist webpages. Still, Peter Calthorpe and other New Urbanists earn a considerable portion of their incomes helping regional and local planning agencies write highly prescriptive New Urbanists zoning codes. As applied by regional planners in Minneapolis–St. Paul, Portland, San Diego, San Jose, and numerous other urban areas, urban planning today is far more authoritarian than any urban renewal or public housing plan of the 1950s or 1960s.

In the end, there are only three or four real differences between Radiant City and New Urbanism. First, one favored high-rises; the other mid-rises. Second, one emphasized modern architecture; the other postmodern architecture. Third, one favored tiny apartments; the other tiny lots. Finally, Radiant City, as envisioned by Le Corbusier but not the authors of *The Ideal Communist City*, supports the automobile as the dominant form of travel; New Urbanism pretends that it is not.

The authoritarianism behind current planning practice inspired Peter Hall to lament that, "in half a century or more of bureaucratic practice, planning had degenerated into a negative regulatory machine, designed to stifle all initiative, all creativity."[10] "Perhaps we came back full circle," he added. "At the end of nearly a century of modern planning, the problems of cities remained much as they had been at the start."[11] More realistically, the problems *as perceived by urban planners* haven't changed because of their focus on design rather than other aspects of human lives.

For urban planners, one major advantage of a prepackaged set of concepts such as Radiant City or smart growth is that they become substitutes for thinking. Rather than do any detailed analyses, planners can simply apply the current planning fad, whatever it is. Planners today often say, for example, that "smart growth is not a one-size-fits-all prescription." Yet no matter what the situation— small towns, suburbs, inner cities—the smart-growth prescription is always the same: increase densities; build mixed-use developments; emphasize walking, cycling, and transit; and discourage auto driving by limiting parking and street flow capacities.

Jane Jacobs specifically warned against this. "I hope no reader will try to transfer my observations [of great cities] into guides as to what goes on in towns, or little cities, or in suburbs which still are suburban. Towns, suburbs and even little cities are totally different organisms from great cities. We are in enough trouble already from trying to understand big cities in terms of the behavior, and imagined behavior, of towns. To try to understand towns in terms of big cities will only compound confusion."[12]

Those planners who say they have learned from Jane Jacobs and now want to apply New Urbanist principles to small towns and suburbs missed Jacobs's real point: that planning will be a "pseudo-science" as long as it relies on "the specious comfort of wishes, familiar superstitions, oversimplifications, and symbols." To really understand the behavior of cities, planners must be willing "to look closely, and with as little previous expectation as possible, at the most ordinary scenes and events."[13] In other words, in Peter Hall's words, planning should be based on "the experience of precedents that have worked well" rather than "abstract ideas." Unfortunately, far too much of what planners did after the war and continue to do today is based on abstract ideas rather than actual experience.

25. Typical Planning Methods

Planners ply their trade in cities as different as Portland, Maine, and Portland, Oregon; and Anchorage, Alaska, and Tampa, Florida. Despite the obvious and significant differences between these cities and regions, planners seem to use the same methodology in all of them.

The first step is to raise public alarm about local issues, especially growth. "The whole aim of practical politics," noted H. L. Mencken, "is to keep the populace alarmed (and hence clamorous to be led to safety) by menacing it with an endless series of hobgoblins, all of them imaginary."[1] It does not matter how fast growth is taking place; planners know that people get upset whenever a former pasture is converted to a subdivision or shopping mall and that people worry about whether their taxes are going to subsidize such developments.

"Over 1,000 people are moving to Washington County every month," says one Portland planner. "Metro needs to figure out how we can accommodate their living, employment, shopping and recreation needs."[2] The implied assumption is that, without Metro planners, these newcomers would be homeless, jobless, hungry, and having nothing to do in their spare time.

Dane County is "adding 60,000 people a decade," frets the county executive of Wisconsin's capital county; "that's adding a Mount Horeb every year."[3] Of course, Mount Horeb is not a particularly large town: 60,000 people a decade is just 500 people a month.

The implied or overt questions behind the growth threat include the following: Where are these people going to live? Who is going to pay for them? Are they going to pave over all of the open space? The answers to these questions should be obvious to anyone with an open mind and a rudimentary knowledge of history.

- Fast-growing areas do not need planners: From 1950 to 1970, Santa Clara County, California, grew by 3,500 people per month and their living, employment, shopping, and recreation needs were fully accommodated by private entrepreneurs with virtually no help from planners.

- Existing residents rarely subsidize growth: The United States has grown from less than 4 million people in 1790 to more than 300 million today. If existing residents had to subsidize growth, then the 4 million original inhabitants must have devoted 10,000 percent of their incomes to subsidize everyone through today. Obviously, they did not.

- We are not running out of farmland or open space: Although four out of five Americans today live in urban areas of 2,500 people or more, the land that they live, work, shop, and play on covers just 2.6 percent of the nation's land area. This suggests that there is still plenty of room for newcomers today.

Planners either are unaware of these facts or assume that their constituents do not know them. They expect people to fear that unplanned growth will lead to high taxes; worsening traffic congestion; and the destruction of the nation's last, precious farmlands. Like knights in shining armor, planners offer to come to the rescue to prevent these problems. Their solutions just happen to produce high taxes; worsening traffic congestion; and the reduction of some of the most valuable urban open spaces, namely people's backyards.

After raising the alarm, the next step, planners say, is for people to envision the future that they want for their city or region. The charter for Metro, Portland's regional planning agency, created a visioning committee that was supposed to envision Portland's future. Planners often call for visioning sessions in which the public are consulted about their desires for their regions.

In a typical visioning session, members of the public are asked leading questions about their preferences. Would you like to have more or less pollution? Would you like to spend more or less time commuting? Would you like to live in an ugly neighborhood or a pretty one? Planners interpret the answers as support for their preconceived notions, usually some form of smart growth. If you want less pollution, you must want less auto driving. If you want to spend less time getting to work, you must want a denser city so you live closer to work. If you want apple pie, you must oppose urban sprawl that might subdivide the apple orchard.

190

Planners asked Portlanders whether they would rather live in a city with six-lane freeways or eight-lane freeways, as if it was an aesthetic decision. Planners did not ask if people wanted to live in a city that wasted 10 minutes of every commuter's time in traffic every day or 30 minutes, or if they wanted to live in a city that wasted 20 million gallons of fuel in congestion each year or 60 million gallons. Yet deciding not to build extra lanes on Portland's six-lane freeways is the same as deciding to greatly increase the time and fuel wasted in Portland's traffic.

Envision Utah, a government-funded planning group, presented the public with a questionnaire asking, among other things, how much air pollution they would like. The graphics in the questionnaire showed a cloud of air pollution associated with no rail transit that was 40 percent larger than the cloud associated with rail transit.[4] The clear implication: if you want less air pollution, you must want rail transit. Yet the numbers actually calculated by Envision Utah estimated that the nonrail alternative produced less than 0.4 percent more pollution than the rail alternative.[5] This tiny difference was far less than the potential errors in the group's analysis, and it is easily possible that the rail alternative would produce the most pollution.

Of course, not everyone has the same preferences, so planners have developed what they call the *urban transect*, which includes several different mixtures of urban uses and densities of housing. But just acknowledging the possibility of low-density suburban housing does not mean that planners will embrace much of it in their plans. Planners know that, just as 98 percent of American commuters think other people should ride transit, many American suburbanites are quite content to think that most newcomers should live in high-density housing so that no development need take place beyond the current urban fringe.

The obvious problem with visioning is that planners cannot accurately predict how many people in the future will want to live in their New Urban villages versus how many would prefer low-density suburbs. But they are quite willing to write 20-, 50-, or even 100-year plans prescribing the amount of land that will be available for each use in the distant future. Envision Utah had no hesitation in proposing that the percentage of families living in single-family homes should be reduced from 68 percent to 62 percent or that average lot sizes should be reduced from 0.37 acres to 0.27 acres.[6] Land-use regulation can force such changes in preferences simply by driving up land prices.

Once the visioning process is done, planners go through numerous steps, most of them behind closed doors, and many of them glossed with a patina of scientific authority, such as a computer model or the hiring of an outside consultant who knows that proposing the solution the planners or politicians want is the key to getting future consulting work. One such consultant justified distorting his results by saying that he was saving the public money by squeezing out competitors who would distort the facts even more than he would.[7] Even if the process is open to the public, the complexity of the computer models is sufficient to prevent 99.999 percent of the people from having any influence.

Most planners present their plan to the public as a utopian future in which congestion will be a thing of the past, the cost of living will be minimized, and the birds and bunnies will have nothing to fear from greedy developers. But this reveals an even more insidious side of planning: once planners identify an ideal future for their regions, they would not dare leave it to chance, or the vagaries of the imperfect market, to produce that future. If you can envision an ideal future, then you must impose that future on your region through prescriptive zoning, design codes, subsidies, and other government controls, as anything else would be less than ideal.

In a few short steps, we have gone from "planners can keep your taxes low and protect farmlands" to "planners know the best use for every parcel in your region and no other use should be allowed." Recall Andrés Duany telling regional planners that they should leave nothing but "the architectural detail" to individual landowners."[8] Planners are willing to be quite draconian in their efforts to ensure that their plans are followed.

In 1971, Robert Goodman wrote of "an insistent pattern of arrogant and repressive programs by many prominent, and not so prominent, planners, politicians and corporate leaders, usually in the cause of solving what has been called the 'urban crisis.'"[9] But Oregon-style smart-growth planning is far more authoritarian than anything done by urban-renewal planners of the 1950s and 1960s.

- To limit development outside of urban-growth boundaries, Oregon planners decreed that 95 percent of the state should have

192

160-acre minimum lot sizes. When that was not restrictive enough, they ruled that even people who owned 160 acres could not build a house on their land unless they earned $40,000 to $80,000 (depending on land productivity) a year farming that land. This rule was needed, said the state, to prevent "lawyers, doctors, and others not really farming [from] building houses in farm zones."[10]

- To ensure high-density development near Portland's city center, the city of Portland gave developers hundreds of millions of dollars worth of subsidies for about 5,000 units of housing. Subsidies included 10-year property tax waivers on $92 million worth of housing, construction of a $55 million streetcar line, and other infrastructure costs totaling more than $100 million.[11]
- Planners ordered the closure of a farmer's popular Blueberry Café because it was located just outside of Salem, Oregon's urban-growth boundary. The café sold more than three tons of local blueberries a year, but because many were mixed with flour and other nonlocal ingredients in pancakes, muffins, and other products, planners said that the café violated a rule that at least 75 percent of things sold at a farmer's stand must be locally grown.[12]
- Although the ruling that allowed a Portland church to have no more than 70 people at one time worship in its 400-seat sanctuary was overturned, other Oregon planners have been just as vigilant against religious sprawl.[13] A Jacksonville, Oregon, church was given a permit to expand provided it would be closed on weeknights and Saturdays and have no weddings or funerals—restrictions needed, said the city, because of traffic concerns.[14]
- When Portland-area residents resoundingly voted against raising their property taxes to build any more light-rail transit, Metro decided to build it anyway and to fund it through tax-increment financing—a surreptitious way of raising property taxes.

Portland has received an enormous amount of publicity for its plans, as well as numerous awards from the American Planning Association and other proponents of planning. The magazine articles and awards rarely mention the huge increase in congestion, the dramatic drop in housing affordability, or the declining urban services because taxes are diverted to rail transit and subsidized high-density housing. Instead, they focus on planners' intentions. Planners often persuade people to judge their plans by their intentions rather than their actual effects because the intentions are concrete today while the effects are in the nebulous future.

Planners are not the only guilty parties and sometimes not the guiltiest parties in such processes. Planners who want to do an honest job often find themselves ordered by politicians to skew the analyses in favor of a favorite pork-barrel project. University of California planning professor Martin Wachs tells the story of a planner who was ordered by a politician to revise rail ridership estimates upward and costs downward. When the project had cost overruns and ridership shortfalls, the politician said, "It's not my fault; I relied on forecasts made by our staff, and they seem to have made a big mistake."[15]

Yet such political shenanigans are an inevitable part of the planning process. Politicians who seek pork or power or who sincerely believe that their programs will improve their communities will gladly use the planning process to justify their whims. Since the professional planners, in effect, work for the politicians, they are unlikely to cross them with plans or analyses that contradict the politicians' preconceived notions. Most likely, the planners support those notions in any case.

In the end, supporters of planning who want to take credit for their good intentions must take the blame for the negative results of their plans. It does not matter whether those results arise from political interference in planning, inadequate funding, unexpected events, or reluctant voters. All these are a part of the world of planning, and planners who assume them away are as guilty as planners who intended from the start to write bad plans.

Part Five
Transportation Planning

O highway I travel! O public road! Do you say to me, Do not
leave me?

*O public road! I say back, I am not afraid to leave you—yet I
love you;*

You express me better than I express myself.

—Walt Whitman[1]

From roughly 1920 through 1990, most transportation decisions in
this country were made by civil engineers whose first priority was
safety and whose second priority was the efficient movement of
passengers and freight. But starting in the 1960s, a growing chorus
of writers argued that highways harmed cities and that transport
agencies needed to account for the effects transportation technologies had on land uses. Urban planners claimed that they could do
a better job of dealing with these effects than civil engineers.

In 1991, Congress turned transportation planning over to the
urban planners when it passed the Intermodal Surface Transportation Efficiency Act, which required metropolitan areas to write long-
range regional transportation plans in order to be eligible for federal
transportation funds. Many urban areas, including Denver, Minneapolis–St. Paul, Portland, San Diego, and the San Francisco Bay
Area, combined their transportation plans with their land-use plans.

Instead of evaluating the effects of transportation technology on
land uses, however, planners turned the formula around and tried
to alter land uses in order to affect people's transportation choices.
Some land uses, they argued, led people to drive more while others
would encourage people to walk, bicycle, or ride transit. Planners'
own data showed that the effects of land use on transportation were
weak, but this did not stop them from proposing costly changes in
urban land uses to reduce driving.

Congress began diverting highway user fees to mass transit in
1982. Since 1956, Congress had distributed highway funds to the

states using a strict formula that accounted for each state's population, land area, and the number of miles of roads in the state. Since state highway bureaus knew how much money they would get each year, they had an incentive to spend their share of funds efficiently. But when the Surface Transportation Act of 1982 allocated some highway user fees to transit, it failed to create such a formula for mass-transit funds. Urban leaders soon realized that the de facto formula was simple: the cities that planned the most expensive projects got the most federal funds.

Soon, scores of cities began planning the construction of expensive rail lines to ensure that they would not lose "their share" of federal funds. Most cities that built rail lines saw transit ridership either decline or grow slower than it had grown when they ran transit systems that relied exclusively on buses. But the needs of the transit riders were forgotten as a powerful coalition of rail consulting, construction, and manufacturing firms; transit agencies; developers; and downtown interest groups was formed to support more rail transit.

Planners jumped on the rail bandwagon because they viewed rail transit as a way to alter land uses. Not only did rail transit provide an alternative to auto driving, but it gave planners an excuse to impose controversial high-density zoning on neighborhoods near rail stations. Rail transit "is not worth the cost if you're just looking at transit," one Portland planner admitted. "It's a way to develop your community at higher densities."[2]

Instead of evaluating the effects of transportation on land use, as promised, planners focused on imposing their design fallacies on cities to socially engineer people out of their automobiles. The result has been a massive increase in urban congestion and billions of dollars wasted on 19th-century rail technologies.

26. Planning vs. Chaos

In the July 2005 issue of *Trains* magazine, columnist Don Phillips applauded the European Union for writing a plan to take freight traffic off highways and put it on rails. A newcomer to Europe, Phillips considered this a good thing because—most *Trains* readers fervently believe—trains are supposed to be more environmentally sound than trucks. "Europe is trying to be a planned economy as far as transportation is concerned," said Phillips approvingly, while "the U.S. continues to be a crisis economy."[1]

Regardless of the merits of trains versus trucks, Phillips should have looked at the numbers before promoting European-style central planning. Although Europe has punitively taxed truckers and subsidized rail for decades, the European Union admits that 75 percent of European freight moves by truck.[2] This compares with just 28 percent in the United States.[3] Moreover, since 1980, the share of European freight that is shipped by rail declined from 22 percent to 14 percent; during the same period, the share of U.S. freight shipped by rail increased from 31 percent to 39 percent.

Phillips made the common mistake of judging planners by their intentions rather than their performance. As a former *Washington Post* writer, he has an inside-the-Beltway view of U.S. transportation, which is why he sees it as lurching from crisis to crisis. In fact, when Congress deregulated the rail and trucking industries in 1980, it placed power in the hands of individual entrepreneurs and businesses, not central planners. This reduced transportation costs and freed the railroads to capture much shipping that would otherwise be on the highway. Similarly, after Britain privatized and deregulated its railways, British rails enjoyed the fastest growth in freight tonnage in Europe.

After spending a year in Europe, Phillips realized his mistake. "I now believe that private enterprise does a far better job of running a freight railroad," he wrote. "No matter how much the European Union pushes European railroads to take freight off the highway,

197

the current system simply cannot hold a candle to what the U.S. system does now every day."[4] Yet, he indicated, he still believes that the government should run passenger trains even though government-run passenger trains have been losing market share in Europe at about the same rate as their freight counterparts.

Railroads are supposed to be the white knights today because they can be more energy efficient than cars and trucks. But in the late 19th century, railroads were considered villains because they acted as monopolies in many parts of the country. Between 1887 and 1907, Congress passed several laws that took from the railroads the power to set rates and make other day-to-day decisions and gave that power to planners in the Interstate Commerce Commission in Washington. This stifled the railroads' ability to compete against truckers and waterways, and it was not until the 1980 deregulation and subsequent closure of the Interstate Commerce Commission— a rare example of a federal agency shutting its doors—that railroads were able to gain back traffic from the trucks.

In the 19th century, many of the nation's highways had been privately built as toll roads. But because railroad monopolies had given private transportation a bad name, when people started promoting highways for 20th-century automobiles, they decided that government should build the roads. In 1919, Oregon became the first state to charge motorists a gasoline tax and dedicate that tax to highways and streets.[5] By 1932, when Congress dedicated the first federal gas tax to roads, every other state had followed Oregon's example and nearly 60 percent of the money spent on roads came from such taxes.[6] Since that time, user fees including tolls and weight-per-mile truck fees have covered an average of 88 percent of all highway construction, maintenance, and operating costs.[7]

Until recently, civil engineers made most of the decisions about how to spend this money. The engineers' first priority was safety, and their second priority was the efficient movement of goods and people. In the 1980s and 1990s, urban planners successfully wrested control of transportation planning from the engineers. The sad result is that transportation now costs far more and does far less than it used to do, and in many respects it is more dangerous.

Although planners pay lip service to congestion reduction and use people's dislike of congestion to gain power, their actual plans show that they have a very different agenda from the engineers.

Instead of improving safety and relieving congestion, planners seek to reduce safety and increase congestion to discourage people from driving. Instead of spending scarce transportation funds as effectively as possible, planners divert funds from cost-effective programs and spend them on expensive urban monuments such as light-rail transit.

Planners gladly joined an informal congestion coalition of interest groups that benefit from increased traffic delays. This coalition includes transit agencies, rail contractors, downtown property owners, and anti-auto environment groups. Any cities or urban areas that rely on urban planners to do or coordinate their transportation planning are likely to find that the resulting plans create far more problems than they solve. Real solutions will be found to America's congestion problems only when transportation decisions are returned to engineers responding to user fees and other signals about what people really need and want from their transportation investments.

It is useful to compare the methods of the engineers with those of the planners. With a narrow focus on safety and efficiency, the engineers carefully studied the effects of any changes or improvements they made to see if those effects were good or bad, and they published their results for other engineers to see. *Practical Traffic Engineering for Small Communities,* published in 1958 by Pennsylvania State University, offers numerous examples of the engineers' method.[8] The guide presents hundreds of case studies asking such questions as

- Will traffic signals reduce pedestrian accidents?
- Is parallel parking less prone to accident than angle parking?
- Will putting grooves in pavement reduce accidents?

Notice the heavy emphasis on *reducing accidents,* in keeping with the engineers' first priority of safety. Improving traffic flows and reducing congestion are important, of course, but only if they can be done without reducing—and preferably by increasing—safety. Most of the studies described in the 1958 engineering manual followed a common method. Data were gathered for a year or more. Then some action—installing a traffic signal, grooving pavement, and so forth—was taken and, sometimes after an adjustment period, data were gathered again. The two periods were compared.

Instead of a before-and-after comparison, engineers sometimes compared two similar streets—say, one with parallel parking and one with angle parking. Sometimes a control street was used for comparison, or perhaps the city as a whole. For example, accidents on a particular street might decline after the pavement was grooved even though accidents increased in the city as a whole. In any case, the point was to carefully evaluate whether the action produced positive benefits and perhaps to assess whether they were worth the cost.

Over time, engineers developed methods to rank roads based on at least three different considerations: safety, pavement quality, and congestion. For example, congestion was ranked with a letter grade, A through F. Roads rated A had very little traffic, while F represented stop-and-go traffic. After fixing safety problems and maintaining pavement quality, engineers gave priority to relieving congestion on the roads rated F, E, and, where funding was available, D.

One of the advantages of this system was that it came with a feedback relationship. If state highway departments built highways that people used, those people would buy more gasoline to drive on the highways and thus provide more funding to the departments. Even though the departments were a part of government, this feedback relationship made them act something like private businesses. While politics played a role in highway location, the departments would tend to resist a "highway to nowhere" that might cost them a large share of their budget but yield little gas tax revenue.

"Highway expenditures can be guided on a more precise basis" than the expenses of most government programs, noted University of Michigan economist Shorey Peterson in 1950. "The inclination of the engineers to whom road-planning is largely entrusted has been to define and apply appropriate standards in transportation terms. It is in the character for the engineer to be mainly concerned, not with broad matters of public interest, but with specific relations between road types and traffic conditions."[9]

Peterson specifically warned against trying to account for the "public interest" when planning roads. This would lead to "the wildest and most irreconcilable differences of opinion," he said. "Control of road improvements through judging its relation to the general welfare is as debatable, as devoid of dependable benchmarks, as deciding the proper peacetime expenditure for national defense or the right quantity and quality of public education," said Peterson. "Controlled in this way, highway projects are peculiarly subject to 'pork barrel' political grabbing."[10]

Accounting for the public interest and broader considerations than just transportation is exactly what planners promise to do. Planners observed that new highways actually generated traffic because they led to new development along the road. In this way, the planners said, the highway engineers were actually influencing land use and, as such, highway decisions should take into account more factors than just safety, pavement quality, and congestion. The planners offered themselves as experts in "comprehensive land-use planning" who could do a better job of transportation planning than the engineers.

To gain power, planners allied themselves with opponents of the automobile. The tradition of auto hating goes back at least to the 1968 publication of *Road to Ruin* by A. Q. Mowbry, who claimed that "highway advocates are already laying plans for an accelerated effort to blanket the nation with asphalt."[11] In 1968, auto critics had some legitimate points: automobile accidents killed nearly 55,000 people per year, and auto pollution obscured skylines and clogged people's lungs in most of our larger cities.

Those problems have been significantly reduced, partly due to improvements in highway construction and other technologies and partly due to congressional legislation mandating safer and cleaner cars. Auto opponents ignore these gains, often claiming that air quality is getting worse when it is getting better or arguing that freeways create dangerous conditions when, by attracting cars away from local streets, they make cities safer. They also add in all sorts of other spurious costs of driving, such as the Iraq War or the cost of making cell phone calls from your car.[12]

"Automobiles are often conveniently tagged as the villains responsible for the ills of cities," observed Jane Jacobs. "But the destructive effects of automobiles are much less a cause than a symptom of our incompetence at city building." Planners "do not know what to do with automobiles in cities because they do not know how to plan for workable and vital cities anyhow—with or without automobiles."[13]

Despite Jacobs's warning, many planners happily used anti-auto arguments to promote the idea that they, rather than the engineers, should plan state and regional transport systems. Finally, in 1991,

Congress required all states and urban areas to undertake comprehensive transportation planning in order to qualify for federal transportation funds.[14] Planners were right in saying that transportation improvements influenced land use, and comprehensive planning might not have been bad if anyone had been capable of doing it. But no one was, and particularly not planners. Instead, planners turned their newly gained power into an anti-automobile crusade.

In doing so, planners turned the engineers' priorities almost completely upside down. Instead of trying to prevent traffic from reaching E or F levels of congestion, they sought to create such congestion. Instead of trying to increase safety, they consciously adopted plans that made roads more dangerous. They hoped that more congested and more dangerous roads would discourage people from driving, yet they lacked any evidence that this was so. Although automobiles provided nearly 90 percent of passenger transport in this country, auto users were not organized to stop the planners. But planners went out of their way to gain the support of well-organized auto haters.

As Peterson predicted, a major consequence of transferring transportation planning from the engineers to the planners is that transportation decisions have become highly politicized. While the engineers based their decisions on quantifiable criteria—safety, efficiency, speed, pavement quality—the criteria used by urban planners were vague and fluid: pedestrian friendly, transit oriented, anti-sprawl. This made them subject to manipulation by special interest groups and politicians interested more in pork barrel than in transportation. Before 1980, for example, Congress was content to let the states decide where to spend federal highway money. But Congress included 10 *earmarks*, or directions that specific projects be funded, in the 1982 transportation bill. Since then, the number of earmarks has steadily increased to more than 6,000 in the 2005 bill. These earmarks severely tie the hands of any states that are truly interested in improving the safety and efficiency of their transportation systems.

27. The Benefits of the Automobile

Since the dawn of the Republic, no invention has enhanced the quality of life of the average American as much as the mass-produced automobile. Americans today are far more mobile, they earn much higher incomes, and they have access to far more consumer goods than a hundred years ago. It is no exaggeration to attribute most of these improvements to the wide availability of automobiles.

Automobiles have also offered Americans an incredible array of social and recreational opportunities as well as many benefits for health, safety, land uses, and even freedom. The only inventions that might come close to the effect of the auto are the railroad and the computer. But gains in personal mobility, income, homeownership, and other lifestyle improvements were far greater between 1900 and 1980 than they were before 1900, when the railroad was the major form of transportation, and after 1980, when the computer began to influence every American's life. Because so much of what planners do today aims to reduce auto driving, it is worth reviewing in detail the benefits that the automobile has produced.

Mobility

People who have grown up in the auto age can hardly imagine how much the automobile has changed people's lives. Automobiles have hugely increased the sheer mobility of the American people. Comparing driving today with transit and train riding in the past clearly reveals the benefits of automobility.

In 1920, the United States had the world's most intensive network of both intercity trains and urban mass transit. This was the apex of the pre-auto public transportation system, with close to 20,000 scheduled intercity trains every day and streetcar or other rail transit systems in nearly every city of 10,000 people or more. Per capita use of both transit and intercity rail peaked in about 1920. In that year, the average American traveled less than 450 miles on intercity passenger trains and about 820 miles on urban transit.[1] Counting only those Americans who lived in urban areas, they rode an average of 1,600 miles per year on transit.

Think about that for a minute. Imagine being confined to one 450-mile out-of-town trip each year. That is less than a roundtrip from Boston to New York City or a one-way trip from Atlanta to Orlando. Meanwhile, 1,600 miles of urban transit per year is only 5.1 miles per workday (at the six workdays per week common before 1920). If you live as much as 2.5 miles from work, that leaves none for shopping, recreation, or socializing. Imagine being limited to one roundtrip per day to anywhere in your city that is further than you can easily reach on foot and to no more than one intercity roundtrip per year.

It is far more likely, of course, that some people—mainly the wealthy and certain white-collar workers—were highly mobile, taking several transit trips each day and numerous intercity train trips each year. Meanwhile, almost everyone else, including factory workers and other low-income urbanites as well as farmers and other ruralites, was confined to travel within walking distance or, in the case of farmers, within horseback-riding distance of their homes.

Lack of mobility was a particular hardship for rural residents. "No burden has ever set quite as heavily on farming and upon the farm family as has the curse of isolation and loneliness," wrote the editor of *American Agriculturalist* in 1927.[2] Women felt the isolation the most, as they made fewer trips beyond the farm.[3] Even small-town residents were isolated in the sense that they rarely met anyone except their neighbors.

Residents of rural areas and small towns were quick to see the benefits of automobility. "We'd rather do without clothes than give up the car," a small-town resident told social scientists in the 1920s.[4] "I'll go without food before I'll see us give up the car," echoed her neighbor.[5] When researchers asked a farmwoman why her family purchased a car when their home still lacked indoor plumbing, she responded, "Why, you can't go to town in a bathtub!"[6]

By comparison with 1920, in 2005, the average American traveled more than 16,000 miles per year by auto, or more than 12 times as many miles as they ever rode on trains and public transit.[7] Although only 21 percent of our population today is rural, 40 percent of the driving is rural, suggesting that urbanites do a lot of intercity driving. The 60 percent that is urban translates to about 12,500 miles per urban resident per year, nearly eight times as many miles as the average urbanite ever rode on mass transit.

Before the railroad, the average American walked perhaps 2,000 miles per year. Railroads and streetcars may have doubled this mobility for some Americans, but automobiles quadrupled the mobility provided by railroads and walking put together.

Not only are we more mobile, this mobility is far more egalitarian than mass transportation was in its heyday. Well over 90 percent of American families have at least one car, and many of those who don't could own one but choose not to. Some new cars cost more than $100,000 while some used cars cost less than $1,000, but they all have more-or-less equal access to nearly all America's highways, roads, and streets.

Admittedly, automobility has not yet reached every American family. Nearly 95 percent of white families own one or more cars, but only about 75 percent of black families do. Yet both these percentages are probably higher than the share of Americans who regularly traveled by train or urban transit in 1920. Low auto-ownership rates among black families should raise a red flag to those who seek to curb future increases in driving and auto ownership: their efforts will make it especially hard for the nation's remaining low-income people to get out of poverty.

Incomes

Auto critics claim that the increased mobility provided by the auto does not translate to increased access to jobs, goods, and services. Instead, they say, urban sprawl has spread things out, thus forcing people to travel more than they would have to in a pedestrian- or transit-oriented city. This is simply untrue. In fact, automobility has produced huge benefits, and low-density urban development simply enables people to take best advantage of those benefits.

The biggest benefit is increased incomes. The incredible mobility provided by the mass-produced automobile has significantly boosted personal incomes in the past century. We typically think that people buy cars only when they can afford to do so, but the reality is more complex. Incomes are increased by auto ownership as much as if not more than ownership is increased by higher incomes.

One hundred years ago, the average American worker earned, after adjusting for inflation to today's dollars, about $10,600 a year.[8]

By 1929, when half of all American families owned an auto, this had increased to $17,000 a year.[9] Today, income per worker (including benefits) exceeds $72,000 per year, more than seven times what it was before the automobile. Much if not most of this increase is due to the automobile.

Compare changes in income during the auto age with changes during the railroad age. In the 70 years from 1830, when the first railroads began operating in the United States, to 1900, per capita gross domestic product (adjusted for inflation) increased by 225 percent. In the 70 years from 1900, when the first autos began appearing in the United States, to 1970, per capita gross domestic product increased by 275 percent. Since then, it has doubled again.[10] Considering that both 1830 to 1900 and 1900 to 1970 included depressions, wars, and the emergence of other technologies, it is clear that the gains in the latter period were greater than the first.

Two factors lead to the conclusion that the mass-produced automobile alone is responsible for most of the increase in income since 1900:

- First, by increasing commuter speeds, autos give workers access to better jobs and employers access to a more highly skilled workforce. Research suggests that this factor alone accounts for around half the increase in incomes.
- Second, mass production not only increased worker pay, enabling workers to buy autos, but mass production itself was enabled by the automobile, because only autos could give large numbers of workers access to the far-flung factories that mass production required.

Autos give people access to far more jobs than they could reach on foot or by mass transit. In Cincinnati, a typical, medium-sized urban area, most residents can reach 99 percent of the region's jobs within 20 minutes of driving. But even allowing 40 minutes—twice as long as the auto trip—most residents can reach only 40 percent of the region's jobs riding public transit.[11]

From the employers' viewpoint, automobiles provide a more productive workforce because autos give them access to more potential employees who are likely to have the skills they need. One study found that a 10 percent increase in travel speeds led to a 3 percent increase in worker productivity, mainly by offering employers a larger pool of potential workers.[12] At this rate, a 900 percent increase in travel speeds from 3 miles per hour walking (which was how most urbanites got to work before 1890) to 30 miles per hour driving would increase worker productivities by 270 percent. Since greater productivities mean that employers can pay their employees more, close to half the increase in incomes since 1900 may be attributable to the increased travel speeds allowed by the automobile.

Automobiles also increased productivity and incomes by ushering in the age of assembly-line production. While Henry Ford did not invent the assembly line, he was the first to use a moving assembly line to build his Model Ts. This method of production turned out to be so boring, yet so profitable, that Ford doubled wages to $5 a day and reduced work from 54 to 40 hours a week—steps he called "one of the finest cost-cutting moves we ever made" because it increased morale and reduced employee turnover.[13]

Modern assembly lines so increased worker incomes that workers could, for the first time, afford to buy the cars they were making. But assembly lines also meant that workers were more likely to use cars to get to work. Before assembly lines, goods were typically manufactured in multistory buildings. A frame might be assembled on the fifth floor, coil springs added on the fourth, stuffing on the third, upholstery on the second, and finishing touches on the first to create a sofa or stuffed chair. Moving assembly lines stretched production out horizontally, so a factory that once occupied a city block now covered many acres. Ford's Rouge River plant, for example, was a mile wide, one-and-a-half miles long, and employed as many as 100,000 workers—far more than could live within easy walking distance.

While workers might be able to walk to the old-style factories, the large expanse covered by the assembly lines dictated that some form of mechanized transportation was needed to get workers to their jobs. This produced a synergistic effect: assembly lines increased worker incomes so they could afford to own cars, and because they could own cars more industries could build far-flung factories using moving assembly lines. These industries moved from urban centers to suburban areas where land was less expensive. This industrial sprawl effectively rules out other forms of commuting, so Americans could not possibly have the incomes they enjoy today without cars. In short, the automobile enabled American workers to find better-paying jobs and live in more desirable low-density neighborhoods.

Numerous studies show that auto ownership continues to help low-income people escape poverty. "Car ownership is a significant factor in improving the employment status of welfare recipients," say University of California (Los Angeles) (UCLA) planners Paul Ong and Ellen Blumenberg.[14] Helping the poor, say Yale economist Katherine O'Regan and University of California (Berkeley) economist John Quigley, means "promoting the mass transit system that works so well for the nonpoor—the private auto."[15]

One Portland study found that people without a high-school diploma were 80 percent more likely to have a job and earned $1,100 more per month if they had a car. In fact, the study found that owning a car was more helpful to getting a job than getting a high-school-equivalent diploma.[16] Another study by University of California researchers found that closing the black-white auto ownership gap would close nearly half the black-white employment gap.[17]

Auto ownership is so important to helping people out of poverty that welfare agencies in more than 50 urban areas in 25 states started "ways-to-work" programs that help low-income people buy their first cars.[18] These programs offer people low-interest loans of up to $4,000 to buy a used car or smaller loans to help people repair a nonworking car they already own.

The director of one of the nation's largest mass-transit agencies responded in horror to this idea. "We can't give cars to low-income people," he said. "It would cause too much congestion!"[19] The Soviet Union proved that poverty is one way to prevent congestion, but that does not mean it is a good thing.

Researchers at New York University have shown that increased incomes are closely tied to increased auto ownership in nations throughout the world.[20] They attribute the growth in auto ownership to rising incomes, but in other countries, as in the United States, the relationship is actually more complex. Countries that have tried to restrict auto driving and penalized auto ownership have lower incomes than those in the United States, partly due to those restrictions.

Western Europeans drive only about 70 percent as many miles per capita as Americans.[21] But that doesn't mean they take transit all that much more: the average Parisian travels 1,300 miles per year on transit; the average Londoner less than 2,400 miles per year, or only a little more than American urbanites used transit in 1920. But they drive close to 4,000 miles per capita per year in cities, plus thousands more between cities.[22]

Though Europeans drive more than they ride transit, they are still less mobile overall than Americans. This could be partly a function of structure: European cities are denser and so people don't need to go as far to get to various destinations. But it is more a function of economics: per capita incomes are lower; unemployment rates are higher; and, thanks to taxes, the cost of driving is higher, so people just don't drive as much.

Several members of the European Parliament recently charged that European policies of heavily taxing autos and fuel to heavily subsidize railroads was "strangling Europe's potential."[23] They cited research showing that, despite these policies, the passenger and freight movements over the roads were 20 times as valuable as those over rail lines.[24] Further increases in taxes aimed at reducing driving would "potentially endanger the European economy with all the consequences, for unemployment in particular, that this would entail."[25]

Americans should heed the same warning. Disincentives to the automobile are likely to harm the economy, with the greatest effect falling on low-income families. Whatever the problems with driving—toxic pollution, greenhouse gas emissions, energy consumption, and so forth—solving them with new technologies will be more successful and have fewer economic effects than attempting to reduce per capita driving.

Freight Transport Costs

Trucks have contributed to a huge reduction in transport costs, which in turn significantly reduces consumer costs. "In the United States transport costs before 1900 were enormously high," say economists Edward Glaeser and Janet Kohlhase.[26] They observe that transportation's share of our economy has fallen from 8 percent in 1929 to just 3 percent today, and the overall cost of moving manufactured goods has fallen by 90 percent.[27]

The biggest decline has been in the cost of shipping by rail, while trucking remains more expensive. But this disguises the fact that the combined cost of rail and truck is far less than the cost of rail alone. Rail costs were once high because of the high cost of gathering cars from various origins, sorting them, breaking them up, and delivering them to various destinations. Today, trucks do these jobs much more economically, while rails are dedicated to moving large volumes of commodities, such as coal, grain, or containers, from one point to another. Without the trucks, and streets on which they can drive—whose costs are shared with car drivers—freight transport would be far more expensive than it is today and modern "just-in-time" manufacturing methods would be impossible.

A major contributor to the reduction in freight costs is the intermodal shipping container. First developed in the 1950s, shipping containers allow easy transfer of freight from ships to railcars to trucks, thus allowing each form of transport to do what it does best: move across oceans and waterways, move large quantities from point to point across land, and move small quantities from their origins or to their final destinations. Development of the modern intermodal container is credited to the owner of a trucking company who sought to gain an advantage over rivals by reducing costs.[28]

The reduction in transport costs combined with the revolution in telecommunications has led *The Economist* writer Frances Cairncross to pronounce the "death of distance."[29] Manufacturers think little of making components in five different countries, shipping them to another country for assembly, and then shipping them elsewhere for final assembly or delivery.

Another symptom of the death of distance is the increasing number of exurbanites: people with urban tastes and occupations living in small towns or rural areas. By some accounts, exurbs are growing faster than either suburbs or cities.[30] Thanks to low-cost delivery of goods by companies such as UPS or FedEx, Americans can live in remote areas without having to give up many of the amenities once exclusively enjoyed in big cities.

Consumer Costs

Thanks to reduced freight costs and the automobile, many consumer goods that were once accessible only to the wealthy are now affordable for almost everyone. In particular, food, clothing, housing, and household good costs have all greatly declined when measured as a share of personal income.

The share of personal incomes spent on food, for example, has declined by nearly 50 percent since 1929 even as the quality and variety of foods available have significantly increased. Clothing costs have declined by nearly two-thirds, while the cost of other household goods has declined by a third.[31]

Housing's share of income has declined by only 8 percent since 1929, yet the average home today is much larger, much higher in quality, and much more likely to be owned by its occupants than housing of 1929.[32] Homeownership rates have increased more than 40 percent, from less than 48 percent in 1930 to nearly 69 percent today.[33] This was almost entirely due to the increased mobility and incomes that automobiles offered to blue-collar workers.

The reductions in these costs have allowed consumers to devote more of their incomes to recreation, education, and charity. Unfortunately, the biggest increases have been in the costs of government and health care, changes largely independent of transportation issues.

Consumer Goods

Americans today have access to an incredible diversity of consumer goods. Grocery stores have grown from stocking a few hundred different products on their shelves in the 1910s to tens of thousands of different products today. A similar diversity of products can be found in clothing, hardware, electronic, and any number of other types of retail outlets.

I first noticed this diversity when I discovered that a nearby supermarket sold more than 50 different kinds of mustard. Baseball fan Barry Levenson had a similar epiphany in 1986 when, depressed after his beloved Boston Red Sox lost game seven of that year's World Series, he wandered into a supermarket and discovered the wide variety of mustards. "I took a vow," he now says, to "collect mustards until the Red Sox win a World Series."[34] By the time that happened in 2004, he had collected 4,257 different varieties of mustard—and continues to collect them for his Mustard Museum in Mount Horeb, Wisconsin.[35]

While you can't find 4,000 varieties of mustard in any single place outside of Mount Horeb, you can still find plenty of variety in most supermarkets. According to a report published by the Dallas Federal Reserve Bank, from the early 1970s to the late 1990s, the number of varieties of milk on a typical supermarket's shelves increased from 4 to 19; the number of breakfast cereals increased from 160 to 340; the number of soft drink brands increased from 20 to 87; and the number of over-the-counter pain relievers increased from 17 to 141.[36]

Variety such as this can be found only in large stores, and only automobiles can bring enough people to a store to support the kind of diversity that such large stores provide. In 1912, the typical neighborhood grocery store served only a few hundred families, and sold just 300 different products, increasing to 600 by 1924.[37]

In 1930, Michael Cullen opened what many regard as the nation's first supermarket on Long Island, New York. Unlike neighborhood grocery stores, the King Kullen Market was located not in a residential area but in a vacant garage in a business district. Cullen's idea was to have a large store offering more than a thousand different products located in an area with plenty of free parking. By marking up prices just 5 percent or less above his cost, Cullen attracted customers from 75 to 100 miles away and made up in volume what he lost in low markups.[38]

A&P, Safeway, Kroger, and other grocery chains soon replaced their neighborhood stores with supermarkets. In 1932, Kroger opened the first *park and shop*: a freestanding store featuring its own parking lot for 75 cars.[39] As more people bought cars, the supermarkets' customer bases grew and so did the stores. Because 25,000 people will have a wider diversity of tastes than 5,000, a store serving 25,000 can offer more products. By 1952, a typical supermarket had 4,000 products for sale; by 2000, it had upward of 30,000 and some had more than 100,000.[40]

Today, traditional supermarkets no longer dominate the grocery business. Instead, they must compete with convenience stores such as 7-Eleven, natural food stores such as Whole Foods, limited-assortment stores such as Trader Joe's, club warehouses such as Costco, and supercenters such as Wal-Mart and Target. The consumer is the winner as each new format offers more choice and lower costs. None of these types of stores would be possible without automobiles.

Automobiles have led to a similar diversity in other retail fields. When Sears, the catalog company, began opening retail stores in 1925, it purchased large lots on the outskirts of downtown retail districts so it could provide free parking. This enabled it to become the nation's leading retailer for many decades.

The adoption of parking areas by retailers and other businesses led to the strip development, which auto critics particularly revile. "The highway strip is not just a sequence of eyesores," says James Kunstler. "The pattern it represents is also economically catastrophic, an environmental calamity, socially devastating, and spiritually degrading."[41] "Strip development is contrary to the basic elements of good planning," says an urban planner. "It consumes open space and depletes natural resources, impedes pedestrian and non-motorized traffic, grows outward from the limits of existing development, and ruins any sense of place."[42] Of course, neither writer documents his claims, which are fundamentally based on aesthetics.

The problem, as sociologist Herbert Gans has noted in another context, is that planners often view the world through the eyes of a tourist rather than those of a resident.[43] While tourists seek aesthetic pleasure, residents want serviceability. From a resident's point of view, strip developments make perfect sense. Strips never exist in isolation. Instead, they are invariably surrounded by low- to moderate-density housing. The commercial development itself is typically just 200 to 400 feet deep. Behind the businesses is often a narrow band of apartments, which buffer the commercial area from neighborhoods of single-family homes.

In other words, businesses and residents have sorted themselves into the places they prefer. Suburban residents want to live on quiet streets, while businesses want to locate on arterials where they are visible to large numbers of potential customers. Illinois historians John Jakle and Keith Sculle traced this sorting process over time on University Avenue, a boulevard connecting Champaign and Urbana, Illinois (see table 27.1). In 1919, University had more than 150 homes, three-fourths of which were owner occupied, but only 9 businesses. As the street became a major automotive corridor, the number of homes declined while the number of businesses grew. By 1989, there were only 18 homes—just 2 of which were owner occupied—and 73 businesses. The number of businesses had declined slightly from 1979 as some grew larger, while smaller businesses such as gas stations moved to other areas.

Planners often blame strip developments on past zoning practices that mandated a separation of uses. In fact, you will find strip developments in cities that have no zoning; zoning that reinforces strip developments merely reflects the preferences of homeowners and businesses.

Table 27.1
HOMES AND BUSINESSES ON UNIVERSITY AVENUE

Year	Dwellings	Businesses
1919	151	9
1929	153	23
1939	145	50
1949	138	71
1959	112	94
1969	69	92
1979	39	96
1989	18	73

SOURCE: John A. Jakle and Keith A. Sculle, *The Gas Station in America* (Baltimore: Johns Hopkins Press, 1994), pp. 212, 214.

Strip developments do "things no city can do without," observes Portland State University planning professor Carl Abbott, noting that they provide low-cost space for start-up companies, specialty businesses, and retailers that serve minorities. Referring in particular to Portland's 82nd Avenue, Abbot says, "This corridor of asphalt, car lots and old-world politics keeps Portland honest."[44]

In 2003, I did a census of businesses along McLoughlin Boulevard, another Portland-area strip development. For a five-mile stretch, McLoughlin featured an average of more than 100 businesses per mile. This represented a density of about 1.3 businesses per acre, only a little less than the density of Oregon's largest shopping mall. This density undermines the claim that strips are a waste of open space. Moreover, the range of businesses available on McLoughlin was much larger than found in any shopping mall.

In addition to 36 car dealerships, 60 other auto-oriented businesses, 70 restaurants, 22 grocery stores, and 24 banks and other financial institutions, McLoughlin offered residents opportunities to

- buy and learn how to play musical instruments;
- buy dance costumes and learn how to dance;
- buy rubber stamps, skateboards, sports cards, flowers, and scuba-diving equipment;
- rent a U-Haul to carry away the things they buy;
- store their purchases in one of three storage facilities;

- buy food for their dog at one of two pet shops, bathe it at a do-it-yourself dog wash, and take it to one of two veterinarians; and
- take whatever they kill when hunting with their dog to a butcher who specializes in making sausages and smoked meats from wild game.

If all these choices are overwhelming to some, there is even a headache clinic to relieve their pain.

Thus, a typical strip development offers a tremendous amount of consumer choice. This choice results largely from the competition that results when people are mobile enough to choose among retailers. In turn, this choice reduces consumer costs. When Wal-Mart begins selling groceries in a community, for example, the average price of groceries in that community falls by 6 to 12 percent.[45] Similar savings follow the introduction of other new retail formats.

Most of the prescriptions planners offer in place of strips would reduce this consumer choice. One critic of strip developments says plans should require "retail clusters or nodes around major intersections, and allow some transitional uses like professional offices along the rest of the road."[46] Limiting the number of street access points to retail sites would drive up the price of retail land, increase consumer costs, and reduce the number and variety of retail establishments available to consumers.

Even more prescriptively, New Urbanism calls for more pedestrian-friendly "main streets," with stores fronting on the sidewalks, parking in the rear, and apartments upstairs. This leads to a very different mix of stores than is found in a strip development. Given the competitive disadvantage of hidden parking, stores on such main streets tend to become boutiques serving niche markets rather than outlets for general consumer goods. Such boutiques attract large amounts of auto traffic because urban densities are rarely great enough to support such stores through walking alone.

Social and Recreational Benefits

Very few Americans today recognize the social and recreational benefits provided by the automobile because few have lived in a society without autos. Before the automobile, rural residents, particularly women, could live for months at a time without seeing anyone except for their immediate family members.[47] Even urban residents could be isolated: people who moved from their hometowns might return to see their families only once or twice in their lifetimes. Passenger trains only partly filled this gap because few could afford to ride them frequently.

The automobile eliminated this social and familial isolation. For the past 50 or so years, Americans have thought little of driving hundreds of miles to visit friends or family. Many happily take trips of several thousand miles every year or so. Whether it is friends across town or grandparents across the country, the automobile has kept Americans in frequent personal contact with one another.

The auto has also opened the door to all sorts of recreational opportunities that previously existed only for the rich, if they existed at all. "Use of the automobile has apparently been influential in spreading the 'vacation' habit," commented the authors of *Middletown* in 1929. "The custom of having each summer a respite, usually of two weeks, from getting-a-living activities, with pay unabated, is increasingly common among the business class, but it is as yet very uncommon among the workers."[48]

Today, of course, nearly every American family takes yearly vacations. Skiing, backpacking, fly-fishing, boating, surfing, and beachcombing are only a few of the many outdoor sports enabled by the automobile. As just one example, in 1904 only about 1 out of every 6,000 Americans visited Yellowstone National Park. By the mid-1960s, it was more than 1 out of every 100 Americans.[49]

Health and Safety

While autos have been accused of killing people, they have also greatly contributed to public health and safety. Thanks to paved streets and automotive technology, fire departments save hundreds of thousands of homes and thousands of lives from fire each year.[50] Paramedics in ambulances also save thousands of lives every year.

As just one example, thousands of Americans suffer from sudden cardiac arrest annually. A rapid response is critical to ensuring the survival of such people. If treated with a defibrillator within two minutes, about 90 percent survive; after six minutes, only 10 percent survive.[51] By reaching victims within six minutes, fire departments and paramedics in America's 50 largest cities alone save close to 1,000 lives a year.[52]

Another benefit of automobiles was vividly demonstrated in the recent flooding of New Orleans caused by Hurricane Katrina. Residents of New Orleans and nearby communities who owned cars

216

were able to evacuate quickly before the hurricane. Residents without cars were left behind.

Natural disasters such as hurricanes tend to be far more devastating to developing nations than developed countries because people in developed countries have greater mobility to escape predictable events and to move to areas with food, safe water, and other essentials after unpredictable events. Due to our own increasing automobility, disaster-related deaths in the United States have steadily fallen from more than 10,000 in 1900, the year of the Galveston hurricane, to a few dozen annually in recent years.

New Orleans was exceptional because, in terms of mobility, it was more like a developing country. According to the 2000 census, more than a quarter of New Orleans households—51,435—do not own an automobile, compared with just 7 percent in the rest of the nation. This makes New Orleans the nation's second-most transit-dependent major city after New York. While many pundits tried to make it a racial issue—"the white people got out," said an article in the *New York Times*—it was not. As the *Times* itself noted, white families with cars got out, as did black families with cars. Families without cars, white and black, for the most part did not.[53]

When Hurricane Rita struck the Gulf Coast a few weeks later, close to three million people evacuated, nearly all by car. While people complained of congestion, anyone who wanted to leave was able to get out before the storm hit. Rita is blamed for only 30 fatalities, 24 of them from a fire on a bus transporting carless people.[54] Automobiles were clearly key to saving lives that might have been lost due to Rita.

Curiously, planners responded by arguing that transit *should* have worked to get people out, ignoring the fact that it did not. Evacuation by automobile would create too much congestion, they added, ignoring the fact that people with cars escaped in spite of congestion. One New Orleans planner who did not own an automobile, but managed to escape Katrina by renting one of the last available rental cars in the city, perversely argued that the problem was "our extreme dependence on cars," implying that transit might have worked better if even fewer New Orleanians had cars.[55] Never mind that this would leave them dependent on the competence of public officials who failed to implement their carefully prepared emergency plans to evacuate transit-dependent people from New Orleans.[56] Rather than

217

find ways to reduce people's transit dependence, this planner held a conference in New Orleans on "Disaster Planning for the Carless Society."[57]

Others fantasized that trains could have evacuated those New Orleans residents who lacked automobiles. But a new Amtrak plan to store 24 passenger railcars in New Orleans and also use cars from regional trains has the capacity to evacuate only about 4,000 people, less than 4 percent of the number of pre-Katrina New Orleanians whose families lacked cars. Rail lines also lack the flexibility of roads: if a road is flooded or knocked out by an earthquake, there are usually plenty of substitute roads; but if a rail line is out of service, there may be no alternatives.

Automobiles give people the freedom to deal with disasters on their own terms and timetables. Even if buses or trains were available, people would be reluctant to take them. Would the bus or train take them where they wanted to go? Would they be available when the people were ready to go? Could people take their pets and precious belongings? Could they come back when they wanted to return? The automobile frees people from dependence on the whims of other people's rules and schedules.

Freedom

As most teenagers know, the key to the family automobile is the key to freedom. And not just for teenagers: auto ownership has helped both women and minorities achieve personal freedom and civil rights.

"Working mothers are much more dependent on driving alone than comparable male parents," says Sandra Rosenbloom, a University of Arizona transportation researcher. Unlike men who tend to drive straight home from work, women use cars to do errands such as shopping and picking up the kids, she says. One advantage of private autos, she adds, is that they offer women greater security than public transit. Efforts to discourage auto driving, she says, penalize women much more than men.[58] When auto hater Jane Holtz Kay responds that it is "grim" that women have to suffer "vehicular bondage," Rosenbloom answers, "You wouldn't believe how owning their first car frees women." Kay's non sequitur response: "How like a man."[59]

"The civil rights movement, which began with the Montgomery (Ala.) Bus Boycott, would have been a failure had it not been for the automobile," says *Washington Post* writer Warren Brown. Because of this, he adds, "I've always viewed automobiles as freedom rides."[60]

Blacks were able to boycott the Montgomery bus system by sharing rides to work, school, and church. Black ministers (and one white minister of a black congregation) organized carpools with hundreds of cars. Black taxi drivers gave rides to fellow blacks for 10 cents (the bus fare) despite threats of legal action if they did not charge the minimum 45-cent taxi fare. Black churches purchased station wagons to help their parishioners support the boycott. In short, says Brown, blacks used "their private automobiles to drive around Jim Crow."[61]

It is no coincidence that the civil rights movement and the women's liberation movement achieved their greatest successes after the automobile became the dominant form of transportation in America. More than any other invention, the automobile offers people freedom and opportunity without regard to race, creed, or gender.

Land Use

Automobiles are blamed for "wasting" land in the form of urban sprawl. Yet autos actually have produced significant land-use benefits.

Consider first the land supposedly wasted by sprawl. According to the U.S. Department of Agriculture, urban land increased from 15 million acres in 1945 (the earliest year for which data are available) to 60 million acres today. During this time, urban populations increased by 160 percent, so if densities had remained the same as in 1945, urban areas would occupy only 39 million acres today. Thus, some 21 million acres of urbanization might be attributed to postwar automobile-oriented sprawl.[62]

Of course, whether this is a waste depends on your point of view. Low-density development brought the American dream of owning a home with a yard to far more people than ever before. Large yards do not destroy open space so much as they convert one form of open space—farms and forests—to another—backyards. From the point of view of watersheds and certain kinds of wildlife, backyards may even be better than intensively managed croplands.

Still, automobiles have more than made up for the 21 million acres of low-density development. Thanks to autos, trucks, and tractors, farmers across the country no longer needed to dedicate tens of millions of acres of land to pasture for horses. As a result, between 1920 and 1970, farmers returned 82 million acres of pastureland to forests.[63] This is almost certainly the largest area of deforested land ever to be reforested. The number of acres reported as forestlands has declined since 1970, but nearly all that decline resulted from the transfer of federal forestlands to the National Park Service, which (by the Department of Agriculture's reckoning) takes them out of the forestland category.[64]

Forests provide much more biodiversity than pastures. Instead of producing fodder for horses, these lands now offer habitat for wildlife, wood for housing, and cleaner water for fish and downstream users.

At the same time, farmers converted millions of other acres of pastures to croplands. When horses were the main source of farm power, virtually all farms had to dedicate a portion of their acreage to pasture. Now, farmers can dedicate their most productive lands to growing crops, while less productive lands are used for range or forests.

As of 2002, the United States had about 442 million acres of cropland, about 40 million more than it had in 1920.[65] Nearly all this increase came from pasturelands. Since pastureland is one of the least valuable uses of agricultural lands, this conversion contributes to overall agricultural productivity.

By any measure, the total amount of urbanized land represents no more than 5 percent of the United States as a whole, and urban sprawl has had a negligible effect on farms, forests, or open space. As the Department of Agriculture says, urbanization is "not considered a threat to the nation's food production."[66]

Yet the automobile's positive effect on the nation's forests and croplands has been much more significant, as it increased croplands by 10 percent and forests by more than 13 percent. When adding the 82 million acres of forestlands to the 40 million acres of croplands, autos improved the management of nearly six times as many rural acres as the 21 million acres that have been developed into low-density urban areas since 1945. On balance, autos, trucks, and tractors did far more good than harm to America's overall land uses.

28. Costs Exaggerated

While they ignore the benefits of auto driving, urban planners and their anti-auto allies greatly exaggerate the costs. They claim that driving imposes unbearable costs on users, requires huge subsidies from taxpayers, generates terrible pollution, and inflicts various other harms on society. At best, these claims are overstated; at worst, they are simply wrong.

Planners in Santa Cruz County, California, somehow calculated that auto drivers spent an average of 86 cents per mile in 2000.[1] This is almost exactly three times the actual amount Americans spent to drive that year. Planners were 200 percent off because they based their calculations on numerous assumptions that they never bothered to verify. Among those assumptions were that everyone buys their cars new, pays the maximum finance charge, drives only 13,000 miles per year, and junks the car as soon as it is fully paid off. Of these assumptions, the only one that is even close is the 13,000 miles per year.[2]

The remaining assumptions, however, are obviously wrong. According to the Department of Commerce, Americans spent $793 billion on driving in 2000, including purchases of new and used autos and trucks, rentals and leasing, parts, repairs, fuel, oil, parking, tolls, insurance, and taxes on those goods.[3] They drove 2.75 trillion miles in 2000,[4] for an average cost per mile of 28.9 cents.

Some of this cost is not truly a cost of driving. Americans use their automobiles to make personal statements about themselves. Thorstein Veblen derisively called this *conspicuous consumption,*[5] but whether or not you approve of it, clearly some spending on autos is not strictly needed for transportation. Do people really need a Cadillac or Lexus when a Chevrolet or Toyota will transport them just as fast, as safely, and more or less as comfortably? About 21 percent of the cost of driving is buying new or used cars, so depending on where your definition of luxury begins, perhaps 5 to 10 percent of the calculated cost of driving isn't truly related to transportation.

One cost counted by Santa Cruz planners that is not included in Department of Commerce calculations is the cost of "travel time (with average delays)," which the planners estimate to be 18.8 cents per mile. This assumes that people don't like to travel and consider all travel time to be a cost. Yet it should not surprise anyone that University of California transportation researcher Patricia Mohktarian has found that people enjoy traveling. Mohktarian even learned that commuters prefer a daily commute averaging about 16 minutes each way.[6] This gives them time to mentally prepare for their day on their way to work and decompress on their way home. Of course, this doesn't mean that commuters look forward to delays caused by congestion. But if that congestion is caused by inept or deliberate planning, it can hardly be counted as a cost of driving.

An anti-auto group known as the Surface Transportation Policy Project claims that driving consumes an inordinate share of people's incomes.[7] In reality, Americans spend almost precisely the same share of their incomes on personal transportation as they did 50 years ago, yet they travel far more today. In 1950, Americans spent 9.8 percent of their personal incomes on driving,[8] and drove an average of less than 3,000 miles per year.[9] By 2005, Americans spent 9.5 percent of their incomes on driving, and drove more than 10,000 miles a year.[10] Despite more than tripling the amount of driving we do, the cost of driving relative to income has stayed flat or declined.

Anti-auto groups act as though the increase in driving is a huge burden on people and have coined the term *auto dependent* to describe modern America. *Auto liberated* is more like it. Anyone who prefers not to drive can find neighborhoods in most cities where they can walk to stores that offer a limited selection of high-priced goods, enjoy limited recreation and social opportunities, and take slow public transit vehicles to some but not all regional employment centers, the same as many Americans did in 1920. But the automobile provides people with far more benefits and opportunities than they could ever have without it.

Auto opponents invariably exaggerate subsidies to highways and driving, usually by counting all government expenditures on highways as subsidies.[11] In fact, gas taxes were specifically created to act as a form of highway user fee. The numbers vary by state, but nationally gas taxes and other user fees, including tolls and weight-per-mile taxes paid by trucks, typically cover nearly 90 percent of the costs of building and operating highways.[12]

Part of the problem for highway finance is that the federal and state governments divert nearly a fifth of highway user fees to mass transit or other nonhighway programs. State and local highway departments must make this up with some other source of funds, but to auto drivers they are still user fees. In 2005, federal, state, and local governments spent $39 billion in general funds on roads, while they diverted $21 billion in highway user fees to other programs. The net subsidy, then, was about $18 billion, or about 12 percent of the $147.5 billion spent on roads in 2004.

If it were done correctly, ending that $18 billion subsidy could produce great benefits for highway users because better user fees would more closely tie the needs of highway users with the agencies that provide the roads. But ending the subsidy probably would not significantly alter driving habits because, as large as $18 billion is, it is trivial when compared with the nearly 4.8 trillion passenger miles carried on American highways in 2005.[13] This is less than 0.4 cents per passenger mile. After adjusting for inflation, back issues of *Highway Statistics* show that the total subsidy over the past 84 years has averaged less than 0.5 cents per passenger mile.[14] The cost per mile is even lower if we attribute part of the cost to the 1.1 trillion ton-miles of freight now carried on highways each year.[15]

On a state-by-state basis, the subsidies range from 2.6 cents per passenger mile in Alaska to minus 0.6 cents in Maryland. Eight states in addition to Maryland divert enough money out of their gas taxes so that highway users pay more fees than the states actually spend on roads. At the other end of the scale, nine states in addition to Alaska contribute more than a penny per passenger mile in subsidies to roads. Subsidies in the remaining 31 states are between 0 and 1 cent per passenger mile.[16]

A case could be made that some of these local expenses are not even subsidies to driving. Streets existed and were paid for by local taxes long before automobiles. In most modern subdivisions, developers build the streets and deed them to the city or county, which then has to pay only for maintenance. Street maintenance, snow removal, and other operations are as important for pedestrians, cyclists, and public safety as for auto drivers. Still, cars dominate many of these streets and auto user fees should pay for most of their maintenance.

Subsidies to highways are particularly insignificant when compared with subsidies to public transportation. Where highway subsidies averaged less than 0.4 cents per passenger mile, taxpayer subsidies to Amtrak are at least 21 cents per passenger mile.[17] Subsidies to urban transit in 2005 averaged 64 cents per passenger mile.[18] (For the record, subsidies to air travel are about a tenth of a penny per passenger mile.)

Total 2005 subsidies to transit amounted to $30 billion, nearly twice subsidies to highways.[19] Yet highways carry a hundred times as many passenger miles, and thousands of times more freight as transit lines. Rail and transit advocates use the myth of major highway subsidies to justify more subsidies to Amtrak and public transit. Yet Amtrak and transit subsidies have been far greater than highway subsidies since at least 1971, the year Amtrak began and the earliest year for which complete transit data are available.

Where highway users pay nearly 90 percent of the cost of building, maintaining, and operating highways, transit fares cover less than a quarter of the cost of building and running transit systems. At 0.4 cents per passenger mile, raising the cost of driving to end highway subsidies would not materially change people's travel habits. But at 65 cents a passenger mile, ending transit subsidies could significantly change people's use of transit.

If lack of funding were the problem, the transit subsidies of the past three decades would have greatly increased transit ridership. Yet actual ridership gains have been modest. Transit carried about 32 percent more trips in 2004 than 1975; during the same time period, driving more than doubled. Chapter 33 will show that, if anything, these subsidies have hampered transit ridership because they encouraged cities to build urban monuments rather than transit systems that would serve the people who want or need to ride transit.

Planners also exaggerate the social costs of driving. Santa Cruz planners, for example, pegged these costs at 33 cents per mile, including 5.6 cents for "land-use impacts," 0.5 cents for "transportation diversity and equity," and 4.2 cents for congestion. After reviewing various similar calculations of social costs and subsidies to the auto, University of California economist Mark Delucchi concluded that most "rely on outdated, superficial, nongeneralizable, or otherwise inappropriate studies."[20] After a lengthy series of studies, Delucchi estimated that the total social costs of driving averaged less than 7 cents a mile. Yet most of these were congestion and accidents, whose costs are paid mainly by auto users. The actual social costs estimated by Delucchi that are not paid by the users—mainly air, water, and noise pollution—averaged 3 cents a mile, two-thirds of which was air pollution.

Air pollution is often cited as a major cost of driving. Yet automotive air pollution has significantly declined in recent years and is expected to continue to decline in the future. Although Americans drove nearly three times as many miles in 2003 than in 1968, their cars produced less than half as much pollution.[21] Outside of Southern California, automotive air pollution is rapidly disappearing as a problem in the United States.[22]

Highways today are also much safer than they were a few decades ago. Highway fatalities peaked at 55,600 in 1972, an average of about 23 deaths per billion passenger miles.[23] Though driving has more than doubled, fatalities declined to less than 40,000 in 1992, an average of 11 per billion passenger miles. Total fatalities have increased slightly since then, but rates continued to drop to around 9 deaths per billion passenger miles in 2005. Urban roads tend to be safer than their rural counterparts, and the safest are urban interstates. People driving on urban interstate freeways suffer fewer than 3.5 fatalities per billion passenger miles, making those roads one of the safest forms of urban transportation anywhere in the world.[24]

One reason driving is safer may be that automobiles are safer, thanks to federal legislation requiring seat belts and other safety features. But the main reason is safer highways. Auto fatality rates have declined steadily from 453 deaths per billion vehicle miles in 1909 to less than 15 in 2003.[25] The rate of decline, about 3.5 percent per year, did not perceptibly increase after the passage of federal safety laws in 1970, showing that better highways, not safer cars, are responsible for most of the improvement. People concerned about automobile accidents should realize that the best remedy is safer roads.

29. The Panic over Peak Oil

The *peak oil* theory says that total world production of oil is about to peak and will thereafter decline even as demand continues to rise. Proponents of this theory say we need to completely redesign our cities because the world is running out of oil and, considering increased demand in China and other Asian nations, fuel prices will rapidly rise. Such high prices will mean an end to life as we know it—life in the suburbs with automobiles, shopping malls, big-box stores, drive-through espresso stands, and other conveniences we take for granted.

Some proponents of peak oil are actually petroleum geologists who have some idea what they are talking about. But many are simply people who hate suburbs and automobiles and are gleeful at the thought that they will soon go away. "Forget Wal-Mart and another $286 billion to pave over good land. Finally!" one group happily reports.[1] The peak-oil theory thereby helps politicians justify intrusive land-use regulations and wasteful transportation projects.

Leading the charge is James Howard Kunstler, author of *The Geography of Nowhere* (which argued that suburbs were "trashy and preposterous"),[2] *Home from Nowhere* (which advocated New Urbanism as a replacement for traditional suburbs),[3] and most recently, *The Long Emergency*, which predicts an apocalypse resulting from declining oil supplies.[4] As summarized in *Rolling Stone*, Kunstler's latest book argues that oil prices are rising to catastrophic levels, and that we will only be saved by building "walkable, human-scale towns."[5]

Kunstler is no petroleum geologist. As evidenced by his earlier books, he simply considers suburbs abominable. If peak oil means an end to the suburbs, then he is all for it. This attitude blinds him to a realistic assessment of his argument.

Broken down, Kunstler's conclusions depend on four separate hypotheses:

1. We are rapidly running out of oil and fuel prices will soon become unaffordable for ordinary auto drivers.

2. There are no substitutes for oil for powering automobiles.
3. Higher prices will necessarily mean less driving.
4. Less driving will favor New Urbanism over low-density suburbs.

If any one of these four hypotheses is wrong, we can throw Kunstler's argument out the car window. All four must be true to support government regulations or subsidies that favor New Urbanism over low-density suburbs or the diversion of highway funds to rail transit. In fact, it is likely that all these hypotheses are wrong.

1. Are We Running Out of Oil?

In 1920, the U.S. Geological Survey officially estimated that the United States had just 6.7 billion barrels of oil left, including undiscovered oil fields.[6] Eighty-two years later, the United States had produced 180 billion barrels of oil[7] and still had 22 billion barrels of proven reserves. The U.S. Geological Survey's 1920 estimate was off by a mere 2,900 percent, not counting oil that remains unproven or undiscovered today.

People have long feared we are about to run out of oil, but their predictions have all proven false. For example, Colin Campbell, author of the 1998 book *The Coming Oil Crisis*, made many predictions of future oil production from various countries in 1991 that were subsequently proven wrong.[8] Given that there is a fixed amount of oil in the world, someday we will doubtless see prices increase due to disappearing supplies. But that hasn't happened yet, and probably won't happen for at least 30 to 100 years.

Virtually all fluctuations in gasoline prices to date have resulted from political events and natural disasters, not to actual shortages of oil in the ground. Though Hurricanes Katrina and Rita briefly drove oil prices to more than $65 a barrel, that was less, after adjusting for inflation, than prices in 1979 through 1981.[9]

The U.S. Geological Survey estimates that the earth's total supply of oil is about 6 to 8 trillion barrels.[10] If we could get it, this would easily last another century. The problem is that most of this is not "cheap oil," and so is not included in listings of "proven reserves," which amount to just over 1 trillion barrels.[11] That trillion is estimated to last about 30 years.

The estimate of 1 trillion barrels of cheap oil is almost certainly conservative. For one thing, there are still parts of the globe that have not yet been fully explored. Thus, the 30-year time horizon for cheap oil is also conservative; while demand is increasing, known reserves of such cheap oil are also increasing.

After the cheap oil is gone, there is still plenty of oil in the ground.

- Venezuela estimates that it has at least 1.2 trillion barrels of tar sand or "heavy" oil, which is more expensive to extract and refine than ordinary oil.[12]
- Canada estimates that Alberta has another 1.8 trillion barrels in tar sands.[13]
- The United States estimates that Colorado, Utah, and Wyoming have 2.6 trillion barrels in oil shales, which will be even harder to extract than oil from tar sands.[14]

Other parts of the world are supposed to have another trillion or so barrels of oil shales. Taken together, these "unconventional" oil reserves add up to more than 6.5 trillion barrels—enough, if they can be extracted, to last more than 40 years even in the unlikely event that everyone in the world increases their oil consumption to U.S. levels of about 24 barrels per person per year.

Increased oil prices do not necessarily mean equivalent price hikes at the gasoline pump. For one thing, the cost of crude oil makes up only about half the total price of gasoline.[15] Between 1998 and 2005, the price per barrel of oil quadrupled, yet the price of a gallon of gasoline only doubled.[16]

More importantly, as new sources come on line, the costs of extracting those sources are bound to drop. Typically, people use the cheapest sources of a raw material first, then move on to the more expensive sources. But when they start on the more expensive sources, they quickly develop techniques for extracting and using the resource much more cheaply. As long as cheap Saudi Arabian oil is available, there is little incentive to find ways to cheaply extract and refine oil from tar sands or shales. But when the incentive arrives, expect the costs of refining and extraction to drop.

For example, U.S. production of iron once centered on the Great Lakes region, where high-grade ores were mined from about 1870 through 1950. When those ores were running out, scientists developed a process for mining low-grade ores, such as taconite, which continued through 1995 or so.[17] Despite having to rely on low-grade ores, U.S. steel production peaked in 1969[18] and 1969 pig iron prices were no greater than in 1900, 1910, or 1920, when top-quality ores were still being mined.[19]

Since then, U.S. steel production has fallen by nearly a third, and someone could easily write a "long emergency" book about "peak iron." Yet after adjusting for inflation, the price of steel today is considerably lower than it was in 1969.[20] Similarly, while the costs of extracting oil may rise—though not for many decades to the levels projected by Kunstler—the cost of gasoline and other refined products may not appreciably increase at all.

In short, there is no clear proof that any shortage-induced price increases will happen soon. For the next 30 years, at least, oil prices will depend more on political events and natural disasters than on actual supplies or extraction costs. After that time, extraction costs may rise, but those costs may not lead to significantly higher fuel prices for many decades.

2. Are There No Substitutes for Oil?

While it seems intuitive that the world's oil supply is ultimately limited, it is not so obvious that there are no substitutes for oil. Yet Kunstler has to take this as a given, because if there are substitutes his entire argument falls apart. "No combination of alternative fuels will allow us to run American life the way we have been used to running it," he asserts.[21]

Yet there are many possible substitutes for our current system of burning a gallon of gasoline for every 17 miles we drive.[22] First, modest increases in gasoline prices could lead carmakers to switch almost entirely to hybrid automobiles, as Toyota has already said it will do.[23] Combining hybrid engines with other improvements, such as less wind-resistant auto designs, could nearly double fuel economy. If other industries could make similar efficiency gains, we could nearly double our effective oil reserves.

We know such a response is possible. Between 1973 and 1991, the fuel efficiency of the average American car increased by 42 percent.[24] Since then, cheap oil has encouraged people to buy heavier cars with bigger engines and more amenities, such as air conditioning and power windows. Yet miles per gallon remained constant, indicating that the auto industry has continued to improve fuel *efficiency*, that is, ton-miles per gallon.[25] If fuel prices rise and remain permanently high, Americans will buy lighter, smaller cars, just as they did in the late 1970s and early 1980s, while the auto industry will continue to improve fuel efficiency.

Second, no one doubts that nuclear power could easily turn water into hydrogen that could be used in fuel-cell-powered automobiles without posing any risk of global warming. While Americans are not enthused about nuclear power, China is building dozens of nuclear power plants using new technologies that are supposed to be far safer and generate less waste than any used in the United States.[26] Kunstler dismisses this possibility by saying Americans won't accept nuclear power. But Americans may be quite willing to accept safe nuclear technologies, especially if rival countries use them to gain economic power and the alternative is giving up the automotive lifestyle.

Third, there are several other potential power sources, only some of which may contribute to global warming. Solar is not yet fully explored. The United States has a huge supply of coal, and coal gasification can keep the automobiles rolling albeit while producing greenhouse gases. The program of turning corn into ethanol is mainly a subsidy to agribusinesses and corn farmers, and it probably saves very little oil.[27] But who knows? Someone might figure out how to do it right.

While hybrid cars may be the short-term response to higher prices, no one can guess what technology will ultimately replace oil. We may not even find out within our lifetimes if oil turns out to be plentiful for the next century. It would be absurdly expensive for the government to promote one technology over others (as it is currently doing by subsidizing ethanol, among other things). Worse, government support could lock us into the wrong technology, leading to long-term waste.

One thing is certain: light-rail transit and other mass transit will never replace petroleum-fueled autos on a large scale. Most people will just not give up the mobility provided by the automobile for a slow, clunky train that doesn't go when and where they want to go.

3. Will Higher Prices Necessarily Mean Less Driving?

At first glance, it may seem obvious that people will drive less if gasoline prices rise, but it is not. Let's take a look at the history of spending on driving and gas and oil.

231

Since 1950, Americans have spent an average of 9.2 percent of their personal incomes on automotive transportation.[28] The year-to-year variation has been quite small, from about 8.1 to 10.1 percent. This suggests that people have a consistent budget for travel based on a percentage of their incomes.

By comparison, the percentage of driving costs that go for gas and oil vary dramatically from year to year.[29] In 1981, when inflation-adjusted oil prices reached an all-time high, Americans spent 40 percent of their driving expenditures on gas and oil. By 1998, it had fallen to 18 percent. This suggests that, when fuel prices rise, people reduce other auto expenses to keep total costs (as a percentage of their incomes) constant. They may keep their cars a little longer: the average age of a car in the United States grew from 6.6 years in 1969 to 8.9 years in 2001.[30] Or they may buy less luxurious cars. However, when fuel prices fall, people spend more on bigger or more luxurious cars.

People also seem to have two different budgets for travel: a dollar budget and a time budget. When incomes are low relative to the cost of driving, the dollar budget is the main limiting factor. When incomes are high enough, the time budget becomes the limiting factor: people won't average more than about 1.1 to 1.3 hours a day traveling no matter how low the cost.[31] When the time budget is limiting, people spend more of their travel budgets on luxuries. Because they can give up those luxuries when fuel prices rise, they are much less sensitive to changes in fuel costs.

Most Americans have already reached the limit of their time budgets. That means their main response to increased fuel prices will be to spend less on other aspects of driving. Of course, some Americans still have incomes low enough that their dollar budgets are limiting, so increased costs will cause them to drive less. The higher gasoline prices that Kunstler eagerly anticipates will have the greatest effects on such low-income people.

We can get some idea of the effects of high prices by looking at Europe, where high taxes have long kept gas prices two to three times higher than prices in America. European incomes are lower than those in America, so even without higher gas taxes you would expect them to drive less. While Europeans drive only about two-thirds as much per capita as Americans, per capita driving in France, Germany, Sweden, and the United Kingdom is growing by more

232

than 10 percent per year, compared with less than 2 percent per year in the United States.[32] High fuel taxes don't seem to slow this growth down.

In short, higher prices will affect driving mainly in low-income families. Moderate- and high-income families will respond by making other changes in their transportation expenses, most likely by keeping their cars a little longer and, when they do buy new cars, buying more fuel-efficient or less luxurious cars.

4. Will Less Driving Favor New Urbanism over Low-Density Suburbs?

Before Americans had cars, they lived in denser "traditional" communities, and many lived in mixed-use neighborhoods. New Urbanists such as Kunstler reason that, when cars disappear, people will cheerfully return to such neighborhoods. But is that the only possible outcome?

Before considering this question, it is worth asking: Is that even a desirable outcome? Kunstler, for one, has no doubt that it would be "a glorious way to live."

"Imagine it's 1881," says Kunstler. "You leave the office on Wabash in the heart of vibrant Chicago, hop on a train in a handsome, dignified station full of well-behaved people, and in thirty minutes you're whisked away to a magnificent house surrounded by deep, cool porches, nestled in a lovely, tranquil, rural setting with not a single trace of industrial hubbub."[33]

That sure sounds glorious. Of course, Kunstler isn't much of a historian, or he would know that only a tiny fraction of American city dwellers lived this way in 1881. Most of them lived in high-density housing, better known as tenements or slums. With sweatshop jobs, poor sanitation, and high crime, their lives were a lot less glorious than Kunstler describes.

Kunstler probably imagines that everyone could live in his traditional neighborhoods. Yet without the mobility provided by the automobile—the same mobility that allowed the children and grandchildren of 19th-century slum dwellers to increase their incomes and escape the tenements—this is unrealistic.

But let's say Kunstler's dream is possible. Is it likely? Or might Americans respond to high gas prices in other ways?

One possibility is that more people will telecommute and move even further away from urban centers than today's suburbs. As Ted Balaker of the Reason Foundation observes, telecommuting is growing faster than commuting by transit.[34] Although the Census Bureau doesn't measure exurbanization, some studies have concluded that the number of exurbanites (rural residents with urban incomes and tastes) is growing far faster than the number of New Urban residents.[35]

Another possibility is that more jobs than ever will move to the suburbs where people live and higher fuel prices will lead many of those people to live in suburbs close to their jobs. Such a "jobs-housing balance" is actually part of the smart-growth platform, but it doesn't mean an end to low-density suburbs or an increase in New Urban residences. Moreover, it effectively destroys the utility of rail or other high-capacity transit because there will be few or no job centers with enough jobs to attract that many transit commuters.

Even less appealing to smart-growth advocates is a third possibility: more people *and* jobs move out of the cities and suburbs to the exurbs. Many companies are already locating their manufacturing facilities in rural areas, where both factories and their employees can avoid high taxes, regulation, and congestion.[36]

Higher fuel prices could actually accelerate all these trends. Why sit in traffic burning expensive gasoline when you can work at home some days and drive 20 or 30 miles to work on uncongested rural roads on other days?

Meanwhile, one retail analyst predicts that, far from putting Wal-Mart out of business, higher fuel prices will "create further opportunities for one-stop-shop retailers like supercenters and warehouse club stores to win more day-to-day shoppers."[37] In other words, people will continue to drive to stores, but they will make fewer trips by going to bigger stores rather than the small shops that New Urbanists such as Kunstler favor.

Fuel costs influence two stages of the retail transaction: first, the cost of getting the customers to the stores, and second, the cost of getting the goods to the stores. Wal-Mart has become dominant by minimizing the second cost, and higher fuel prices may actually help that company. Higher-priced fuel will hit retailers located in congested urban areas the hardest, as their trucks are forced to burn fuel in stop-and-go traffic. Retailers located in rural areas and on urban fringes can keep these costs down, providing a net savings to customers who drive to their stores.

There's a Ford in Your Future

Proponents of the peak-oil theory use apocalyptic visions of an energy-poor future to advocate government subsidies and regulations aimed at ending the American dream of a home with a yard and freedom to move when and where people choose. Yet their visions critically depend on four assumptions that, when closely examined, do not stand up.

Peak oil will not devastate our economy because the earth has vast reserves of petroleum that are not counted by the peak-oil theorists. Any increases in energy prices that do take place will lead Americans to become more fuel efficient and explore new energy technologies. No matter what technology they select, they are not likely to drive significantly less than they do today.

To the extent that higher fuel prices change Americans' travel habits at all, those changes may actually accelerate the suburbanization and exurbanization trends that James Kunstler and other New Urban planners find offensive. If anything devastates our economy, it will be the intrusive government regulations and expensive rail transit systems that those planners want to impose on our urban areas.

30. Planning for Congestion

In the early 1960s, the great entrepreneur Henry J. Kaiser built Hawaii Kai, a development of thousands of homes east of Honolulu. One problem was that the narrow, two-lane Kalanianaole Highway that stretched five miles from Honolulu's edge to Kaiser's development was clearly inadequate to support the traffic Hawaii Kai would generate.[1]

To rectify this, the state of Hawaii announced an expensive study to examine whether it should add two new lanes to the highway. Kaiser, whose resumé included roads, dams, liberty ships, cement plants, steel and aluminum refineries, automobiles, and the world's first health maintenance organization, called then Governor William Quinn to offer to build the highway for the cost of the study. The governor told Kaiser that the state would have to put the project out for public bid. Kaiser submitted the low bid, and in four months the four-lane road was complete for less than the cost of the study.[2]

Kaiser's can-do attitude contrasts sharply with the many years needed to plan, study, and eventually build new highways today. Most states require that gasoline taxes be spent exclusively on highways, roads, and streets. But this includes funding planning studies for those roads. Rather than take steps to reduce congestion, many state and regional governments spend a large part of their share of gas taxes on endless studies.

According to the Texas Transportation Institute, congestion in 85 major urban areas wasted more than 420,000 person-years of time in 2003. Cars sitting in traffic unnecessarily burned 2.3 billion gallons of fuel. The Institute estimates that the time and fuel wasted were worth more than $60 billion.[3] Other costs of congestion include higher consumer costs from delays to freight deliveries and property losses and deaths from delays to fire trucks and other emergency service vehicles. Some would say that congestion also contributes to urban sprawl as people and jobs move to the urban fringes to avoid traffic snarls.

Polls of urban residents repeatedly show that congestion is one of the greatest sources of dissatisfaction with their areas. Planners use this dissatisfaction to argue that more planning is needed. The problem is that planning does not reduce congestion, and in fact many plans actively seek to increase congestion. Just as Le Corbusier once argued that the problem with cities was that they were too dense, and the solution was even more density, planners seem to say that the problem is that cities are too congested, and the solution is more congestion.

"Congestion signals positive urban development," says Portland's Metro.[4] "Transportation solutions aimed solely at relieving congestion are inappropriate."[5] When asked why Metro found high levels of congestion to be acceptable, Metro's leading transportation planner replied that any effort to relieve congestion "would eliminate transit ridership."[6]

Similarly, in 1996 planners in the Twin Cities decided "expansion of roadways will be very limited in the next 25 years." They hoped that "as traffic congestion builds, alternative travel modes will become more attractive."[7]

"Congestion is a sign of a healthy community which has resisted the ruinous temptation to build its way out of congestion with monster roads," says smart-growth advocate Dom Nozzi. "It is only dead, stagnant, dying cities and downtowns that do not have congestion."[8]

Nozzi is wrong: many fast-growing cities have relatively low rates of congestion, and many other cities are so congested that their growth has stagnated. Yet many planners and planning advocates put their faith in congestion. Portland U.S. Representative Earl Blumenauer, the leading smart-growth advocate in Congress, calls congestion "exciting. It means more business to the merchants. It means an exciting street life. It's the sort of hustle and bustle—and people don't mind going slow."[9] Blumenauer is confusing cause and effect: exciting places may be congested, but that doesn't mean planners can make boring places exciting, or bring more money to local merchants, by reducing street capacities to make them congested.

Planners often say that "we can't build our way out of congestion." The corollary is that new roads simply "induce" more traffic, so there is no point in building new highway capacity. These absurd myths grew out of the combination of inflation and the growing anti-auto movement in the 1970s.

238

The urban interstate freeways built in the late 1950s and 1960s did a great deal to reduce urban congestion. Freeways make up less than 3 percent of the road mileage in urban areas, but carry 37 percent of the traffic.[10] Freeways, especially those built to interstate highway standards, are also the safest forms of transportation in urban areas.

The U.S. Department of Transportation has more than two decades' worth of highway data for all major urban areas in the United States. These data, which include the number of freeway lane miles, the miles driven on freeways each day, and the total miles driven in the urban area each day, can be used to test the claim that more freeways simply lead to more driving. The data reveal a strong correlation (correlation = 0.48 with 1.0 meaning perfect correlation) between the growth in new freeway lane miles and per capita freeway driving. But there is virtually no correlation (correlation = 0.01) between growth in per capita total driving and new freeway lane miles.

In other words, new freeways attract traffic off other, more dangerous streets, but do not lead to more total per capita driving. This means freeways are one of the most "pedestrian-friendly" investments cities can make, because they leave streets safer and less congested.

University of California planning professor Robert Cervero agrees that the induced-demand myth has caused enormous harm. "Claims of induced demand have stopped highway projects in their tracks," says Cervero. "This is wrongheaded. . . . The problems people associate with roads—e.g., congestion and air pollution—are not the fault of the road investments," he adds. They result "from the *use* and *mispricing* of roads"[11] (emphasis added).

The real cause of increasing congestion is inflation. Highways are paid for out of gas taxes, and those taxes are proportional to the number of gallons of gasoline sold, not the price of those gallons. During the 1970s, inflation caused construction costs to increase much faster than gas tax revenues. On top of this, Americans bought more fuel-efficient cars after 1974, which meant they could drive more without contributing more to highway funds. While Congress and many states eventually increased gas taxes, people today pay only half as much inflation-adjusted gas tax for every mile they drive as their parents paid in 1960.

The result was that the congestion relief of the 1960s turned into the congestion growth of the 1970s. Those roads that could be built with the limited funds that were available were often delayed by anti-highway activists. So much time was required to plan and build roads that when new roads finally opened, they were often more congested than existing roads had been when construction began simply because of the growth in driving. This fed the fantasy that new roads simply resulted in more congestion.

In 1989, a national conference on transportation planning brought together opponents of the automobile with opponents of low-density suburbs.[12] They agreed that more congestion, not less, would help them achieve their goals. Opponents of the automobile hoped that congestion would encourage people to use transit. Opponents of the suburbs hoped that congestion would encourage people to live in dense cities. They formed a congestion coalition that was soon joined by companies that made money designing and building rail transit lines, downtown property owners who didn't want to see more businesses move to the suburbs, and big-city mayors who didn't want to see more people move to the suburbs.

All the members of the congestion coalition benefited from increased congestion, particularly in the suburbs. To get that congestion, they convinced Congress to include detailed planning requirements in the 1991 transportation bill, known as the Intermodal Surface Transportation Efficiency Act (ISTEA). This bill set the rules for spending federal gasoline taxes for the following six years.

ISTEA required all states and urban areas to write detailed regional transportation plans and to update those plans every five years. This meant that millions of dollars that could have gone for congestion relief was spent on planning instead. Moreover, many parts of the planning process were biased against new roads:

- Regional planners were directed by the U.S. Department of Transportation to get transit, bicycle, and pedestrian groups involved in planning, but were not required to involve auto groups.
- Funding was tied to air quality, and even though congestion is a major source of pollution, regions with dirty air were discouraged, and in some cases forbidden, from using federal funds to build new highway capacity.

- Starting in 1983, Congress dedicated 20 percent of all increases in gas taxes to mass transit. But in addition to this fixed mass-transit fund, ISTEA created a "flexible fund" allowing states and regions to spend money on either highways or transit. The result was that highways received a declining share of the total.
- ISTEA created a new grant program, called the *Congestion Mitigation/Air Quality* (CMAQ) fund, of a billion dollars a year. Despite the name, many regions spent CMAQ grants on high-density housing, rail transit, traffic calming, and other activities designed to increase, not mitigate, congestion. For example, in 2000, a typical recent year, 53 percent of CMAQ funds were spent on transit, which has a negligible effect on congestion, while only 18 percent were spent on traffic signal improvements.[13]

Although ISTEA expired in 1997, most of these requirements were included in reauthorizations of the law passed in 1998 and 2005.

During the Clinton administration, the Environmental Protection Agency gave millions of dollars in grants to national and regional anti-auto groups with the stated objective of reducing "the growth of vehicle miles traveled throughout the U.S."[14] For example, the Surface Transportation Policy Project received more than $1 million, the Bicycle Federation of America received $465,000, and the pro-transit Association for Commuter Transportation received $315,000. Many of these groups used their funds to participate in the planning process and oppose new roads.[15]

In the 1998 update to ISTEA, Congress legislated more such grants by creating the Transportation and Community and Systems Preservation Pilot Program, which encouraged regional and local governments to transfer federal transportation funds to local nonprofit groups. Many of those groups used those funds to campaign against new roads and promote congestion-building activities such as high-density developments and rail transit.[16]

By exaggerating the costs of automobiles, ignoring the benefits of driving, and imagining apocalyptic energy shortages, planners promote the congestion coalition's platform. As described in chapter 12, this includes land-use plans that seek to increase population densities and create more congestion. In addition, planners want to rebuild streets to reduce their ability to safely move traffic and divert funds needed for congestion relief to wasteful rail transit projects.

31. Building Auto-Hostile Streets

Someone once suggested that the best way to ensure safe driving would be to attach a sharp knife to automobile steering wheels aimed at the driver's heart. While this might be an amusing thought to some, the reality is that auto fatalities were greatly reduced in the past 40 years by making cars and highways safer, not more dangerous. Safety devices like collapsible steering columns, padded dashboards, seat belts, and air bags reduce the effects of accidents without leading people to drive more recklessly.

Urban planners, however, have adopted the knife-to-the-heart theory of safe driving. Their prescription for city streets is to reduce speeds and flow capacities by making the streets more dangerous. Planners call this *traffic calming*, which is a euphemism for congestion building. Planners say their goal is to create streets that are more pedestrian and bicycle friendly, but many things they do make streets more dangerous for both walkers and cyclists.

At its simplest, traffic calming consists of putting barriers in roads to slow traffic. The barriers might be rotaries at intersections, center dividers between intersections, and curb extensions or bump-outs at crosswalks. Planners also advocate converting one-way streets to two-way operation. A more extreme version of traffic calming is *boulevarding*, a planning term for removing or slowing travel lanes on arterial streets. The most extreme version, promoted by a Dutch planner, is the "naked street," from which all signs, stripes, and other safety devices are removed on the theory that more dangerous streets will encourage people to drive more safely.[1]

The stated goal of all these devices is to slow traffic, supposedly to make the streets more inviting to pedestrians. Many traffic-calming barriers make the streets far more risky for cyclists, as they make the lanes too narrow to comfortably accommodate both a bicycle and an automobile. Moreover, any perception of safety generated by traffic calming is entirely imaginary and is more than made up for by the problems traffic calming creates for emergency service vehicles. Studies have shown that, for every pedestrian whose life might be saved by traffic calming, more than 30 people are likely to die due to delays to fire trucks and paramedics.[2]

Converting one-way streets to two-way presents similar problems. In the 1950s, traffic engineers consistently found that one-way streets had numerous advantages over two-way. One study found that converting two-way streets to one-way led to a 19 percent increase in traffic at speeds that averaged 37 percent faster. This wasn't because the maximum speed limit on the one-way streets was any greater than on the two-way streets, but because drivers experienced 60 percent fewer stops. To top it off, there was a 38 percent decrease in accidents.[3]

Engineers reported similar results in city after city:

- Portland found 51 percent fewer accidents at intersections and 37 percent fewer between intersections.[4]
- The Oregon State Highway Department found that one-way streets in a dozen Oregon cities, ranging from Astoria to Eugene, led to an average of 10 percent fewer accidents and 23 percent more traffic—meaning the accident rate per million vehicle miles declined by 27 percent.
- Sacramento found 14 percent fewer accidents on streets converted to one-way operation despite a 17 percent increase in accidents in the city as a whole.[5]

Pedestrians particularly benefit from one-way streets. Two-way streets produced 163 percent more pedestrian accidents in Sacramento, and 100 percent more pedestrian accidents in Portland, Oregon; Hollywood, Florida; and Raleigh, North Carolina. One study called one-way streets "the most effective urban counter-measure" to pedestrian accidents.[6]

Many downtown businesses initially resisted one-way streets, worrying that customers going in the other direction would miss them or not bother to drive around the block to shop. But after some streets were converted, most businesses saw the benefits of increased traffic—meaning more customers—and became believers.

In 1949, the Traffic Engineering Department of the City of Fresno, California, made a nationwide survey of cities with one-way streets. A questionnaire to traffic engineers and police came back with unanimous responses in favor of one-way streets. This was so striking that the city worried that "officials might have been prejudiced." So it sent a second survey to merchant associations, and that survey came back almost as favorable: only 10 percent reported opposition to one-way streets.[7]

Engineers in Olympia, Washington, and in Sacramento compared actual retail sales before and after one-way streets. Olympia found that businesses on one-way streets were doing better than comparable businesses on two-way streets.[8] Sacramento also found that businesses grew faster (or, in some cases, shrank less—the study was done at the beginning of a recession) than similar businesses in the city as whole.[9]

Despite these advantages, planners began proposing the restoration of two-way traffic to one-way streets in the 1970s. As early as 1976, the city of Denver considered converting several one-way streets to two-way operation. The city's director of traffic engineering wrote a lengthy memo predicting that this action would increase accidents, congestion, and air pollution. He could find no evidence to support claims that property values on two-way streets were greater than on one-way streets. He concluded that "the benefits to the total neighborhood [of converting to two-way] would be negligible."[10]

The report may have delayed one-way conversions in Denver, but it did not stop them. About a decade later, Denver converted several one-way streets to two-way operation. A 1990 review of the conversions found that virtually all the engineer's predictions had come true. Accidents increased an average of 37 percent "as is expected with two-way operations" (not that the planners told anyone they expected more accidents when they proposed the changes).[11] Congestion increased as well, along with the pollution that accompanies congestion.

The review claimed that downgrading some one-way collector streets to two-way local streets "strengthened the residential status of those streets." It did not provide any evidence for this or even offer a way to measure it, but of course any local street will be more attractive to residences than busy collector streets, regardless of whether they are one- or two-way. The only real benefit the report could find for turning other one-way collector streets to two-way collectors was "a *perceived preference* for two-way operations"[12] (emphasis in original). Again, the report did not document this, suggest how it could be measured, or even mention whose preferences were perceived to favor two-way streets. Despite this negative finding, Denver continues to convert one-way streets to two-way.

Other cities have gone through similar experiences. In 1993, Indianapolis converted a major route to two-way operation. After three years, accidents on that route had increased 33 percent.[13] In 1996, Lubbock, Texas, converted several one-way streets to two-way. Two years later, monitoring found a 12 percent decrease in traffic on those routes, but 25 percent more accidents causing 34 percent more property damage.[14]

Despite these results, proposals to convert one-way streets to two-way are being taken seriously in Austin, Berkeley, Cambridge, Chattanooga, Cincinnati, Columbus, Louisville, Palo Alto, Sacramento, San Jose, Seattle, St. Petersburg, and Tampa, among other cities. Though the benefits are meager—and may be limited to a "perceived preference" for two-way streets—the proposed conversions are costly:

- St. Petersburg estimates that restriping, signal changes, and other changes required to convert streets from one-way to two-way cost more than $140,000 per intersection;[15]
- Conversion of 9 one-way streets to two-way in downtown Austin is expected to cost $15 million;[16]
- San Jose spent $15.4 million converting 10 streets to two-way;[17] and
- A plan to turn a one-way couplet in Hamilton, Ontario, to 2 two-way streets is estimated to cost Can$3.2 million (about US$2.0 million).[18]

Conversions are costly in other ways as well, namely, in terms of accidents, congestion, and pollution. Austin planners admit that their plan of converting nine streets will increase traffic delays by 23 percent and downtown air pollution by 10 to 13 percent.[19]

A more extreme form of traffic calming consists of turning major expressways into "boulevards." Planners start with an arterial that might have four main travel lanes, a center left-turn lane, and right-turn lanes at major intersections. They replace the left-turn lane with a tree-filled median strip. They block the right-turn lanes with curb extensions. The four main travel lanes remain, but traffic suffers delays whenever anyone wants to make a turn.

A minor arterial road might consist of four travel lanes with few or no auxiliary right- or left-turn lanes. Planners might convert this to two main travel lanes with a center left-turn lane and convert the space that had been used by the fourth lane into bike lanes.

Boulevarding seriously impairs a highway's ability to move traffic. Portland-area planners want to boulevard McLoughlin Avenue, which currently carries more than 40,000 cars per day, into a street capable of moving no more than 30,000 cars a day. Other Portland expressways that planners want to boulevard include Barbur and Sandy.

The most extreme version of traffic calming comes from the Netherlands, where a planner named Hans Monderman proposes to make streets safe by making them as dangerous as possible. He modifies urban streets by removing all safety devices, including signs, stripes, signals, and even the curbs separating pedestrians from automobiles.[20] By taking the knife-to-the-heart theory of traffic safety to its logical conclusion, Monderman's ideas undo a century of safety research by traffic engineers. They are just idiotic enough that some American planners are likely to make similar proposals soon.

32. The Rail Transit Hoax

More than 750 U.S. cities boasted electric streetcars in 1910. Yet gasoline- or diesel-powered buses were more flexible; cost less to operate; and did not require rails, trolley wires, and other expensive infrastructure. Transit companies began converting streetcar lines to buses as early as 1918. Forty-eight years later, in 1966, St. Louis completed its conversion from streetcars to buses, leaving rail transit in just eight American cities.

Yet the past 30 years have seen a resurgence of rail transit. Today, 25 urban areas operate rail transit lines, and several more have lines under construction. This does not even count the many vintage trolley lines that serve tourist districts of such cities as Little Rock, Memphis, Tampa, and Tuscan.

Federal funding of urban mass transit goes back to 1964, when Congress passed the Urban Mass Transportation Act. The law offered capital grants to cities that operated their own transit systems. At that time, the vast majority of transit systems were privately owned. Although ridership was declining, the industry as a whole earned a profit. Spurred by federal funding, in the next eight years cities purchased the vast majority of private transit systems and poured billions of dollars into their operations. Yet ridership had fallen another 21 percent.

The gasoline shortages of the 1970s did more to reverse this trend than any public investments. By 1980, ridership recovered to 1964 levels and then some, growing by 30 percent from 1972. Had the industry remained private, it probably would have responded to gas shortages with innovative, low-cost solutions to urban transportation problems. Such solutions could have included frequent bus service with limited stops in major corridors (known today as bus rapid transit), express service from individual suburban centers to major job centers, and door-to-door demand-responsive services to low-density areas. Government assistance to low-income and other transit-dependent people, if required, could come in the form of transit vouchers that could be used like food stamps on buses, taxis, or other public conveyances.

Instead of allowing private operators to develop innovative solutions to the energy crisis, most states passed laws forbidding private operators to compete with government transit monopolies.[1] Since transit agencies receive more than three-fourths of their funds from taxpayers and less than a fourth from transit fares, they are more dependent on appropriations committees than fare-paying riders. The plodding planning processes of government bureaucracies stifled innovations, while the incentives associated with federal funding encouraged transit agencies to select high-cost, high-risk solutions such as high-capacity buses and rail transit rather than the low-cost solutions that private entrepreneurs might have chosen.

Initially, public agencies continued the transit industry's history of replacing obsolete streetcar lines with buses. Los Angeles's Metropolitan Transit Authority replaced the last Pacific Electric streetcars with buses in 1961 and St. Louis's Bi-State Transit System replaced that city's last streetcars with buses in 1966. While Atlanta, San Francisco, and Washington, D.C., planned to build high-speed rail systems, until Congress created incentives to waste money on expensive transit, most other cities were content to rely on buses.

Those incentives began in 1973, when the state of Massachusetts convinced Congress to pass a law allowing cities to cancel interstate highway projects and use the funds for mass transit instead—but only for capital projects.[2] This created a dilemma for cities that wanted to cancel such freeways. The cost of an interstate highway would be enough to buy hundreds of new buses, but no transit agency could afford to operate that many new buses. However, failure to spend all the money released by canceling the highway would open elected officials to charges that they "lost" federal funds, and the jobs associated with them, to other regions of the country.[3]

Officials in Boston, Portland, and a few other cities hit upon an answer: rail transit. Rail transit's high cost became its virtue: it was costly enough to absorb the costs of the cancelled interstate highway and provide at least as many local construction jobs as the highway would have required. Rail's operating costs were also a bit higher than the cost of operating buses, but agency officials entranced by "free" federal money convinced themselves that this would not be a problem. In addition to Boston and Portland, cities such as Chicago and Sacramento took advantage of this law.[4]

In 1982, Congress repealed the 1973 law but dedicated a share of federal gasoline taxes to a special mass-transit fund.[5] The mass-transit fund represented a departure from the previous history of the federal highway trust fund. The term *trust fund* implies an obligation to manage the fund on behalf of the beneficiaries of that fund, in this case the auto drivers who pay into it. By diverting some of the money to transit, Congress was breaching that obligation.

Moreover, in creating the mass-transit fund, Congress neglected an important feature of the highway fund: a strict formula allocating that fund to the states based on the population, land area, and road mileage of each state. Congress quibbled over this formula every six years when it reauthorized transportation funding, but once the formula was set, each state knew how much money it would get. Thus, states had an incentive to spend their share of the money as effectively as possible.

Congress did not bother to write such a formula for the mass-transit fund. Cities such as Portland that built new rail lines quickly grabbed a huge share of the funds. Other cities soon realized that, in effect, there *was* a formula for the mass-transit fund: the cities that proposed the most expensive transit projects received the most money. Soon, dozens of cities that had once happily dismantled their expensive and obsolete streetcar lines started developing proposals to build new ones.

To disguise the fact that they were using an obsolete technology, many transit agencies substituted the term *light-rail* for trolleys or streetcars. In fact, there is little that is light about light-rail: the rails weigh the same as those used for any other rail transit project, and at 50 tons apiece, the vehicles typically weigh more than those used for other forms of rail. While light-rail refers to railcars that sometimes run in the streets, *heavy-rail* has come to refer to subways and elevateds that never intersect streets or pedestrian paths. The terms "light" and "heavy" refer to the volume of passengers they carry, not the weight.

A third type, *commuter rail*, uses existing or former freight lines that sometimes cross streets but rarely operate in streets. While each car on a light- or heavy-rail train generally has its own motors, most commuter trains consist of a locomotive pulling unpowered passenger cars. Recently, some cities have also built *vintage trolleys*, which are mainly tourist attractions, and *modern streetcars*, which are mainly downtown circulators.

Many rail transit lines cost as much to build, per mile, as a four- to eight-lane freeway. Yet, mile for mile, the New York City subways are the only U.S. rail transit lines that carry as many people as a single freeway lane. Rail transit's huge cost translates into huge profits for engineering and design firms, contractors, railcar manufacturers, bond dealers, and many other businesses. Naturally, these businesses were only too happy to contribute to political campaigns favoring rail transit.

If you accept, as most urban planners do, that cities should try to get people out of their cars and onto transit, then rail transit is an extraordinarily expensive way to do this. The Federal Transit Administration developed a formula for calculating the *cost per new rider*, which is roughly the cost of getting someone out of his or her car and onto transit (though in fact some new riders may not have previously been driving). This formula is, basically, the capital cost amortized over the expected life of the project plus the annual operating cost divided by the annual number of new riders attracted by the transit improvements. Using this formula, improvements in bus service typically attract new riders at a cost of $1 to $6 per trip, but construction of rail lines typically cost $10 to $100 per new trip.

By 1989, enough cities had built new rail lines to evaluate the benefits those lines produced. A U.S. Department of Transportation researcher named Don Pickrell reviewed several lines completed by that year and found that the planners of those early rail projects had almost all overestimated ridership and underestimated costs to justify federal grants and local matching funds for the projects.[6] "The systematic tendency to overestimate ridership and to underestimate capital and operating costs," said Pickrell, "introduces a distinct bias toward the selection of capital-intensive transit improvements such as rail lines."[7] Rather than improve its procedures to ensure that estimates were more accurate, the Federal Transit Administration responded to Pickrell's report by having him transferred to another part of the Department of Transportation and ordered never to analyze transit projects again.[8]

"I have interviewed public officials, consultants and planners who have been involved in these transit planning cases," comments University of California planning professor Martin Wachs, "and I am absolutely convinced that the cost overruns and patronage overestimates were not the result of technical errors, honest mistakes or inadequate methods. In case after case planners, engineers and economists have told me that they had to 'revise' their forecasts many times because they failed to satisfy their superiors. The forecasts had to be 'cooked' in order to produce numbers that were dramatic enough to gain federal support for the projects."[9]

A group of Danish researchers led by Bent Flyvbjerg found that U.S. rail transit projects cost an average 41 percent more[10] and attracted fewer than half the riders than originally projected.[11] In contrast, U.S. road projects went only 8 percent over budget and actually underestimated use. Rail cost "underestimation cannot be explained by error," says Flyvbjerg, "and is best explained by strategic misrepresentation, that is, lying."

"Undoubtedly, most project proponents believe their projects will benefit society and that they are thus justified in cooking costs and benefits to get projects built," Flyvbjerg adds. "The ends justify the means, or so the players reason."[12]

Even after cooking the books, planners' analyses nearly always show that rail is the least cost-effective transportation solution. Yet cities and transit agencies usually propose to build new rail lines anyway. For example, Denver transportation planners compared the cost of new freeway lanes, bus/high-occupancy vehicle (HOV) lanes, and rail transit between downtown and Denver International Airport. Planners projected that the rail line would cost at least 50 percent more and be less than half as effective at reducing congestion than new freeway lanes. This made the freeway lanes more than three times as cost-effective at reducing congestion as the rail line. The bus/HOV lanes were twice as cost-effective as the rail line. Of course, planners ignored these results and selected the rail alternative.[13] Since then, the estimated cost of the rail line has increased by 75 percent, suggesting that it is even less cost-effective than the early analysis indicated.[14]

The pre-1990 projects reviewed by Pickrell had cost overruns averaging 50 percent. Planners today claim that new forecasting techniques have greatly improved the accuracy of these projections. Yet in 2005, researchers at Northeastern University and Booz Allen Hamilton looked at more recent light- and heavy-rail transit projects and concluded that they had suffered cost overruns averaging 40 percent.[15]

Moreover, there is no indication that the accuracy of cost projections is improving over time: the most recent project in the Northeastern University study, the Minneapolis Hiawatha light-rail, went 49 percent over budget. A Seattle light-rail line that is now under construction has gone well over its original budget. Cost overruns projected for the Seattle monorail line led voters to shut down that project in November 2005, but transit agencies rarely give voters an opportunity to stop horrendously expensive projects.[16] Ridership projections may be more accurate in some cases, but many recently completed lines, including the light-rail lines in New Jersey, carry far fewer passengers than originally projected.

Transit agencies routinely deceive people about these estimates, often claiming that rail projects whose costs far exceeded the original estimates were finished "under budget." For example, Portland's Westside light-rail line was initially projected to cost $175 million ($350 million in constant dollars). Its final cost turned out to be $944 million, or 170 percent over the projected cost. Yet Portland claims that it came in under budget. By "budget," however, they mean not the originally projected cost but the final budget, including all gold-plated changes made to the project after politicians agreed to build it.

In the early stages of planning, when they are trying to persuade politicians to build rail transit as opposed to spending transportation funds on some other project, planners make optimistic cost and ridership projections. As the planning proceeds and construction begins, planners revise cost estimates upward and ridership estimates downward. When the project is complete, they claim they finished under budget even though that budget may be twice the originally projected cost. After the rail line opens, they claim that ridership exceeds expectations even though those expectations may be only half the original projections. The agencies then claim that their excellent record justifies funding and building more rail transit lines.

Agency managers know that, once the first spade of dirt is turned on a construction project, politicians will rarely bring that project to a halt no matter what the cost overruns. Economists call this the *Concorde effect*, after the French-British plane that went far over budget and produced negligible benefits for anyone except those wealthy enough to pay $5,000 or more for a transatlantic flight.[17]

In the past 15 years alone, the United States has spent more than $100 billion on rail transit capital projects.[18] That is two-thirds of all transit capital spending even though rail transit carries only about a third of transit trips (mostly on existing lines in the New York area).[19] Economists from the Brookings Institution and the University of California examined U.S. rail systems to see whether the net social benefits of those systems outweighed the costs. They compared the benefits to transit riders and the benefits of reduced congestion with the costs of the rail systems and found that, "with the single exception of BART in the San Francisco Bay area, *every* U.S. [rail] transit system actually reduces social welfare"[20] (emphasis in original).

Even the net benefits of the Bay Area Rapid Transit (BART) system are questionable as the economists only counted the benefits to the transit riders who actually rode BART. Yet, to pay the high cost of constructing BART to distant suburbs, Bay Area transportation planners cannibalized the budgets of San Francisco Muni, Oakland's AC Transit, and other area bus systems that serve the dense cities where most potential transit riders live. The result has been a net decline in total regional transit ridership since 1984.

Many transit advocacy groups, including the BayRail Alliance[21] and the San Francisco Chapter of the Sierra Club,[22] have come out against further extensions of BART because they would take resources away from more effective but lower-cost transit services. A founder of the Regional Alliance for Transit and member of the Alameda Contra Costa Transit Board calls BART a "vampire" because it "sucks the lifeblood out of every transit agency with which it comes in contact."[23] These controversies led low-income advocates to sue the Metropolitan Transportation Commission (the Bay Area's regional transportation planning agency) for funding BART to wealthy suburbs while denying funds to low-cost bus improvements in low-income neighborhoods.[24]

The San Francisco Bay Area is not the only region to see a decline in transit ridership since building rail transit. The real tragedy of rail transit is that it has actually harmed transit riders in cities across the nation. In most cases, this is because rail transit is so expensive to build and operate that transit agencies have had to cannibalize their bus systems to finance the rail lines—either cutting bus service, raising bus fares, or both.

We can track the effects of rail transit on transit ridership using two sources of data. First, since at least 1960, the decennial census has asked about one out of six households how workers in those households "usually" get to work. From this we can calculate the percentage of workers that usually take transit. The Census Bureau counts taxis as a form of public transit; the numbers in this book exclude taxis.

It should be noted that census data actually overstate the share of workers who take transit on any given day. U.S. Department of Transportation surveys reveal that people who say they usually take transit to work often drive instead, while people who say they usually drive rarely take transit.[25] Correcting for this would reduce transit's share by about 23 percent. The numbers in this book do not reflect this correction.

The second source of data is annual transit and driving numbers reported by the U.S. Department of Transportation. The National Transit Database reports passenger miles by transit agency, which can be totaled for each urban area.[26] *Highway Statistics* is an annual report that presents, among other things, total miles of driving by urban area.[27] To get passenger miles, miles of driving should be multiplied by 1.6, which is the U.S. Department of Transportation's estimate of average vehicle occupancy.[28]

Of the urban areas that had rail transit in 2003, nearly half actually lost transit riders over the past 20 years (Table 32.1).[29] For example, despite a doubling of the region's population and nearly tripling of the miles of rail transit lines, Atlanta's transit system carried fewer transit riders in 2004 than in 1985. While other rail regions saw ridership gains, it was mainly because their populations grew. Between 1984 and 2004, transit's share of total travel increased only in Boston; San Diego; and Washington, D.C.

The picture for transit commuting in rail cities was even bleaker than that for total transit travel. With the exceptions of Los Angeles, San Diego, and San Jose, transit carried a smaller share of commuters in 2000 than in 1980.[30] Between 1990 and 2000, some urban areas with supposedly excellent rail networks, such as Chicago and Washington, D.C., actually saw a large decline in the total number of transit commuters.

The sad part of this tragedy is that the rail transit lines were built largely to serve relatively wealthy suburban commuters who already have lots of mobility, while the reductions in bus services mainly harmed low-income inner-city residents, many of whom did not own automobiles. As Brookings Institution economist Clifford Winston

Table 32.1
Transit Ridership in Rail Urban Areas

			Transit's Share of			
	Transit Trips		Total Travel[1]		Commuting[2]	
Urban Area	1984	2004	1984	2004	1980	2000
Atlanta[3]	141.1	147.0	1.9	1.1	9.1	4.1
Baltimore	109.5	107.3	2.4	1.5	12.3	7.4
Boston	270.3	393.1	2.5	3.4	13.5	12.5
Buffalo	35.1	23.1	1.3	0.6	16.4	4.1
Chicago	735.7	577.6	5.7	3.6	18.7	12.6
Cleveland	94.4	58.1	2.6	1.1	11.5	5.0
Dallas–Ft. Worth	47.9	83.9	0.7	0.6	4.0	2.2
Denver	50.7	81.4	1.4	1.3	6.4	4.9
Los Angeles[4]	551.3	600.2	2.0	1.6	5.9	6.0
Miami	77.9	141.3	1.1	0.9	4.3	3.3
New Orleans	84.0	51.3	3.2	1.4	11.5	7.1
New York	3,493.3	3,357.4	12.6	9.7	30.7	29.0
Philadelphia	394.8	348.2	3.8	2.5	15.1	10.1
Pittsburgh	88.2	65.8	2.1	1.3	13.8	8.1
Portland	51.7	104.5	2.5	2.3	9.8	7.7
Sacramento	16.6	32.0	0.9	0.7	4.1	2.9
Salt Lake City	16.4	25.3	1.1	1.0	5.5	3.6
San Diego	39.2	86.6	1.0	1.1	3.5	3.6
San Francisco	488.5	402.6	4.0	3.9	16.8	14.6
San Jose[5]	38.5	39.5	1.1	0.9	3.1	3.6
St. Louis	50.8	46.7	0.9	0.7	6.7	2.9
Washington, D.C.	309.4	447.9	3.9	4.2	16.7	13.7

1. Transit's share of total travel is calculated by comparing the passenger miles of transit travel in each urban area, available from the U.S. Department of Transportation's (DOT) National Transit Database, with the passenger miles of auto travel in each urban area, available from table HM-72 of U.S. DOT's *Highway Statistics*. To get passenger miles, vehicle miles of travel in table HM-72 are multiplied by 1.6, the average occupancy of automobiles according to U.S. DOT's National Household Travel Survey.
2. Transit's share of commuter travel is calculated from decennial census data, which reports how workers "usually" get to work. Taxis are excluded from transit.
3. Atlanta transit carried 155.7 million trips in 1985.
4. Between 1985 and 1995, Los Angeles transit ridership fell by 17 percent; see text.
5. Due to a financial crisis caused by the high cost of rail, San Jose lost a third of its transit riders between 2001 and 2004; see text.

observes, the average incomes of rail transit riders are more than 25 percent greater than bus riders.[31]

Cities that build rail transit leave transit riders vulnerable to cuts in service during three main periods:

- *Construction*: Cost overruns during construction often require transit agencies to cut services or raise fares to cover the higher costs. Although the federal government may pay 50 percent or more of the original projected cost, it will usually not pay for any cost overruns.
- *Recessions*: Transit agencies often go heavily into debt to pay for the local share of rail construction costs, and repay that debt out of sales taxes or other tax revenues. A recession that reduces tax revenues by 10 percent might force a bus-only agency to cut service by 10 percent, but a rail agency that spends half its income paying its debt would have to reduce service by 20 percent.
- *Reconstruction*: Rail systems must be completely rebuilt, at a substantial fraction of the original construction cost, every 30 years or so. Transit agencies rarely account for this in their original plans (whose time horizons often conveniently end in 30 years or less) and so may not have funds available for such reconstruction.

Transit systems in Portland, Sacramento, and other cities suffered during construction due to cost overruns, but the worst case was in Los Angeles. Los Angeles's transit agency had increased ridership by more than 8 percent per year in the early 1980s by keeping fares low. But rail transit costs forced it to raise fares and cut back on bus service. Between 1985 and 1995, ridership fell from 584 million to 484 million trips per year. In 1995, the National Association for the Advancement of Colored People sued the Los Angeles Metropolitan Transit Authority on behalf of a Bus Riders' Union, charging the transit agency with discrimination because it cut bus service to low-income minority neighborhoods in order to build rail lines into white, middle-class neighborhoods. In a settlement agreement, the agency agreed to restore bus service.[32] This led to a 32 percent increase in transit ridership. After spending billions on rail lines, rail transit carried fewer riders in 2004 than the bus riders lost between 1985 and 1995.[33]

258

The worst-case example of the effects of a recession on transit ridership is San Jose. In the late 1980s and early 1990s, San Jose built several light-rail lines that enjoyed modest ridership. But when the 2001 recession caused a dramatic decline of the sales taxes that supported the transit system, the financial crisis forced the agency to make severe cuts in bus and rail service.[34] As a result, total ridership fell by a third in just three years.[35]

Portland's transit system also suffered from the recent recession. Between 2001 and 2005, the number of jobs in downtown Portland declined by 5 percent. But declining tax revenues forced Portland's transit agency to make significant cuts in bus and rail service.[36] These led to a 21 percent decline in the number of downtown commuters taking transit to work and a full 33 percent decline in the number taking light-rail. Meanwhile, the number of people driving to work downtown increased.[37] Even higher gasoline prices did not help Portland transit: Tri-Met, Portland's major transit agency, actually carried fewer riders in the first nine months of 2006 than the same period of 2005, when gas prices were much lower.[38]

Currently, the city facing the biggest burden of rail reconstruction is Washington, D.C. Washington's Metro Rail system first opened in 1976, and today nearly two-thirds of it is more than 20 years old.[39] The federal government paid for much of the construction, and the transit agency did not make any provision for funding reconstruction. The agency estimates that it faces a $3.5 billion funding shortfall over the next 10 years because of the high cost of replacing outdated equipment and maintaining the system.[40] To reduce its maintenance costs, Metro has seriously considered replacing many of its subway escalators with stairways.[41]

To make matters worse, many regions, including Los Angeles, Portland, and San Jose, had enjoyed rapid increases in bus ridership before they began building rail transit. These increases resulted from increased frequencies and other low-cost improvements to bus service accompanied by minimal fare increases. Other cities, such as Dallas, Denver, Sacramento, Salt Lake City, and San Jose, also saw faster growth in ridership before building rail lines than after those lines opened.

In contrast with declining ridership in rail regions, numerous regions with bus-only transit systems have seen huge increases in ridership over the past two decades. They include Austin, Charlotte,

Houston, Las Vegas, Phoenix, and Raleigh-Durham. On average, between 1984 and 2004, transit trips in regions with bus-only transit grew by 30 percent, whereas trips grew by less than 1 percent in regions with rail transit.[42] In many bus-only urban areas, transit ridership has grown much faster than driving. Among rail regions that built rail in the past 30 years, only San Diego can say the same.

San Diego built the nation's first modern light-rail line. Its success stems from an intensive effort to keep the costs of both rail and bus transit down. This allowed the region to double bus service even as it built light-rail transit without increasing taxes or getting huge federal grants. The result was a doubling of transit riders—mostly due to the improved bus service, not the light-rail.[43] Other cities that built light-rail transit failed to achieve San Diego's success because they relied on "free" federal dollars to build "gold-plated" rail transit lines that included many unnecessary frills. Cost overruns often led to reductions in bus service.

Another rail transit story reveals another problem with federal transit grants. In 2002, the Vermont legislature agreed to fund an experimental commuter-rail service in Burlington. The legislature set specific performance criteria that the transit service had to achieve to receive continued funding. After 18 months, analysis revealed that the commuter trains were taking very few cars off the road and that the diesel locomotives produced more pollution than was saved by taking cars off the road. The legislature stopped funding it and the trains stopped running.[44]

Vermont could terminate its failed experiment because it was funded entirely with state and local taxes. But federally funded rail transit projects cannot have such happy endings because the federal government requires transit agencies to return to the federal treasury funds spent on any transit projects that are terminated. Since most of the cost of rail transit is in right-of-way improvements that have little cash value, no transit agency can afford to admit that rail transit is a failure. Thus, regardless of the reality, transit agency press releases must claim that all federally funded rail transit projects are a great success.

Most of the eight cities that kept some of their rail systems through the 1960s and 1970s— Boston, Chicago, Cleveland, New Orleans, New York, Philadelphia, Pittsburgh, and San Francisco—haven't done any better than cities that built new rail transit lines. Since

1984, transit ridership has either stagnated or declined in all these regions except Boston.

One argument for rail transit is that it will reduce sprawl. But census data reveal that rail transit has done little to stem the growth in auto commuting or the movement of jobs to the suburbs. The Chicago urban area gained more than 300,000 new jobs during the 1990s, and because nearly all the new jobs were in the suburbs, virtually every one of those new workers drove to work. Meanwhile, despite Chicago's extensive rail transit system, the region lost more than 40,000 transit commuters during the decade. Similarly, the Washington, D.C., urban area gained more than 100,000 new jobs, yet lost more than 20,000 transit commuters.[45] Some regions with rail transit gained transit commuters in the 1990s, but all rail regions combined lost more than 14,000 transit commuters. By contrast, bus-only regions gained more than 53,000 transit commuters.[46]

Obviously, if rail transit results in a loss in transit ridership, it can hardly be credited with relieving congestion. But even in the few cities where rail transit is associated with increasing transit ridership, transit carries so few people that its effect on congestion is negligible and certainly not cost-effective. Moreover, because light-rail transit often occupies lanes in streets that were formerly open to automobiles and both light-rail and commuter-rail trains often cross streets, these forms of rail transit can actually increase congestion.

Two cities opened new rail lines in 2004, both with disastrous results. Minneapolis proudly opened its first modern light-rail line, promising that it would attract enough people out of their cars to relieve congestion on the parallel Hiawatha Avenue (State Highway 55).[47] Instead, motorists on Hiawatha immediately experienced a huge increase in congestion. While signals on Hiawatha had previously been coordinated to allow smooth progression of traffic, the new arrangement gave the light-rail line signal priority over autos. While the line did not cross Hiawatha itself, it crossed numerous Hiawatha cross streets, which led the signals on those streets to interrupt the normal cycle of signals on Hiawatha. This added 20 or more minutes to the trips of people driving on Hiawatha.[48]

Although the state tried to fix the problem,[49] by December it had given up, with officials admitting traffic on Hiawatha would never be the same. A Federal Highway Administration report blamed the problem on poor planning. "More time, effort and money should have been allocated to ensuring that [signals] operate as efficiently as possible before committing to construction," said the report.[50]

"This is not a sinister plot to make traffic as miserable as possible and move everybody onto the train," claimed an official with the state Department of Transportation, which both built the rail line and maintains Hiawatha Avenue.[51] However, documents uncovered by state representative Phil Krinkie proved him wrong. In 1999, state records revealed, a consultant warned that giving light-rail signal priority would severely disrupt traffic. Yet the state decided to give the trains priority because, said a state engineer, "transit had to have an advantage" over autos. The Federal Transit Administration requires that all new light-rail lines give trains priority at traffic signals, thus promising to expand this problem to other regions.[52]

Also in 2004, Houston opened a light-rail line that soon earned the name "Wham-Bam Tram" because it collided with automobiles every four to five days.[53] Running in downtown streets did more to add to congestion than relieve it. Transit systems in both Houston and Minneapolis carried fewer riders in 2004 than 2003, partly because the high cost of the rail lines forced the agencies to curtail bus service. Minneapolis transit recovered in 2005, but Houston did not.

Regions that build rail transit must spend a huge share of their transportation funds on transit systems that carry only a tiny share of regional travel. The regional transportation plan for the San Francisco Bay Area calls for spending 65 percent of the region's total transportation budget, and 68 percent of the capital budget, on transit even though transit carries only 4 percent of passenger travel and virtually no freight.[54] The Twin Cities' regional transportation plan calls for spending 71 percent of that region's funds on a transit system that carries just 1 percent of travel.[55] Portland's plan calls for spending 61 percent of funds on a transit system that carries just 2 percent of travel.[56] Similar disparities are found in almost all rail regions.[57] Note that these numbers indicate how planners want to spend each region's money; actual expenditures may differ.

Despite rail's poor track record, dozens of urban areas are planning rail projects—including, ironically, many regions with fast-growing bus ridership. Rail was endorsed by politicians seeking "their share" of federal pork, but it was especially promoted by planners on a moral crusade to get commuters out of their automobiles. They reasoned that middle-class commuters who would not ride a bus would be attracted to trains. Yet, researchers have found, "there is no evident preference for rail travel over bus when quantifiable service characteristics such as travel time and cost are equal."[58] Rail attracts riders because transit agencies typically operate it more frequently than buses and, since it stops fewer times per mile than buses, at higher average speeds. When buses are put on similar schedules, they "should be as effective as rail in generating patronage," another study concluded.[59]

The focus on suburban riders creates an equity issue, says University of California (Los Angeles) planning professor Brian Taylor. "The growing dissonance between the quality of service provided to inner-city residents who depend on local buses and the level of public resources being spent to attract new transit riders is both economically inefficient and socially inequitable," comments Taylor.[60] "While low-income residents generally benefit from the public transit subsidy," Taylor adds, "the benefits of subsidies disproportionately accrue to those least in need of public assistance."[61]

Rail transit takes these inequities to extremes. The General Accounting Office observed that rail transit could cost 50 times as much to build as it would cost to start bus service on comparable frequencies and schedules.[62] Moreover, the General Accounting Office found, buses in comparable corridors cost less to operate and can run as fast and sometimes faster than rail transit.[63]

The equity problems of sacrificing bus service to central-city neighborhoods filled with transit-dependent families to build rail to middle-class suburbs where families often own more than one automobile per driver have been highlighted by lawsuits brought by low-income bus riders in Los Angeles and the San Francisco Bay Area. In 2005, low-income groups in the Bay Area filed a lawsuit against that region's Metropolitan Transportation Commission that was similar to the National Association for the Advancement of Colored People suit in Los Angeles. The commission's transportation plan called for spending billions of dollars on suburban rail lines that, in some cases, are expected to cost $100 for each new ride. Meanwhile, the commission's plan denied funds for improving bus service to a low-income minority neighborhood that was expected to attract new riders at a cost of just 75 cents per trip.[64]

Many planners point to Europe as an example of a place that has successfully invested in rail transit instead of highways. Yet the truth is Europe's experience with rail transportation is nearly as dismal as that in the United States. Since World War II, European countries have discouraged auto driving with punitive auto and fuel taxes and promoted rail transit with heavy subsidies. Europe's policy, like that of many U.S. urban planners, is to "shift the balance" from autos to transit, relieving road traffic "by developing other means of transport," especially "major rail works."[65]

This policy has not worked. According to the European Union, between 1980 and 2000, the automobile's share of European passenger travel increased from 76 percent to 78 percent, whereas intercity rail and transit's share declined from 21 percent to 16 percent.[66] A recent conference on European transport policy concluded that rail transit "has never successfully reduced road traffic and, except in a few city centres, cars remain largely predominant almost everywhere in urban and suburban areas."[67] As a result, says one member of the European Parliament, "the current European transport policy steers towards a prohibitively expensive and inefficient utopian ideal."[68] If rail transit has not halted suburbanization and reduced auto usage in dense European cities, it certainly cannot do these things in American cities whose densities are much lower.

Spotter's Guide to Rail Transit

The most common kinds of rail transit are vintage trolleys, modern streetcars, light-rail, heavy-rail, and commuter rail. Unfortunately, these terms are often misused, which leads to confusing debates. This guide presents the basic characteristics of each type.

Vintage trolleys are usually designed to appear old-fashioned and mainly serve as tourist attractions to popular shopping areas. They are powered by electricity, connecting to the overhead wires with a single pole.

Modern streetcars appear streamlined and most often run in streets as single cars. Like vintage trolleys, they are powered by electricity, connecting to the overhead wires with a single pole or pantograph. They are designed to serve downtown residents and shoppers.

Light-rail may run in streets or on exclusive rights of way, often runs in trains of two or three cars, and is powered by electricity, connecting to the overhead wires with a pantograph. The "light" refers to the load capacity, not the weight of the cars or rail.

Heavy-rail runs in subterranean or elevated lines, always on exclusive rights of way, in trains of four to eight or more cars, and is powered by electricity. The "heavy" refers to load capacity, not weight.

Commuter rail usually runs on existing or abandoned freight railroad tracks, which may cross streets or pedestrian paths. It is typically powered by diesel locomotives pulling several unpowered passenger cars, though in the New York–Connecticut areas it is usually powered by electric locomotives.

33. Transportation Myths

Two major myths drive transportation planning in American cities today. First is the assumption that public transit is drastically underfunded and that more people would ride transit if only it were available. "When public policy allows a real choice between the auto and mass transit," writes a professor in the Rutgers University planning school, "a far higher percentage of the population travels by mass transit."[1] Second is the oft-stated claim that "we can't build our way out of congestion."

These myths have led Portland, the San Francisco Bay Area, and many other urban areas to make almost no attempt to relieve congestion by building new roads. Instead, they put most of their transportation funds into expensive transit projects. The result is more congestion and few new transit riders.

Supporting the underfunded-transit myth is the fable urban planners love to tell about how the big bad General Motors (GM) conspired to rid the nation of efficient streetcar systems, supposedly so that people would have to buy GM automobiles and drive rather than take transit. No matter how often researchers at the University of California (Berkeley),[2] University of California (Irvine),[3] Portland State University,[4] and elsewhere[5] have debunked this myth, it continues to persist among rail advocates and auto opponents.

General Motors *was* convicted of conspiring to monopolize the market for buses by having National City Lines, which it partially owned, purchase buses from GM rather than its competitors. But this does not mean it was out to destroy transit systems or that it played a significant role in converting streetcar lines to buses. If anything, GM's infusion of capital into National City Lines may have helped transit systems and transit riders.[6]

As previously noted, transit companies throughout the nation began converting from streetcars to buses as early as 1918, and continued to do so through the 1960s. More than half of the nation's streetcar systems had gone out of business or been replaced by buses long before National City Lines was formed in 1933. From 1933 to 1949, the years during which General Motors is supposed to have carried out its nefarious deeds, more than 300 streetcar systems converted to buses.[7] National City Lines owned or had an interest in fewer than 30 of these systems.[8] In most of the systems, the conversion of streetcars to buses had begun long before National City purchased an interest in the line. National City purchased 12 systems in the very year they converted to buses, suggesting that the decision to convert had been made even before National City got involved.

In 1949, 50 American cities still had streetcars. Although GM divested itself of National City Lines by that year, transit companies (and, in some cases, public transit agencies) continued to convert to buses over the next 17 years. St. Louis was the last to complete its conversion in 1966, leaving just eight U.S. cities with rail transit (including two, Chicago and New York, which converted their street-car lines to buses in the 1950s but maintained subway, elevated, and commuter rail lines). In short, General Motors was involved, through its partial ownership of National City Lines, in less than 5 percent of the conversions of streetcars to buses.

Transit companies had excellent reasons to convert streetcars to buses: buses were more flexible and less expensive to buy, cost less to operate, and did not require installation and maintenance of expensive rail and trolley infrastructure. "The faithful electric trolley had sunk into such a state of obsolescence as to be scarcely tolerable," *Fortune* magazine wrote in 1936.[9] The new buses were popular among transit riders: when New York streetcar companies replaced trolleys with buses, ridership increased by as much as 50 to 60 percent.[10] GM took advantage of this transition to sell more of its buses, but the transition would have taken place with or without GM's involvement. "Buses were clearly a better way to go and would have taken over with or without GM," says University of Arizona transportation researcher Sandra Rosenbloom.[11]

The General Motors conspiracy myth is popular because it supports the larger myth that a powerful highway lobby promoted huge subsidies to highways and auto driving, leaving the transit industry unable to compete. This myth is used to justify increased subsidies to transit today, with an emphasis on rail transit to undo the damage supposedly caused by the GM conspiracy.

Although autos and oil are two of the largest industries in America, auto manufacturers and oil companies barely lifted a finger in support of the Interstate Highway Act of 1956 or any federal or state highway legislation since. Instead, most lobbying has come from truckers and construction companies. But most construction companies can profit equally from building rail lines as building highways, so the notion of an all-powerful highway lobby is a myth. In fact, what remains of a highway lobby has been losing ground to an increasingly powerful transit lobby since 1981, when Congress first diverted highway user fees to transit. The transit lobby has been dominant at least since 1991, when Congress directed cities to undertake comprehensive transportation planning that, in many cases, favored transit funding over highways.

The transit lobby is represented by the American Public Transportation Association, whose membership includes

- close to 400 U.S. transit agencies;
- more than 70 other government agencies, such as regional councils of governments and state departments of transportation;
- nearly 400 engineering and consulting firms;
- more than 450 manufacturers and suppliers;
- 20 companies that manage transit services for public transit agencies;
- 7 contractors and land developers; and
- more than 70 quasi-governmental and nonprofit organizations.

Collectively, the U.S. transit industry spent more than $40 billion in 2004. Since more than three-quarters of that comes from taxpayers, the various agencies and companies within the industry have a huge incentive to lobby Congress and state and local governments.[12] A typical transit-planning program may work as follows.

First, the regional transit agency and local governments form a *transportation management association*. Normally, state laws prevent local governments from lobbying taxpayers, but the transportation management association offers a way around this. The association accepts money from private companies, such as potential rail contractors, as well as tax dollars from the transit agency and local governments. The association uses some of this money to conduct "public involvement processes," which are really little more than propaganda exercises in favor of increased transit funding.

The association or the transit agency itself will also hire a consultant such as Parsons Brinckerhoff to study transit alternatives in the region or one corridor in the region. Parsons Brinckerhoff built New York City's first subway line and since then has probably been involved in one way or another in a majority of U.S. rail transit projects. The company knows that if it recommends that a rail line be built, it is likely to get the contract to engineer the project, so it has a strong incentive to slant the analysis toward rail. This does not mean that the consultant will "cook the books," only that it will find justifications for building rail even when other alternatives would make more sense.

A transportation management association in Madison, Wisconsin, hired Parsons Brinckerhoff to analyze a rail transit proposal. The company compared several alternatives. If Madison continued to grow but did nothing to improve its bus system, the consultant estimated buses would carry 12.4 million passengers a year by 2020. But if Madison spent $60 million "enhancing" its bus system, it would carry more than 18.8 million passengers in 2020.[13] The cost of each new rider (using the Federal Transit Administration formula) would be about $1.50, much of which would be offset by fares.

Next, Parsons Brinckerhoff prepared an alternative that included both the bus enhancements plus one new commuter rail line costing $180 million, or three times as much as all the bus enhancements. To its disappointment, the company's computer models projected that this alternative would actually carry *fewer* riders than the bus enhancements alone.[14] So the consulting firm crippled the enhanced bus alternative by "deleting duplicative service and the least-productive routes."[15] The crippled bus alternative was projected to carry 18.5 million riders in 2020, or 0.3 million less than the rail alternative. Even if these numbers were valid, the 0.3 million additional rail riders would cost an average of $65 apiece—more than 40 times as much as new riders under the enhanced bus alternative.

At least Parsons Brinckerhoff was honest enough to admit that this is how it prepared the alternatives. The transportation management association was not so candid. When presenting the alternatives to the public, they not only deleted the enhanced bus alternative, they deleted the crippled-enhanced alternative. That left only the do-nothing alternative and rail, making it appear that rail transit was needed to increase ridership from 12.4 to 18.8 million trips per year.[16]

Planners let everyone know their numbers were backed by a report written by experts—a report so filled with jargon and technical terms that few members of the public ever read it.

Similarly, Denver's transit agency hired consultants to review rail transit proposals in each of several corridors (several of which were supported by transportation management associations). Every single study that compared rail transit with bus transit or highway expansions found that rail transit was the least cost-effective way of reducing congestion.[17] But in public presentations, the transit agency and its supporters emphasized how little rail transit would cost and how much it would reduce congestion and air pollution.[18]

Although the federal government will sometimes pay up to half the cost of rail transit projects, local governments must come up with the other half. If local voters are allowed to vote on taxes for rail transit, most of the money for the pro-rail campaign will come from engineering and construction companies and other firms expecting to profit from rail construction. For example, Parsons Brinckerhoff donated more than $65,000 to the pro-rail campaign in Denver; Kiewit Western, a contractor that is also a member of the American Public Transportation Association, donated $55,000; and Siemans, a railcar manufacturer, donated $50,000. These companies also often contribute to the campaigns of elected officials who support rail transit.

Once the decision is made to build rail, huge amounts of money are spread around to numerous groups: realtors, bond dealers, railcar manufacturers, engineering consultant firms, electrical contractors, power companies, concrete tie manufacturers, union construction workers, and many more. In contrast, buying buses creates profits for bus manufacturers—which are rarely located in the same city—and jobs for drivers and maintenance workers. These groups are obviously nowhere near as powerful as the groups that benefit from rail construction.

Rail transit also influences property values in parts of an urban region, and that leads to political support from the landowners who benefit. Contrary to frequent claims, rail transit does not stimulate new investment in a region. An analysis by University of California planning professor Robert Cervero and Parsons Brinckerhoff consultant Samuel Seskin found that "urban rail transit investments rarely 'create' new growth." However, they added, rail investments may

271

"redistribute growth that would have taken place without the invest-ment." The main redistribution was from the suburbs to downtown, which explains why downtown property owners tend to strongly support rail transit projects.[19]

While rail transit does not by itself stimulate new investments, the Federal Transit Administration has required most cities that have built rail transit to attempt to boost ridership by promoting transit-oriented developments. Many if not most of these developments are supported by tax-increment financing, tax breaks, or other subsidies. This has spawned a new industry of realtors and developers who thrive on tax subsidies to high-density developments.

Portland claims that its streetcar line has generated $2.3 billion worth of development.[20] What it fails to mention is that the streetcar line passes through three urban-renewal districts, and that the city has spent more than two-thirds of a billion dollars subsidizing the redevelopment of those districts.[21]

Between the transit bureaucracies, consulting firms, contractors, developers, and other special interest groups, the one interest group that is often forgotten is the group for which transit ostensibly exists: transit riders. Curiously, few if any members of the American Public Transportation Association truly represent this group. Even the "public interest groups" that the association counts among its mem-bers are mostly special interests such as the Concrete Reinforcing Steel Institute and the National Railroad Construction and Mainte-nance Association.

Transit riders themselves divide into two groups: transit-depen-dent people who cannot drive and transit-choice people who can drive but prefer to ride transit. Normally, both groups tend to settle in cities that have intensive transit service rather than in the suburbs. Rail transit, and most transit planning, seem to be aimed at expand-ing the second market by attracting suburbanites out of their cars. Since rail transit so often ends up sacrificing bus services to or raising fares for transit-dependent people, it would seem to make much more sense instead to increase bus services in the cities and corridors where most people who prefer or depend on transit already reside. But planners, bedazzled by the mantra of "transportation choices," have focused instead on rails: in addition to the 25 urban areas that had rail transit in 2004, at least three dozen more cities are planning or proposing rail projects.

In supporting rail transit, urban planners allowed themselves to become tools of powerful special interests whose main goal is to transfer dollars from taxpayers to their own pockets. Planners justify this by the need to "redevelop" cities to reduce auto driving.[22] But the hard cold truth is that rail transit does little to shape cities, especially when it so often actually reduces transit ridership. At most, it offers planners an excuse to rezone neighborhoods to higher densities.

If rail transit cannot significantly relieve congestion, is there an alternative that can? Or are we doomed to be "stuck in traffic," as Brookings Institution economist Anthony Downs named his book about congestion problems?[23] The answer is that we *can* build our way out of congestion if new construction is combined with better road pricing.

Downs points out that people respond to congestion in one of several ways. Some may simply suffer through it, but others change their times of travel or travel routes. A few switch to public transit or other modes, and some may not travel at all. When a new highway opens, or a highway's capacity is increased, people respond by switching back to the times or routes that were most convenient to them.[24] This creates the impression that new roads are just as congested as the old ones and fuels the claim that new roads simply "induce" more traffic.

The induced-demand myth—the claim that it is pointless to build new highways because they merely increase driving—is especially peculiar because it is so irrational. It is the dream of every private entrepreneur to find a product so desirable that people will consume more the more it is made. Only the government would be criticized for building things that people use and urged instead to build things, such as rail transit lines, that receive little use.

If it were really true that new freeways merely induce more traffic, then the interstate freeways of Sioux Falls, South Dakota, or Cheyenne, Wyoming, would be just as congested as the freeways of Los Angeles or San Francisco. Of course, they are not. Instead of speaking of "induced demand," it would be more accurate to describe such demand as "suppressed demand" that is relieved by new roads. Even University of California planning professor Robert Cervero admits that most induced-driving studies "have suffered from methodological problems" and that "wrong-headed . . . claims of induced demand have stopped highway projects in their tracks."[25]

The Tampa-Hillsborough Expressway Authority recently completed an innovative new highway that proves cities can build their way out of congestion. The authority manages an east-west tollway through Tampa, part of which was congested at near-gridlock levels during morning and evening rush hours. The authority knew that three-fourths of its morning traffic moved in the direction of downtown Tampa and three-fourths of the afternoon traffic moved in the opposite direction.

Without buying any significant new right of way, the authority built three new lanes that it uses for inbound traffic in the morning and outbound traffic in the afternoon. For a considerable portion of the highway, the new lanes were elevated above the existing road and built on piers that occupy just six feet in the median strip of the existing highway. Since the authority effectively has six new lanes—three in bound and three out bound—it says it built six lanes in six feet.[26]

The new elevated lanes were expected to cost a total of $7 million per lane mile, but turned out to cost twice that due to an engineering error made by a consultant hired by the authority. Even $14 million per lane mile is less than a third of the cost per mile of the average light-rail line that is currently proposed or under construction.[27] Moreover, 100 percent of the elevated expressway cost is being paid for by tolls; the road cost taxpayers nothing. The new lanes are electronically tolled; people who buy a transponder pay $1.50 every time they use it; the authority photographs the license plates of cars without transponders and sends them a bill for $1.75.

Since the lanes first opened in July 2006, congestion on both the new and existing lanes dropped from level of service F, meaning near-gridlock or stop-and-go traffic, to level of service B, meaning traffic moves at a "reasonably free flow." If congestion increases, the authority plans to use value-priced tolls—tolls that increase during heavy traffic periods—to ensure that the new lanes are never congested. This means that the local transit agency can put express buses on such lanes and those buses can move as fast or faster than any rail line.[28]

The new, elevated express lanes did not result from the long-range transportation planning that has been required by federal law since 1991. In fact, it would be more accurate to say that the lanes were built in spite of such planning. Instead of express lanes, the

Hillsborough County Metropolitan Planning Organization had written a light-rail line into its plans. This line would have required huge tax subsidies and done little or nothing to relieve traffic congestion. Fortunately for Tampa commuters, the Tampa-Hillsborough Expressway Authority is funded out of tolls, not federal tax dollars, so it could build the lanes regardless of the planners' wishes.

One lesson here is that the solution to congestion has as much to do with institutional design as with infrastructure. Many of the cities that are doing the most to relieve congestion are doing so with independent toll road authorities that are funded out of user fees. Such authorities have an incentive to relieve congestion because such relief increases their revenues.

The 1956 law creating the Interstate Highway System forbade the use of tolls for any new roads built with federal funds. This provision was supported by truckers who feared that tollbooths would simply create traffic jams and by the U.S. Bureau of Public Roads that may have feared that independent toll road authorities might demonstrate that there was no need for a federal roads program. Congress repealed this restriction in 1991, and several innovations have rekindled interest in tolling.

First, in 1975, Singapore pioneered the use of value pricing, that is, charging higher tolls during congested times of the day. Since then, France, Norway, and other countries have found that variable road pricing can significantly reduce congestion.[29] The first notable experiments with value pricing in the United States were on State Route 91 in Orange County, California, and Interstate 15 in San Diego.[30]

Second, the introduction of electronic tolling has eliminated the problem of delays at tollbooths. Hong Kong may have been the first city to try electronic tolling in 1986.[31] Since then, almost all toll road authorities have adopted the use of transponders, which can cost as little as $10 per automobile, to collect tolls. Toronto was the first city to have a toll road with no tollbooths: as in the Tampa expressway, a camera photographs the license plates of cars lacking transponders whose owners then receive a bill in the mail.

The third development is the increasing use of public-private partnerships to finance new and existing roads. Many European nations routinely give concessions to private companies to build toll roads. Typically, the companies contract with the government to build and manage the roads and collect tolls for 50 to 99 years, after which time they are expected to turn the facility over to the government. Interest in public-private partnerships in the United States increased when Chicago and Indiana sold franchises in existing toll roads to a Spanish company, receiving billions of dollars for the franchises. Now highway agencies in Colorado, Oregon, and other states are exploring the use of public-private partnerships to construct new toll roads.

The use of private financing to fund variable-priced, electronically collected tolls allows highway agencies to circumvent the anti-auto planners who dominate the long-range transportation planning process mandated by federal law. For private financing to work, state legislatures must authorize the creation of toll road authorities, either within or (probably better) separate from the existing state department of transportation.

New highways are not the only way to relieve traffic congestion. The most cost-effective way of reducing congestion is coordinating traffic signals. According to the Federal Highway Administration, three out of four traffic signals in the nation are obsolete and poorly coordinated with other signals. Without laying any new pavement, every dollar spent on signal improvements can produce a $40 saving in time and fuel to auto users.[32] Coordinating signals also reduces air pollution.

Engineers in San Jose estimated that coordinating 223 traffic signals on the city's most congested streets reduced travel times by 16 percent, eliminated 107,000 pounds of toxic air emissions per year, and saved 471,000 gallons of gasoline per year, all for just $500,000.[33] Despite these benefits, anti-auto planners often resist signal coordination because they want to increase, rather than reduce, congestion, and would rather spend scarce transportation dollars on costly rail projects.

Other low-cost solutions to congestion are also on the horizon. A considerable amount of congestion is caused by drivers' slow reaction times. In heavy traffic, one car slowing down can create a wave of slower traffic that can take hours to work itself out. Improving reaction speeds can eliminate such waves. Some new cars today have *adaptive cruise control*, also known as laser-guide cruise control, which allows the car to instantly respond to changes in speed of the car before it. Traffic engineers at the University of Minnesota estimate that, when 20 percent of cars on the road have adaptive cruise control—which is expected by 2010—much of this congestion will disappear.[34] In effect, adaptive cruise control increases roadway capacities without building any new roads.

An even longer-term solution to congestion will come in the form of intelligent highways that are wired to control vehicles. Some state highway agencies are already placing wires in roads capable of sending signals to vehicles. Meanwhile, automakers are introducing cars that can accelerate, brake, and steer themselves. It would be a simple matter to put a receiver in the car that can get signals from the roads. Since computer-controlled cars could safely drive within a few feet of one another, this system could triple road capacities. Such systems should be available by about 2020.

Until such systems are operating, more highway capacity will be needed in the nation's most congested cities. If built with public-private partnerships and funded out of tolls, such capacity may not require any taxpayer subsidies. If built as elevated roads similar to the Tampa expressway, road capacities can be increased with minimal purchases for new rights of way. Such capacity increases can save people time and money while reducing air pollution and fuel consumption. One of the main obstacles to such solutions to congestion is the urban planning process that gives undue influence to the minority of people who oppose the automobile.

Urban planners promised to provide balanced transportation planning that considered a wide range of social benefits and costs. Instead, they focused on extremely narrow concerns: promoting downtown property owners over suburban property owners; promoting rail construction over road construction; and creating auto-hostile environments. Planners assumed that anything that might reduce driving was good, no matter what the cost to auto users or society in general. Even if reducing driving is a good thing, planners rarely asked whether their tools—more congestion and more money spent on rail transit and other nonroad projects—would actually reduce driving. In fact, many recent transportation plans produce more congestion and air pollution, not less, and end up wasting people's time, money, and health.

Part Six
Why Government Fails

The American Constitution is designed to be run by crooks, just as the British constitution is designed to be operated by gentlemen. . . . If ever a World Government should come into existence, it had better be a government designed to be run by crooks rather than a government designed to be run by gentlemen. Gentlemen are too often in short supply.

—Freeman Dyson[1]

The fundamental premise behind government planning is that government can be benignly objective and even altruistic. Whereas private individuals and corporations work only in their own self-interest, only government can protect the common good. Yet this runs counter to almost every experience Americans have with their governments.

"I have come to the conclusion that the making of laws is like the making of sausages," said an Illinois legislator in about 1878; "the less you know about the process the more you respect the result."[2] The people most likely to believe in government altruism are those who have never closely observed government in action.

Government is run by people who are just as human—which means just as self-interested—as the people who run private businesses. Legislators primarily aim to get reelected. Bureaucrats mainly want to increase their budgets and power. As soon as government begins to exercise power over people or resources, special interest groups rise up to influence that power. Though everyone in and around government is careful to use terms like "the common good" and "the public interest," even those with the best intentions are biased by their experiences and incentives.

Given that there are so many special interest groups, some people argue that the political process ends up producing an accurate reflection of the public good. But nearly all special interest groups assert that their problems can be solved with more government spending. For everyone who lobbies to reduce the budget of a government

279

agency, at least 100 people lobby to increase that budget—and many of those who want to reduce agency budgets merely hope to transfer the money to their pet projects.[3] The result is that one interest group is heavily underrepresented: taxpayers—which explains why government budgets tend to keep growing.

Government has grown not only in size but in power, passing laws and regulations today that residents of the most autocratic nations would not have tolerated a century ago. That power is no more likely to be used in the public interest than the money government spends in support of various special interest groups.

Given this situation, it is absurd to expect that government planners with the best of intentions and the finest planning tools will be able to develop a rational plan that truly serves the common good. Instead, plans are likely to be so heavily warped by the special interests that lobby the hardest and the politicians who receive contributions from those interest groups that they will in fact do more harm than good. People who truly want to solve social problems must find solutions that do not involve government planning.

34. Power and Rationality

Danish planning professor Bent Flyvbjerg distinguishes between rationality, as in the ideal of "rational planning," and *Realrationalität*, meaning what really happens when planners plan.[1] In Flyvbjerg's home city of Ålborg, "planners, administrators, and politicians thought that if they believed in their project hard enough, rationality would emerge victorious; they were wrong." The plans they wrote were "transformed by power and *Realrationalität* into environmental degradation and social distortion." This was partly because "institutions that were supposed to represent what they themselves called the 'public interest' were revealed to be deeply embedded in the hidden exercise of power and the protection of special interests."[2]

In many ways, Flyvbjerg's experience in Ålborg resembles my own experience in Portland. As Flyvbjerg points out, "Most people interested in politics know one or more 'Aalborg Stories.'"[3]

Planners claim that government planning is rational, meaning "based on reason and logic rather than emotion or prejudice."[4] But planning is driven by political power, not reason and logic. As Flyvbjerg says, "Power defines reality."[5] That power may be derived from wealth, rhetorical skills, or coalition building, but it has little to do with rational thinking and analyses. Government planning cannot be analytical and efficient if government bureaus, elected officials, and special interest groups all try to manipulate the planning process to achieve their own ends.

This is true whether planning is done by federal, state, regional, county, or city governments. Since no level of government can avoid self-interest on the part of these groups, government planning will inevitably produce more problems than it solves.

Thanks to transportation planners who dedicate two-thirds of the region's transportation funds to a transit system that carries 4 percent of passenger travel, the San Francisco Bay Area has the nation's second-worst traffic congestion. Thanks to land-use planners who make it impossible for homebuilders to meet the demand for new housing, the Bay Area is the nation's least affordable major housing market. So it is particularly ironic that a San Francisco planner named John Hirten has repeatedly called for bringing the "benefits" of planning to the national level.

Hirten points out that the federal government requires regions such as the San Francisco Bay Area to plan for housing and transportation, telling the regions that "it is important to plan and coordinate their various programs." So Hirten thinks it is strange that "no such formal planning or coordination mechanism exists at the national level."[6]

"What we need is: an organized, rational, efficient way to give guidance and direction to the use of federal resources, programs and funds which affect the country's future," argues Hirten. "This means an Office of Policy, Planning and Programming in the Office of the President or administration, to help establish an agreed upon National Growth Plan and related policies."[7] Because such planning has worked so well in the San Francisco Bay Area.

Hirten observes that the federal government has previously engaged in national planning, first during World War I, when it took control of the entire economy; then the New Deal, when it tried to recover from the Depression; and most recently during the Nixon administration, when it imposed wage-and-price controls to reduce inflation.[8] Hirten neglects to mention that all those efforts failed: the government mismanaged the First World War economy so badly that it did not repeat its mistake in the Second; the New Deal actually prolonged the Depression, which lasted far longer in the United States than in European countries that did not have a new deal; and inflation raged on for years after Nixon gave up on wage-and-price controls.

Why can't government plan? Part two showed that technical barriers render government planning impossible. Part four showed that the people who are trained as planners are not qualified to plan. But, if the technical barriers could be overcome and the right people found to do the planning, could government planning work? This chapter will show that it cannot because the other groups involved in government—elected officials, bureaucracies, and special interests—will warp planning to their own ends rather than to the public interest.

For planning to be the "organized, rational, efficient" process that Hirten advocates, everyone involved must be altruistic or, at the least, completely detached from its outcomes. But almost no one involved in government is altruistic or detached. Elected officials are mainly interested in getting reelected. Government agencies are motivated by their budgets. Special interests want subsidies and favors from government. The result is that any semblance of rationality in government planning is lost in a miasma of self-interest.

Having fought monarchists, fascists, and communists in the past century, Americans have come to believe that democracy is without question the best form of government. Many political scientists and other experts on government have an almost childlike faith in the democratic process. Special interests fight over social issues such as education, abortion, and gay rights as well as fiscal issues such as how much to spend on defense and welfare and how much taxes people and corporations should pay. Since the battles over these issues often seem evenly balanced, many people actually believe that the final result, whatever it is, must be "right" because it grew out of the democratic process.

This is a recent attitude. Before the Great Depression, most Americans agreed with Thomas Paine's statement, "Government even in its best state is but a necessary evil; in its worst state an intolerable one."[9] "A government in which the majority rule in all cases cannot be based on justice," said Henry David Thoreau two generations later.[10] "A wise man will not leave the right to the mercy of chance, nor wish it to prevail through the power of the majority."[11] "If all life were determined by majority rule," P. J. O'Rourke explained more recently, "every meal would be a pizza and every pair of pants, even those in a Brooks Brothers suit, would be stone-washed denim."[12]

Democracies suffer so many scandals that no one can seriously believe that democracy is perfect. Yet when any problem arises, too many people expect the government to solve it. Typically, this means creating a new government agency or giving more money and power to an existing one. Elected officials then pat themselves on their backs for solving the problem. When a few years later someone notices that the program is hemorrhaging money and the problem is worse than ever, people blame incompetent bureaucrats instead of recognizing that government simply can't solve most problems.

Freeman Dyson's comparison of the American and British constitutions refers to the checks and balances that keep any of the three branches of American government—legislative, executive, and judicial—from dominating the others. These checks and balances indeed allow for a president, or members of Congress, to be "crooks" without doing too much damage to the nation because their powers will be checked by one of the other branches of government. The British system has fewer checks—notably, the executive and legislative branches are always the same party, so neither checks the other— so it only works so long as everyone is a gentleman (or lady).

What Dyson does not note is that roughly 100 years after the Constitution was written, a fourth branch of the American government emerged that was not contemplated by the Framers of the Constitution, and there have been few or no checks on its growth. This branch is the bureaucracy that has grown since the creation of the civil service system in the late 1870s and 1880s. The civil service system implicitly assumes that no one in the civil service is a crook. But even if every member of the civil service is honest, the bureaucracy itself still tends to look out mainly for its own interests, not for the public interest.

The growth of bureaucracy has contributed in turn to the creation of special interest groups, which could be considered a fifth branch of government because they have as much or more to say about what our government does as any of the original three branches. Political scientists call bureaucracies, interest groups, and elected officials the *Iron Triangle* because they form a practically unbeatable combination favoring government growth.

When Henry David Thoreau gave his lecture on "Civil Disobedience" in 1849, Washington, D.C., was a swampy town of no great importance in the world. The president hired a staff of, at most, two people. He had time to meet with any citizen who had a request to make or a favor to ask. Most members of Congress had no staff at all; Congress as a whole, including its many committees, hired fewer than one staff member per senator or representative. No more than a half dozen people worked as lobbyists. The federal government, whose costs amounted to about 2 percent of the American economy, had less than 25,000 civilian employees, 80 percent of whom worked for the Post Office.[13]

By 1930, the federal government had grown but was still less than 4 percent of the nation's economy. President Hoover had the services of a few score staff members. Washington tourists could visit the

White House most afternoons and shake his hand. Congress employed an average of 20 people per elected senator and representative. The federal government employed about 600,000 civilian workers, about half of whom worked for the Post Office.[14] But the federal budget was still so small that fewer than 100 people spent time lobbying in Washington, D.C.

Since 1950, Washington, D.C., has been completely transformed. The president has a personal staff of over 1,500. Congress employs 40,000 people, more than 75 for every senator and representative. Some 35,000 people have registered as congressional lobbyists. The federal budget now consumes more than a fifth of the national economy and, after adjusting for inflation, has grown by more than 50 times since 1930, and 1,700 times since 1850. More than 2.5 million civilians work for the federal government, and if government contractors are included, the total is four times that many.[15]

This growth in the federal government, which has been paralleled by a similar growth in state governments, was so incremental that few really noticed it. As *Newsweek* columnist Robert Samuelson observed in 1993, "We gradually moved from an era when people were loath to use government for almost anything to an era (today) when people use government for almost everything."[16] Despite the incremental nature of government growth, there have been several notable steps along the way.

War: Every major war led to a massive increase in the size of the federal government. After most wars, government shrank but to a size that was still considerably larger than before the war. The exception was World War II; because it was followed by the Cold War, the federal government simply continued to grow.

Civil service reform: Before 1878, every federal civilian employee, down to the lowest postal clerk, got his or her job through the patronage or spoils system. The election of every new president saw a complete replacement of the entire federal government. The spoils system often put inept and venal people in charge of federal programs. Civil service reforms, which began during the Hayes administration and accelerated in the Arthur administration, solved this problem but created a new one. Since civil service employees—or, as they were soon called, bureaucrats—were effectively appointed for life, they became a significant voice for government growth that in many ways equals or outweighs the other three branches in power and influence.

The Depression: Many economists today believe that, by itself, the stock market crash of 1929 might have had no more influence on the U.S. economy than the crash of 1987. But the effects of the 1929 crash were significantly worsened by mistaken Federal Reserve Bank policies and a trade war that erupted when Congress passed a protective tariff in 1930.[17] In the 1930s, however, people blamed the Depression on market failure and looked to the federal government to fix the problem. By today's standards, the New Deal was a modest government program, but with the help of key precedents set by the U.S. Supreme Court in response to pressure from Roosevelt, the New Deal created the conditions for government growth long after the Depression ended.

Payroll deductions: When the income tax was created in 1913, people paid taxes out of their savings at the end of each year. But in 1942, Congress started withholding taxes from payrolls so that soldiers going to war would not have to pay taxes on the higher salaries that many earned before the war out of the lower pay they were earning in the military. As the U.S. Treasury notes, payroll deductions had the unexpected effect of greatly reducing "the taxpayer's awareness of the amount of tax being collected, i.e. it reduced the transparency of the tax, which made it easier to raise taxes in the future."[18]

Watergate: In 1969, Aaron Wildavsky observed that the House Appropriations Committee, which was dominated by conservative Southern Democrats, viewed itself as "defenders of the public purse."[19] Wildavsky, founder of the Goldman School of Public Policy at the University of California, believed this kept the federal budget within bounds, and in fact the federal government actually produced a surplus in the year his book on the politics of the federal budget was published. But the Watergate scandal led to a huge turnover of Congress in the 1974 election, and incoming freshmen viewed the House seniority system as an obstacle to their liberal agenda. They replaced the seniority system with one based more on popularity, and the best way to be popular in Congress is to give out pork. With no one acting as a defender of the public purse, the result was a distinct acceleration in the growth of federal budgets and deficits.

These recent events have forged and hardened all three legs of the Iron Triangle. The bureaucracies were first formed after the civil service reforms of the 19th century but did not really build up until the New Deal and its expansion of federal powers. Increased federal spending and regulation that started during the New Deal but greatly escalated after World War II led to the rise of the special interests. And post-Watergate congressional reforms took the cap off federal spending.

35. Legislators: Seeking Reelection

In recent years, Congress and various state legislatures have demonstrated a remarkable faith in planning as a substitute for markets and a cure-all for bureaucracies. This is particularly puzzling because planning has so clearly failed in the Soviet Union and Eastern Europe. The National Forest Management Act of 1976, which required the Forest Service to plan the national forests, and the Intermodal Surface Transportation Efficiency Act of 1991, which required urban areas to write five-year regional transportation plans, were only two of the many laws Congress passed since 1969 that required federal, state, and local agencies to prepare detailed, long-range plans. Meanwhile, legislatures in Florida, Hawaii, Oregon, Tennessee, Vermont, Washington, Wisconsin, and many other states wrote laws requiring cities and counties to write land-use plans and to ensure that local zoning conformed to those plans.

As the most visible leg of the Iron Triangle, members of Congress have many worthwhile goals. But to achieve their goals, the paramount duty of any member is to get reelected.[1] "All members of Congress have a primary interest in getting re-elected," says one former congressman. "Some members have no other interest."[2] For representatives, whose terms are just two years, the fundraising and publicity campaign for reelection begins the day after the previous election. Even senators, who are elected for six years, often find that their offices are so hotly contested that they must raise money throughout their terms to defend their seats.

Congress has developed several strategies to get reelected, not all of which directly involve pork. One is to pass vaguely worded laws that offend as few people as possible. Implementation of the laws is the duty of the bureaucracy, which can be conveniently blamed if anyone complains that the laws are too strict or too loose. Most laws are passed amid conflicts between interest groups. As former Natural Resources Defense Council attorney David Schoenbrod observes, "It is the job of Congress in our constitutional scheme of things to resolve such conflicts, but that requires legislators to make hard choices, and making hard choices is not conducive to reelection."[3] So Congress passes the buck to government agencies, telling them to make the hard choices.

This explains why Congress and other legislative bodies are so willing to pass planning laws: not because planning has proven so successful, but because it offers legislators plausible deniability. If the plans succeed, those who wrote the laws are heroes, but if plans fail, legislators can blame the bureaucracy. "The legislators designed the system so they can claim maximum credit and take minimum responsibility," says Schoenbrod.[4]

Another reelection strategy is to provide services to constituents. Congress employs thousands of people who do nothing else but provide direct services to potential voters. The classic example is the little old lady whose social security check was lost in the mail. But an increasing share of constituent services today results from the vaguely worded laws Congress has passed. Instead of bringing itself under criticism for passing vague legislation, Congress creates for itself a whole new clientele for constituent services.

If most laws are vague, most pork is specific. In 1982, Congress passed a transportation bill that contained fewer than a dozen earmarks—requirements that specific transportation projects be built. The 2005 transportation bill had more than 6,000 earmarks. In various appropriations, Congress will go so far as to specify how stoplights should operate in small Pennsylvania towns or how boat landings should be designed on a Tennessee River.

To get pork for their states or districts, members of Congress engage in *logrolling*, which means, "I'll vote for your pork if you'll vote for mine." Alaska Representative Don Young wanted to include some very expensive bridges and other Alaskan projects in the 2005 transportation bill. So he issued a call to all members of Congress asking them to include their favorite projects in the bill as well, which explains how so many earmarks ended up in the bill.

If Congress is quick to blame the bureaucracy for poor laws, it is quick to take credit for the pork it spends. The latest trend is for senators and representatives to name highways, buildings, bridges, and other structures after themselves or close relatives. The most recent transportation bill not only included a $200 million bridge that was to be named after the chair of the House Transportation Committee, the bill itself was named after his wife.[5]

The emphasis on pork warps the way legislators view the economy. Members of Congress love to brag about the number of jobs their programs have created. But economically, jobs are a cost, not a benefit; no one wants to work 24 hours a day. The real benefit is net revenue, sometimes called profits. If jobs cost taxpayers more than the workers are paid, which is typical for many government programs, they are a drag on the economy, not a boost.

One kind of pork that is kept quiet is the tax breaks that key members of Congress give to their friends and constituents. The people who get the tax breaks are well aware of them and no doubt show their gratitude in many ways. But as *Washington Post* editor Brian Kelly says, "One man's tax break is another man's tax bill," so Congress wouldn't want ordinary voters to know much about them.[6]

For example, one line in the 1986 tax code read, "In the case of any pre-1987 open year, neither the United States nor the Virgin Islands shall impose an income tax on non–Virgin Island source income derived from transactions described in clause (ii) by one or more corporations which were formed in Delaware on or about March 6, 1981."

In other words, William Lansdale, a friend of Ronald Reagan, wouldn't have to pay about $4.5 million in taxes.

Congress will change course only when a major crisis hits. In response to the expanding deficits of the late 1980s, Congress made several important reforms, including an internal requirement that spending could not increase without an equal increase in revenues. Those reforms were quickly forgotten when the budget deficits briefly disappeared in the 1990s. The next crisis may not take place until about 2017, when social security revenues are expected to fall below social security payments and Congress must increase taxes or deficits to both meet social security obligations and maintain the rest of the federal government.

36. Special Interests: Looking for Handouts

A representative democracy could not exist without a legislature. Special interest lobbies, however, are a relatively new phenomenon; they exist only when government is big. And that, primarily, is the problem with big government: big government means big lobbies. Big lobbies mean that government doesn't do what we want it to do; it does what the lobbies want it to do. This means that we now have a government that is of the special interests, by the special interests, and for the special interests.

Some people have argued that, since there are so many special interest groups, they merely cancel one another out, allowing Congress to make decisions that truly reflect the national interest.[1] But the reality is that some interest groups are better represented than others. Most notably, those groups that want Congress to spend money are far better represented than those that want Congress to spend less.

The basic goal of any special interest group is to concentrate the benefits of some government activity on itself while diffusing the costs to as many people as possible. Millions of people pay taxes, and the cost to a single taxpayer of any single government activity is low. Taxpayers thus have little incentive to complain about any particular program, no matter how wasteful it is.

But the beneficiaries of a government program may make millions of dollars from that program. This gives them a huge incentive to lobby for the creation or continuation of that program. With almost everyone clamoring for dollars and few complaining, legislators have little incentive to do anything but put the country further into debt each year.

Each February, the president presents a budget proposal to Congress for the fiscal year beginning the following October. The House and Senate appropriations committees hold hearings at which people testify on the budget. These hearings are a long succession of people asking for more money for their pet projects. One study found that, for every hearing witness who asks for a reduction in the funding for some activity, an average of nearly 150 witnesses ask that funding be increased.[2] Most people who do want to reduce funding for any agency usually just want the funds transferred to another agency.

Few, if any, lobbyists are as crass as those in Eddie Murphy's 1992 movie *The Distinguished Gentleman*. Most are earnest, well-meaning people who see their work as educational rather than arm-twisting. But lobbyists, like everyone else, are subject to incentives.

Lobbyists actually come in two forms. There are paid lobbyists who represent a special interest group, such as the American Forest and Paper Association, the National Audubon Society, or the National Rifle Association. And there are people who are actual members of a special interest group, such as a timber company executive, a bird watcher, or a hunter. The incentives facing these two types are slightly different.

The paid lobbyists have an incentive to work on hot issues that will get their names in the paper and help them attract new members or clients. But they also have an incentive to readily compromise on many issues so they can appear reasonable and be people who members of Congress can deal with. Interest group members themselves tend to be concerned with less sexy issues, but have a harder time compromising because they don't expect to come back to the bargaining table on other issues in the future.

One result is that there is a powerful incentive to polarize issues and demonize the opposition. Paid lobbyists benefit from polarization because it brings in new members and clients. Interest group members benefit because, they hope, it moves the middle ground in their direction. Yet there always remains a tension between the paid lobbyists and the members themselves.

Close scrutiny of the relationship between any interest group and legislators reveals that interest groups cannot always get what they want just by hiring an expensive lobbyist. Congress can deny access to interest groups that fail to come up with politically persuasive arguments.[3] Interest groups have developed a number of techniques to be most persuasive:

1. *Generate a crisis*: When overseeing a multitrillion-dollar budget, members of Congress have little time to deal with problems of

mere inefficiency or waste. To get their attention, you need to show that the end of the world, or a significant part of it, is at hand.

2. *Build a coalition*: The most successful interest groups are really combinations of groups, each of which expects to benefit from legislation in different ways. Economist Bruce Yandle describes some of these coalitions as "bootleggers and Baptists," referring to an unspoken coalition supporting prohibition laws. "'Baptists' point to the moral high ground" and their "moral message forms a visible foundation for political action." Meanwhile, the bootleggers "expect to profit" from the laws desired by Baptists, so they "grease the political machinery with some of their expected proceeds."[4] In urban transportation debates, for example, environmentalists are the Baptists while rail contractors are the bootleggers.

3. *Develop warm-and-fuzzy terms*: The battle over federal forestlands turned when some environmentalist substituted the term "ancient forests" for the more traditional "old-growth forests." Urban planning advocates use terms like "smart growth," "traffic calming," and "lively streets" to mean "congestion, more congestion, and even more congestion."

4. *Be as bipartisan as possible*: Pork is naturally bipartisan, so many groups have little problem increasing spending. To do more than spend money, successful interest groups carefully cultivate friends on both sides of the aisle. When the Republicans were in charge of Congress, environmentalists had little chance of passing new legislation but could prevent any anti-environmental laws from being passed because they were assured the votes of a majority of Democrats and a minority of Republicans.

Naturally, every special interest group is convinced that its agenda is completely justified. "Above all, any government activity almost at once becomes 'moral,'" says Peter Drucker. "No longer is it viewed as 'economic,' as one alternative use of scarce resources of people and money. It becomes an 'absolute.' It is in the nature of government activities that they come to be seen as symbols and sacred rather than as utilities and means to an end."[5]

In other words, once a special interest group gets its foot in the door, it reshapes the debate to make those subsidies a moral question, not a political one. Subsidies to agriculture "protect the small family farmer." Subsidies to ranchers "protect the Western way of life." Subsidies to rail transit car manufacturers "help stop global warming."

Occasionally an issue, such as $90 hammers or $600 toilet seats, becomes so well known that members of the public react. Then the special interests just hunker down and wait for the public to go away. The special interests can afford to wait because they never go away.

Special interests rely on the fundamental law of pork: concentrate the benefits on a few while spreading the costs to many. About 110 million people pay federal taxes each year. Take a penny from each one, and none will notice. Give that million dollars to one person or interest group, and they will most certainly notice. Conversely, give the taxpayers back their pennies and again they won't notice. But take away the interest group's million dollars and their hollering will be heard for miles or, at least, within the halls of Congress or whatever legislature granted the million dollars in the first place.

Every system works on feedback. If you water a garden that receives enough sunshine, your tomatoes will turn red. If Chrysler designs enough cars that everyone likes, it will make money and survive to compete against Toyota. If members of Congress find that spending money helps them get reelected, they will spend more money.

Some feedback systems are stable while others are not. A ball in a basin is stable. Push it up the side of the basin, and it rolls back down. A ball on a hilltop is unstable. Push it off the top, and it accelerates downward in an uncontrollable direction. The feedback system in government is unstable. Everyone has an incentive to spend more; few have an incentive to fight for smaller government.

Big government wouldn't be so bad if government actually produced anything. But much of what government does is take from those who produce and give to those who don't. Some might approve of this if it were taking from the rich and giving to the poor. Mostly, it is the other way around, for the simple reason that the rich can afford better lobbyists.

37. Bureaucrats: Maximizing Budgets

In 1988, Robert Redford invited a group of environmental leaders, timber company executives, and Forest Service officials to his Sundance resort in the hope that they could reach a consensus about national forest management. After a long debate between the environmentalists and industry leaders, Forest Service Chief Dale Robertson asked for an opportunity to speak.

"We can talk a lot of philosophy about how the national forests ought to be managed," said Robertson, "but let me tell you it is the budget that energizes the Forest Service." Former U.S. senator Dan Evans, who chaired the meeting, was stunned: he had imagined that Forest Service officials would act in the best interests of the national forests no matter what their budgets. "If Congress changed your budget so that it had no relationship to outputs," he asked Robertson in a shocked voice, "would that change your operations?"

"I think it would change," Robertson quietly replied.[1] In other words, Forest Service officials, like everyone else, are influenced by the incentives they face.

Evans is not the only one with an inordinate faith in bureaucrats. Students at Syracuse University's Maxwell School of Public Administration, which turns out many future bureaucrats, are not taught about the Iron Triangle. Instead, they are told of a "Golden Triangle" of bureaucrats, special interests, and legislators—"with bureaucrats at the top of the triangle," of course. Instead of being a problem, their professors consider it "an ideal that hasn't quite yet been achieved."[2]

Far from being unbiased, bureaucrats have their own set of incentives. Individual bureaucrats may all have their own unique goals. A Forest Service fisheries biologist may want to increase salmon habitat. A Bureau of Land Management hydrologist may want to reduce erosion. A Fish and Wildlife Service biologist may want to promote ecosystem diversity.

But one common element is needed to do any of these things: money. When the objectives of all the individual officials and employees are combined, the natural goal of every agency becomes identical: maximize the budget. "Few people outside government pay any attention to budget systems," affirmed David Osborne and Ted Gaebler in their 1992 best seller, *Reinventing Government*. "But budgets control everything an agency does."[3]

Whatever the conscious goals of anyone in the agency, almost everything a government agency does can be understood by assuming that the agency's primary goal is to maximize its budget.[4] Anthony Downs of the Brookings Institution points out that a large and growing bureaucracy has several advantages over a small or stagnant one:

- Its leaders enjoy greater power, income, and prestige.
- Internal conflicts are minimized because everyone can share the spoils.
- It is more likely to be noticed by funders and better able to attract funding advocates.
- It can attract more capable personnel.[5]

A Forest Service official once told me that after he was promoted to head a staff of 17 people, he soon realized that only 9 of those people actually did any work—the rest just pushed paper around. But as a supervisor of 9 people, his pay level would have been lower than as a supervisor of 17, so he made no effort to reduce his staff.

Budget maximization does not mean that agency leaders are venal or corrupt. Instead, budget maximizing takes place through a process of natural selection. Agency officials whose policies help increase agency budgets are most likely to be promoted. As a result, the firm and sincere beliefs of the officials at the top just happen to correspond with the policies that maximize their budgets. "You would not think that it would be proper for me to be in charge of this work and not be enthusiastic about it and not think that I ought to have a lot more money, would you?" an assistant chief of the Forest Service once asked an appropriations committee. "I have been in it for thirty years, and I believe in it."[6]

Bureaucracy can be found in private business as well as in government. As documented by *Dilbert*, any company department that does not contribute directly to the bottom line, such as accounting or human resources, tends to become bureaucratic, meaning that rather than maximize profits or revenues it engages in budget-maximizing behavior. But private companies that become excessively bureaucratic soon face competition from leaner companies in the same industry and must either trim down or become takeover targets. Government bureaucracies rarely face such competitive checks.

Through the civil service system, government employees have effectively insulated themselves from attempts to trim bureaucratic fat. "If I could have had just one power that could make the Forest Service work better," said Forest Service Chief Jack Ward Thomas shortly after his retirement, "it would have been the power to fire one person each year. I wouldn't have necessarily have used that power, but just knowing that I had the power to fire someone would have made everyone in the agency work better."[7]

Effectively appointed for life, civil service bureaucrats gain a huge amount of expertise about their areas that is not shared by the other branches of government. In a sense, the three million civilian employees of the federal government become three million lobbyists for their own programs. With the civil service system protecting them from interference by the president, they set their own goals and performance standards and measure their success by the amount of money they get from legislators.

People commonly assume that since the public pays government officials, they will automatically work in the public interest. Members of the public get outraged when they find out that this isn't so. "I'm paying your salary," is a common response, "why aren't you working for me?" Yet the *public interest* is an elusive goal about which there is little agreement. Bureaucrats have no better insights than anyone else about what it is. They may try to work in the public interest, but their ideas of the public interest are shaped by the feedback they get from their work. If they are rewarded with bigger budgets for doing certain things, they soon identify those things with the public interest. Since they believe in their program, they believe that "what's good for my program is good for the country."

This means that government agencies that get a large share of their funds from taxes end up with a warped sense of values. In 1989, a reporter for *The Economist* visited several factories in the Soviet Union. The factories were going to have a hard time adjusting to markets, the reporter concluded, because their managers didn't understand such basic concepts as "sales," "profits," or "costs."[8]

Why should they, when all their lives the government provided them with all the raw materials they requisitioned and bought all the products they produced?

Government agencies in the United States are not much better off, even those that actively market the goods they produce. Agency officials tend to count taxes that they receive as "revenues" and user fees that they must return to the general treasury as "costs." This gives them incentives to do things that enhance their tax revenues rather than their user fees. Transit agencies are more interested in building expensive rail projects than serving transit riders. The Forest Service designs timber sales to minimize returns to the Treasury and maximize the share of timber receipts that it keeps for itself.

Bureaucracies are adept at manipulating elected officials to increase their budgets. When Congress cut the Park Service's budget in 1968, the agency's director, George Hartzog, responded by shutting down the elevator to the Washington Monument. When the thousands of tourists who visit the monument each day complained, a park ranger directed them to talk to their senators and representatives located a few blocks away. Congress quickly restored the budget.[9]

This has since become known as the *Washington Monument strategy*, and most agencies use it at one time or another. When President Clinton asked the Forest Service for a proposal to reduce money-losing timber sales, it developed a plan that would virtually shut down over half the national forests. The agency leaked the plan to the press before showing it to Clinton, and members of Congress who opposed "Clinton's plan" to shut down their forests soon besieged the president.

Another strategy agencies use to manipulate elected officials is to spread the benefits of their programs to as many states or legislative districts as possible. In 1964, after learning that some members of congressional appropriations committees had little interest in his agency, the director of the Park Service resolved to expand the park system so that it had a national park in every state and a historic site in every congressional district.[10] Similarly, Amtrak tries to run trains in as many states as possible even if it could get more riders by focusing on a few high-use corridors.

The Forest Service recognized this strategy 80 years ago, when it began supplementing the 140 million acres of national forests in the

West by purchasing another 50 million acres of forestlands in the East. Originally located in just 11 states, the agency now manages land in 40 states. This gives it a broad range of support in Congress not enjoyed by, say, the Bureau of Land Management, whose lands are largely confined to the 12 western states.

A popular attention-getting technique that is used by both bureaucracies and special interest groups is to generate crises, often by predicting shortages of the goods they deal with. In 1910, Gifford Pinchot, then chief of the Forest Service, wrote, "The United States has already crossed the verge of a timber famine so severe that its blighting effects will be felt in every household of the land."[11] In fact, the nation had such a glut of timber that, over the next 30 years, major timber companies lobbied to prevent the Forest Service from selling any trees in order to keep their wood prices high. But in the meantime, Pinchot convinced Congress to expand the Forest Service's empire by buying more forestlands.

Each agency also enjoys alliances with various special interest groups. The Forest Service has more than 100 line items in its budget. When the Clinton administration tried to "simplify" the budget by combining various line items, it soon discovered that each line item had a special interest group that existed partly just to support the growth of that line item. These groups resisted combining line items because they would be unable to demonstrate to their members that they had successfully defended their members' interests.

Political scientists often argue that agencies become "captured" by the special interests that they were designed to regulate. But in many cases, it is the bureaucracies that manipulate the special interests in order to increase their budgets. The Forest Service routinely countered criticism from one special interest group by inviting criticism from another interest group with the opposite view. At a public meeting I once attended of loggers, ranchers, and environmentalists, the one thing everyone could agree on was that off-road vehicles were bad because they eroded the soil. As I left the meeting, I noticed the Forest Service official who called the meeting had written on his notepad, "Invite off-road vehicle users to next meeting."

It might seem self-defeating to cultivate criticism from everyone. Yet in the short run, the Forest Service could say, "If everyone hates us, we must be doing something right." Its long-run view was even more pragmatic. "Our problem is in dividing up the pie," officials

301

would say. When too many interest groups wanted a piece of the pie, the easy solution was to expand the pie. And the way to do that was to give the agency a bigger budget.

The agencies that are most successful in getting large budgets tend to be those with the strongest special interest supporters. Yet the alliances between bureaucrats, special interests, and members of Congress are, for the most part, unwritten and unspoken—more like a symbiosis than a conspiracy. This is what makes the Iron Triangle so strong: by following its own incentives, each part of the triangle ends up supporting the other two parts.

38. The Executive: Distracted by Detail

Yes, Prime Minister was a popular BBC comedy produced in the 1980s. In each episode, the prime minister comes up with some great idea to streamline government. The leading bureaucrats would tell him it was a wonderful idea, but behind his back they would prevent it from happening.

American politicians often feel the same frustration with our bureaucrats. Richard Nixon was angered when the Park Service director George Hartzog first used the Washington Monument strategy, but in 1969 Nixon, who had barely won the 1968 election, lacked the political muscle to fire the director. After decisively winning reelection in 1972, he told an assistant that the Park Service director "has been screwing with us for four years. . . . He's got to go."[1] Hartzog was fired within weeks of the election, but other officials within the agency were able to prevent Nixon and successive presidents from making radical changes in its structure or programs— except, of course, for changes that enhanced the Park Service's budget.

The president is supposed to be one of the constitutional checks and balances that prevent the American system from going out of control. This worked when the federal government was small and people expected it to stay that way. Nineteenth-century presidents often vetoed spending bills that they thought were unconstitutional. For example, in 1887, Grover Cleveland vetoed a $10,000 appropriation to provide seed to Texas farmers who were suffering from a drought.

Not only could he not find any justification for such spending in the Constitution, said Cleveland, "I do not believe that the power and duty of the General Government ought to be extended to the relief of individual suffering which is in no manner properly related to the public service or benefit." He suggested that if members of Congress wanted to send seed to those farmers, they should send some of the seed that the Department of Agriculture routinely provided to members for distribution to their constituents.[2]

Today, people expect federal handouts for every disaster and presidents usually love to be seen giving such handouts away. But as the government grows larger, the president's job becomes impossibly complex. The federal government expects to spend $2.8 trillion in 2007, or more than $1 million every 12 seconds.[3] No one, even with a staff of 1,500, can effectively monitor such profligate spending.

Even a president who is determined to take a stand on pork or any other issue must deal with 535 members of Congress who will each demand his or her own concessions. Canny senators and representatives will refuse to support the president until the last minute, knowing that this puts them in a good negotiating position.

State governors, most of whom work under constitutions modeled after the U.S. Constitution, are not much better off. Even after adjusting for inflation, the average state budget today is two and a half times larger than the entire federal budget was in 1910.[4] The pressures to spend more are the same at the state as at the federal level, and state civil service programs put bureaucrats as much out of reach of governors as the president.

One of the major problems executives face is that government agencies and special interest groups all view the treasury as a commons. A commons, or common pool resource, is a resource whose costs are shared by many but whose benefits can be grabbed by a few. The classic example is a community-owned pasture that might support, say, 10 cows for each farmer in the community. Each farmer knows that putting out more cows will cause the pasture to deteriorate. But the cost of the deterioration is shared by all the farmers, while the benefits are concentrated on the farmer who put out the extra cows.

In real life, small communities that share a commons carefully monitor to prevent overuse. When the commons is shared by many, such as an entire nation, monitoring is more difficult because the cost of overuse to each person is so much smaller than the cost of monitoring.

U.S. and state treasuries are common pool resources, viewed by the Iron Triangle—bureaucrats, special interests, and legislators—as a way to finance their objectives. These groups have jointly overgrazed the federal Treasury to the detriment of the taxpayers.

Almost everyone can think of good, worthwhile things they could do if only they had more money. The federal government spends so much, and there are so many taxpayers, that it is an easy step to think that the government ought to finance those good things. After all, the cost to any one taxpayer will be negligible, while the benefits will be so large. The cumulative effect of this attitude is the federal debt, which currently stands at around $8.4 trillion or more than $28,000 per resident.[5] The debt will continue to grow until the Treasury is so overgrazed that there is nothing left—or until people start to monitor spending more carefully and forcefully.

Most states are not allowed to go heavily into debt without voter approval, but that doesn't prevent problems. Typically, during boom years state revenues increase and legislators respond by creating new programs. Each new program creates a new constituency whose aim is to defend that program. When a recession hits, declining revenues force legislators to choose between cutting program budgets or increasing taxes. Since lobbyists for the programs are louder than lobbyists for taxpayers, the taxpayers are often hit with an increased bill just when they can least afford to pay it.

39. Courts and Voters: The Last Lines of Defense

Courts and voters should be able to prevent Congress and the administration from overspending. With Congress's focus on pork and the president's hands tied by the civil service system, the courts in particular could help defend against needless government growth and bureaucracy. Unfortunately, the U.S. Supreme Court has withdrawn from the battle.

Before 1937, the U.S. Supreme Court frequently voided federal programs that went beyond a strict reading of the Constitution. But after the Court blocked several New Deal programs, President Franklin Roosevelt urged Congress to increase the number of members on the Court, which is not set by the Constitution. That would allow Roosevelt to "pack" the Court with justices favorable to his views. Seemingly to avoid such Court packing, Justice Owen Roberts did an about-face and started voting in favor of Roosevelt's programs. Cases that had previously been five-to-four against big government switched to five-to-four in favor. From then on, the Court upheld virtually all big-government programs.

In one famous case, the U.S. Department of Agriculture regulated the amount of wheat farmers could grow so as to keep wheat prices high. Congress claimed that it had the authority to regulate farmers under the interstate commerce clause of the Constitution. But an Ohio farmer named Roscoe Filburn argued that the federal government could not regulate how much he grew because he fed all his grain to his own livestock. The Court ruled, however, that if Filburn had not grown his own grain he would have had to buy it and the grain he bought might have crossed a state line.[1] This precedent was recently used by the U.S. Supreme Court to justify the enforcement of federal marijuana laws against people who grew their own marijuana for medical purposes in states where such use is legal.[2] In effect, the Court places almost no limit on the powers of the federal government.

In another recent case, the U.S. Supreme Court granted extremely broad powers to federal bureaucracies. The Natural Resources Defense Council had convinced a circuit court that the Environmental Protection Agency was not doing enough to clean the air. Chevron, whose plant would be affected by the ruling, appealed to the U.S. Supreme Court, arguing that, though the law was vague, the agency's interpretation of the law was "reasonable." The Court ruled that so long as an agency's interpretation was reasonable, the courts should defer to that interpretation.[3] This *Chevron deference doctrine* means that when Congress writes vague laws, it effectively gives bureaucracies the power to do just about anything they want.

In a 1997 case involving the Forest Service, the Sixth Circuit Court openly challenged Chevron deference. The Forest Service, said the court, had an incentive to lie about its timber sale program because that program enhanced the agency's budget. For this reason, the court argued, courts should be more skeptical of the agency's policies.[4] When the case went to the U.S. Supreme Court, it was overturned on other grounds, so we don't know if the Court would have agreed with the circuit court's argument.

The Chevron ruling has become one of the most frequently cited cases in American law as court after court has been forced by it to defer to agency policies. It pretty much renders the courts ineffective as a check on government bureaucracy.

Voters are the Constitution's ultimate check against a federal government out of control. Yet voters have as much incentive to study the federal budget as farmers do to study meteorology. Although the weather is the most important factor in determining the profitability of most farmers, it is completely beyond their ability to predict or control. Thus, few students at agricultural colleges study meteorology.

To voters, taxes are distasteful but ultimately unavoidable. Nor can they do much about them. Although the average taxpayer pays nearly $5,000 per year in personal federal income taxes, taking the time to successfully lobby Congress to reduce the tax burden would cost anyone far more than any likely reduction. Thus, taxpayers form a weak lobby, at best, for reducing federal spending.

When federal spending is financed out of borrowing, taxpayers have even less of an incentive to complain. Although public borrowing saps the economy because it takes money from productive activities and spends it on things like $900 toilet seats and below-cost timber sales, taxpayers do not immediately notice this in their paychecks.

When it comes to voting, taxpayers face a dilemma. They do not like paying taxes to Washington that they can only hope to get back in the form of pork and entitlements. But everyone can justify his or her own personal pork. As long as the system is rigged, it makes sense for them to vote for the incumbent to maximize their own take. Everyone has become a member of some special interest group, whether it favors the arts, education, defense-related jobs, or family farms. Congressional incumbents have made their seats virtually invulnerable simply by giving pork to enough special interest groups in their districts to gain the groups' votes each election.

Part Seven
Instead of Planning

If all the men who have worked for me, directly and indirectly for the past ten years, and who are now scattered through the four quarters of the earth, were marshaled on the plain outside of the city, organized and equipped for war, I could march to the proudest capital of the world and the armies of Europe could not withstand me. I am the master of all the world. But during all my life I have worked for other men, and thus I am every man's servant, and so are we all—servants to many masters and masters of many servants. It is thus that men are gradually becoming organized into one vast body-politic, every one striving to serve his fellow man and all working for the common welfare.

—John Wesley Powell[1]

Human societies have developed four ways of allocating scarce resources: violence, religion, politics, and markets. Most people agree that violence is not the appropriate means of settling disputes, and most Americans agree that religion is only appropriate for members within a particular religious group. That leaves politics and markets.

Government planning is the almost inevitable result of using politics to allocate resources on any large scale. On a small scale, elected officials or other government leaders can make decisions on a case-by-case basis. But when the area or resources being managed become large enough, the leaders turn decisions over to a planning bureaucracy.

Planning is not the only means governments have of allocating resources. Markets and trade result partly from government policies that define property rights and help people defend their property rights against theft and trespass. There are many cases of people spontaneously developing and defending property rights without government assistance, such as in mining areas of the Old West and certain fishing areas. However, government assistance can ensure

311

that allocations are fair and trades or transfers of property take place without compulsion or violence.

Where planners see their role as providing a substitute for markets, this alternative view sees the role of government as ensuring that markets work. Many so-called market failures are, in reality, government failures. Markets require property rights, which means that property must be clearly defined, defendable from trespass or theft, and that the owner must be allowed to divest or sell the property. Government rules prevent people from owning or selling many resources, including wildlife and water. Problems with these resources are not the results of market failure but of the government failure to define and allow the trading of property rights in those resources.

When markets are free to work, they work very well, providing people with a wide variety of abundant, affordable goods. Environmental threats, such as timber cutting threatening wilderness or air pollution threatening public health, take place when resources such as wilderness or clean air are excluded—usually by government action—from the marketplace.

Some resources, such as endangered species, may be truly non-marketable. Yet government planning has failed to protect these resources any better than the free market. One alternative is to use fiduciary trusts to protect such resources. Trusts have a long history of helping people protect assets and resources that otherwise might be looted by unscrupulous managers (including government managers). The biggest advantage of trusts may actually be mistrust: whereas courts traditionally presume that government managers and planners have the public's best interests at heart, courts presume that trust managers are strictly self-interested and place the burden on those managers to prove that they are acting responsibly.

It is likely that roads and sewers and schools and libraries can all be produced by private parties with little or no government involvement. Yet government agencies will continue to provide many of these functions. To ensure that they work effectively, legislatures should design each agency to have a very narrow mission and align its incentives with that mission. As far as possible, road, transit, sewer, water, and other agencies should be funded out of user fees. This will help the agencies define and achieve their objectives while minimizing the pitfalls of comprehensive, politically driven planning.

The best solutions to society's problems will come from a respect for property rights, the use of trusts to protect nonmarketable resources, and narrowly defined government agencies whose incentives are aligned as closely as possible with their goals. While implementing these solutions will never be as easy as stating them, these tools will go far toward solving the problems that planning tends to make worse.

40. 246 Varieties of Cheese

When plans go astray, planners and planning advocates blame failure on politics or say that the wrong people were put in charge. This book has shown instead that failure is inevitable. We should not be surprised that a planning agency created to save Portland from turning into Los Angeles decides instead to replicate Los Angeles in Portland. Nor should we be surprised that a government agency created to protect forests from overcutting should overcut them. Neither should anyone be surprised when planners charged with increasing mobility end up reducing mobility. All these things are predictable effects of applying government planning principles to complex problems.

Comprehensive government planning does not work because no one can understand the total complexity of the world in which we live. As a result, planning has two very predictable results. First, it produces surpluses of things that people do not really want. Second, it produces shortages of things that people do want.

Fortunately, people have developed an alternative system for dealing with that complexity. This system can easily solve complex problems because it does not require any one person to deal with more than a tiny part of those problems. This system is called the market.

The market uses a simple tool, prices, to give everyone in the market signals about the costs and values of various goods in the market. When the price of a good goes up, buyers will find substitutes or otherwise curtail their use of that good. At the same time, producers of the good will find ways to produce more. In this way, shortages and surpluses tend to be small and short-lived.

Think, for example, about all that is involved in producing a seemingly simple good such as milk. People laugh when they hear that children do not know that milk comes from cows. But few people really understand all the complexity involved in getting milk from farms to people's refrigerators.

First, dairy farmers must choose the breed of cow they raise. Holsteins produce the most milk, while Jerseys produce the highest percentage of butterfat. Other breeds have other advantages and disadvantages. Farmers must also decide whether to produce milk year-round, for the fresh-milk market, or seasonally, for the cheese and other processed-food market. Of course, farmers also need land and food for the cows.

Once cows are milked, the milk must be quickly transported to a processor that can pasteurize it. Pasteurized milk, of course, can be made into many products, including cheese, butter, ice cream, cottage cheese, yogurt, and fresh milk. Each of these breaks down into many other products; fresh milk, for example, is sold as skim milk, 1/2 percent butterfat, 1 percent, 2 percent, 3.5 percent or whole milk, 5 percent, half-and-half (10 to 12 percent), whipping cream (30 percent), and heavy cream (36 to 40 percent), not to mention buttermilk and other variations. Although no dairy offers every variety of dairy foods, most make several different products and have to decide which ones and how much of each to make.

Once processed, the milk must be packaged in cardboard, plastic, or other cartons. The production of such cartons would be a lengthy story in itself. Then, the products must be transported to distribution centers and from there to grocery stores. Since fresh milk has a short shelf life, warehouse companies and supermarkets must be careful not to order so much that milk spoils while ordering enough to give customers the selection of products they want. Other milk products, such as cheese, have a longer shelf life but can also come in so many varieties that grocers despair of finding space for them all.

All these decisions—from which breed of cow to raise to what kinds of products to make to how to package and ship those products to how much of each product grocery warehouses and stores will carry—are made by individuals in response to prices: the prices offered by dairy processors for raw milk, the prices of various types of milk containers, the price of transporting raw and processed milk, and the prices of various varieties of milk and other dairy products in the market. Unlike the demands placed on comprehensive planners, no single player in the market needs to know everything about the entire chain of events from calf to supermarket, because it is all coordinated by prices.

Suppose instead that the government were producing and distributing milk to people and you were in charge of planning dairy operations. Would you be able to know all that was needed about dairy land, dairy cow breeds, transportation, packaging, the hundreds of varieties of dairy products, and what consumers wanted or expected out of dairy foods? You would probably start with some rules of thumb, such as that people drink an average of so much milk and eat so much cheese each year. Would you distribute that much to every person or use the intermediary of a grocery store? Would you remember not to send so much milk to grocery stores in communities that have a high percentage of lactose-intolerant people? To simplify your job, you might dispense with certain varieties. Who really needs 2 percent milk when they can mix skim milk and whole milk together?

Now multiply these questions and problems by all the other major kinds of food in your supermarket: fruits, vegetables, fish, poultry, red meat, baked goods, and so forth. Then add all the products you can get in department stores, variety stores, automotive stores, clothing stores, and all the other specialty stores in the world. The problem of planning the production and distribution of these goods becomes impossible. No wonder soviet supermarkets in the 1980s had an average of fewer than a dozen items on their shelves at any given time, whereas American supermarkets had thousands of times that many.

"How can you govern a country that has 246 varieties of cheese?" Charles de Gaulle once asked.[1] The answer is: if you rely on planners—as France did at the time de Gaulle said this—you can't. But if you rely on prices and markets, you can easily have hundreds or thousands of kinds of cheese and other dairy products.

The Soviet Union had a bureau called *Goskomtsen* whose task was to set prices for all goods in the economy. The 200,000 items it was able to price each year represented less than half the items in the economy, which in turn was only a small fraction of the items in a Western market economy.[2] The prices they set were usually "wrong," meaning they resulted in surpluses of some goods and shortages of many others.

The market does not work for everything, but when it works, it works very well. Thanks to the workings of the market, Americans have an incredible abundance of goods and services available to them. Institutions such as the futures market and title companies smooth market transactions so that nearly everyone can benefit from reasonably priced goods and affordable housing.

One minority school of planning, led by University of Southern California (USC) planning professors Peter Gordon and Harry Richardson, says that the role of planners should be to make the market work, not to act as a substitute for it. "We are not against planning," they say, "but we are against inefficient and inequitable interventions" in the market. Instead, they support "innovations in the employment of price incentives in land use planning."[3] Notably, the USC planning department is associated with a real estate school, not an architecture school.

The problem with Gordon and Richardson's aspiration is that planners—with the possible exception of those graduating from USC—are not suited by either training or disposition to apply market incentives to planning. Moreover, once markets are in place, the number of planners or others needed to monitor them is far less than the number of planners needed to implement ordinary plans. Rather than train and hire planners to apply markets, legislators and municipal councilors should learn how to directly use markets themselves. The following chapters provide a basic guide to doing so.

41. Make the Market Work

Markets cannot solve every environmental and social problem. But they can solve a lot of problems that are poorly handled today using government planning and regulation. Markets can work for any resource, good, or service that has clearly defined property rights. Economists James Gwartney and Richard Stroup say there are three requirements for property rights: property must be *definable*, *defendable*, and *divestible*. In other words, you must be able to define where your property ends and someone else's begins; you must be able to protect your property from being used by people who you do not want to use it; and you must be able to sell your property.

When the market does not work, people call it "market failure." But many cases of market failure are really government failure: the government has prevented the market from working for certain goods and services, often by making it impossible for people to defend or sell their property.

Wildlife, fisheries, and water are some examples of government failure. Under our legal system, no one is allowed to own wildlife living in the forests, fish swimming in the rivers, or water flowing in the streams. But if someone shoots an elk, hooks a salmon, or draws water out of the creek, then he or she can own it. This system gives people incentives to use these resources but no incentives to conserve them.

American bison nearly became extinct, and some species of bison and elk did become extinct, because of this system. Even if you had wanted to conserve these species, under 19th-century laws you could not have done so. If you decided not to kill a particular buffalo or elk to preserve the species, you could not have prevented the next person from killing it. You would have given up whatever benefit you could have gained from killing it but not gotten anything in return.

Cattle replaced buffalo on the plains because cattle could be owned and protected. If you owned a herd of cattle, only you could legally

319

decide to kill them. If someone else did so, they would be guilty of theft and could be prosecuted. So you had an incentive to maintain your cattle herd, something that no one had for a herd of buffalo or elk. In short, property rights for wildlife did not work because wildlife, by law, failed the defendability test: no one could legally stop others from killing them.

Water is a similar issue. In the western United States, only people who owned land next to streams could own the water in those streams. Plus, they could only own the water if they took it out of the stream; if they left it in the stream, someone else could take it out. Water was distributed among landowners based on a *prior appropriations* doctrine. This meant that if you or previous owners of your land were the first to take water from a stream, you would have the senior right to take as much water as you regularly consumed. Other people could also take water from that stream as long as they did not interfere with your consumption. In years when water was short, only the people with the most senior rights could take the water.

One aspect of this legal policy was a *use-it-or-lose-it* doctrine. If you stopped using your water, you would lose your rights to that water. Water rights accompanying land were often worth as much or more than the land itself, so farmers would not risk losing those rights by leaving water in streams even if they wanted to protect fish in droughty years. This gave everyone incentives to use their entire allocation of water whether or not they really needed it. Modern irrigation systems use far less water than those used a century ago, but no one had an incentive to install efficient irrigation systems because doing so would mean losing their water rights. In droughty years, irrigators would suck a stream dry, leaving no water for fish or wildlife—not because they hated fish or wildlife but because they didn't want to lose their water rights. By law, water failed the divestability test: people could own a water right, but they couldn't sell that right without selling their land.

In *Cadillac Desert*, Mark Reisner showed how the prior appropriations doctrine wastes water in California and other arid states. The least valuable crop in California is pasture, which is also the most water-intensive crop. The most valuable crop, almonds, is one of the least water-intensive crops. Farmers with water rights who grow almonds must dedicate a portion of their farms to pasture just so they can use their full allocation of water.[1] The result is less profit for the farmers and less water for everyone else.

Problems with wildlife becoming extinct, overfishing, and water shortages are not market failures. They are government failures. They could easily be resolved by creating markets for these resources. History shows that this works.

In the early 20th century, the states began claiming the right to control when and how wildlife could be killed and charged people who wanted to hunt and fish. The fees they collected gave wildlife managers both an incentive and a source of revenue to protect huntable wildlife from extinction. The results are some of the most successful recoveries of endangered species in history: species whose numbers had declined to a few thousand or even a few hundred in 1920 had grown to hundreds of thousands by 2000. This worked because the state wildlife agencies began treating wildlife as property, with themselves as the owners. But the system was only effective with game species, and many states did little to protect nongame species.[2]

Markets can solve numerous problems that are poorly addressed by regulation and planning. Broadly speaking, there are two major kinds of so-called market failure: *open-access resources* and *public goods*. Markets can easily solve the problems of open-access resources, but not public goods. It is easy to confuse these two kinds of resources, and many people who fear markets try to define every problem as a public good so that they can claim there are no market solutions to that problem.

An open-access resource is one that is shared by a large number of people. The classic example is "the tragedy of the commons," the commons being (in Garrett Hardin's prime example) a rangeland that many people shared to feed their cattle. The problem, Hardin said, was that everyone would have an incentive to overgraze the land because each individual would get the benefit of overgrazing but would share the cost with everyone else.

A rangeland may have been a poor choice of examples for Hardin's story because, in actual practice, the small numbers of people who share rangelands are usually able to develop formal or informal agreements about who gets to use the land so that it is not overgrazed. For example, in the 19th-century West, ranchers who raised cattle or sheep grazed them on federal lands and divided up the

321

pastures among themselves. Yet problems occurred when owners of transient sheep herds—people who had no lands themselves but simply moved the sheep from one public pasture to another—entered an area because the sheep would eat all the forage that landowning ranchers expected to use themselves. Ranchers would sometimes try to keep the transient sheep herds away by deliberately overgrazing the range before the sheep arrived.[3]

A similar situation occurred in the beaver-trapping era of the early 19th century. Beaver were effectively an open-access resource, but Hudson Bay Company instructed its trappers to always leave some beaver behind in every watershed so that there would be more beaver in the future. When American trappers affiliated with the Rocky Mountain Fur Company crossed west of the Rocky Mountains into areas that Hudson Bay Company regarded as "its" land, the latter company instructed its trappers to take every last beaver so as to discourage the American trappers.

In short, open-access resources can be effectively and conservatively managed by small groups of people who know and trust one another. But when too many people get involved, when strangers are involved, or when people start acting competitively, some form of property rights must be used to protect the resource. Fortunately, any open-access resource can be treated as property simply by dividing it up among the shared owners.

A public good is not so easily fixed by markets. A public good is a good that benefits everyone whether or not they pay for it. In other words, public goods fail the defendability test because no one can keep other people from using them. The classic example is national defense; an army or weapon that protects some residents of a nation from foreign invaders will generally protect them all. So asking people to pay for national defense through voluntary contributions will probably not work because too many people will be tempted to be *free riders*, enjoying the benefits without paying the costs.

Peter Gordon and Harry Richardson point out that true public goods are rare. Most of "what passes for public goods," they say, "can be provided by the private sector almost as easily as by the public sector."[4] Although certain historical and cultural resources and endangered species might be public goods, most of the environmental problems that planners deal with are not public goods at all but are really open-access resources. Even many resource problems that truly involve public goods can best be solved through private means because government action is usually too slow and too politicized to effectively address the issue.

Unfortunately, the very factors that make it difficult for markets to handle public goods also make it difficult for government to deal with them. "It is not enough that there is something government *could* do that would give a better outcome" than the market, says economist David Friedman. "There must also be a reason to *expect* government to do it. . . . The incentives of the relevant political actors have to be such that it is in their interest to act in ways that result in the improved outcome"[5] (emphasis added).

Planning advocates often use other kinds of market failures to justify government planning, including externalities, monopolies, and inequitable distribution of wealth. Externalities result when someone can impose some of their costs on others. But most externalities exist because of open-access resources, such as air or water. The solution for them is the same as for open-access resources. In general, the goal should be to internalize externalities, that is, ensure that the people who get the benefits of their actions are also the ones who pay the costs.

True monopolies, like public goods, are in fact very rare, and usually exist only if they are protected by government laws or regulation. Technological change takes place so quickly that even if someone manages to gain a monopoly in one field, consumers can quickly find substitutes. For example, the development of the telephone ended Western Union's near monopoly on telegraphic communication. In turn, the telephone's near monopoly on modern communications was broken up by the development of cell phones and the Internet. Even if the government had not broken up AT&T, its monopoly power would be greatly diminished today. If real monopolies exist, the solution is government antitrust laws, not regulation and planning.

Government planning is also a poor solution to inequitable wealth distribution because the wealthy tend to have far more political power than the poor. Thus, planning programs that start with the aim of reducing inequitable distributions of wealth often end up concentrating it instead. This can be seen in the various land-use programs that enrich wealthy homeowners while they impoverish low-income families who do not own their own homes.

For all the problems with markets, they tend to work much better than government. When the market does not work perfectly, government intervention should be limited to improving the incentives, not planning and regulating to try to achieve some predetermined outcome.

42. Turn Open-Access Resources into Property

What is the best way to deal with an open-access resource? Some answers can be gained by looking at the experiences in former soviet nations that, after 1990, had to deal with all kinds of state-owned factories, properties, and resources. In general, countries that quickly privatized those properties did better than countries that held onto some state-owned programs in the hope that state management could be made more efficient. It is easier for governments to let private companies go bankrupt if they are poorly managed than to let government-owned companies go out of business. This means government managers have less of an incentive to become efficient to avoid bankruptcy.

The Western world has numerous successful examples of open-access resources being converted to property. To protect fish and conserve streams, in 1987 the state of Oregon changed its water laws to allow irrigators who install more efficient irrigation equipment to sell some of the water they save or use it for other purposes, including dedicating the water to in-stream flows.[1] Irrigators who save water get to keep, sell, or reallocate 75 percent of the water they save and the other 25 percent is dedicated to in-stream flows.

Another 1987 Oregon law allows people to buy or lease a water right from a landowner and then leave the water in the stream.[2] This led people to form the Oregon Water Trust, which raises money from donors to buy water rights. The trust has developed several ways that it can efficiently protect in-stream flows. For example, it may buy an option to lease water in low-water years. When water is abundant, irrigators can use the water they need and still leave water in the stream. In droughty periods, the Oregon Water Trust can exercise its option and pay irrigators to leave water in the streams. The irrigators get paid enough to be compensated for any losses they incur by not using their full water rights that year, while fish have water every year.[3] The owner retains the rights to leased water so leasing the rights does not reduce the owner's property values.

In the 1980s, the government of New Zealand created markets for its ocean fisheries by giving fishing rights to the people who had historically fished in the area. Someone who had historically taken 1 percent of a particular fishery would be given the right to 1 percent of future harvests of that fishery. Instead of having an incentive to deplete the fishery—because any fish they left behind would be taken by someone else—the people who own fishing rights have an incentive to have a growing fishery because it means the value of their share of the fish is growing.[4] Similar laws exist in Iceland. As a result, New Zealand and Iceland have the only ocean fisheries in the world that are growing rather than shrinking.[5]

In these two cases, resources that had previously been publicly owned were effectively privatized. Yet the public ownership was more imaginary than real. If a publicly owned stream is drained dry by irrigators or a publicly owned fishery is fished to extinction by commercial fishers, the public gets little benefit. Allowing irrigators to sell water rights or allowing fishers to own a portion of a fishery helps ensure that those resources will be available for future generations.

Property does not have to be privately owned for it to be treated as property. As previously noted, state management of sports fisheries and huntable wildlife has been remarkably successful. Government construction of highways, and in particular the Interstate Highway System, has produced huge benefits. In both cases, government agencies had incentives to act like private owners because their revenues came from the resources they produced. State wildlife agencies received most or all of their revenues from hunting and fishing licenses and, later, from sales taxes on guns, ammunition, and fishing tackle. These sources of revenues gave the agencies incentives to promote wildlife herds and fisheries production, because more wildlife and fish meant more license revenues. Similarly, state highway agencies received most or all of their revenues from gas taxes and other highway user fees. So they had an incentive to build roads in places that would receive the most use, thus generating the most revenues.

For whoever owns or manages a resource, then, the key is to fund that management out of user fees. It does no good to privatize a resource if the new private owner expects to get significant tax subsidies. The United States has about 600 million acres of federal lands and about 400 million acres of privately owned croplands. If the $5 billion in annual subsidies to federal land agencies discourages efficient management of those lands, just think what the $16 billion in annual subsidies given to farmers does to efficient management of private farms.[6]

Beyond user fees, it is important to properly design the incentives that will face resource managers. When New Zealand first privatized its ocean fisheries, it got the incentives wrong. It allocated to each fisher so many tons of fish to catch each year.

"That turned out to be wrong because what we needed to be able to do was allocate more as the fishery grew in size and allocate less if it shrunk in size," says former New Zealand cabinet minister Maurice McTeague. "So we changed that to not be a number of tons that you were entitled to catch, but a proportion of the total allowable catch for that species in that area."[7] This meant that if the fishery grew, each fisher would get the benefit of that growth, thus giving the fishers an incentive to promote conservation and growth.

Correcting this mistake was expensive: having given each fisher the right to harvest so many tons each year, the government had to buy back those rights and then give the fishers the right to harvest a particular percentage each year. While it proved worthwhile because it led to more fish and more fisheries-related jobs, getting the incentives right in the first place would have been better.

43. Protect Public Goods with Trusts

Although a pure free market may not produce an optimal level of public goods, government bureaucracy has not proven to be a notably effective savior of such goods either. The Department of Defense is charged with providing the ultimate public good, national defense, yet due to political pressures, much of what it does is pork barrel rather than defense.

The Forest Service can apply user fees, mainly from timber, to some of its management activities but relies on congressional appropriations for most of its remaining budget. When faced with a conflict between timber and a nonmarket resource such as an endangered species, the agency often favors the resource that generates revenues for its budget. Biologists who are attempting to help recover endangered species have observed that they get as much resistance from public agencies such as the Forest Service as they do from private landowners.

- Biologist Ken Alvarez says that attempts to recover the Florida panther encountered "resistance" or at least a "lack of official enthusiasm" on the part of agencies ranging from the Florida Department of Natural Resources to the National Park Service.[1]
- Mississippi State University biologist Jerome Jackson says that the Forest Service, the army, and even the Fish and Wildlife Service have put up "professional obstacles" to the recovery of the red-cockaded woodpecker.[2]
- Noel Snyder, who led efforts to save the California condor, says that conflicts between the U.S. Fish and Wildlife Service and California Department of Fish and Game sometimes led to a near-gridlock in the recovery program.[3]

Obviously, it is not enough for Congress to order agencies to do something. It must also give them incentives to do it or, at the very least, ensure that their existing incentives do not conflict with the new task.

However, agencies that are funded entirely out of appropriations are not necessarily any better caretakers of public goods. The Fish and Wildlife Service is charged with protecting and recovering all terrestrial and freshwater endangered species in the United States. But long before the passage of the Endangered Species Act, the Fish and Wildlife Service had the goal of eliminating or controlling wildlife species that were regarded as pests, such as coyotes and prairie dogs. For decades, the Fish and Wildlife Service and its predecessor agency, the U.S. Biological Survey, killed thousands of prairie dogs each year, usually by poisoning. To advertise its prowess, the Biological Survey once distributed a photo showing its name spelled out on the landscape using the bodies of dead prairie dogs.

When the Endangered Species Act was passed, one of the first species listed as endangered was the black-footed ferret, which the Fish and Wildlife Service called "the rarest mammal in North America." It was endangered because it depended entirely on prairie dogs for both food and—because it lived in abandoned prairie dog dens—shelter. The Fish and Wildlife Service was fully aware of the ferret's dependence on prairie dogs, yet for more than a decade after passage of the Endangered Species Act, the agency continued to poison thousands of prairie dogs each year. As a result, the ferret nearly went extinct.[4]

Why did the agency kill prairie dogs when not killing them could make the difference for the black-footed ferret's survival? The answer is simple: key members of Congress who funded the Fish and Wildlife Service cared more about killing prairie dogs than saving ferrets. In fact, they cared so much that in 1986, worried that the Fish and Wildlife Service might stop killing prairie dogs to save the ferret, Congress took the mandate to kill pests away from the Fish and Wildlife Service, which is in the Department of the Interior, and gave it to an agency in the Department of Agriculture.[5] That agency continues to kill prairie dogs in spite of the Endangered Species Act. The point is that politics creates incentives that can prevail over laws and agencies intended to protect public goods.

If neither markets nor government can be relied on to protect public goods, then what else is there? University of California natural resources professor Sally Fairfax suggests that we consider *fiduciary trusts* to protect such resources. A fiduciary trust is based on centuries of common law and is designed to ensure accountability when one person or institution holds and manages property for the benefit of another.

There is a clear difference between a trust and a public agency. When Congress or another legislative body creates a public agency and gives that agency a mission, it expects the employees in the agency to faithfully carry out that mission. Yet if the incentives facing the agency run counter to the agency's mission, the agency will often follow the incentives rather than the mission. The problem is that there are no checks and balances designed to return the agency to its mission rather than its incentives.

The agency missions defined by Congress are usually vague, and the agency's incentives usually spawn a new set of special interest groups who benefit when the agency follows its incentives. So agencies often end up doing something completely different from what they were intended. When agency actions are challenged by members of the public, the U.S. Supreme Court has ruled that courts must defer to agency interpretations of any vaguely worded law. This eliminates a potential check on agency mismanagement.

In contrast, the fundamental presumption behind a trust is that the trustee's incentives are absolutely the opposite of the trust's mission. To put it bluntly, trust law assumes the trustee will want to steal from the trust and leave the beneficiary poor and starving. Trust law therefore includes checks and balances designed to ensure that does not happen—checks and balances that are absent from an ordinary government agency.

Many institutions that are called "trusts" are not true fiduciary trusts. Neither the Social Security Trust Fund nor the Highway Trust Fund is a fiduciary trust; if they were, they would be managed quite differently. However, something can be a fiduciary trust even if it is not called a trust. Many western states own lands that were given to them by the federal government to provide funds for schools. Without using the word "trust," state constitutions have defined how these lands are to be managed, and the courts have interpreted these constitutions as if the lands are to be managed as a fiduciary trust.

A fiduciary trust has the following elements:

- A *settlor* who creates the trust and sets aside resources to be used by the trust;

- A *trust instrument* written by the settlor that defines the goal of the trust and how the trust is to be managed;
- The *property* that is to be held or managed by the trust;
- A *trustee* who is designated to manage the property; and
- The *beneficiary* for whom the property is to be managed.

Congress or another legislative body can be a settlor. The law or ordinance they write can be the trust instrument. The property can be the land, buildings, funds, or other resources to be managed by the trust. The trustee can be a public agency or private organization such as a nonprofit group. The beneficiary can be the general public or a particular part of that public. Although the trust might be set up to protect wildlife or historic sites or for some other purpose, that wildlife or historic site is *not* the beneficiary. The reason for creating the trust is that people want or somehow benefit from that wildlife or historic site, so ultimately people are the beneficiaries.

Once the trust is created, a number of checks and balances are immediately put in place by common-law interpretations of fiduciary trusts. First, the trustee is obligated to act with *undivided loyalty* to the beneficiary. The trustee cannot make a decision that enriches any person or any other public purpose, no matter how meritorious, at the expense of the beneficiary. Since any beneficiary can bring suit challenging a decision that seems to benefit someone else at the beneficiary's expense, trustees tend to be cautious about the decisions they make. This, incidentally, is the reason why the resource to be protected is not the beneficiary; since only beneficiaries can challenge a decision, it is essential that beneficiaries be people.

The second check on the trustee is an obligation to *disclose to beneficiaries* all information necessary to evaluate trust management. In essence, common law includes a built-in freedom of information act for fiduciary trusts. Trustees are required to keep records of all trust transactions and make them and other pertinent information available to beneficiaries to assure that the trustee is acting with undivided loyalty.

A third check on the trustee is an obligation to *preserve the corpus of the trust*. This is particularly important for trusts with perpetual durations, as they would be for most public goods. This obligation means that the trustee cannot manage a trust for short-term gains at the expense of long-term productivity. Although a beneficiary can challenge a trustee if the trustee is acting for the benefit of someone other than the beneficiary, even the beneficiary cannot force the trustee to exploit the trust at the expense of its long-term value. This obligation is probably the strongest legal requirement for what has become popularly known as "sustainability."

As previously noted, states have created trusts whose beneficiaries are public school children and whose properties are state lands. The state of Washington, for example, has earned tens of millions of dollars for public schools by selling timber from its trust lands. During a recession in the 1980s, timber companies said that they had bid too much for Washington State timber and convinced the legislature to relieve them from the obligation of cutting and paying those high prices for that timber. But the schools sued and the courts agreed that this law violated the obligation of undivided loyalty to the trust. However, when schools have sued the trust asking it to cut timber at faster than sustainable rates to increase revenues to the schools, the courts have ruled that this would violate the obligation to preserve the corpus of the trust.

Trusts can be created for many purposes. Many museums have trusts whose purpose is to preserve the cultural or historic resources managed by those museums. Museums that get in trouble for selling paintings or other assets are usually charged with violating their trust obligations.

It is worthwhile to consider the use of trusts to oversee income-producing assets and other nonpublic goods as well as public goods. The full-disclosure requirement is a very effective freedom of information act. The requirement to preserve the corpus of the trust is an excellent sustainability requirement. But if public resources are to be managed as trusts, it is still important to get the incentives right. That means, as far as possible, funding revenue-producing activities out of a share of those revenues, not out of tax dollars. It also means promoting competition by encouraging or requiring agencies to contract out as many of their activities as possible.

333

44. Understand Government's Limits

Part six detailed the problems with government. But sometimes, for political, historical, or other reasons, there is no choice but to use a government agency to address a problem. In designing such agencies, keep the following in mind:

1. Give government agencies a single, precisely defined mission.
2. Design agency incentives so they complement rather than conflict with the mission.
3. Write performance criteria against which agencies can be evaluated.
4. Open agencies to competition.
5. Fund revenue-generating agencies exclusively out of their user fees.
6. Create a competitive environment for agencies or branches of agencies that do not generate revenue.

1. *The mission*: Government agencies must have a single, easy-to-measure mission. "Government will malperform if an activity is under pressure to satisfy different constituencies with different values and different demands," says Peter Drucker. "Performance requires concentration on one goal."[1] That means that separate agencies for local sewer, water, solid waste, and other functions will work better than a superagency that tries to handle all those functions. It also means that numerous local agencies work better than a massive regional agency.

It is also important to prevent "hidden" missions from being added to agency mandates. Overtly, urban transit and Amtrak are supposed to have the missions of moving people. Both have failed to be effective because Congress saddled these institutions with a hidden mission of maintaining union jobs. To apply for federal grants, transit agencies are required to gain the approval of their unions. Until 1997, to delete unproductive routes, Amtrak had to give displaced employees six years severance pay. These requirements stifled innovation and productivity improvements.

2. *The incentives*: Give each agency incentives that encourage it to fulfill its mission as efficiently as possible. Whenever possible, this means funding the agency through user fees rather than tax dollars. When the agency must be funded through tax dollars, tie those dollars to measurable targets relating to the agency's mission. It would be far better to let the agency suffer staff and budget cuts than to reward the agency for failure by giving it more money to waste.

3. *Performance criteria*: Give each agency specific performance criteria against which it can be judged. Legislative oversight committees should reevaluate agencies every few years and, if they have not met their performance standards, the committees should find ways to reorganize the agencies and give them new incentives to meet those standards.

4. *Competition*: Recognize that a government monopoly is no better, and could be far worse, than a private monopoly. Whenever possible, allow the agency to be confronted with competition. The Postal Service is much more efficient today than it was 30 years ago because it has to compete with FedEx and UPS. In most cities, private transit operators such as Supershuttle are only allowed to provide airport service. Public transit agencies might operate more efficiently if they had to face more competition from such private operators on other routes.

5. *Funding out of user fees*: Agencies that can generate revenue should be funded exclusively out of a share of their revenues or, better yet, net revenues. As net revenue is a measure of the true value of a program, an incentive to maximize net revenue is better than one to maximize gross revenue. Suppose an agency is funded out of half its net revenue. If it spends $3 million (out of the previous year's revenue) to earn $9 million, its net revenue is $6 million. It would then get $3 million to spend next year.

6. *Intrapreneuring*: Agencies or divisions that cannot generate revenue should be opened to competition from inside or outside the agency. For example, almost every government agency has an accounting department, yet there are many private accounting companies. Agencies should open services such as accounting to bidding, allowing their own departments to bid but ensuring that the process

is competitive. Gifford Pinchot III, the grandson of the founder of the Forest Service, calls this "intrapreneuring."[2]

These guidelines will help government agencies be as efficient as private enterprise, but they are no guarantee. Remember Peter Drucker's rule that "any government activity almost at once becomes 'moral.'" In other words, special interest groups will try to use the mantle of morality to twist the direction of government agencies in their favor. The greatest danger is for agencies that rely on tax dollars rather than user fees. But even federal gasoline user fees for the Interstate Highway System became a moral issue once transit advocates saw that they could divert those fees to their pet programs.

Should the federal government continue to manage the national forests and national parks, or should it turn them over to the states or sell them to private parties? Some people argue that the states have a better record of managing lands than the federal government, although my own research indicates that the state record is better only for state trust lands; state lands not managed as trusts are managed as poorly and inefficiently as federal lands.[3]

Should the federal government continue to collect highway user fees or should it allow the states exclusive jurisdiction over collection and use of those fees? Arizona Representative Jeff Flake argues that, since the Interstate Highway System is complete, the federal gas tax should be eliminated or, at most, reduced to an amount needed to maintain the system. But others argue that eliminating the federal gas tax will leave states short of funds because many states will not be able to raise their taxes to compensate.

The debate over the appropriate role of federal, state, and local governments is as old as the Republic and beyond the scope of this book. The point of this book is that, at whatever level of government, the solution to resource problems will come not from comprehensive, long-range planning but from markets, trusts, and government agencies with clear, narrowly defined missions. The next few chapters offer some ways these ideas can be applied to public land management, transportation, and land-use issues.

45. Reforming Public Land Management

Shortly before leaving office, President Clinton created an Upper Missouri River Breaks National Monument. The monument consisted of 377,346 acres of federal land in Montana managed by the Bureau of Land Management. Under Clinton's proclamation, the monument would still be managed by the bureau, but under a stricter set of rules. However, the proclamation left unclear the monument's exact goal and whether historic activities such as livestock grazing and oil exploration would have to end.

The Foundation for Research on Education and the Environment asked people for proposals on how to manage the monument and resolve conflicts among users. University of California natural resources professor Sally Fairfax and I submitted a proposal for turning this monument into a fiduciary trust. The trust would collect fees for recreation, livestock grazing, and mineral exploration and extraction and use those revenues to restore the monument's 377,346 acres to approximately the condition they were in when Lewis and Clark visited the area in 1803.

To assist the trust, we also proposed the creation of a nonprofit group known as the Friends of the Upper Missouri River. The Friends would educate the public, help raise funds, and provide a structure for volunteers to help restore the area. Anyone would be allowed to join the Friends for a nominal annual fee, say $25.

The trust itself would be overseen by a board of nine trustees, three of whom would be appointed by the secretary of the interior, three of whom would be appointed by the governor of Montana, and three of whom would be elected by the Friends of the Upper Missouri River. This would ensure that national, state, and grassroots interests would all be represented on the board.

Funding of the trust would come from user fees as well as an initial endowment provided by Congress. The trust could use the interest from the endowment but not the principle and could not expect any future appropriations from Congress. We did not propose this, but some state land trusts require that revenues from nonrenewable resources be placed in the endowment fund.

Oil and gas and other extractive uses would be allowed only if they did not degrade the river or otherwise conflict with the trust purpose. In practice, this would mean that recreationists would have first priority on the river, while extractive uses would be allowed that were out of sight of the river.

The Missouri Breaks involved only three different activities that might conflict: river recreation, livestock grazing, and oil and gas. National forests that manage timber, grazing, wildlife, fisheries, watershed, motorized and nonmotorized recreation, and wilderness face a formidable array of potential conflicts. National parks can also suffer significant conflicts between recreation use and preservation of natural or historic resources, such as the debate over snowmobiling in Yellowstone Park.

To address these issues, I developed a trust proposal that is somewhat more complicated than the Missouri Breaks trust. For each national forest, park, or appropriate combination of forests or parks, I proposed the creation of *two* trusts. The first trust would manage the marketable resources: recreation in the case of parks, and recreation, timber, grazing, and minerals in the case of forests. The second trust would manage the nonmarket resources, such as nongame wildlife habitat, historic sites, and to a certain extent watershed values. Water is potentially a marketable resource, but that is a matter of state law, so management will vary from state to state.

The purpose of the market trust is to maximize revenues for the nonmarket trust. To ensure that it does so, the market trust would be funded out of a percentage of its revenues or, even better, a percentage of its net revenues. For example, if a forest earns $12 million in one year and spends $4 million to get that, and if it were funded out of 50 percent of its net revenues, then it would get to keep $4 million of the total revenues for its budget for the following year. The remaining revenues, in this case $8 million, would go to the nonmarket trust.

The purpose of the nonmarket trust is to maximize the nonmarket stewardship values in the region it serves. To do this, it could use its share of market revenues to buy land or easements from private landowners or buy easements from the state or federal land trusts. For example, suppose a nonmarket trust decides that a particular endangered species needs a particular kind of forest to survive. The trust could pay private landowners or market trust managers to produce that kind of forest.

Each national forest in the West, or in some cases pairs of national forests, could be made into individual market trusts. Eastern national forests tend to be smaller, so more forests would likely be combined into trusts. Large national parks such as Yellowstone and Yosemite would be individual trusts, whereas smaller ones might be combined. The nonmarket trusts would cover larger areas, perhaps entire states, collecting all the revenues from the market trusts in those areas. However, separate nonmarket trusts would be created for natural and historic resource conservation, and the revenues from individual forests or parks would be dedicated to one or the other nonmarket trust.

As in the Missouri Breaks case, each trust would have an associated friends group that would, among other things, elect some or all of the trustees on the trust board. Personally, I would support having all trustees elected by the friends group, but it might be politically necessary to "buy" the support of state governors or other officials by letting them appoint some members. Whoever is on the board is obligated by trust law to solely represent the beneficiaries of the trust, not the people who appointed them. The actual method of selecting board members may be less important than ensuring that the members clearly understand this obligation.

Together, management of the national forests, national parks, Bureau of Land Management lands, and federal fish and wildlife refuges costs taxpayers well over $5 billion per year. Yet I am confident that these lands could be managed as revenue-producing trusts. Managers today are not allowed to collect a full range of user fees and do not have an incentive to collect all the fees they are allowed to collect. However, administrative costs are much higher than necessary due to bloated bureaucracies and budgets. Managing these lands as trusts would lead to innovative methods of collecting fees and rapid reductions in bloat.

Nor do I fear that managing public lands for maximum revenues is likely to lead to the destruction of the environmental values of those lands. The Forest Service estimates that recreation is by far the most valuable use of the national forests, and outdoor recreationists are highly sensitive to unsightly activities. Forest Service data also show that recreationists are willing to pay the most to use wilderness and other unspoiled landscapes. If managers were allowed to charge a wide range of recreation user fees, they would have powerful incentives to protect scenery, water quality, wildlife habitat, and other environmental resources. The nonmarket trusts would provide backup to ensure that recreation and other uses do not harm any values that are not protected by managers seeking to attract recreation users.

If Congress is unwilling to convert national forests, national parks, and other federal lands into trusts on a wholesale basis, Congress should at least experiment with trusts and other institutional arrangements on a portion of federal lands. The Forest Options Group, a group of industry and environmental leaders, identified five different institutional packages, including trusts, and suggested that each package be tested on two national forests per package.[1] A few years of such testing will help Congress identify which package or combination of reforms will best apply to the various federal lands.

46. Reforming Transportation

One of the biggest obstacles to saving our nation from the planners' grip is federal transportation legislation, which Congress reauthorizes every six years. This legislation defines how the billions of dollars in gasoline taxes that the federal government collects will be spent. The 1991 reauthorization, known as ISTEA, required state and regional governments to prepare long-range transportation plans and to update those plans every five years, which effectively put these agencies in a permanent planning mode. The law should have been called the "urban planners' full-employment act."

Planning requirements were retained in the 1998 and 2005 updates to the law. But each successive update has included more and more earmarks, that is, mandatory funding for particular projects. These earmarks raise the suspicion that Congress does not really trust the plans it has required states and regions to write. In fact, members of Congress just want to be able to brag to their constituents that they delivered juicy pieces of pork to their states or districts. Since the decline in defense spending that followed the fall of the Soviet Union, transportation has become Congress's biggest source of pork, and the House Transportation Committee is the largest committee in congressional history as almost every member of Congress wants to get in on the action.

Arizona Representative Jeff Flake has proposed that the federal gas tax be eliminated. Now that the Interstate Highway System has been completed, Flake argues, state and local taxes should be sufficient to handle state and local transportation needs. He managed to get about eight votes for his point of view. At the same time, members of Congress are clearly embarrassed by the pork fest that went into the 2005 transportation bill. When President Bush committed federal resources to help rebuild the Gulf Coast after Hurricanes Katrina, Rita, and Wilma, many people suggested that Congress should give up the pet projects earmarked in the transportation bill to provide funding for reconstruction.[1] Some members of Congress, including the then House minority leader Nancy Pelosi, took the proposal seriously.[2] This suggests that there may be an opportunity for a major revision of the law in the next reauthorization.

What Congress Should Do

Congress should undertake the following actions:

1. Congress must eliminate the long-range transportation planning requirements in the law. Such planning requirements have as much value for transportation as long-term weather forecasts had for the Army Air Corps in World War II.

2. Congress should also untie transportation funding from air pollution. While clean air is important, 35 years of cleanup programs have proven that reducing tailpipe emissions is far more successful and cost-effective than programs aimed at shaping behavior and influencing transportation choices.

3. Congress should require that annual transportation plans, known as *transportation improvement plans*, be cost-effective in providing safe transportation. All potential urban transportation capital improvements, for example, should be ranked by regional transportation commissions according to their dollar cost per hour of reduced congestion delay. Funding should go to only the highest-ranked projects unless safety or some other consideration takes an overriding priority.

4. Congress should specify that federal funds be based on transportation considerations alone and *not* be used to try to stimulate urban or regional development. Such efforts merely politicize transportation funding and promote the creation of insider networks of people who benefit from pork at everyone else's expense.

5. Congress should allocate transit funds to urban areas based on a formula that considers the population and transit ridership of those areas. While Congress can argue over the details of this formula, once the formula is established Congress should not disrupt it with earmarks.

6. Congress should specify that no federal transportation funds be given to nonprofit groups or be used in any way to support political lobbying.

7. Congress should eliminate labor requirements that discourage innovative solutions to transportation problems.

8. Congress should encourage experimentation and remove requirements that states or regions reimburse the federal government when experiments fail.

After passing this law, members of Congress can still brag that they brought billions of dollars of funding to their states—and only some constituents will know that the funding formulas would have ensured that much funding in any case. The funding formulas will reduce the incentive for regions to pork out on expensive projects and encourage them to use their share of the funds as effectively as possible.

What the Administration Should Do

The administration should reorganize the Department of Transportation. The current organization, which is by mode, discourages an even-handed evaluation of the benefits and costs of each mode. The Federal Transit Administration and Federal Highway Administration each fight for its own turf and make little effort to ensure that urban transportation funding is truly balanced. A reorganized department would consist of agencies based on geography: for example, an Urban Transportation Agency, Interstate Transportation Agency, and International Transportation Agency. Grants given by the Urban Transportation Agency would be based on the cost-effectiveness of each mode in providing urban mobility.

What State and Regional Governments Should Do

Whether or not Congress reforms federal transportation funding, state governments and regional transportation commissions can do much to improve urban transportation. Since state as well as federal gasoline taxes are spent on urban transportation, state legislatures can impose the same cost-effectiveness requirements on the use of state funds.

In the long run, gasoline taxes will not be sufficient to fund urban transportation. As cars get more fuel-efficient or use alternative fuels, gas tax revenues per mile driven will continue to decline. Gas taxes are not a very efficient user fee in any case because they do not let users know that some highways are more expensive than others or let highway departments know that people are willing to pay more to drive on some roads than others. The decline in gas tax revenues therefore offers an opportunity to try new forms of user fees.

Many analysts believe that electronic toll collection is the highway user fee of the future. A toll road in Toronto relies exclusively on electronic tolls and has no formal tollbooths. Most users purchase toll transponders, which can be made for as little as about $10. Transponders can be treated like phone cards, loaded with credits, and used without invading anyone's privacy. Or users can choose to have tolls charged to their credit card. People driving on the Toronto toll road without a transponder can expect to have their license plates photographed and receive a bill in the mail, including a small surcharge to cover the cost of billing.

Modern tolls are applied mainly to limited access highways. But construction of other arterials can also be costly. The state of Oregon is testing tolls using transponders tied into the global positioning system. If all cars in Oregon had such transponders, it would allow the state to charge tolls on any or all state highways, and local governments would have the option of using the system as well. Although this proposal has generated concern among privacy advocates, tolling advocates think the system can be designed in a way that protects people's privacy.

Whatever system is used, the institutional structure for tolling should recognize that any government agency must have a single, easily defined mission. This means that state legislatures should create independent tolling authorities for each urban area. The toll agency could sell bonds, build roads, collect tolls, and use those tolls to repay the bonds and operate and maintain the roads. No tolls should be transferred to transit agencies, although toll road authorities may be authorized to provide transit services if they find it is the most cost-effective use of their funds.

What Transit Agencies Should Do

Tolls can relieve congestion, but a minority of American households still lacks access to an automobile. Public transit should cost-effectively provide mobility for people who cannot or do not want to drive. This will rarely mean new rail transit, which is far from cost-effective, but even bus service could be made much more effective than it is today. Some ways this could be done include the following:

- Contract out bus routes to private operators. The Colorado legislature requires Denver's transit agency to contract out at least half its bus routes. The buses that it contracts out cost only half as much per bus hour or bus mile as buses that are operated directly by the agency.

- Allow companies that provide airport shuttle services to provide similar services to and from other destinations. Such services are typically between buses and cabs in price and speed.
- Legalize the operation of *collectivos* or other privately operated transit services. *Collectivos* are vans or other private vehicles that may be licensed and certified by a transit agency but are operated on schedules, routes, and fares determined by the owner. Atlantic City's transit system consists entirely of privately owned vans and is the only transit system in the United States that runs without subsidies.
- Provide people who are truly transit dependent, whether for income or other reasons, with transit vouchers that they can use toward fares on existing trains, buses, *collectivos*, taxis, or other public transportation. In effect, give transit subsidies to transit riders rather than transit agencies.

The main obstacles to many of these ideas are political, not technical. Transit unions object to contracting out transit because private operators do not always hire union workers (though they typically pay close to union wages). Taxicab companies object to expanding shuttle services, *collectivos*, or other private transit. Yet implementation of these ideas would do far more for urban mobility than rail transit, dedicated busways, or other expensive transit projects that are so beloved by planners and politicians.

47. Reforming Land Use

Zoning was invented in the 1910s to stabilize and protect property values in neighborhoods of single-family homes. In the past decade or so, planners have used zoning as a weapon to impose changes on neighborhoods of single-family homes. In between, zoning has been used for all sorts of purposes, some worthwhile, but many simply drive up the cost of housing and commercial and industrial development.

The alternative way to protect neighborhood property values is covenants. Some 50 million Americans live in neighborhoods with protective covenants, though in most cases they are in addition to, not a substitute for, zoning. However, many cities in Nevada, Texas, and other states have no zoning and numerous developments in those cities rely exclusively on covenants. Homes in neighborhoods with covenants sell for 5 percent more than homes elsewhere, and since the cost of writing such covenants is low, developers have a strong incentive to use them.[1] The developer also creates a homeowners' association that has the power to enforce and change the covenants.

Houston permits residents of neighborhoods with no covenants to petition to create a homeowners' association and write new covenants. This requires approval of the majority of the voters in the neighborhood. University of Maryland Professor Robert Nelson has suggested that states create a process to allow neighborhoods in cities that have zoning to opt out of the zoning and write covenants instead.[2] The neighborhoods governed by homeowners' associations tend to be much smaller than the neighborhood associations found in many cities; the average homeowners' association has around 200 homes, whereas the average neighborhood association can have thousands or tens of thousands of homes.

Like zoning, homeowners' associations are not perfect. They are somewhat tainted because covenants written in the early part of the 20th century explicitly forbade homeowners from selling to blacks or other minorities. But zoning has a similar tainted history, and there is arguably more implicit racism in many modern zoning codes that make housing unaffordable than in modern covenants, which have been applied to neighborhoods of a wide assortment of incomes.

A more serious problem with homeowners' associations is that some have been overzealous in enforcing their covenants. Covenants will lapse if they are not enforced, and many associations worried that if they allowed even a tiny infraction of the covenants, all their covenants would lapse. The Community Association Institute, which helps and advises homeowners' associations, has encouraged associations to be flexible and compassionate in enforcing their covenants.

Houston inadvertently created another problem when it allowed homeowners' associations that won enforcement actions against their members to make the member pay the association's attorney fees and place a lien on the member's home until the fees were paid. This led to attorneys roaming neighborhoods looking for minor infractions and sending letters to homeowners telling them to fix the problem along with a bill for their services and a threat to put a lien on their homes if they did not pay the bill. This kind of system is unnecessary.

Despite these problems, homeowners' associations and covenants have many advantages over zoning.

- Homeowners can feel confident that the character of their neighborhood will not change without their approval.
- At the same time, no one feels they have any say over land use outside their neighborhoods, so development can take place to market needs without major regulatory obstacles.
- If developers see a market in changing an existing neighborhood, they can negotiate with that neighborhood's homeowners' association and offer to buy homeowners out or to compensate them for the changes. In this way, neighborhoods can evolve to meet changing tastes with the approval of the homeowners and without the iron fist of government planners imposing changes on the neighborhood.

This system of covenants and owners' associations can be applied to industrial, commercial, and retail developments as well.

What States Should Do

Florida, Minnesota, Oregon, Tennessee, Washington, Wisconsin, and other states that have passed legislation requiring cities and counties to do comprehensive planning should repeal those laws. If there are specific problems that such planning legislation was intended to address, such as funding for roads, schools, and other infrastructure, then the states should ensure that an appropriate combination of taxes and user fees allows growth to pay for itself without creating housing shortages or other artificial land shortages. Legislatures should also consider Robert Nelson's proposal to allow neighborhoods and other landowners to opt out of zoning and develop and apply their own covenants instead.

What Local Governments Should Do

Ideally, cities and counties should shut down their planning departments, phase out their zoning codes, and create a process for neighborhoods and other landowners to replace zoning with covenants. This may seem radical, especially when it is recognized that zoning itself is not the problem: the real problems arise when planners try to manage growth or socially engineer the people in their regions.

There are systems of zoning that could be used in place of smart growth or other forms of growth-management planning, for example, cumulative zoning and performance zoning.

- *Cumulative zoning* may limit some areas to single-family housing, but other zones would allow a mixture of uses: single-family and multifamily in multifamily zones; housing and commercial in commercial zones; housing, commercial, or industrial in industrial zones. This form of zoning does not prevent developers from building mixed-use projects in retail or commercial zones and is much less likely to lead to shortages of land in any category.
- *Performance zoning* specifies the maximum effects—traffic, noise, water runoff, and so forth—that are allowed in any zone without dictating the actual use in that zone. It could be used to protect watersheds, for example, or other regional resources that might not receive protection from neighborhood covenants. However, care must be taken to ensure that it does not descend into some form of growth management.

351

In the end, however, the arguments in favor of any zoning system are offset by the danger that the system will lead to more problems than it solves. Cities and counties will be better off finding ways to deal with land-use issues that do not require any form of government-imposed regulation.

48. The American Dream

The best role government can play in our economy is to give people the freedom to choose their own destinies but ensure that people pay the costs of their own choices. In most cases, the best way to do this is to ensure that the market works, not to act as a regulatory substitute for the market.

- Turn open-access resources into private property or ensure that some public agency has the incentives to treat them as private property;
- Internalize externalities;
- Use fiduciary trusts to manage public goods and publicly owned marketable resources;
- Give government agencies (including trusts) precise, easy-to-measure missions and performance standards;
- Maximize the opportunity for competition for both private and public services; and
- Ensure that the incentives facing public or private managers are right, that is, that they are rewarded for doing good things for people and penalized for doing bad things.

When I present these sorts of ideas to people, I am often asked, "What will it look like?" People want to know my vision for the future, in the same way that planners have presented their vision for smart growth or their ideal forest condition for public lands. Will cities be compact or sprawling? Will more people drive or take transit? Will public land managers clearcut the forests or preserve them as wilderness?

The short answer is, I don't know. I am no more capable of predicting the future than planners. What I do know is that markets give people what they want, and because we have a diversity of tastes, markets produce a similar diversity of products. New Urbanists say more people would rather live in tightly knit communities where they can walk to services and ride transit to work. If that is true, builders will cater to those people once regulatory zoning that stands in the way of New Urban development is lifted. Rail advocates say that rail transit can be less expensive than buses or autos, and if so, transportation companies will build more rail lines. That would make me happy because at heart I am a rail fan.

My suspicion, however, is that more freedom, even with the responsibility to pay the full costs of our choices, will lead to more auto driving and low-density development. This is not necessarily my preference, but it is happening in Europe and Asia, despite the fact that many of the countries in those regions have restricted low-density development and heavily taxed autos and fuel for decades.

I also suspect that most federal lands will end up being managed more like national parks than industrial forest or agricultural lands. The best lands for growing trees and crops are mostly in private ownership, whereas public lands can provide high-quality remote recreation unavailable on private land. But I have no doubt that some public lands will be managed for timber, oil and gas, and other extractive uses. I would rely on the nonmarket stewardship trusts, rather than planning and regulation, to ensure that such uses do not permanently damage the land or harm endangered species.

Instead of paying for water, fire, and other services through my taxes, I can imagine a future in which I pay separate bills to public or private water, sewer, fire, and street agencies or companies just as today I pay separate bills to electric and telephone companies. The bills I pay would depend on how much water I use, how many miles I drive—and when and where I drive them—and how much it costs to provide sewer and fire protection services for my neighborhood. When I use public lands, I imagine paying fees, either daily or annual, for basic entry, plus additional fees for hunting, fishing, camping, hiking in wilderness or other special areas, and so forth. I would not mind paying such fees because I know that my fees give managers the incentive to provide me with the kind of recreation I prefer just as buying a gallon of nonfat milk gives the dairies an incentive to make that milk and the grocer an incentive to stock it.

Just as grocers offer filet mignon, hamburger, Gardenburgers®, and many other choices, the markets for housing, urban transportation, and public land recreation will offer similarly broad choices. I can imagine premium fees for certain uses, such as driving on roads that are guaranteed to be uncongested even in the busiest time of the day or hiking in a particular wilderness area in the knowledge that I am one of the few people allowed to be in that area on that particular day. But I also imagine a range of other fees that will be more affordable even though they may not provide quite as exclusive an experience. The market is about choices and tradeoffs, and experience shows that there is more money to be made by serving large numbers of people of moderate incomes than by catering to a few wealthy people.

I may not always be able to afford everything I want. But that will give me an incentive to work a little harder to produce things that other people want so that I can earn the income to get what I want. As Adam Smith realized 230 years ago, that is the best thing about the market: when we all work in our own interest, we also work in everyone else's interest. Thus, the market relies on the very traits that keep government planning from working.

In short, my vision of the future is that we all have the freedom to choose our own lifestyles and the opportunity to earn the money to afford the choices we have made. For more than 200 years, that has been the American dream. If government will stay out of the way, we can continue to achieve that dream for another 200 years.

Notes

Introduction

1. The Intermodal Surface Transportation Efficiency Act of 1991 required that, to be eligible for federal transportation funding, regional planning organizations in every metropolitan area must write long-term regional transportation plans for their urban areas. The law also required states to write long-term transportation plans.

2. *Encarta Dictionary*, tinyurl.com/2qov3z.

Part One

1. James C. Scott, *Seeing Like a State: How Certain Schemes to Improve the Human Condition Have Failed* (New Haven, CT: Yale University Press, 1998), p. 11.

2. Dale Bosworth, "A Process in Need of Change" (speech before the Forest Policy Summit, Forest Service, Rapid City, SD, August 15, 2001), tinyurl.com/3d6sf7.

Chapter 1

1. Dale Champion, "U.S. Rangers' Admission: 'Fake Forests' in California," *San Francisco Chronicle*, April 13, 1985, p. 1.

2. U.S. House of Representatives, *Oversight Hearing before the Subcommittee on General Oversight, Northwest Power, and Forest Management on Region 5 U.S. Forest Service Silvicultural Program, July 8, 1985* (Washington, DC: GPO, 1986), pp. 6–7.

3. Ibid, p. 10.

4. Ibid., p. 8.

5. "Fabulous Bear, Famous Service Fight Annual Billion-Dollar Fire." *Newsweek*, June 2, 1952, pp. 50–54.

6. Herbert Kaufman, *The Forest Ranger: A Study in Administrative Behavior* (Baltimore: Johns Hopkins Press, 1960).

7. Jerry F. Franklin and Dean S. DeBell, "Effects of Various Harvesting Methods on Forest Regeneration," in *Even-Age Management: Symposium held August 1, 1972,* ed. Richard K. Hermann and Denis P. Lavender (Corvallis: Oregon State University, 1973), pp. 29–57, says, "Biologically, no types or species appear to require large clearcuttings for successful regeneration—by 'large' we mean clearcuttings that exceed 10 acres."

8. Senate Committee on Agriculture and Forestry, *National Forest Environmental Management Act: Hearing before Subcommittee on Environment, Soil Conservation, and Forestry*, 93rd Cong., 1st sess., 1973, p. 250.

9. See, for example, the statement of Region 6 Regional Forester H. J. Andrews in the "Hearing Record for the Proposed Shelton Cooperative Sustained Yield Unit," on file at the Olympic Forest supervisor's office, Olympia, WA, September 18, 1946, pp. 10–11.

10. *Douglas-Fir Supply Study* (Portland, OR: Forest Service, 1969), p. 14.

11. "Emergency Directive No. 16," memo from Chief of the Forest Service to regional foresters, May 1973.

Chapter 2

1. Joseph Cone, "Public Involvement and Computer Programs: An Interview with the Director of Forest Service Land Management Planning," *Forest Planning*, April 1980, pp. 15–16.

2. Tom Wolf, "Black Box Ethics," *Forest Planning*, March 1981, p. 11.

3. Anonymous memo apparently from Malheur National Forest employee to Oregon Natural Resources Council, "Malheur Timber Inventories," December 1989.

4. Randal O'Toole, *Review of the Okanagon National Forest Plan* (Eugene, OR: CHEC, 1982), p. 7.

5. Randal O'Toole, "Affidavit of Randal O'Toole on the Santa Fe National Forest Plan," December, 1983.

6. Randal O'Toole, *Review of Region 5 Timber Yield Tables* (Eugene, OR: CHEC, 1986), p. 7.

7. Alan McQuillan, "Yield Tables Used in the Clearwater National Forest Plan" (report to the Sierra Club Legal Defense Fund, January 29, 1988).

8. According to the University of Idaho *Big Tree List*, the tallest tree in Idaho is 229 feet; see tinyurl.com/2n54v7. The tallest tree in the world is 379 feet; see tinyurl.com/qlzxq.

9. Gerry Mackie, "Speculative Bidding: A Prophecy," *Forest Planning*, December 1981, p. 5.

10. Randal O'Toole, *Review of the Beaverhead National Forest Draft Plan and EIS* (Eugene, OR: CHEC, 1983), pp. 2–3.

11. Mackie, "Speculative Bidding," p. 5.

12. "Timber Value Trends in Forest Planning," memo from Region 6 economists to the Washington Office of the Forest Service, Portland, OR, November 23, 1983, pp. 2–4.

13. "Real Price Trends for Timber," memo from Washington office to Region 6, on file at Forest Service Region 6 office, Portland, OR, January 16, 1984, p. 1.

14. Jeffrey M. Stone, "Giving Computer Hardware the Soft Touch," *Forest Planning*, August 1982, pp. 18–20.

15. "Review Draft of Analysis of the Management Situation," unpublished Forest Service memo on file at Hoosier National Forest supervisor's office in Bedford, IN, November 1982 (handwritten note).

16. *Final Environmental Impact Statement for Gallatin National Forest Plan* (Bozeman, MT: Forest Service, 1987), pp. II-64–66.

17. "Procedure for Estimating the Effects of Alternative Forest Plan Prescriptions on Five Flathead National Forest Grizzly Bear Productivity Areas." Unpublished document on file in the Flathead National Forest supervisor's office, Kalispell, MT, 1982.

18. "Managed Yield Table Adjustment Percentage," memo on file at the Mt. Hood National Forest supervisor's office, Gresham, OR.

Chapter 3

1. Quoted in Dale Champion, "U.S. Rangers' Admission: 'Fake Forests' in California," *San Francisco Chronicle*, April 13, 1985, p. 1.

2. U.S. House of Representatives, *Oversight Hearing before the Subcommittee on General Oversight, Northwest Power, and Forest Management on Region 5 U.S. Forest Service Silvicultural Program, July 8, 1985* (Washington, DC: GPO, 1986), pp. 10–11.

3. Tom Barlow et al., *Giving Away the National Forests* (Washington, DC: Natural Resources Defense Council, 1980), appendix 1.

4. *Forest Service Handbook 2409.19.03(5)* (2004).

5. Randal O'Toole, "Cross-Subsidization—The Hidden Subsidy," *Forest Planning*, May 1984, pp. 15–17.

6. Ibid.

7. Richard Behan, *Plundered Promise: Capitalism, Politics, and the Fate of the Federal Lands* (Covelo, CA: Island Press, 2001), p. 33.

8. Richard M. Alston, *FOREST: Goals and Decisionmaking in the Forest Service* (Ogden, UT: Forest Service, 1972), p. 63.

Chapter 4

1. "National Forest Land Management Planning," memo from John Crowell to the Chief of the Forest Service, January 19, 1983.

2. "Draft AMS Direction," memo from Region 6 Regional Forester to Forest Supervisors, May 1984.

3. Fred Trevey, Clearwater National Forest Supervisor, "Timber Resource Strategy Update," memo to Region 1 Regional Forester, February 26, 1990.

4. "Timber Resource Situation on the Wasatch-Cache National Forest," draft Wasatch-Cache National Forest memo to Region 4 Regional Forester, June 7, 1991.

5. *The Flathead National Forest Cannot Meet Its Timber Goal* (Washington, DC: General Accounting Office, 1991).

6. "Forest Engineers Meeting, April 20–21, 1989," memo from Milroy Teigen, Region 5 Assistant Regional Engineer to Forest Engineers, May 5, 1989.

7. *Up from the Ground* (Region 6 Forest Supervisors, November 1989), videotape.

8. "An Open Letter to the Chief of the Forest Service" from Region 1 Forest Supervisors, November 1989.

9. "Feedback," memo to the Chief of the Forest Service from Region 1, 2, 3, and 4 Forest Supervisors, October 2, 1989.

10. Forest Service, *Budget Explanatory Notes for Committee on Appropriations, FY 1992* (Washington, DC: USDA, 1991), pp. 6–47; Forest Service, *Budget Explanatory Notes for Committee on Appropriations, FY 1994* (Washington, DC: USDA, 1993), pp. 7–43; Forest Service, *Budget Explanatory Notes for Committee on Appropriations, FY 1996* (Washington, DC: USDA, 1995), pp. 8–52.

11. Forest Service, *Budget Justification, FY 2001* (Washington, DC: USDA, 2000), pp. 6–79; Forest Service, *Budget Justification, FY 2008* (Washington, DC: USDA, 2007), pp. 9–47.

12. For more information on the incentives that influence national park management, see Randal O'Toole, *Tarnished Jewels: The Case for Reforming the Park Service* (Bandon, OR: Thoreau Institute, 1995).

13. For a detailed analysis of more than 150 state land and resource agencies, see Randal O'Toole, *State Lands and Resources* (Bandon, OR: Thoreau Institute, 1995).

14. Jerry Franklin said, "Old-growth forest ecosystems are not only more complicated than we understand, they are more complicated than we can understand."

This is a version of Haldane's law, "The universe is not only queerer than we suppose, but queerer than we can suppose."

15. Dale Bosworth, "A Process in Need of Change" (speech before the Forest Policy Summit, Forest Service, Rapid City, SD, 2001), tinyurl.com/3d6sf7.

Chapter 5

1. Stephen Pyne, *Fire in America: A Cultural History of Wildland and Rural Fire* (Princeton, NJ: Princeton University Press, 1982), p. 196.

2. Ibid., p. 290.

3. Ashley L. Schiff, *Fire and Water: Scientific Heresy in the Forest Service* (Cambridge, MA: Harvard University Press, 1962), pp. 29–44.

4. U.S. Forest Service, *Budget Explanatory Notes* (Washington, DC: USDA, 1990, 1991).

5. Michael Milstein, "Firefighters Spent with a Blank Check, Auditors Say," *The Oregonian*, January 5, 2003, p. A1.

6. Michael Milstein, "Gambler Fleeced Fire Funds," *The Oregonian*, November 16, 2006, p. B1.

7. Office of Inspector General, *Implementation of the Healthy Forests Initiative* (Washington, DC: USDA, 2006), p. 1.

8. Dale Bosworth, "A Process in Need of Change" (speech before the Forest Policy Summit, Forest Service, Rapid City, SD, 2001), tinyurl.com/3d6sf7.

Part Two

1. P. J. O'Rourke, *Parliament of Whores* (New York: Atlantic Monthly Press, 1991), p. 36.

2. James Gleick, *Chaos: Making a New Science* (New York: Viking, 1987), p. 8.

3. Jane Jacobs, *The Death and Life of Great American Cities* (New York: Vintage, 1963), p. 13.

Chapter 6

1. Henry Diamond and Patrick Noonan, *Land Use in America: The Report of the Sustainable Use of Land Project* (Washington, DC: Island Press, 1996), p. 7.

2. Chris Norby, *Redevelopment: The Unknown Government* (Fullerton, CA: Municipal Officials for Redevelopment Reform, 2004), p. 2.

3. Bernard Siegan, *Land Use Without Zoning* (Lexington, MA: Lexington Books, 1972), p. 6.

4. Anthony Downs, *Inside Bureaucracy* (Boston: Little, Brown, 1967), p. 266.

5. *2040 Plan: Design Types* (Portland, OR: Metro, 1996), p. 3.

6. Peter Bernstein, *Against the Gods: The Remarkable Story of Risk* (New York: John Wiley, 1998), p. 203.

7. E. F. M. Durbin, *Problems of Economic Planning* (London: Routledge & Kegan Paul, Ltd., 1949), p. 51.

8. Gerald Sirkin, *The Visible Hand: The Fundamentals of Economic Planning* (New York: McGraw-Hill, 1968), p. 4.

9. Martin Wachs, "Ethics and Advocacy in Forecasting for Public Policy," *Business and Professional Ethics Journal* 9, nos. 1 & 2 (1990): 148–49.

10. Ibid., p. 149.

11. Ibid., p. 150.

12. Ibid.

13. Quoted in James C. Scott, *Seeing Like a State: How Certain Schemes to Improve the Human Condition Have Failed* (New Haven, CT: Yale University Press, 1998), p. 345.

14. Andrés Duany, Elizabeth Plater-Zyberk, and Jeff Speck, *Suburban Nation: The Rise of Sprawl and the Decline of the American Dream* (New York: North Point Press, 2000), p. 228.

15. Scott, *Seeing Like a State*, p. 141.

16. Herman E. Daly, *Steady-State Economics: Second Edition with New Essays* (Covelo, CA: Island Press, 1991), p. 4.

Chapter 7

1. Real Estate Research Corporation, *The Costs of Sprawl* (Washington, DC: CEQ, 1973).

2. Helen Ladd, "Population Growth, Density and the Costs of Providing Public Services," *Urban Studies* 29, no. 2 (1992): 273–95.

3. Robert Burchell, George Lowenstein, William Dolphin, and Catherine Galley, *The Costs of Sprawl 2000* (Washington, DC: National Academy Press, 2002), p. 13.

4. Wendell Cox and Joshua Utt, *The Costs of Sprawl Reconsidered: What the Data Really Show* (Washington, DC: Heritage Foundation, 2004), p. 10.

5. Robert Putnam, *Bowling Alone: The Collapse and Revival of American Community* (New York: Simon & Schuster, 2000), pp. 140, 143.

6. Ibid., p. 206.

7. Ibid., p. 205.

8. Ibid., p. 283.

9. Ibid., p. 408.

10. Katherine J. Curtis White and Avery M. Guest, "Community Lost or Transformed: Urbanization and Social Ties," *City and Community* (September 2003): 239–59.

11. Jan Brueckner and Ann Largey, *Social Interaction and Urban Sprawl* (Munich: Center for Economic Studies, 2006), tinyurl.com/25bxwa.

12. Melvin Webber, "Order in Diversity: Community Without Propinquity," in *Cities and Space*, ed. Lowdon Wingo Jr. (Baltimore: Johns Hopkins Press, 1963), pp. 25–54.

13. Based on data from the 2002 Behavioral Risk Factor Surveillance System downloaded from the Centers for Disease Control website, www.cdc.gov/brfss.

14. Reid Ewing, Tom Schmid, Richard Killingsworth, Amy Zlot, and Stephen Raudenbush, "Relationship between Urban Sprawl and Physical Activity, Obesity, and Morbidity," *American Journal of Health Promotion* 18, no. 1 (September–October 2003): 47–57.

15. Wendell Cox, "Sprawl and Obesity in Chicago: Why All the Fuss?" Heartland Institute, August 29, 2003, tinyurl.com/2rqjhd.

16. Smart Growth America, "Research Links Sprawl and Health," news release, August 28, 2003, tinyurl.com/2qudlc.

17. Ewing et al., "Relationship," p. 47.

18. Jean Eid, Henry G. Overman, Diego Puga, and Matthew A. Turner, *Fat City: Questioning the Relationship between Urban Sprawl and Obesity* (Toronto: University of Toronto, 2006), p. 1.

19. Andrew J. Plantinga and Stephanie Bernell, "The Association between Urban Sprawl and Obesity: Is It a Two-Way Street?" *Journal of Regional Studies* (forthcoming), tinyurl.com/2dtbwh.

20. R. Sturm and D. A. Cohen, "Suburban Sprawl and Physical and Mental Health," *Public Health* 118, no. 7 (2004): 488–96, tinyurl.com/26yde4.

21. James S. House et al., "Excess Mortality among Urban Residents: How Much, for Whom, and Why?" *American Journal of Public Health* 90, no. 12 (2000): 1898–1904.

22. See, as examples, Howard Frumkin, Lawrence Frank, and Richard Jackson, *Urban Sprawl and Public Health: Designing, Planning, and Building for Healthy Communities* (Washington, DC: Island Press, 2004); Michael Dudley, "Childhood Obesity and the Built Environment," *Planetizen*, tinyurl.com/3ag85u; and Christian Peralta, "Suburbs Are Making Canadians Fatter," *Planetizen*, tinyurl.com/3xz883.

23. Metro Means Business Committee, *Public Opinion Survey* (Portland, OR: Metro, 1996).

24. Howell Baum, "Problems of Governance and the Professions of Planners: The Planning Profession in the 1980s," in *Two Centuries of American Planning*, ed. Daniel Schaffer (Baltimore: Johns Hopkins Press, 1988), pp. 279–302.

25. Ibid.

26. Linda Saul-Sena, acceptance speech at 2005 conference of the Florida Chapter of the American Planning Association, St. Petersburg, September 9, 2005.

27. Lopes de Sousa, "Urban Planning and Management," p. 3.

28. Various researchers have questioned the seriousness of the fire problem, including Tania Schoennagel, Thomas T. Veblen, and William H. Romme, "The Interaction of Fire, Fuels, and Climate across Rocky Mountain Forests," *BioScience* 54, no. 7 (July 2004): 661–76; and A. L. Westerling, H. G. Hidalgo, D. R. Cayan, and T. W. Swetnam, "Warming and Earlier Spring Increase Western U.S. Forest Wildfire Activity," *Science*, August 2006, pp. 940–43.

29. Scott Learn, "Last-Minute Donations Come into Campaigns," *The Oregonian*, May 16, 2000, p. B2.

Chapter 8

1. *Village of Euclid v. Ambler Realty Co.*, 272 U.S. 365 (1926).

2. Peter Gordon and Harry W. Richardson, "The Sprawl Debate: Let Markets Plan," *Publius* (Fall 2001): 131–49.

3. David Rusk, *Cities Without Suburbs* (Washington, DC: Woodrow Wilson Center Press, 1993).

4. Jane Jacobs, *The Death and Life of Great American Cities* (New York: Random House, 1961), p. 410.

Part Three

1. Quoted in Charles R. Metzger, "Whitman on Architecture," *Journal of the Society of Architectural Historians* 16, no. 1 (March 1957): 25–27.

2. Andrés Duany, Elizabeth Plater-Zyberk, and Jeff Speck, *Suburban Nation: The Rise of Sprawl and the Decline of the American Dream* (New York: North Point Press, 2000), p. 228.

3. *Using Income Criteria to Protect Commercial Farmland in the State of Oregon* (Salem: Department of Land Conservation and Development, 1998), p. 2.

4. Greg Winterowd, *Woolen Mill Refinement Plan* (Portland, OR: WinterBrook Planning, 2004), p. 15.

Chapter 9

1. *Kelo v. City of New London*, 545 U.S. 469 (2005).

2. Ibid., concurrence.

3. American Planning Association, "Kelo Decision Emphasizes the Importance of Planning," news release, June 23, 2005.

4. Scott Greer, *Urban Renewal and American Cities* (Indianapolis: Bobbs-Merrill, 1964), p. 3.

5. Herbert J. Gans, *The Urban Villagers: Group and Class in the Life of Italian Americans*, updated ed. (New York: Free Press, 1982), pp. 380–81.

6. *Berman v. Parker*, 348 U.S. 26 (1954).

7. Jane Jacobs, *The Death and Life of Great American Cities* (New York: Random House, 1961), p. 13.

8. Ibid.

9. Ibid., pp. 150–51.

10. Ibid., p. 14.

11. Ibid., pp. 16, 18.

12. Gans, *The Urban Villagers*, p. 300.

13. Herbert J. Gans, "City Planning and Urban Realities: A Review of *The Death and Life of Great American Cities*," *Books in Review* (1961): 170–73.

14. Ibid.

15. Gans, *The Urban Villagers*, p. 393.

16. Gans, "City Planning." Gans also feared *Death and Life* would attract "ultra-right-wing groups who oppose planning." Though Gans supports the idea of planning, none of his books presents a persuasive case of anyone who benefited from such planning.

17. "Jane Jacobs Still Helping to Shape Cities," Associated Press, November 23, 2000, archives.cnn.com/2000/books/news/11/23/jane.jacobs.ap.

18. "Jane Jacobs: Anatomiser of Cities," *The Economist*, May 11, 2006.

19. Carol Lloyd, "A Blight on Urban Renewal: Are Bay Area Cities Abusing Eminent Domain as a Redevelopment Tool?" *San Francisco Chronicle*, March 4, 2005.

Chapter 10

1. *Dark Side of the American Dream* (San Francisco: Sierra Club, 1998), p. 4.

2. David Schrank and Tim Lomax, *The 2005 Urban Mobility Report* (College Station: Texas A&M University, 2005), p. 12.

3. Anita Manning, "California Has the USA's Worst Air Quality," *USA Today*, May 1, 2002.

4. Federal Highway Administration, *Highway Statistics 2003* (Washington, DC: U.S. DOT, 2004), table HM-72.

5. *Metro Measured* (Portland, OR: Metro, 1994), p. 7.

6. Testimony of Michael Burton, Metro executive, before the State Senate Natural Resources Committee, April 1, 1998, West Linn, OR.

7. *Metro Measured* (Portland, OR: Metro, 1994), p. 25.

8. Jane Jacobs, *The Death and Life of Great American Cities* (New York: Vintage, 1963), p. 14.

9. The full story of what happened in my neighborhood can be read at ti.org/ogt.html and is illustrated at ti.org/og.html.

10. "Zoning Acres by County—1986," internal LCDC memo, Salem, OR.

11. *Making the Connections: A Summary of the LUTRAQ Project* (Portland, OR: 1000 Friends, 1997), pp. 8–10.

12. Genevieve Giuliano, "The Weakening Transportation–Land Use Connection," *Access* 6 (Spring, 1995): 8.

13. Ibid.

14. *Transportation Planning Rule* (Salem, OR: LCDC, 1991), OAR 660-012-0035(4). A 1998 amendment reduces the 30-year goal to 15 percent.

15. Oregon Administrative Rule 660-012-0045.

16. Dionne Peeples-Salah, "Rezoning for Transit Traps Downtown Homeowners," *The Oregonian*, January 18, 1996, p. A1.

17. *Region 2040 Technical Appendix* (Portland, OR: Metro, September 15, 1994), transportation tables.

18. *1999 Regional Transportation Plan* (Portland, OR: Metro, 1999), tables 2.7, 2.9, 5.9, and 5.11.

19. Testimony of Michael Burton, April 1, 1998.

20. Testimony of Richard Benner, director of Oregon Department of Land Conservation and Development, before the State Senate Natural Resources Committee, April 1, 1998, West Linn, OR.

21. Oregon Administrative Rule 660-012.

22. *Region 2040 Technical Appendix* (Portland, OR: Metro, September 15, 1994), parking memo.

23. John Charles, *The Mythical World of Transit-Oriented Development* (Portland, OR: Cascade Policy Institute, 2001), tinyurl.com/336pt6.

24. Kennedy Smith, "Cascade Station Stops Short of New Urbanism," *Daily Journal of Commerce*, December 5, 2005.

25. Joseph Roth, "Swedish Retailer IKEA Plans to Grow Pacific Northwest Presence with Portland Store," news release, October 20, 2005, tinyurl.com/37dczj.

26. John Charles and Michael Barton, *The Mythical World of Transit-Oriented Development: Light Rail and the Orenco Neighborhood* (Portland, OR: Cascade Policy Institute, 2003), tinyurl.com/2kh6s.

27. Bruce Podobnik, *Portland Neighborhood Survey Report on Findings from Zone 2: Orenco* (Portland, OR: Lewis & Clark College, 2002), p. 1, tinyurl.com/37rwx3.

28. Randy Gragg, "The New Urbanism: Laboratory Portland," *The Oregonian*, June 11, 2000, p. E10.

29. "EPA Says N.Y., Calif. Have Worst Air," Associated Press, March 22, 2006, tinyurl.com/2vzjp9.

Chapter 11

1. Smart Growth Network, "About Smart Growth," tinyurl.com/2su246.

2. John W. Frece, "Lessons from Maryland's Smart Growth Initiative," *Vermont Journal of Environmental Law* 6 (2004–2005), tinyurl.com/8sj28.

3. Andrés Duany, presentation to the Preserving the American Dream Conference, Washington, DC, February 2003.

4. Dowell Myers and Elizabeth Gearin, "Current Preferences and Future Demand for Denser Residential Developments," *Housing Policy Debate* 12, no. 4 (2001): 633–59, tinyurl.com/2skfah.

5. Timothy Egan, "Vibrant Cities Find One Thing Missing: Children," *New York Times*, March 24, 2005, p. A1.

6. Rebecca R. Sohmer and Robert E. Lang, *Downtown Rebound* (Washington, DC: Fannie Mae, 2001), p. 1, tinyurl.com/32yvy2.

7. Ibid., p. 3.

8. National Family Opinion, *Consumers Survey Conducted by NAR and NAHB* (Washington, DC: National Association of Realtors, 2002), p. 3, tinyurl.com/y5n9yd.

9. Ibid., p. 6.

10. Douglas Porter, "Regional Governance of Metropolitan Form: The Missing Link in Relating Land Use and Transportation," in *Transportation, Urban Form, and the Environment* (Washington, DC: Transportation Research Board, 1991), p. 65.

11. Ahwahnee Principles, 1991, tinyurl.com/2v4xap.

12. "New Urbanism Basics," Congress for the New Urbanism, 2000, tinyurl.com/2qvoub.

13. "Charter of the New Urbanism," Congress for the New Urbanism, 1998, tinyurl.com/3aggl6.

14. Anthony Downs, *Stuck in Traffic: Coping with Peak-Hour Traffic Congestion* (Washington, DC: Brookings Institution, 1992), p. 133.

15. John R. Stilgoe, *Borderland: Origins of the American Suburb, 1820–1939* (New Haven, CT: Yale University Press, 1988).

16. Quoted in Robert Fishman, "The Post-War American Suburb: A New Form, A New City," in *Two Centuries of American Planning*, ed. Daniel Schaffer (Baltimore: Johns Hopkins Press, 1988), p. 266.

17. Henry Ford, *Ford Ideals: Being a Selection from 'Mr. Ford's Page' in the Dearborn Independent* (Dearborn, MI: Dearborn Independent, 1922), pp. 426–27.

18. Census Bureau, *2000 Census*, table GCT-PH1. For a state-by-state comparison of populations and land areas of urban and rural areas from the 2000 census, download tinyurl.com/3arenr.

19. National Resources Conservation Service, *1997 Natural Resources Inventory* (Washington, DC: USDA, 2001), table 1.

20. Joel S. Hirschhorn, *Sprawl Kills: How Blandburbs Steal Your Time, Health and Money* (New York: Sterling & Ross, 2005).

21. Peter Gordon and Harry Richardson, "Congestion Trends in Metropolitan Areas," in *Curbing Gridlock: Peak-Period Fees to Relieve Traffic Congestion* (Washington, DC: National Academy Press, 1994), 2:1–31.

22. Don Pickrell, "Transportation and Land Use," in *Essays in Transportation Economics and Policy: A Handbook in Honor of John R. Meyer*, ed. Jose A. Gomez-Ibanez, William B. Tye, and Clifford Winston (Washington, DC: Brookings Institution, 1999), p. 425.

23. Melvyn D. Cheslow and J. Kevin Neels, "Effect of Urban Development Patterns on Transportation Energy Use," *Transportation Research Record* 764 (1980): 70–78.

24. Paul Schimek, "Household Motor Vehicle Ownership and Use: How Much Does Residential Density Matter?" *Transportation Research Record* 1552 (1996): 120–25.

25. Census Bureau, "Census 2000 Summary File 3, Journey to Work," table QT-P23, 2002.

26. Andrew Carter, Gordon Ewing, and Murtaza Halder, *Could "New Urbanism" Policies Reduce Car Dependency in Cities? Evidence from Old Urbanism* (Montreal: McGill University, 2004), p. 28.

27. Ibid., p. 35.

28. Ibid., p. 30.

29. Patricia Mokhtarian and Ilam Salomon, "Travel for the Fun of It," *Access* 15 (Fall 1999): 27.

30. Robert Cervero, "Jobs-Housing Balance Revisited," *Journal of the American Planning Association* 62 (4): 492.

Chapter 12

1. John Berlau, "Smart-Growth Plan Riles Black Farmers," *Insight*, August 26, 2002.

2. *Valley Transportation Plan 2030* (San Jose, CA: Valley Transportation Authority, 2005), p. 145.

3. David Schrank and Tim Lomax, "Appendix: Mobility Data for San Jose," in *The 2005 Urban Mobility Report*, ed. David Schrank and Tim Lomax (College Station: Texas A&M University, 2005), tinyurl.com/2ngbg4.

4. Nico Calavita, "Vale of Tiers: San Diego's Much-Lauded Growth Management System May Not Be as Good as It Looks," *Planning*, March 1997, pp. 18–21.

5. "2020 Cities/County Forecast Land Use Alternatives," SANDAG Board of Directors Report No. 99-2-7, February 26, 1999.

6. David Peterson, "Mondale Says Met Council Has Big Plans," *Minneapolis Star Tribune*, October 11, 1999.

7. Bruce Liedstrand, "Ten Common Sense Rules for TOD," *Planetizen*, tinyurl.com/35h3wc.

8. *Regional Transportation Plan Update* (Portland, OR: Metro, 1996), p. 1-20.

9. *1999 Regional Transportation Plan* (Portland, OR: Metro, November, 1999), p. 638.

10. "Minutes of the Metro Council Transportation Planning Committee Meeting," Portland OR, July 18, 2000, p. 7.

11. *Transportation Policy Plan* (St. Paul, MN: Metropolitan Council, 1996), p. 54.

12. Dom Nozzi, "Traffic Congestion: Friend or Foe?" tinyurl.com/3dfwbu.

13. Joel Garreau, *Edge City: Life on the New Frontier* (New York: Doubleday, 1991), p. 8.

14. Wendell Cox, "Paris Arrondissements: Post 1860 Population and Population Density," tinyurl.com/346k43.

15. Jeffrey R. Kenworthy and Felix B. Laube, *An International Sourcebook of Automobile Dependence in Cities 1960–1990* (Boulder: University of Colorado, 1999).

Chapter 13

1. "2006 Home Price Comparison Index," Coldwell Banker, September 27, 2006, tinyurl.com/2kd7dh.

2. Census Bureau, "Historical Census of Housing Tables," tinyurl.com/2m5j5j.

3. Census Bureau, "Housing Vacancies and Homeownership, Historical Tables, Table 14," tinyurl.com/gsucz.

4. European countries from Michael Ball, *European Housing Review* (London: Royal Institution of Chartered Surveyors, 2005); Mexico from *Nation's Building News Online*, May 10, 2004, tinyurl.com/3cr36l.

5. Irving Schiffman, *Alternative Techniques for Managing Growth* (Berkeley, CA: IGS Press, 1999).

6. Paul Krugman, "That Hissing Sound," *New York Times*, August 8, 2005.

7. Edward L. Glaeser and Joseph Gyourko, *The Impact of Zoning on Housing Affordability* (Cambridge, MA: Harvard Institute of Economic Research, 2002), p. 3.

8. G. Donald Jud and Daniel T. Winkler, "The Dynamics of Metropolitan Housing Prices," *Journal of Real Estate Research* 23, No. 1/2 (2002): 29–45.

9. Hernando de Soto, *The Mystery of Capital: Why Capitalism Triumphs in the West and Fails Everywhere Else* (New York: Basic Books, 2000), p. 6.

10. Ibid., p. 53.

11. Donald R. Haurin, *The Private and Social Benefits of Homeownership* (Americus, GA: Habitat for Humanity University, 2003), tinyurl.com/2nnl6t.

12. Ibid., p. 14.

13. Joseph Harkness and Sandra Newman, "Differential Effects of Homeownership on Children from Higher- and Lower-Income Families," *Journal of Housing Research* 14, no. 1 (2003): pp. 1–19.

14. Peter H. Rossi and Eleanor Weber, "The Social Benefits of Homeownership: Empirical Evidence from National Surveys," *Housing Policy Debate* 7, no. 1 (1996): pp. 1–35.

15. Andrew Oswald, "Theory of Homes and Jobs," preliminary paper, 1997, tinyurl.com/2pfwvv.

16. Haurin, *The Private and Social Benefits of Homeownership*, p. 16.

Chapter 14

1. Eric A. Hanushek and John M. Quigley, "What Is the Price Elasticity of Housing Demand?" *Review of Economics and Statistics* 62, no. 3 (1980): 449–54, tinyurl.com/766wq.

2. All references to 1969 median home values or median family incomes are from *1970 Census of Housing Volume 1 Housing Characteristics for States, Cities, and Counties Part 1 United States Summary*, table 17, "Financial Characteristics for Areas and Places; *1970 Census of the Population, Volume 1 Characteristics of the Population, Part 1 United States Summary Section 2*, table 366, "Median Income in 1969 of Families by Type of Family and Race of Head for Standard Metropolitan Statistical Areas of 250,000 or More."

3. Irving Schiffman, *Alternative Techniques for Managing Growth* (Berkeley, CA: IGS Press, 1999), p. 6.

4. Ibid.; *Draft Petaluma General Plan 2025* (Petaluma, CA: City of Petaluma, 2004), p. 57, tinyurl.com/2sj4yz.

5. Peter Pollack, "Controlling Sprawl in Boulder: Benefits and Pitfalls," *Proceedings of the 1998 National Planning Conference* (Chicago: AICP, 1999), tinyurl.com/2rmv5h.

6. Bernard J. Frieden, *The Environmental Protection Hustle* (Cambridge, MA: MIT, 1979), p. 6.

7. David E. Dowall, *The Suburban Squeeze: Land Conservation and Regulation in the San Francisco Bay Area* (Berkeley: University of California Press, 1984), p. 15.

8. Ibid., pp. 141–42.

9. *At Risk: The Bay Area Greenbelt* (San Francisco: Greenbelt Alliance, 2006), p. 4, tinyurl.com/ys3d4n.

10. Ibid., p. 143.

11. All references to 1979 median home values or median family incomes are from *1980 Census of Population, Volume 1 Characteristics of the Population, Chapter C General Social and Economic Characteristics, Part 1 United States Summary (PC80-1-C1)*, table 247, "Summary of Economic Characteristics for Areas and Places"; *1980 Census of*

Housing, Volume 1 Characteristics of Housing Units, Chapter A General Housing Character-istics, Part 1 United States Summary (HC80-1-A1), table 76, "Financial Characteristics for SCSA's and SMSA's."

12. Edward Glaeser, Jenny Schuetz, and Bryce Ward, *Regulation and the Rise of Housing Prices in Greater Boston* (Cambridge, MA: Rappaport Institute, 2006), pp. 1-i–1-iv, tinyurl.com/ad8g4.

13. All references to 1989 median home values or median family incomes are from *1990 Census of Population*, tables P107A and H061A, available at www.census.gov.

14. For an explanation of how 2005 value-to-income ratios were calculated, see Randal O'Toole, *The Planning Penalty: How Smart Growth Makes Housing Unaffordable* (Bandon, OR: American Dream Coalition, 2006), pp. 9–10.

15. All references to 1999 median home values or median family incomes are from *2000 Census of Population*, tables P77 and H85, available at www.census.gov.

16. The discussion of housing prices and housing penalties in this and the following several paragraphs is documented in greater detail in O'Toole, *The Planning Penalty*.

17. Robert Burchell, Anthony Downs, Barbara McCann, and Sahan Mukheri, *Sprawl Costs: Economic Impact of Unchecked Development* (Covelo, CA: Island Press, 2005).

18. Caroline S. Latham, "Occupancy Declines While Rent Remains Anemic," *Real-Facts*, January 27, 2006, tinyurl.com/2o7vua.

19. Matthew E. Kahn, "Does Sprawl Reduce the Black/White Housing Consump-tion Gap?" *Housing Policy Debate* 12, no. 1 (2001): 77–86.

20. Randal Pozdena, *Smart Growth and Its Effects on Housing Markets: The New Segregation* (Washington, DC: National Center for Public Policy Research, 2002), p. 40, tinyurl.com/38ybkt.

21. Peter Geoffrey Hall, *Cities of Tomorrow: An Intellectual History of Urban Planning and Design in the Twentieth Century* (Cambridge, MA: Blackwell, 2002 ed.), pp. 421–22.

22. Teresa Tico, "A Brief History of Land Acquisition in Hawaii," tinyurl.com/2rfcwg.

Chapter 15

1. Office of Federal Housing Enterprise Oversight, *3q 2006 Manipulable Data for Metropolitan Statistical Areas* (Washington, DC: Department of Commerce, 2006), tinyurl.com/2qqgr7.

2. Alan W. Evans and Oliver Marc Hartwich, *Unaffordable Housing: Fables and Myths* (London: Policy Exchange, 2005), p. 9, tinyurl.com/a4njl.

3. Edward Glaeser, *The Economic Impact of Restricting Housing Supply* (Cambridge, MA: Rappaport Institute, 2006), p. 1.

4. Ibid.

5. Dean Baker, *The Run-Up in Housing Prices: Is It Real or Is It Another Bubble?* (Washington, DC: Center for Economic and Policy Research, 2004), p. 8.

6. PMI Mortgage Insurance Company, "Local Economic Patterns and MSI Indica-tors," *Economic and Real Estate Trends*, Spring 2005, p. 4.

7. Jack Guynn, "Adjusting to the Next Stage of the Housing Cycle" (speech before the Council for Quality Growth, Atlanta, June 7, 2006), tinyurl.com/hj55g.

8. PMI Mortgage Insurance Company, "Metropolitan Area Indicators as of May 2005," *Economic and Real Estate Trends*, Spring 2005, p. 6.

9. Joe Hurd, *The Bay Area Economy: The Meltdown Isn't Over* (Los Angeles: UCLA, 2003), p. 4.4.

10. Office of Federal Housing Enterprise Oversight, *3q 2006 Manipulable Data.*

11. "The Sun Also Sets," *The Economist,* September 9, 2004.

12. "After the Fall," *The Economist,* June 16, 2005.

13. "Going through the Roof," *The Economist,* March 28, 2002.

Chapter 16

1. Eric Schmidt, "The Price of Smart Growth," *Boulder Daily Camera,* May 21, 2006.

2. "List of Projects," San Jose Housing Department, tinyurl.com/2l4rrn.

3. Edward L. Glaeser and Joseph Gyourko, *The Impact of Zoning on Housing Affordability* (Cambridge, MA: Harvard Institute of Economic Research, 2002), p. 22.

4. "What Is a Housing Impact Fee?" San Diego Housing Commission, tinyurl.com/35rdea.

5. Jerald Johnson, *Issues Associated with the Imposition of Inclusionary Zoning in the Portland Metropolitan Area* (Portland, OR: Hobson Johnson & Associates, 1997); Benjamin Powell and Edward Stringham, *Housing Supply and Affordability: Do Affordable Housing Mandates Work?* (Los Angeles: Reason Foundation, 2004).

6. Powell and Stringham, "Executive Summary," *Housing Supply and Affordability,* p. 2.

7. Ibid.

8. Glaeser and Gyourko, *The Impact of Zoning,* pp. 21–22.

9. Edward Glaeser, Joseph Gyourko, and Raven Saks, Abstract, *Why Have Housing Prices Gone Up?* (Cambridge, MA: Harvard Institute of Economic Research, 2004).

10. "Report: 98 Percent of U.S. Commuters Favor Public Transportation for Others," *The Onion,* November 29, 2000.

Chapter 17

1. E. Kimbark MacColl, *The Growth of a City: Power and Politics in Portland, Oregon 1915 to 1950* (Portland, OR: Georgian Press, 1979), pp. 300–301.

2. Ken Hamburg, "Study Links Affordable Housing to Land-Use Laws," *The Oregonian,* October 10, 1991, p. D16.

3. Foster Church, "Portland Becomes Pricey," *The Oregonian,* July 31, 1995, p. A1.

4. R. Gregory Nokes, "Portland Housing Ranks as 2nd Least Affordable in U.S.," *The Oregonian,* July 19, 1997, p. A1.

5. MacColl, *The Growth of a City,* p. 301.

6. Quotes from the October 23, 1996, city council meeting were transcribed from a videotape of that meeting made by the city of Portland.

7. Gordon Oliver, "Once a Solution, Row Houses Fall Out of City Favor," *The Oregonian,* August 11, 1999, p. C2.

8. Gordon Oliver, "Apartment Hunters Move in on Deals in the Glutted Portland-Area Rental Market," *The Oregonian,* December 6, 1999, p. A1.

9. *Displacement: The Dismantling of a Community* (Portland, OR: Coalition for a Livable Future, 1999).

10. Clifton Chestnut and Shirley Dang, "Suburbs Drain City Schools," *The Oregonian,* October 12, 2003, p. A1; NewsMax.com, "U.S. Cities Have Fewer Kids, More Singles," June 13, 2001.

11. Dana Tims, "Land Value 'Tipping Point' Hits Suburbs," *The Oregonian,* October 20, 2005, Metro Southwest ed., p. 1.

Chapter 18

1. Claire Lomax, "Path Has Led to Dramatic Increase in Crime," *Telegraph and Argus*, November 22, 2001.

2. Al Zelinka and Dean Brennan, *SafeScape: Creating Safer, More Livable Communities through Planning and Design* (Chicago: American Planning Association, 2001).

3. Ibid., p. 13.

4. Oscar Newman, *Defensible Space: Crime Prevention through Urban Design* (New York: Collier, 1973).

5. Zelinka and Brennan, *SafeScape*, p. 19.

6. Newman, *Defensible Space*, p. 112.

7. Peter Knowles, "Designing Out Crime: The Cost of Policing New Urbanism," tinyurl.com/qkhl.

8. Zelinka and Brennan, *SafeScape*, p. 50.

9. Ibid., p. 219.

10. Oscar Newman, "Defensible Space," *Shelterforce Online*, May–June 1997, tinyurl.com/2nj2py.

11. Zelinka and Brennan, *SafeScape*, p. 204.

12. "Charter of the New Urbanism: The Block, the Street, and the Building," Congress for the New Urbanism, tinyurl.com/m6k4q.

13. Oscar Newman, personal correspondence with Stephen Town, February 5, 2003, and December 1, 2003.

Chapter 19

1. Janet Christ, "Land-use officer decides her last case," *The Oregonian*, July 6, 2000, p. D1.

2. Anthony Downs, *Stuck in Traffic: Coping with Peak-Hour Traffic Congestion* (Washington, DC: Brookings Institution, 1992), p. 133.

3. Testimony of Michael Burton, Metro executive, before the Senate Natural Resources Committee, April 1, 1998, West Linn, OR.

4. Ron Buel, "The Goldschmidt Era," *Willamette Week: 25 Years*, special issue, 1999, tinyurl.com/2aher2.

5. "Say It Ain't So, Neil," *Daily Astorian*, January 6, 2004.

6. Nigel Jaquiss, "The 30-Year Secret: A Crime, a Cover-Up, and the Way It Shaped Oregon," *Willamette Week*, April 27, 2004, tinyurl.com/36g9jj.

7. Jim Redden, "Neil's Network," *Portland Tribune*, May 21, 2004.

8. Jim Redden, "Can Goldschmidt Come Back?" *Portland Tribune*, May 21, 2004.

9. Bob Young, "Big Dog," *Willamette Week*, August 26, 1998, tinyurl.com/2n4gah.

10. *Urban Renewal History Appendix* (Portland, OR: Portland Development Commission, 2006), p. 3, tinyurl.com/yo2zde.

11. Steve Duin, "An Agenda, Not an Inferiority Complex," *The Oregonian*, May 16, 2006.

12. "Death Investigation: Interview with Homer Williams," Portland Police Bureau, tinyurl.com/y2vbtu.

13. Steve Duin, "The Fix Is In," *The Oregonian*, October 21, 2006, tinyurl.com/2rzcnm.

14. *Community Policing in Portland* (Portland, OR: City Club, 2003), p. iii, tinyurl.com/yh9jk6.

15. Rosie Sizer, "The Death of James Chasse Jr.," *The Oregonian*, October 25, 2006, tinyurl.com/yme6bz.

16. Maxine Bernstein, "Files Detail Chasse's Final Days," *The Oregonian*, November 10, 2006, tinyurl.com/y5oeu6.

17. Jack Bogdanski, "A Tale of Two Cities," bojack.org/2006/11/tale_of_two_cities.html.

18. Young, "Big Dog."

19. Don Larson, "Why Build Just One Tram? Why Not an Aerial Network?" *The Oregonian*, July 4, 2003, p. D7.

20. Ryan Frank and Jeff Manning, "Tram's Price Tag Unrealistic from Get-Go," *The Oregonian*, April 2, 2006, p. A1.

21. Jim Redden, "$4 Ticket Has Tram Watchers Crying Foul," *Portland Tribune*, January 9, 2007, tinyurl.com/yvz45d. For a complete history of projected and actual construction and operating costs, see "Tram on Budget," tinyurl.com/2kqtp2.

22. Dylan Rivera, "As South Waterfront Towers Rise, So Does District's Price," *The Oregonian*, February 23, 2006, p. A1.

23. Ryan Frank, "Apartment Builder Follows City's Instructions but Gets No Tax Relief," *The Oregonian*, August 25, 2005, p. B2.

24. Jim Redden, "Transit Puzzle Presents Itself," *Portland Tribune*, May 5, 2006.

25. S. Renee Mitchell, "Bridge Money Drowns in Troubled Process," *The Oregonian*, February 25, 2004, p. C1.

26. Tomas Alex Tizon, "Portland Jail Empty, Despite Rise in Crime," *Seattle Times*, March 20, 2006, tinyurl.com/ykehso.

27. Jim Pasero, "The City That Shrinks," *BrainstormNW*, March 2002, tinyurl.com/7kpql.

28. Helen Jung, "Tim Boyle Faces Off with Tom Potter over the City's Business Climate," *The Oregonian*, May 19, 2005, p. A1.

29. Editorial, "Problems of Abundance," *BrainstormNW*, November 2005, tinyurl.com/2spgmb.

30. Fred Leeson, "Land Value's Uncertain, but PDC, Developer Want Tower," *The Oregonian*, December 15, 2006.

31. Paige Parker, "Middle Class Losing Faith in Schools, City," *The Oregonian*, March 5, 2006, p. A1.

32. Jim Parker, "Portland Public School Leaders Back Away from Mayor's School Tax Plan," KGW News, February 9, 2006, tinyurl.com/2qzzfp.

33. bojack.org and portlandfreelancer.blogspot.com.

34. Phil Stanford, "Tram's Sure to Take Us All for a Ride," *Portland Tribune*, November 22, 2005, tinyurl.com/2l8g6j.

35. *The Cost of Congestion to the Economy of the Portland Region* (Boston: Economic Development Research Group, 2005), p. ES-1.

36. Jim Redden, "Road to Ruin?" *Portland Tribune*, December 2, 2005, p. 1.

37. *Cost of Congestion*, p. ES-2.

Part Four

1. *Olmsted v. U.S.*, 277 U.S. 479 (1928).

Chapter 20

1. Alex Anas, Richard Arnott, and Kenneth A. Small, "Urban Spatial Structure," *Journal of Economic Literature* 34: 1444.

2. Bruce Hamilton, "Wasteful Commuting," *Journal of Political Economy* 90 (1982): 1035–51.

3. See, for example, John Pucher, "Urban Travel Behavior as the Outcome of Public Policy," *Journal of the American Planning Association* 54, no. 4 (1988): 509–20.

4. "National Occupational Employment and Wage Estimates," Bureau of Labor Statistics, May 2005, tinyurl.com/3dxfre.

5. "History," American Planning Association, tinyurl.com/2m4m2k.

6. RWA Consulting, Inc., *Regulatory Problems Tying You Up?* flyer.

7. Joel Garreau, *Edge City: Life on the New Frontier* (New York: Doubleday, 1991), p. 222.

8. Melvin M. Webber and Frederick C. Collignon, "Ideas that Drove DCRP," *Berkeley Planning Journal* 12 (1998): 1–19.

9. Joel Garreau, *Edge City*, p. 222.

10. Oscar Newman, *Defensible Space: Crime Prevention through Urban Design* (New York: Collier, 1972).

11. "Report: 98 Percent of U.S. Commuters Favor Public Transportation for Others," *The Onion*, November 29, 2000.

12. Cindy Shea, "Franklin Street Pedestrian Mall," Florida Sustainable Communities Center, tinyurl.com/2tsw94.

13. Neil Fraser, "A Pedestrianised City Is Not the Answer," 2005, tinyurl.com/2vlby6.

14. Matt Branaugh, "More Pedestrian Malls Fail Than Succeed, Observers Say," *Boulder Daily Camera*, July 18, 2002, web.dailycamera.com/pearl/19xwor.html.

15. Greg Flisram, "Post-Modern or Post-Mortem? The Kalamazoo Mall Revisited," American Planning Association, March 2000, tinyurl.com/3bux7l.

16. Steinhauer, Jennifer, "When Shoppers Walk Away from Pedestrian Malls; Downtown Retailing Trend Again Favors a Car Culture," *New York Times*, November 5, 1996, p. D1.

17. Branaugh, "More Pedestrian Malls Fail than Succeed."

18. City of Buffalo Planning Department, survey data on U.S. shopping malls, n.d.

19. Michelle Wallar, "How to Create a Pedestrian Mall," *Culture Change*, no. 14 (2003), tinyurl.com/2jne59.

20. Kathryn Beaumont, "Ketchum Pedestrian Mall Is a No-Go—For Now," *Ketchum Express*, July 22, 1998, tinyurl.com/277yxn.

21. Christopher Walker, "Downtown Stroll: Pedestrian Mall Proposed," *Patriot Ledger*, November 27, 2004, tinyurl.com/r3p2l.

22. Jane Jacobs, *The Death and Life of Great American Cities* (New York: Vintage, 1963), p. 12.

23. Peter Geoffrey Hall, *Cities of Tomorrow: An Intellectual History of Urban Planning and Design in the Twentieth Century* (Cambridge, MA: Blackwell, 2002 ed.), p. 415.

Chapter 21

1. Peter Geoffrey Hall, *Cities of Tomorrow: An Intellectual History of Urban Planning and Design in the Twentieth Century* (Cambridge, MA: Blackwell, 2002 ed.), p. 7.

2. Ibid., p. 17.

3. Ibid., pp. 8–10.

4. Ibid., p. 3.

5. Ibid., p. 5.

6. Ibid.

7. Ibid., p. 219.

8. Quoted in Robert Fishman, *Urban Utopias in the Twentieth Century: Ebenezer Howard, Frank Lloyd Wright, and Le Corbusier* (New York: Basic Books, 1977), p. 190.

9. Le Corbusier, *The City of Tomorrow and Its Planning* (London: John Rodher, 1929), p. 310.

10. Hall, *Cities of Tomorrow*, pp. 7–8.

11. Walden E. Sweet, "The Denver City Plan," *Western City*, May 1930, p. 16 in Mark S. Foster, "The Western Response to Urban Transportation: A Tale of Three Cities, 1900–1945," *Journal of the West* 3, no. 18 (1979): 37.

12. Stephen Town, *Permeability, Access Opportunities, and Crime* (Bradford, England: West Yorkshire Police Department, 2005), p. 9.

13. Hall, *Cities of Tomorrow*, p. 79.

14. Ibid., p. 80.

15. Ibid.

16. John R. Stilgoe, *Borderland: Origins of the American Suburb, 1820–1939* (New Haven, CT: Yale University Press, 1988), p. 4.

17. Hall, *Cities of Tomorrow*, p. 84.

18. Thomas Sharp, *Town and Countryside: Some Aspects of Urban and Rural Development* (London: Oxford University Press, 1932) p. 11.

19. C. E. M. Joad, "The People's Claim," in *Britain and the Beast*, ed. Clough Williams-Ellis (London: J. M. Dent, 1937), pp. 72–73.

20. Ibid., pp. 81–82.

21. Thomas Sharp, *English Panorama* (London: Oxford University Press, 1936), p. 107.

Chapter 22

1. Alexei Gutnov et al., *The Ideal Communist City* (New York: George Braziller, 1971), pp. 69–70.

2. Ibid., p. 66.

3. Ibid., p. 74.

4. Ibid., pp. 79–80.

5. Christine Hanneman, *Architecture as Ideology: Industrialization of Housing in the GDR* (Berlin: Humboldt University, 2004), p. 9, tinyurl.com/2pxgef.

6. Ibid., p. 23.

7. Karin Book and Lena Eskilsson, *Transport, Built Environment and Development Control: A Comparative Urban Study* (Lund, Sweden: Dept. of Social and Economic Geography, 1998), pp. 109–10.

8. Ibid., p. 104.

9. Ibid., p. 111.

10. Ibid.

11. Shrinkingcities.com, "Halle/Leipzig," tinyurl.com/2o4aze.

12. "The Future of the Slab," Goethe Institute, tinyurl.com/2ptmag.

13. "Halle, Saxony-Anhalt," Wikipedia, tinyurl.com/3x4ztz.

14. Personal observations during a tour of Halle-Neustadt in April, 2005; see tinyurl.com/2vc74g.

15. David Popenoe, *Private Pleasure, Public Plight: American Metropolitan Community Life in Comparative Perspective* (New Brunswick, NJ: Transaction, 1985), p. 61.

16. Ibid., p. 44.

17. Ibid., p. 61.

18. Ibid., p. 43.

19. Ibid.

20. Ibid., p. 42.

21. Ibid., p. 43.

22. Peter Hall, *Cities in Civilization* (New York: Pantheon Books, 1998), p. 863.

23. Ibid., p. 872.

24. Ibid., p. 873.

25. Ibid., p. 874.

26. Ibid., p. 875.

27. Ibid., pp. 877–78.

28. Jeffrey R. Kenworthy and Felix B. Laube, *An International Sourcebook of Automobile Dependence in Cities 1960–1990* (Boulder: University of Colorado, 1999).

29. Hall, *Cities in Civilization*, p. 878.

30. Ibid., p. 879.

31. Ibid., p. 239.

32. Peter Geoffrey Hall, *Cities of Tomorrow: An Intellectual History of Urban Planning and Design in the Twentieth Century* (Cambridge, MA: Blackwell, 2002 ed.), p. 242.

33. Ibid., p. 244.

34. Wendell Cox, "Democratizing Prosperity: The Role of Home Ownership" (presentation to the 2005 Preserving the American Dream conference, Bloomington, MN, June 25, 2005).

35. Hall, *Cities of Tomorrow*, p. 246.

36. Ibid., pp. 246–47.

37. Ibid., p. 246.

Chapter 23

1. Melvin M. Webber and Frederick C. Collignon, "Ideas that Drove DCRP," *Berkeley Planning Journal* 12 (1998): 4.

2. Campbell Gibson, *Population of the 100 Largest Cities and Other Urban Places in the United States: 1790 to 1990* (Washington, DC: Census Bureau, 1998), tables 18 and 20.

3. Kenneth T. Jackson, *Crabgrass Frontier: The Suburbanization of the United States* (New York: Oxford University Press, 1985), p. 149.

4. Peter Geoffrey Hall, *Cities of Tomorrow: An Intellectual History of Urban Planning and Design in the Twentieth Century* (Cambridge, MA: Blackwell, 2002 ed.), p. 253.

5. Alexander von Hoffman, "Why They Built Pruitt-Igoe," in *From Tenements to the Taylor Homes: In Search of an Urban Housing Policy in Twentieth-Century America*, ed. John F. Bauman (University Park: Pennsylvania State University Press, 2000).

6. Hall, *Cities of Tomorrow*, p. 256.

7. Ibid., pp. 258–59.

8. Carl Greene, "Philadelphia's Housing Renaissance," Philadelphia Housing Authority, 2005, p. 5, tinyurl.com/3bktav.

9. "What Is the Relationship between TIFs and Public Housing?" Neighborhood Capital Budget Group, tinyurl.com/2snmgd; "Tearing Down Cabrini-Green," CBS News, July 23, 2003, tinyurl.com/cov4.

10. Mark Rose, *Interstate: Express Highway Politics, 1939–1989* (Knoxville: University of Tennessee Press, 1990), p. 20.

11. Ibid., pp. 56–57.

12. Darwin Stolzenbach, interview with Professor Alan Altshuler, former secretary of transportation, Massachusetts, AASHTO Interstate Highway Research Project, June 8, 1981, pp. 3–4.

13. Rose, *Interstate*, pp. 20, 25.

14. Jane Jacobs, *The Death and Life of Great American Cities* (New York: Vintage, 1963), p. 3.

15. Hall, *Cities of Tomorrow*, p. 261.

Chapter 24

1. Peter Geoffrey Hall, *Cities of Tomorrow: An Intellectual History of Urban Planning and Design in the Twentieth Century* (Cambridge, MA: Blackwell, 2002 ed.), p. 402.

2. George Dantzig and Thomas Saaty, *Compact City: A Plan for a Livable Urban Environment* (San Francisco: Freeman, 1973), p. 26.

3. Edwin S. Mills, *Studies in the Structure of the Urban Economy* (Baltimore: Johns Hopkins Press, 1972), pp. 123–26.

4. U.S. Congress, *Compact Cities: A Neglected Way of Conserving Energy: Joint hearings before the Subcommittee on the City of the Committee on Banking, Finance, and Urban Affairs and the Subcommittee on Oversight and Investigations of the Committee on Interstate and Foreign Commerce, U.S. House of Representatives, Ninety-sixth Congress, first session, December 11 and 12, 1979* (Washington, DC: GPO, 1981).

5. Andrés Duany and Elizabeth Plater-Zyberk, "The Second Coming of the American Small Town," *Wilson's Quarterly*, Winter 1992, pp. 19–48.

6. Peter Calthorpe, *The Next American Metropolis: Ecology, Community, and the American Dream* (New York: Princeton Architectural Press, 1993), p. 17.

7. Ahwahnee Principles, tinyurl.com/2v4xap.

8. Ibid.

9. "New Urbanism Basics," Congress for the New Urbanism, tinyurl.com/2k7pvr; "Charter of the New Urbanism" (Chicago: Congress for the New Urbanism, 1998), cnu.org.

10. Hall, *Cities of Tomorrow*, p. 11.

11. Ibid., p. 421.

12. Ibid., p. 16.

13. Jacobs, *Death and Life*, p. 13.

Chapter 25

1. H. L. Mencken, "Women as Outlaws," in *A Mencken Chrestomathy* (New York: A. A. Knopf, 1949), p. 29.

2. Jim Redden, "Caution: Growth Ahead," *Portland Tribune*, July 8, 2005.

3. Kathleen Falk, Dane County executive, presentation to Special Joint Meeting of the Comprehensive Planning Strategy Committee and the Strategic Growth Management Committee, Madison, WI, February 23, 2004.

4. *Growth Questionnaire* (Salt Lake City: Envision Utah, 1998), tinyurl.com/227tr5.

5. Envision Utah, "Transportation Choices," newspaper ad, August 2000, tinyurl.com/yucdwg.

6. Ibid.

7. Martin Wachs, "Ethics and Advocacy in Forecasting for Public Policy," *Business and Professional Ethics Journal* 9, nos. 1 & 2 (1990): 152.

8. Andrés Duany, Elizabeth Plater-Zyberk, and Jeff Speck, *Suburban Nation: The Rise of Sprawl and the Decline of the American Dream* (New York: North Point Press, 2000), p. 228.

9. Robert Goodman, *After the Planners* (New York: Simon & Schuster, 1971), p. 11.

10. Using Income Criteria to Protect Commercial Farmland in the State of Oregon (Salem: Department of Land Conservation and Development, 1998), p. 2.

11. Anna Griffin, "City Council Stops to Think on Tax Breaks for Developers," *The Oregonian*, October 19, 2005.

12. Cheryl Martinis, "Blueberry Café Will Close March 1," *The Oregonian*, February 20, 2000.

13. Wade Nkrumah, "Portland Church at Center of Gathering Storm," *The Oregonian*, February 11, 2000.

14. Associated Press, "Church Will Appeal Land-Use Decision," *The Oregonian*, March 17, 2000.

15. Wachs, "Ethics," p. 144.

Part Five

1. Walt Whitman, "Song of the Open Road," *Leaves of Grass*, 82.

2. Dee J. Hall, "The Choice: High Density or Urban Sprawl," *Wisconsin State Journal*, July 23, 1995.

Chapter 26

1. Don Phillips, "Reasoned Policy vs. Crisis Decision-Making," *Trains*, July 2005, pp. 16–17.

2. *Key Facts and Figures about the European Union* (Brussels: EU, 2004), p. 51.

3. Bureau of Transportation Statistics, *National Transportation Statistics 2003* (Washington, DC: US DOT, 2004), table 1-46.

4. Don Phillips, "European Lesson: Freight and Passenger Don't Mix," *Trains*, August 2006, pp. 12–13.

5. Robert Bradley, *Oil, Gas, and Government: The U.S. Experience* (Lanham, MD: Rowman & Littlefield, 1996), 2:1370.

6. Federal Highway Administration, *Highway Statistics Summary to 1995* (Washington, DC: US DOT, 1996), table HF-210.

7. Ibid.; annual issues of *Highway Statistics* since 1995, table HF-10.

8. Calvin G. Reen, *Practical Traffic Engineering for Small Communities* (University Park: Pennsylvania State University, 1958).

9. Shorey Peterson, "The Highway from the Point of View of the Economist," in *Highways in Our National Life: A Symposium*, ed. Jean Labatut and Wheaton J. Lane (Princeton, NJ: Princeton University Press, 1950), p. 194.

10. Ibid.

11. A. Q. Mowbry, *Road to Ruin* (Philadelphia: J. B. Lippincott, 1969).

12. Jane Holtz Kay, *Asphalt Nation: How the Automobile Took over America and How We Can Take It Back* (New York: Crown, 1997), p. 121.

13. Jane Jacobs, *The Death and Life of Great American Cities* (New York: Vintage, 1963), p. 7.

14. Intermodal Surface Transportation Efficiency Act (ISTEA), Public Law 102-240.

Chapter 27

1. Intercity data from *Historical Statistics of the United States: Colonial Times to 1970* (Washington, DC: Census Bureau, 1975), series Q307; urban transit data from *Transit Factbook* (Washington, DC: American Public Transportation Association, 1998), assumes an average of 5.6 miles per transit trip.

2. Edward R. Eastman, *These Changing Times: A Story of Farm Progress during the First Quarter of the Twentieth Century* (New York: Macmillan Company, 1927), p. 7.

3. Michael Berger, "Farmers, Flivvers, and Family Life: The Impact of Motoring on Rural Women and their Kin," in *Women's Travel Issues: Proceedings from the Second National Conference*, ed. Sandra Rosenbloom (Washington, DC: US DOT, 1997), p. 111, tinyurl.com/kcutw.

4. Robert S. Lynd and Helen Merrell Lynd, *Middletown: A Study in Contemporary American Culture* (New York: Harcourt, Brace, 1929), p. 255.

5. Ibid., p. 256.

6. Franklin M. Reck, *A Car Traveling People: How the Automobile Has Changed the Life of Americans—A Study of Social Effects* (Detroit: Automobile Manufacturers Association, 1945), p. 8.

7. Federal Highway Administration, *Highway Statistics 2005* (Washington, DC: US DOT, 2005), table VM1; Census Bureau, *Annual Estimates of the Total Population of the United States, 2000–2006* (Washington, DC: Department of Commerce, 2007), table 1, tinyurl.com/2lnso6.

8. *Historical Statistics of the United States: Colonial Times to 1970* (Washington, DC: Census Bureau, 1976),[AQ: 1975?] series D5 and F73. Because personal incomes are not available before 1929, the "flow of goods to consumers" is used as a proxy. Price indexes are from series E23.

9. "Personal Income and Its Disposition," table 2.1, Bureau of Economic Analysis, www.bea.gov; number of workers from "Seasonally Adjusted Employment," Bureau of Labor Statistics, www.bls.gov.

10. Louis D. Johnston and Samuel H. Williamson, "The Annual Real and Nominal GDP for the United States, 1790–Present." Economic History Services, April 1, 2006, eh.net/hmit/gdp.

11. *OKI 2030 Regional Transportation Plan* (Cincinnati: Ohio Kentucky Indiana Regional Council of Governments, 2001), p. 16-10.

12. Rémy Prud'homme and Chang-Woon Lee, "Size, Sprawl, Speed and the Efficiency of Cities," *Urban Studies* 36, no. 11 (October 1999): 1849–58.

13. "Assembly Line Production and the Model T," tinyurl.com/25e7ue.

14. Paul Ong and Evelyn Blumenberg, "Job Access, Commute, and Travel Burden among Welfare Recipients," *Urban Studies* 31, no. 1 (1998): 77–93, tinyurl.com/zd9e5.

15. Katherine M. O'Regan and John M. Quigley, "Cars for the Poor," *Access* 12 (Spring 1998): 20–25.

16. Kerri Sullivan, *Transportation and Work: Exploring Car Usage and Employment Outcomes* (Cambridge, MA: Harvard, 2003), tinyurl.com/yonw9f.

17. Steven Raphael and Michael Stoll, "Can Boosting Minority Car-Ownership Rates Narrow Inter-Racial Employment Gaps?" (Berkeley, CA: Berkeley Program on Housing and Urban Policy, 2000), p. 2, tinyurl.com/2yeuvq.

18. "Ways to Work Local Sites," Alliance for Children and Families, tinyurl.com/hsykp.

19. Cal Marsella (director of Denver Regional Transit District), comments made in debate with the author, May 7, 2004, Aurora, CO.

20. Joyce Dargay and Dermot Gately, *Income's Effect on Car and Vehicle Ownership, Worldwide: 1960–2015* (New York: New York University, 1997), p. 1.

21. Federal Highway Administration, *Highway Statistics 2002* (Washington, DC: US DOT, 2003), table IN-4.

22. Jeffrey R. Kenworthy and Felix B. Laube, *An International Sourcebook of Automobile Dependence in Cities 1960–1990* (Boulder: University of Colorado, 1999).

23. Ari Vatanen and Malcolm Harbour, *European Transport Policy: Strangling or Liberating Europe's Potential?* (Brussels: European Parliament, 2005), p. 1, tinyurl.com/7j7s5.

24. Rémy Prud'homme, "The Current EU Transport Policy in Perspective" (paper prepared for the Transport Conference in the European Parliament, July 12, 2005).

25. Vatanen and Harbour, *European Transport Policy*, p. 8.

26. Edward L. Glaeser and Janet E. Kohlhase, *Cities, Regions, and the Decline of Transport Costs* (Cambridge, MA: Harvard, 2003), p. 2, tinyurl.com/kiwf.

27. Ibid., pp. 1, 6.

28. Marc Levinson, *The Box: How the Shipping Container Made the World Smaller and the World Economy Bigger* (Princeton, NJ: Princeton University Press, 2006).

29. Frances Cairncross, *The Death of Distance: How the Communications Revolution Will Change Our Lives* (Cambridge, MA: Harvard Business School Press, 1997).

30. Arthur Nelson and Kenneth Dueker, "The Exurbanization of America and Its Planning Policy Implications," *Journal of Planning Education and Research* 9, No. 2 (1990): p. 93; Rick Lyman, "Living Large, by Design, in the Middle of Nowhere," *New York Times*, August 15, 2005.

31. "Personal Incomes Expenditures by Type of Expenditure," table 2.5.5, Bureau of Economic Analysis, bea.gov.

32. Ibid.

33. "Homeownership Database," Fannie Mae Foundation, tinyurl.com/2jspn7.

34. Barry Levenson, *Mustard Museum Newsletter*, February 2003.

35. Ibid., July 2005.

36. W. Michael Cox and Richard Alm, *The Right Stuff: America's Move to Mass Customization* (Dallas: Dallas Federal Reserve Bank, 1999), p. 4.

37. William I. Walsh, *The Rise and Decline of the Great Atlantic and Pacific Tea Company* (Secaucus, NJ: Stuart, 1986), pp. 29, 34.

38. Lloyd Singer, "They Called Him the Price Wrecker," *Long Island Business Journal*, tinyurl.com/gra9t.

39. Ryan Mathews, "1926–1936: Entrepreneurs and Enterprise: A Look at Industry Pioneers like King Kullen and J. Frank Grimes, and the Institution They Created (Special Report: Social Change and the Supermarket)," *Progressive Grocer* 75, no. 12 (December 1996): 39–43.

40. "Time Capsules from 50 Years of Annual Reports," *Progressive Grocer*, April, 1983, p. 120; Richard Turcsik, "Super Success," *Progressive Grocer*, December, 2000, p. 51.

41. James Howard Kunstler, "Home from Nowhere," *Atlantic Monthly*, September 1996, p. 43.

42. Ross Moldoff, "Controlling Strip Development," *Planning Commissioners Journal* no. 53 (Winter 2004), tinyurl.com/2f56jp.

43. Herbert J. Gans, "City Planning and Urban Realities: A Review of The Death and Life of Great American Cities," *Books in Review* (1961): 170–73.

44. Carl Abbott, "It's a Vital Artery That Keeps Portland Honest," *The Oregonian*, August 20, 2006.

45. Emek Basker, "Selling a Cheaper Mousetrap: Wal-Mart's Effect on Retail Prices," *Journal of Urban Economics* 58, no. 2 (September 2005): 203–29, economics. missouri.edu/Working_Paper_Series/2004/wp0401_basker.pdf.

46. Moldoff, "Controlling Strip Development."

47. Michael Berger, *The Devil Wagon in God's Country: The Automobile and Social Change in Rural America, 1893–1929* (Hamden, CT: Archon Books, 1979), pp. 55–74.

48. Lynd and Lynd, *Middletown*, p. 261.

49. Public Use Statistics, National Park Service, www2.nature.nps.gov/stats/.

50. U.S. Fire Administration/National Fire Data Center, *All Structure Fires in 2000* (Washington, DC: FEMA, 2004), p. 2.

51. Ray Bowman, "Deaths Expected from Delayed Emergency Response Due to Neighborhood Traffic Mitigation," testimony submitted to Boulder, CO, City Council, April 3, 1997.

52. Robert Davis, "The Price of a Few Seconds: People Die," *USA Today*, July 28, 2003.

53. Jason DeParle, "What Happens to a Race Deferred," *New York Times*, September 4, 2005, tinyurl.com/adgjx.

54. Rick Lyman, "Bus Caught Fire after a Waiver Put It Back into Service," *New York Times*, September 25, 2005, tinyurl.com/lek.

55. John Renne, "Car-less in the Eye of Katrina," *Planetizen*, September 6, 2005, tinyurl.com/yteduh.

56. David Brooks, "The Best-Laid Plan: Too Bad It Flopped," *New York Times*, September 11, 2005.

57. John Renne, "National Conference on Disaster Planning for the Carless Society," October 25, 2006, carlessevacuation.org.

58. Sandra Rosenbloom and Elizabeth Burns, "Do Environmental Measures and Travel Reduction Programs Hurt Working Women?" Drachman Institute for Land and Regional Development Studies, University of Arizona, October 1993.

59. Jane Holtz Kay, *Asphalt Nation: How the Automobile Took over America and How We Can Take It Back* (New York: Crown, 1997), pp. 22–23.

60. Warren Brown, "Automobile Played Role on Long Ride to Freedom," *Washington Post*, September 5, 2004, p. G2.

61. Ibid.

62. Ruben N. Lubowski, Marlow Vesterby, Shawn Bucholtz, Alba Baez, and Michael J. Roberts, *Major Uses of Land in the United States, 2002* (Washington, DC: USDA, 2006), p. 5.

63. *Historical Statistics of the United States: Colonial Times to 1970* (Washington, DC: Census Bureau, 1975), series J73–74.

64. Lubowski et al., *Major Uses of Land*, p. 5.

65. Ibid.; Census Bureau, *Historical Statistics*, series J72.

66. Natural Resources Conservation Service, *Natural Resources Inventory: Highlights* (Washington, DC: USDA, 2001), p. 1.

Chapter 28

1. *Calculate Your Cost of Driving* (Santa Cruz, CA: Santa Cruz County Regional Transportation Commission, 2002), p. 1, tinyurl.com/2b2898.

2. Federal Highway Administration, *Highway Statistics 2000* (Washington, DC: US DOT, 2001), tables MV-1, VM-1.

3. Bureau of Economic Analysis, *National Income and Production Accounts* (NIPA) (Washington, DC: Department of Commerce, 2005), table 2.5.5.

4. Federal Highway Administration, *Highway Statistics 2000*, table VM-1.

5. Thorstein Veblen, *The Theory of the Leisure Class* (New York: Macmillan, 1899).

6. Patricia Mokhtarian and Ilam Salomon, "Travel for the Fun of It," *Access* 15 (Fall 1999): 27.

7. *Transportation Costs and the American Dream* (Washington, DC: Surface Transportation Policy Project, 2003).

8. Bureau of Economic Analysis, *NIPA*, table 2.5.5.

9. *Historical Statistics of the United States: Colonial Times to 1970* (Washington, DC: Census Bureau, 1975), series Q 1–11.

10. Bureau of Transportation Statistics, *National Transportation Statistics 2003* (Washington, DC: US DOT, 2004), table 1-37.

11. Friends of the Earth, "Balance of Transportation Funding Tipping More Toward Highways: Congress Blindly Supporting Broken, Unfair System," *Economics for the Earth*, August 29, 2000, p. 1.

12. Federal Highway Administration, *Highway Statistics* (Washington, DC: US DOT, various years), table HF-10. Calculated by deducting diversions to nonhighway purposes and mass transportation from "other taxes and fees."

13. Ibid., table VM-1.

14. Federal Highway Administration, *Highway Statistics Summary to 1995* (Washington, DC: US DOT, 2005), table HF-210, plus annual issues since 1995, table HF-10.

15. Bureau of Transportation Statistics, *National Transportation Statistics 2004* (Washington, DC: US DOT, 2005), table 1-46a.

16. Federal Highway Administration, *Highway Statistics 2004*, tables LGF-1, SF-1, DF, FE-9, and VM-2.

17. Bureau of Transportation Statistics, *Federal Subsidies to Passenger Transportation* (Washington, DC: US DOT, 2004), table 3.

18. Federal Transit Administration, *National Transit Database* (Washington, DC: US DOT, 2006), tables 1, 11, 12, and 19.

19. Ibid.

20. James J. Murphy and Mark A. Delucchi, "A Review of the Literature on the Social Cost of Motor Vehicle Use in the United States," *Journal of Transportation and Statistics* 1, no. 1 (January 1998): 15–42.

21. Federal Highway Administration, *Highway Statistics Summary to 1995* (Washington, DC: US DOT, 1997), tables VM-201, FI-201; and *Highway Statistics 2003* (Washington, DC: US DOT, 2004), tables VM-1, FI-1; Environmental Protection Agency, *National Air Quality and Emissions Trends Report, 2003* (Washington, DC: EPA, 2003), pp. 1–24.

22. Joel Schwartz, *Air Quality: Much Worse on Paper than in Reality* (Washington, DC: American Enterprise Institute, 2005), tinyurl.com/2df3bs; Joel Schwartz, *No Way Back: Why Air Pollution Will Continue to Decline* (Washington, DC: American Enterprise Institute, 2003), tinyurl.com/yqev6q.

23. Federal Highway Administration, *Highway Statistics Summary to 1995*, table FI-200.

24. Federal Highway Administration, *Highway Statistics 2004*, tables FI-20 and VM-20.

25. Federal Highway Administration, *Highway Statistics Summary to 1995*, table FI-200; subsequent years, tables FI-20 and VM-20.

Chapter 29

1. Jan Lundberg, "Termination of the Fossil-Fuels Society," *Culture Change*, August 11, 2005, tinyurl.com/dmout.

2. James Howard Kunstler, *The Geography of Nowhere: The Rise and Decline of America's Manmade Landscape* (New York: Simon & Schuster, 1993), p. 112.

3. James Howard Kunstler, *Home from Nowhere: Remaking Our Everyday World for the Twenty-First Century* (New York: Simon & Schuster, 1996).

4. James Howard Kunstler, *The Long Emergency* (Boston: Atlantic, 2005).

5. James Howard Kunstler, "The Long Emergency," *Rolling Stone*, March 24, 2005, tinyurl.com/coyxh.

6. Bill Kovarik, "The Oil Reserve Fallacy: Proven Reserves Are Not a Measure of Future Supply—Timeline," tinyurl.com/7l6cx.

7. *Historical Statistics of the United States: Colonial Times to 1970* (Washington, DC: Census Bureau, 1975), series M138; "World Crude Oil Production, 1960–2004," Department of Energy, tinyurl.com/2f9er.

8. Michael C. Lynch, "Crying Wolf: Warnings about Oil Supply," tinyurl.com/co4zk.

9. Judith Crosson, "Oil Prices Prompt Another Look at Shale," Reuters, November 23, 2004, tinyurl.com/7na59.

10. *2004 Corporate Citizenship Report* (Irving, TX: Exxon-Mobil, 2005) p. 13, tinyurl.com/29jep3.

11. Piero Scaruffi, "Oil Reserves, Production, and Consumption in 2001," tinyurl.com/4t9sx.

12. Bill Kovarik, "The Oil Reserve Fallacy: Proven Reserves Are Not a Measure of Future Supply—Defining Oil Reserves, Part III," tinyurl.com/an5rd.

13. Brendan J. Koerner, "The Trillion-Barrel Tar Pit," *Wired*, July 2004, tinyurl.com/9drod.

14. Bureau of Land Management, "Nominations for Oil Shale Research Leases Demonstrate Significant Interest in Advancing Energy Technology," news release, September 20, 2005, tinyurl.com/24olg5.

15. Energy Information Administration, "A Primer on Gasoline Prices," tinyurl.com/egj43.

16. Energy Information Administration, "Retail Motor Gasoline Prices, 1990–2005," tinyurl.com/ystsms; "Cushing, OK WTI Spot Price," tinyurl.com/25krc6; "Europe Brent Spot Price," tinyurl.com/295hta.

17. "Taconite," Minnesota Historical Society, tinyurl.com/984fa.

18. "The Reader's Companion to American History: Iron and Steel Industry," Houghton Mifflin, tinyurl.com/84lsh.

19. *Historical Statistics of the United States*, series M218.

20. Michael Fenton, "Annual Average Hot-Rolled Steel Bar Price," tinyurl.com/9z5ew.

21. Kunstler, "The Long Emergency," pp. 45–48.

22. Federal Highway Administration, *Highway Statistics 2004* (Washington, DC: US DOT, 2005), tables MF-21 and VM-1.

23. "Toyota Says It May Put Gas-Electric Engines in All Its Vehicles," September 13, 2005, Bloomberg.com, tinyurl.com/b9g2w.

24. Federal Highway Administration, *Highway Statistics Summary to 1995* (Washington, DC: US DOT, 1996), tables MF-221 and VM-201.

25. Nicholas Lutsey and Daniel Sperling, "Energy Efficiency, Fuel Economy, and Policy Implications," *Transportation Research Record* 1941 (2005): 8–17.

26. Spencer Reiss, "Let a Thousand Reactors Bloom," *Wired*, September 2004, tinyurl.com/5fcu6.

27. Greg Breining, "Five Reasons Corn Ethanol Won't Save the Planet," *Minnesota Magazine*, January–February 2007, tinyurl.com/38ky8x.

28. "National Economic Accounts," Bureau of Economic Analysis, tinyurl.com/cb7f9, line 69 (user-operated transportation) of table 2.5.5 with line 1 (personal income) or line 26 (disposable personal income) of table 2.1.

29. Ibid., compare line 75 with line 69 of table 2.5.5.

30. Bureau of Transportation Statistics, *Preliminary Results from the 2001 NHTS: Changes in Demographics and Travel* (Washington, DC: US DOT, 2003), p. 3, tinyurl.com/2bknjt.

31. Patricia L. Mokhtarian and Cynthia Chen, *TTB or Not TTB, That Is the Question: A Review and Analysis of the Empirical Literature on Travel Time (and Money) Budgets* (Davis, CA: Institute of Transportation Studies, 2002), p. 1.

32. Federal Highway Administration, *Highway Statistics 1995* and *Highway Statistics 2002*, table IN-4.

33. James Howard Kunstler, "Remarks to the Florida AIA," 1998, tinyurl.com/8ogt9.

34. Ted Balaker, *Telecommuting's Impact on Transportation and Beyond* (Los Angeles: Reason Foundation, 2005), reason.org/ps338.pdf.

35. Arthur Nelson and Kenneth Dueker, "The Exurbanization of America and Its Planning Policy Implications," *Journal of Planning Education and Research* 9, no. 2 (1990): 93.

36. Arthur C. Nelson, William J. Drummond, and David S. Sawicki. "Exurban Industrialization: Implications for Economic Development Policy," *Economic Development Quarterly* 9, no. 2 (May 1995): 119–33, tinyurl.com/bb3r2.

37. "2005 Gas Prices Changing How Consumers Shop," *Facts, Figures, and the Future*, September 13, 2005, Food Marketing Institute, tinyurl.com/88nvg.

Chapter 30

1. "7-syllable highway," *Honolulu Star-Bulletin*, July 20, 1999, starbulletin.com/1999/07/20/news/briefs.html.

2. Albert P. Heiner, *Henry J. Kaiser: Western Colossus* (San Francisco: Halo Books, 1991), p. 351.

3. David Schrank and Tim Lomax, *The 2005 Urban Mobility Report* (College Station: Texas A&M University, 2005), p. 1.

4. *Regional Transportation Plan Update* (Portland, OR: Metro, March 1996), p. 1-20.

5. *1999 Regional Transportation Plan* (Portland, OR: Metro, November, 1999), p. 6-38.

6. "Minutes of the Metro Council Transportation Planning Committee Meeting," Portland, OR, July 18, 2000, p. 7.

7. *Regional Blueprint* (St. Paul, MN: Metropolitan Council, 1996), p. 54.

8. Dom Nozzi, *Traffic Congestion: Friend or Foe?* tinyurl.com/3dfwbu.

9. Steve Inspkeep, "Commuting, Part IV," *All Things Considered*, May 30, 1997.

10. Federal Highway Administration, *Highway Statistics 2003* (Washington, DC: US DOT, 2004), table HM-71.

11. Robert Cervero, "Are Induced Travel Studies Inducing Bad Investments?" *Access* 26 (Spring 2005): 27, tinyurl.com/34nesx.

12. *Annual Report 1990* (Chicago: Joyce Foundation, 1990).

13. Federal Highway Administration, *CMAQ F.Y. 2000 Annual Report* (Washington, DC: US DOT, 2004), tinyurl.com/2oqvsp and tinyurl.com/346f66.

14. "Executive Summary," *Transportation Partners 1997 Annual Report* (Washington, DC: Environmental Protection Agency, 1998), p. 1.

15. Peter Samuel and Randal O'Toole, *Smart Growth at the Federal Trough* (Washington, DC: Cato Institute, 1999).

16. Randal O'Toole, *Department of Transportation Funds Smart-Growth Groups* (Bandon, OR: Thoreau Institute, 2002), ti.org/vaupdate23.html.

Chapter 31

1. Sarah Lyall, "A Path to Road Safety With No Signposts," *New York Times*, January 22, 2005.

2. Leslie W. Bunte, Jr., "Traffic Calming Programs and Emergency Response: A Competition of Two Public Goods," professional report prepared in partial fulfillment of the requirements for the degree of Master of Public Affairs, University of Texas at Austin, 2000; Ronald Bowman, "Deaths Expected from Delayed Emergency Response Due to Neighborhood Traffic Calming," April 1997, members.aol.com/raybowman/risk97/eval1.html.

3. W. S. Homburger, *Transportation and Traffic Engineering Handbook*, 2nd ed. (Englewood Cliffs, NJ: Prentice Hall, 1982).

4. Fred T. Fowler, "One-Way Grid System of Portland, Oregon," *Traffic Engineering*, April 1953, p. 231.

5. D. J. Faustman, "Improving the Traffic Access to Sacramento's Business District," *Traffic Quarterly*, July 1950, p. 249.

6. *National Highway Safety Needs Study* (Chapel Hill, NC: Research Triangle Institute, 1976).

7. Robert D. Pier, "One-Way Street Experience," *Traffic Engineering*, January 1950, p. 153.

8. Traffic Engineering Division, State of Washington, *A Study of Vehicle Traffic and Business Trends "Before" and "After" One-Way Streets in Olympia, Washington* (Olympia: Highway Commission, 1952).

9. D. J. Faustman, "Improving the Traffic Access to Sacramento's Business District," *Traffic Quarterly*, July 1950, p. 239.

10. James L. Brown (Director of Traffic Engineering), *One-Way Street Study* (Denver, CO: City of Denver, 1976).

11. *One-Way Street Monitoring Study: Phase 1 Conversion Report* (Denver, CO: City of Denver, January 1990), p. 29.

12. Ibid., p. 31.

13. Pflum, Klausmeier & Gehrum Consultants, Inc., *Pennsylvania Street/Delaware Street/Central Avenue Analysis of Impacts Conversion to Two-Way Operation* (Indianapolis: City of Indianapolis, 1999), p. 3.

14. *Main and 10th Street Accident Analysis Before/After Study* (Lubbock, TX: City of Lubbock, 1998).

15. Marc Levin, "Two-Way Streets No Walk in the Park," *Austin Review*, July 1, 2002.

16. Eddie Safady, "Great Streets a Boondoggle," *Austin Business Journal*, July 12, 2002.

17. Janice Rombeck, "Council Restores 10 Streets to 2-Way," *San Jose Mercury News*, June 5, 2002.

18. Andrew Dreschel, "City Should Say No Way to Two-Way Street Switch," *Hamilton Spectator*, March 6, 2002.

19. Levin, "No Walk in the Park."

20. Tom McNichol, "Roads Gone Wild," *Wired*, December 2004, tinyurl.com/6vw9w.

Chapter 32

1. Wendell Cox, *Competition, Not Monopolies, Can Improve Public Transit* (Washington, DC: Heritage Foundation, 2000), tinyurl.com/ypqok8.

2. George M. Smerk, *The Federal Role in Urban Mass Transportation* (Bloomington: Indiana University Press, 1991), pp. 120–21.

3. Darwin Stolzenbach, interview with Professor Alan Altshuler, former secretary of transportation, Massachusetts, AASHTO Interstate Highway Research Project, June 8, 1981), p. 36.

4. Gregory L. Thompson, "Defining an Alternative Future: Birth of the Light Rail Movement in North America," in *Ninth National Light Rail Transit Conference*, ed. Transportation Research Board (Washington, DC: US DOT, 2004), p. 35.

5. William Buechner, *History of the Gasoline Tax* (Washington, DC: ARTBA, 1998), tinyurl.com/ejgst.

6. Don Pickrell, *Urban Rail Transit Projects: Forecast Versus Actual Ridership and Costs* (Washington, DC: US DOT, Urban Mass Transportation Administration, 1989), table S-2.

7. Ibid., p. xi.

8. James Dunn, "Mobility Contested: Ethical Challenges for Planners, Administrators and Policy Analysts" (paper prepared for the Conference on Ethics and Integrity of Governance, Leuven, Belgium, June 2005), p. 6, tinyurl.com/35cfne.

9. Martin Wachs, "Ethics and Advocacy in Forecasting for Public Policy," *Business and Professional Ethics Journal* 9, nos. 1 & 2 (1990): 141.

10. Bent Flyvbjerg, Mette Skamris Holm, and Søren Buhl, "Underestimating Costs in Public Works Projects: Error or Lie?" *Journal of the American Planning Association* 68, no. 3 (2002): 279–95.

11. Bent Flyvbjerg, Mette K. Skamris Holm, and Søren L. Buhl, "How (In)accurate Are Demand Forecasts for Public Works Projects?" *Journal of the American Planning Association* 71, no. 2 (2005): 131–46.

12. Bent Flyvbjerg, "Misrepresentation Drives Projects," *Engineering News-Record*, January 5, 2004, p. 87, flyvbjerg.plan.aau.dk/Misrepr4-0.pdf.

13. Kimley-Horn & Associates, *East Corridor Major Investment Study Final Report* (Denver, CO: DRCOG, 1997), pp. 37–39.

14. *FasTracks Plan* (Denver, CO: Regional Transit District, 2003), appendix M.

15. Nasiru A. Dantata, Ali Touran, and Donald C. Schneck, "Trends in U.S. Rail Transit Project Cost Overrun" (paper presented to the Transportation Research Board, 2006), table 3, tinyurl.com/34g9rd.

16. Larry Lange, "Voters Reject Shortened Monorail Line," *Seattle Post-Intelligencer*, November 9, 2005, seattlepi.nwsource.com/local/247655_monorail09.html.

17. Hal R. Arkes and Peter Ayton, "The Sunk Cost and Concorde Effects: Are Humans Less Rational Than Lower Animals?" *Psychological Bulletin* 125, no. 5 (1999): 591–600.

18. *Public Transportation Fact Book* (Washington, DC: APTA, 2006), table 37.

19. Ibid., table 7.

20. Clifford Winston and Vikram Maheshri, "The Social Desirability of Urban Rail Transit Systems," *Journal of Urban Economics*, in press.

21. Edward Carpenter, "Transit Advocates Blast SJ BART Funding as Wasteful," *Peninsula Examiner*, February 3, 2007, tinyurl.com/35lc2t.

22. Letter from Robert Piper, Sierra Club San Francisco Bay Chapter, to U.S. Representative Ellen Tauscher, July 6, 2004.

23. Belinda Griswold, "Tunnel Vision," *San Francisco Bay Guardian*, November 5, 1997.

24. Bob Egelko, "Inequality in Funding Discriminates against AC Transit Riders, Plaintiffs Claim in Suit," *San Francisco Chronicle*, April 20, 2005, p. B-5, tinyurl.com/8otrw.

25. Nancy McGuckin and Nanda Srinivasan, *Journey-to-Work Trends in the United States and Its Major Metropolitan Areas, 1960–2000* (Washington, DC: US DOT, 2003), p. 1-19.

26. Federal Transit Administration, *National Transit Database* (Washington, DC: US DOT, various years), "Service Supplied and Consumed." Tables can be downloaded from ntdprogram.com.

27. Federal Highway Administration, *Highway Statistics* (Washington, DC: U.S. DOT, various years), table HM-72. Tables can be downloaded from tinyurl.com/2cc3oj.

28. Pat S. Hu, *Summary of Travel Trends: 2001 National Household Travel Survey* (Washington, DC: US DOT, 2004), p. 31, tinyurl.com/2xsqa6.

29. Federal Transit Administration, *National Transit Database* (1983–2004, table titled "service supplied and consumed." These numbers are analyzed in Randal O'Toole, *Rail Disasters 2005* (Bandon, OR: American Dream Coalition, 2005), americandream coalition.org/rail2005.html.

30. Census Bureau, *Census of Population and Housing* (Washington, DC: Department of Commerce, 1982, 2002), means of transportation to work for urbanized areas.

31. Clifford Winston and Chad Shirley, *Alternate Route: Toward Efficient Urban Transportation* (Washington, DC: Brookings Institution, 1998), p. 9.

32. "Bus Riders Union," Labor/Community Strategy Center, busridersunion.org.

33. Federal Transit Administration, *National Transit Data Base*, various years, "Service supplied and consumed."

34. Gary Richards, "VTA Backs Major Cuts," *Mercury News*, May 10, 2003.

35. *Transit Ridership Report* (Washington, DC: APTA, various years).

36. Nick Budnick, "TriMet Feels Its Own Squeeze," *Portland Tribune*, June 6, 2006, tinyurl.com/yoqnq4.

37. *2005 Downtown Portland Business Census and Survey* (Portland, OR: Portland Business Alliance, 2006), p. 11.

38. *Transit Ridership Report Third Quarter 2006* (Washington, DC: APTA, 2006), agency totals, p. 21, tinyurl.com/yupav7.

39. Richard White, *WMATA Performance and Funding Requirements Update* (Washington, DC: WMATA, 2004), p. 6.

40. *Information on the Federal Role in Funding the Washington Metropolitan Area Transportation Authority* (Washington, DC: Government Accountability Office, 2005), p. 11.

41. Lena H. Sun, "Hoofing It Out of the Subway: System Considers Converting Some Escalators to Stairs to Save on Repairs," *Washington Post*, October 10, 2006.

42. Federal Transit Administration, *National Transit Data Base*, various years, "Service supplied and consumed."

43. Gregory L. Thompson, "Defining an Alternative Future: Birth of the Light Rail Movement in North America," *Planning and Forecasting for Light Rail Transit: 9th National Light Rail Transit Conference* (Washington, DC: US DOT, 2003), p. 3.

44. Neil Schickner, *Audit of the Champlain Flyer Commuter Rail Service Pursuant to 2002 Session, Act 141, Sec. 18* (Burlington, VT: Joint Legislative Fiscal Office, 2003).

45. Census Bureau, 2000 census, table P30, "Means of Transportation to Work"; 1990 census, table P049, "Means of Transportation to Work," for urbanized areas.

46. Census Bureau, 2000 census, table P30; 1990 census, table PO49.

47. "Light Rail and Congestion: A Sympathetic Argument," tinyurl.com/3caxxf.

48. Laurie Blake, "Light-Rail Trains Run; Motorists Seethe," *Minneapolis Star-Tribune*, June 30, 2004.

49. Laurie Blake, "Mixed Signals: Officials Try to Undo Snarls along Rail Line," *Minneapolis Star-Tribune*, June 25, 2004.

50. Laurie Blake, "Light Rail Will Always Slow the Flow," *Minneapolis Star-Tribune*, December 12, 2004.

51. Blake, "Mixed Signals."

52. Blake, "Light Rail Will Always Slow the Flow."

53. "Wham-Bam Tram Ram Counter," Action America, tinyurl.com/ysf98b.

54. *Final Transportation 2030 Plan* (Oakland, CA: Metropolitan Transportation Commission, 2005), p. 35.

55. *Regional Transportation Plan* (St. Paul, MN: Metropolitan Council, 1999), pp. xii, 95, 98.

56. *2004 Regional Transportation Plan Project List* (Portland, OR: Metro, 2004), tinyurl.com/3yrdtv.

57. Randal O'Toole, "Planners Waste Money on Rail Transit," *Vanishing Automobile Update No. 24*, 2002, ti.org/vaupdate24.html.

58. Moshe Ben-Akiva and Takayuki Morikawa, "Comparing Ridership Attraction of Rail and Bus," *Transport Policy Journal* 9, no. 2 (2002).

59. Graham Currie, "The Demand Performance of Bus Rapid Transit," *Journal of Public Transportation* 8, no. 1 (2005): 41.

60. Mark Garrett and Brian Taylor, "Reconsidering Social Equity in Public Transit," *Berkeley Planning Journal* 13 (1999): 6–27.

61. Hiroyuki Iseki and Brian Taylor, *Demographics of Public Transit Subsidies: A Case Study of Los Angeles* (Berkeley: University of California Transportation Center, 2003), p. ii.

62. *Bus-Rapid Transit Shows Promise* (Washington, DC: General Accounting Office, 2001), p. 17.

63. Ibid., pp. 23, 26–27.

64. Bob Egelko, "Inequity in Funding Discriminates against AC Transit Riders, Plaintiffs Claim in Suit," *San Francisco Chronicle*, April 20, 2005, p. B-1.

65. Ari Vatanen and Malcolm Harbour, *European Transport Policy: Strangling or Liberating Europe's Potential?* (Brussels: European Parliament, 2005), p. 5.

66. *Key Facts and Figures about the European Union* (Brussels: European Union, 2004), p. 52.

67. Vatanen and Harbour, *European Transport Policy*, p. 6.

68. Ari Vatanen, "Transport Conference Breaks the Camel's Back," news release, July 12, 2005.

Chapter 33

1. John Pucher, "Urban Travel as the Outcome of Public Policy," *Journal of the American Planning Association* 54, no. 4 (1988): 509–20.

2. Scott Bottles, *Los Angeles and the Automobile: The Making of the Modern City* (Berkeley: University of California Press, 1987), pp. 3–4.

3. Christine Cosgrove, "*Roger Rabbit* Unframed: Revising the GM Conspiracy Theory," *ITS Review Online* 3, no. 1 (2004–05), tinyurl.com/2bcg2t.

4. Martha J. Bianco, "Kennedy, 60 Minutes, and Roger Rabbit: Understanding Conspiracy-Theory Explanations of the Decline of Urban Mass Transit" (Portland State University Center for Urban Studies Discussion Paper 98-11, Portland, OR, November 1998).

5. Cliff Slater, "General Motors and the Demise of Streetcars," *Transportation Quarterly* 51, no. 3 (Summer 1997): 45–66, tinyurl.com/yuth5m.

6. Bottles, *Los Angeles and the Automobile*, p. 240.

7. "List of Town Tramway Systems—United States," Wikipedia, tinyurl.com/yhrjxg.

8. Bill Vandervoort, "Cities Served by National City Lines," hometown.aol.com/chirailfan/holdbun.html.

9. Quoted in Bottles, *Los Angeles and the Automobile*, p. 241.

10. Slater, "General Motors and the Demise of Streetcars," p. 57.

11. Quoted in "Divided Highways: The Interstates and the Transformation of American Life," Florentine Films, 1997, tinyurl.com/yt45dk.

12. *Public Transportation Fact Book* (Washington, DC: APTA, 2006), tables 37, 48, and 51.

13. Parsons Brinckerhoff, *Transportation Alternatives Analysis for the Dane County/ Greater Madison Metropolitan Area* (Madison, WI: Transport 2020, 2002), pp. 7-6, 10-22.

14. Ibid., p. 7-6.

15. Ibid., p. 10-2.

16. *Transport 2020 Oversight Advisory Committee (OAC) Summary Report* (Madison, WI: Transport 2020, 2002), p. 21.

17. Kimley-Horn & Associates, *East Corridor Major Investment Study Final Report* (Denver, CO: DRCOG, 1997), pp. 37–39; BRW, Inc., *West Corridor Major Investment Study Final Report* (Denver, CO: RTD, 1997), pp. 108, 110; CH2M Hill, *I-70 Denver to Golden Major Investment Study Final Report* (Denver, CO: RTD, 2000), pp. 5-17, 5-18, 6-13; Carter-Burgess, *US 36 Major Investment Study Final Report* (Denver, CO: RTD, 2001), pp. 5-7, 5-9, 6-24, 6-25, 6-26; S. R. Beard & Associates, *I-225 Major Investment Study Parker Road to Interstate 70: Detailed Evaluation Technical Report* (Denver, CO: RTD, 2001), pp. 19–20, 27, 32.

18. See, for example, Regional Transportation District, *FasTracks* (Denver, CO: RTD, 2004), pp. 4 and 6 of a brochure delivered to hundreds of thousands of households in the Denver metropolitan area.

19. Robert Cervero and Samuel Seskin, *An Evaluation of the Relationship between Transit and Urban Form* (Washington, DC: Transportation Research Board, 1995), p. 3.

20. Office of Transportation, *Portland Streetcar: Development-Oriented Transit* (Portland, OR: City of Portland, 2006), p. 1, tinyurl.com/22uoxe.

21. Portland Development Commission, *Urban Renewal History Appendix* (Portland, OR: City of Portland, 2005), pp. 1–4, tinyurl.com/yo2zde.

22. Dee J. Hall, "The Choice: High Density or Urban Sprawl," *Wisconsin State Journal*, July 23, 1995.

23. Anthony Downs, *Stuck in Traffic: Coping with Peak-Hour Traffic Congestion* (Washington, DC: Brookings Institution, 1992).

24. Ibid., pp. 27–28.

25. Robert Cervero, "Are Induced-Travel Studies Inducing Bad Investments?" *Access* 22 (Spring 2003): 22–27.

26. Martin Stone, "The Tampa Elevated Expressway" (presentation to the Hawaii Highway Users Alliance, Oahu, October 23, 2006).

27. "North American Light Rail and Trolley Systems," Lightrail.com, lightrail.com/LRTSystems.htm.

28. Stone, "The Tampa Elevated Expressway."

29. John E. Evans et al., *Road Value Pricing: Traveler Response to Transportation System Charges* (Washington, DC: Transportation Research Board, 2003), pp. 6–14.

30. Ibid., pp. 20–24.

31. Ibid., p. 6.

32. Federal Highway Administration, *Traffic Signal Timing* (Washington, DC: US DOT, 2005), ops.fhwa.dot.gov/traffic_sig_timing/index.htm.

33. Gary Richards, "A Sea of Greens for S.J. Drivers: City Tweaks 223 Intersections to Ease Delays," *San Jose Mercury-News*, November 6, 2003.

34. Xi Zou, *Simulation and Analysis of Mixed Adaptive Cruise Control/Manual Traffic* (Minneapolis: University of Minnesota, 2001), rational.ce.umn.edu/Theses/XiZou_Thesis.pdf.

Part Six

1. Freeman Dyson, *Infinite in All Directions* (New York: Harper & Row, 1988), p. 205.

2. Quoted in Frank Tracy, "The Report of the Committee on Uniform Laws, of the American Bankers' Association," *Banking Law Journal* 15 (1898): 542. A similar quote has often been attributed to Otto von Bismarck, but there is no evidence that he said such a thing.

3. James L. Payne, *The Culture of Spending: Why Congress Lives Beyond Our Means* (San Francisco: ICS, 1991), p. 12.

Chapter 34

1. Bent Flyvbjerg, "The Dark Side of Planning: Rationality and 'Realrationalität,'" in *Explorations in Planning Theory*, ed. Seymour J. Mandelbaum, Luigi Mazza, and Robert W. Burchell (New Brunswick, NJ: Center for Urban Policy Research Press, 1996), p. 383.

2. Bent Flyvbjerg, "Rationality and Power" in *Readings in Planning Theory*, 2nd ed., ed. Scott Cambell and Susan S. Fainstein (Oxford: Blackwell, 2003), p. 318.

3. Ibid., p. 319.

4. Encarta.msn.com, tinyurl.com/28kbxv.

5. Flyvbjerg, "Rationality and Power," p. 319.

6. John E. Hirten, "Planning for Our Nation's Future!" (paper presented at American Planning Association National Conference, New Orleans, March 13, 2001, tinyurl. com/yvpnyn.

7. Ibid.

8. Ibid.

9. Thomas Paine, *Common Sense* (Bartleby.com), p. 1, tinyurl.com/22adz. Although often attributed to Paine or Thomas Jefferson, there is no evidence that either made the similar statement that "government is best which governs least." Instead, the phrase quoted by Thoreau was from *The United States Magazine and Democratic Review*, which in 1838 adopted as its motto "The best government is that which governs least." See tinyurl.com/yzydkj and tinyurl.com/ym4bv3.

10. Henry David Thoreau, "Civil Disobedience," in, *Henry David Thoreau: Walden and Other Writings*, ed. Brooks Atkinson (New York: Modern Library, 1992), p. 668.

11. Ibid, p. 673.

12. P. J. O'Rourke, *Parliament of Whores* (New York: Atlantic Monthly Press, 1991), p. 5.

13. *Historical Statistics of the United States: Colonial Times to 1970* (Washington, DC: Census Bureau, 1975), series Y308, Y314.

14. Ibid.

15. Christopher Lee, "Big Government Gets Bigger," *Washington Post*, October 6, 2006, p. A21, tinyurl.com/fhyvv.

16. Robert Samuelson, "Clinton's Nemesis," *Newsweek*, February 1, 1993, p. 51.

17. Milton Friedman and Anna Schwartz, *A Monetary History of the United States, 1867–1960* (Princeton, NJ: Princeton University, 1963).

18. "History of the U.S. Tax System," U.S. Treasury, tinyurl.com/2emtt8.

19. Aaron Wildavsky, *The Politics of the Budgetary Process*, 3rd ed. (Boston: Little, Brown, 1979), p. 163.

Chapter 35

1. David R. Mayhew, *Congress: The Electoral Connection* (New Haven, CT: Yale, 1974), pp. 14–16.

2. Frank E. Smith, *Congressman from Mississippi* (New York: Random House, 1964), p. 127.

3. David Shoenbrod, *Saving Our Environment from Washington: How Congress Grabs Power, Shirks Responsibility, and Shortchanges the People* (New Haven, CT: Yale University Press, 2005), p. 35.

4. Ibid., p. 231.

5. The Safe, Accountable, Flexible, Efficient Transportation Equity Act: A Legacy for Users (SAFETEA-LU), Public Law 109-59. Representative Don Young's spouse is named Lula.

6. Brian Kelly, *Adventures in Porkland* (New York: Villard, 1992), p. 156.

Chapter 36

1. See, for example, Raymond A. Bauer, Ithiel de Sola Pool, and Lewis Anthony Dexter, *American Business and Public Policy* (Chicago: Aldine, Atherton, 1972), p. 414.

2. James L. Payne, *The Culture of Spending: Why Congress Lives Beyond Our Means* (San Francisco: ICS, 1991), p. 12.

3. John Mark Hansen, *Gaining Access: Congress and the Farm Lobby, 1919–1981* (Chicago: University of Chicago Press, 1991), p. 7.

4. Bruce Yandle, "Bootleggers and Baptists in Retrospect," *Regulation* 22, no. 3 (1999): 5–7, tinyurl.com/yo8mzv.

5. Peter Drucker, *The New Realities* (New York: Harper & Row, 1989), p. 64.

Chapter 37

1. Quotes taken from my notes from the August 1988 meeting held at Sundance, Utah.

2. I learned this from a Maxwell student who interned with the Thoreau Institute in 1992.

3. David Osborne and Ted Gaebler, *Reinventing Government: How the Entrepreneurial Spirit Is Transforming the Public Sector* (New York: Plume, 1992), p. 117.

4. William Niskanen, *Bureaucracy and Representative Government* (Chicago: Aldine, Atherton, 1971), p. 38.

5. Anthony Downs, *Inside Bureaucracy* (Boston: Little, Brown, 1967).

6. Assistant Chief Thayer, as quoted in Aaron Wildavsky, *The Politics of the Budgetary Process*, 3rd ed. (Boston: Little, Brown, 1979), p. 193.

7. Jack Ward Thomas, interview with Randal O'Toole, 1998.

8. "Life in a Soviet Factory," *The Economist*, December 22, 1990, pp. 21–24

9. George Hartzog, *Battling for the National Parks* (Mt. Kisko, NY: Moyer Bell, 1988), pp. 154–55.

10. Ibid., pp. 117–18.

11. Gifford Pinchot, *The Fight for Conservation* (New York: Doubleday, Page and Co., 1910), p. 15.

Chapter 38

1. George Hartzog, *Battling for the National Parks* (Mt. Kisko, NY: Moyer Bell, 1988), p. 477.

2. *Congressional Record*, 49 Cong., 2nd sess., vol. 18, pt. 2, 1887, p. 1875.

3. White House, *Historical Tables: Budget of the United States Government Fiscal Year 2008* (Washington, DC: GPO, 2007), p. 22.

4. Census Bureau, *Statistical Abstract of the United States 2004–2005* (Washington, DC: Department of Commerce, 2004), table 442.

5. White House, *Historical Tables*, p. 127.

Chapter 39

1. *Wickard v. Filburn*, 317 U.S. 111 (1942).

2. *Gonzales v. Raich*, 352 F. 3d 1222.

3. *Chevron v. Natural Resources Defense Council*, 467 U.S. 837 (1984).

4. *Sierra Club v. Wayne National Forest*, 1997 Fed. App. 0022P (6th Cir.).

Part Seven

1. John Wesley Powell, "From Savagery to Barbarism," *Transactions of the Anthropological Society of Washington*, III: 173–96.

Chapter 40

1. Ernest Mignon, *Les Mots du General de Gaulle* (Paris: Fayard, 1962).

2. Francis Fukuyama, *The End of History and the Last Man* (New York: Free Press, 1992), p. 94.

3. Harry W. Richardson and Peter Gordon, "Market Planning: Oxymoron or Common Sense?" *Journal of the American Planning Association* 59, no. 3 (Summer 1993): 347–52.

Chapter 41

1. Mark Reisner, *Cadillac Desert: The American West and Its Disappearing Water*, rev. ed. (New York: Penguin Books, 1993), pp. 514–16.

2. Fish and Wildlife Service, *National Survey of Fishing, Hunting, and Wildlife-Associated Recreation* (Washington, DC: Department of Interior, 1993).

3. Wesley Calef, *Private Grazing and Public Lands* (Chicago: University of Chicago Press, 1960).

4. Harry W. Richardson and Peter Gordon, "Market Planning: Oxymoron or Common Sense?" *Journal of the American Planning Association* 59, no. 3 (Summer 1993): 347–52.

5. David Friedman, "Do We Need Government?" *Liberty*, December 2005, p. 16.

Chapter 42

1. State of Oregon, Conserved Water Program, Oregon Revised Statute 537.455.

2. State of Oregon, Instream Water Rights Act of 1987, Oregon Revised Statute 537.348.

3. "Our Approach," Oregon Water Trust, tinyurl.com/29reyj.

4. Maurice McTeague, "The New Zealand Solution," *Different Drummer*, no. 14, pp. 51–54, ti.org/nzsolution.html.

5. Michael de Alessi, *Fishing for Solutions* (London: IEA, 1998).

6. Brian M. Riedl, *Still at the Federal Trough: Farm Subsidies for the Rich and Famous Shattered Records in 2001* (Washington, DC: Heritage Foundation, 2002), p. 1, tinyurl.com/y362wo.

7. McTeague, "The New Zealand Solution."

Chapter 43

1. Ken Alvarez, "The Florida Panther Recovery Program: An Organizational Failure of the Endangered Species Act," in *Endangered Species Recovery: Finding the Lessons, Improving the Process*, ed. Tim Clark, Richard Reading, and Alice Clarke (Covelo, CA: Island Press, 1994), pp. 205, 219.

2. Jerome Jackson, "The Red-Cockaded Woodpecker Recovery Program: Professional Obstacles to Cooperation," in Clark, Reading, and Clarke, *Endangered Species Recovery*, p. 157.

3. Noel Snyder, "The California Condor Recovery Program: Problems in Organization and Execution," in Clark, Reading, and Clarke, *Endangered Species Recovery*, pp. 188–89.

4. Karl Hess, Jr., *Saving the Black-Footed Ferret: Policy Reforms and Private Sector Incentives* (Bandon, OR: Thoreau Institute, 1996), ti.org/bffhess.html.

5. Randal O'Toole, *Audit of the USDA Animal Damage Control Program* (Bandon, OR: Thoreau Institute, 1994), p. 3, ti.org/adcreport.html.

Chapter 44

1. Peter Drucker, *The New Realities* (New York: Harper & Row, 1989), p. 66.

2. Gifford Pinchot III, *Intrapreneuring: Why You Don't Have to Leave the Corporation to Become an Entrepreneur* (New York: Harpercollins, 1986); Gifford Pinchot III and Ron Pellman, *Intrapreneuring in Action: A Handbook for Business Innovation* (San Francisco: Berrett-Koehler, 1999).

3. Randal O'Toole, *Should Congress Transfer Federal Lands to the States?* (Washington, DC: Cato Institute, 1997), tinyurl.com/2728yk.

Chapter 45

1. Forest Options Group, *The 2nd Century Report: Options for the Forest Service* (Bandon, OR: Thoreau Institute, 2001), ti.org/2c.html.

Chapter 46

1. Ronald D. Utt, *The Katrina Relief Effort: Congress Should Redirect Highway Earmark Funding to a Higher Purpose* (Washington, DC: Heritage Foundation, 2005), tinyurl. com/2r6hz2.

2. Edward Epstein, "Pelosi Willing to Give Up S.F. Funds for Recovery," *San Francisco Chronicle*, September 21, 2005.

Chapter 47

1. Amanda Agan and Alexander Tabarrok, "What Are Private Governments Worth?" *Regulation* Fall 2005, pp. 14–17.

2. Robert Nelson, "Privatizing the Neighborhood: A Proposal to Replace Zoning with Private Collective Property Rights to Existing Neighborhoods," *George Mason Law Review* 7, no. 4 (Summer 1999): 827–80.

Index

About the Author

Randal O'Toole is a senior fellow at the Cato Institute working on urban growth, public land, and transportation issues. Described by *U.S. News & World Report* as a researcher who "has earned a reputation for dogged legwork and sophisticated number crunching," he was also named by *Newsweek* magazine as one of 20 "leading movers and shakers in the West." His previous books, *Reforming the Forest Service* and *The Vanishing Automobile and Other Urban Myths*, have significantly influenced public land management and urban planning in this country.

O'Toole was formerly senior economist at the Thoreau Institute. In 1998, Yale University named O'Toole its McCluskey Conservation Fellow. He was the Scaife Visiting Scholar at UC Berkeley in 1999 and 2001, and the Merrill Visiting Professor at Utah State University in 2000.

An Oregon native, he currently resides in Bandon, Oregon.

Cato Institute

Founded in 1977, the Cato Institute is a public policy research foundation dedicated to broadening the parameters of policy debate to allow consideration of more options that are consistent with the traditional American principles of limited government, individual liberty, and peace. To that end, the Institute strives to achieve greater involvement of the intelligent, concerned lay public in questions of policy and the proper role of government.

The Institute is named for *Cato's Letters,* libertarian pamphlets that were widely read in the American Colonies in the early 18th century and played a major role in laying the philosophical foundation for the American Revolution.

Despite the achievement of the nation's Founders, today virtually no aspect of life is free from government encroachment. A pervasive intolerance for individual rights is shown by government's arbitrary intrusions into private economic transactions and its disregard for civil liberties.

To counter that trend, the Cato Institute undertakes an extensive publications program that addresses the complete spectrum of policy issues. Books, monographs, and shorter studies are commissioned to examine the federal budget, Social Security, regulation, military spending, international trade, and myriad other issues. Major policy conferences are held throughout the year, from which papers are published thrice yearly in the *Cato Journal.* The Institute also publishes the quarterly magazine *Regulation.*

In order to maintain its independence, the Cato Institute accepts no government funding. Contributions are received from foundations, corporations, and individuals, and other revenue is generated from the sale of publications. The Institute is a nonprofit, tax-exempt, educational foundation under Section 501(c)3 of the Internal Revenue Code.

CATO INSTITUTE
1000 Massachusetts Ave., N.W.
Washington, D.C. 20001
www.cato.org